The Heresy of Jacob Frank

The Heresy of Jacob Frank

From Jewish Messianism to Esoteric Myth

JAY MICHAELSON

OXFORD
UNIVERSITY PRESS

Oxford University Press is a department of the University of Oxford. It furthers
the University's objective of excellence in research, scholarship, and education
by publishing worldwide. Oxford is a registered trade mark of Oxford University
Press in the UK and certain other countries.

Published in the United States of America by Oxford University Press
198 Madison Avenue, New York, NY 10016, United States of America.

© Oxford University Press 2022

All rights reserved. No part of this publication may be reproduced, stored in
a retrieval system, or transmitted, in any form or by any means, without the
prior permission in writing of Oxford University Press, or as expressly permitted
by law, by license, or under terms agreed with the appropriate reproduction
rights organization. Inquiries concerning reproduction outside the scope of the
above should be sent to the Rights Department, Oxford University Press, at the
address above.

You must not circulate this work in any other form
and you must impose this same condition on any acquirer.

Library of Congress Cataloging-in-Publication Data
Names: Michaelson, Jay, 1971– author.
Title: The heresy of Jacob Frank : from Jewish messianism to esoteric myth
/ Jay Michaelson.
Description: New York, NY : Oxford University Press, [2022] |
Includes bibliographical references and index.
Identifiers: LCCN 2022012686 (print) | LCCN 2022012687 (ebook) |
ISBN 9780197530634 (hardback) | ISBN 9780197651025 (paperback) |
ISBN 9780197530658 (epub)
Subjects: LCSH: Frank, Jacob, approximately 1726-1791. |
Pseudo-Messiahs—Biography. | Jewish messianic movements—Europe,
Eastern—History. | Mysticism—Judaism—History—18th century. |
Judaism—Europe, Eastern—History—18th century.
Classification: LCC BM755.F68 M53 2022 (print) | LCC BM755.F68 (ebook) |
DDC 296.8/2—dc23/eng/20220605
LC record available at https://lccn.loc.gov/2022012686
LC ebook record available at https://lccn.loc.gov/2022012687

DOI: 10.1093/oso/9780197530634.001.0001

Perhaps Frank's mythology is threatening and dangerous; I believe nevertheless that I am more qualified than others to perceive its dangers.
—Gershom Scholem, Letter to Isaiah Sonne, 1943

> We are, I am, you are
> by cowardice or courage
> the one who find our way
> back to this scene
> carrying a knife, a camera
> a book of myths
> in which
> our names do not appear.
> —Adrienne Rich, "Diving into the Wreck"

Contents

Introduction: The Boundary Crosser   1

1. "I tell you everything and tell you nothing": Charlatan, Fool, Deviant, Heretic—Who Was Jacob Frank?   13

2. "I do not look to heaven but at what God does here on Earth": Frankist Antinomianism as Materialist Skepticism   46

3. "Everything that is of the spirit has to be turned into flesh": Magic, Myth, and the Material *Imaginaire*   71

4. "To make a man in wholeness, stable and possessing eternal life": The Occult Quest for Immortality   91

5. "With this deed we go to the naked thing": Sexual Antinomianism as Mystical Messianism   114

6. "We don't need the books of Kabbalah": Rejecting Kabbalah and Sabbateanism   152

7. "The gods of the freemasons will have to do what those two have done": Frankism as Western Esotericism   168

8. "All religions change and go beyond the borders laid down by their ancestors": Foreshadowing Secularism and Spirituality   182

Acknowledgments   207
Appendix: Review of Scholarship and Textual Notes   209
Bibliography   225
Index   253

Introduction

The Boundary Crosser

Jacob Frank (1726–1791) was once the most notorious Jew in Europe, widely regarded as a villain, a scoundrel, a pervert, and a heretic. After rumors of secret orgies and heretical rituals, Poland's rabbinic leadership reported him to the Christian authorities as a heretic, and in 1759, Frank led the largest mass apostasy in Jewish history, leading thousands to convert, en masse, to Catholicism. But the conversion was not sincere (Frank told his followers it was only a step toward territorial independence, or perhaps the messianic age) and when this was discovered, he was thrown in jail for twelve years. Frank's infamy faded, but upon his release in 1772, he had a second career as a kind of eighteenth-century cult leader, revered by his followers and involved in political intrigues, alchemical experiments, and underground esoteric movements until his death in 1791. Frank's late career borders on the unbelievable: Frankist sect members ran guns for the French Revolution, founded a Masonic order, and conducted secret rituals and bizarre paramilitary exercises at a borrowed castle in Moravia. Eventually they would help create Poland's professional class, bring about the Jewish Enlightenment in Prague, and count among their descendants Polish national poet Adam Mickiewicz and US Supreme Court Justice Louis Brandeis. Frankism, though an utter failure on its own terms, also foreshadowed developments that would transform the Jewish world including secularist, Reform, and Zionist critiques of Jewish religion, and contemporary Jewish spiritual movements which attempt to integrate them. Frankist teachings have even made it into the writings of contemporary antisemites on the internet, who put them forth as evidence of secret Jewish conspiracies,[1] and into a masterpiece of

---

[1] The infamous antisemite and notorious conspiracy theorist David Icke has said that "to understand Sabbatian Frankism is to understand the world." Icke, "To Understand Sabbatian Frankism." Icke claims that Zionists (as well as the Rothschilds and the Saudi royal family) are actually Frankists and *doenmeh* who have infiltrated political and religious entities across the globe. Remarkably, Icke accurately describes several aspects of Frankist and Sabbatean history and doctrine in his unhinged presentations. See Icke, *The Trigger*; Icke, "To Understand Sabbatian Frankism."

twenty-first-century literature by the Nobel Laureate Olga Tokarczuk.[2] Indeed, Frank's life story is even more bizarre than the myths he told to his disciples of immortal races and magical beings that populate the earth.

But what—if anything—did Jacob Frank believe? History is written by the victors, and Frank's name was indeed "blotted out" (in the traditional Jewish idiom) by those who successfully persecuted him. Most of his teachings were either lost or preserved only by a small handful of his sect's descendants— indeed, most were not even known to the first scholars to study him. To the extent Frank is known today, it is as a false messiah riding the coattails of his more famous forbear, Sabbetai Zevi (1626–1676), whose 1666 messianic activity and subsequent apostasy destabilized the Jewish world, undermined rabbinic authority, and ultimately led both to the popularization of Jewish mysticism and to its suppression. (We will survey the Sabbatean movement in chapter 1.) In the words of Gershom Scholem, the pioneering scholar of Kabbalah, Frank was

> a religious leader who, whether for purely self-interested motives or otherwise, was in all his actions a truly corrupt and degenerate individual ... a man who could snuff out [Sabbateanism's] last inner lights and pervert whatever will to truth and goodness was still to be found in the maze-like ruins of the "believers"' souls.[3]

Yet almost all of these accounts, popular and scholarly alike, are incorrect, at least by the time of Frank's later teachings, recorded in 1784 and 1789–1790 in a Polish-language anthology now known as the *Collection of the Words of the Lord* (*Zbiór Słów Pańskich* in the original, abbreviated here as ZSP).[4] In that text, Frank weaves a shocking, original theology at the intersections of Western esotericism, liberated sexuality, and, strangely enough, rationalist skepticism. Frank was not a messiah in any usual sense—he rejected

---

[2] Tokarczuk, *The Books of Jacob*.
[3] Scholem, *The Messianic Idea in Judaism*, 126–27.
[4] This title appeared together with the oldest copy of the manuscript known to scholars, published in 1866. As discussed in the Appendix, it is not known which of Frank's disciples recorded the teachings or even their original language. The English title *Words of the Lord* is somewhat misleading, as it can be read as signifying that Frank claimed divinity, whereas the Polish word *pan* was the standard title of address for nobility at the time, while today it roughly means "sir." The Hebrew translation *Divrei Ha-Adon* comes closer. See Maciejko, "Sabbatean Charlatans," 368–69. In this book, quotations from *Zbiór Słów Pańskich* are based on the 1997 printed Polish edition compiled by Jan Doktór (Frank, *Księga Słów Pańskich*), with translations by myself and Dr. Luiza Newlin-Lukowicz. The English translation by Harris Lenowitz and the Hebrew translation by Fania Scholem (edited by Rachel Elior) were also consulted.

the Jewish, Kabbalistic, and Sabbatean conceptions of the messianic age, replacing them with his own worldly blend of militaristic triumphalism and the alchemical pursuit of immortality. Nor, contrary to some popular and scholarly presentations, was Frank some kind of sex fiend; in fact, while antinomian sexual ritual was practiced in the Frankist sect, it was extremely limited and rare. Frank, at least according to the texts available to us today, did not perpetuate the Sabbatean project (although after his death, many of his followers did); on the contrary, he rejected it, Kabbalah, Judaism, and religion in general as ineffectual nonsense. None of this is to suggest that Frank was a good man: He was manipulative, abusive, conniving, and cruel. But he was, as the etymology of the word "heretic" suggests, one who chose his own path.

This book is about what this great Jewish heretic believed, at least at the time of *ZSP*, with the intention of complementing the historical scholarship on Frank with a close analytical reading of the Frankist corpus. As we will see, Frank preaches a combination of antinomianism—the view that the law ought to be broken—and myth. On the one hand, he heavily critiqued religion as oppressive, ineffectual, and overly parochial. Obedience to the law is foolish, Frank holds, because religion's promises are false and adherence to religious stricture needlessly restrains human potential. Frank believes only in the material—in what could be seen and touched—denying any notion of the spiritual, and preaches a radical skepticism and a quasi-humanist gospel of sensuality, power, and worldly success. He reminds us again and again how much he enjoys good food, sex, money, and wine.

And yet, Frank was no rationalist. He inhabited a mythic world of superhuman beings who live forever, elf-like creatures who dwell in caves, and occult hero-mages such as Balaam, the Queen of Sheba, Solomon, and Asmodeus. Frank describes a hidden world, separated from this one by an impassable curtain (*zasłona*), where Frank's counterpart, the Big Brother, leads a sect parallel to Frank's own, except that the Big Brother's cohort has learned to live forever because they possess the secret *Das* (gnosis) which Frank's sect seeks. The gateway to this other world is a syncretic, messianic figure Frank calls the *Panna*, or Maiden, the incarnation of sexuality and materiality, combining elements of the Shechinah, Frank's daughter Eve, and the Black Virgin of Częstochowa, where Frank had been imprisoned and where a portrait of the Virgin is venerated and worshiped. As discussed in detail in chapter 7, the later teachings of Frank ought to be understood in the context of Western esotericism, which flourished in the eighteenth century; Frank's combination of libertinism and occultism reflects his contacts with contemporaries including Casanova, Freemasons, alchemists, and "Illuminist" esoteric societies of his day.[5] As a result, his theology is perhaps closer to Mormonism (which, by way of Freemasonry, shares many of the same themes as Frank's) than Kabbalah. And as discussed in chapter 8, Frankist and Sabbatean ideas influenced the Haskalah (though not in the way Scholem had proposed) and Hasidism, and foreshadowed many of the tenets of contemporary Jewish spirituality. Nothing about Frank is predictable. Having spent over fifteen years studying Frank's words, I remain surprised by them every single day.

* * *

Until very recently, most of Frank's teachings were unknown even to scholars. The *Words of the Lord* exists in only three manuscripts, was only printed in Polish in 1997, and has only been partially translated into Hebrew and English, with neither of those translations in wide circulation. (The handful of other Frankist primary sources are also not well known; they are discussed in chapter 1.) Fortunately, while *ZSP* remains difficult to access, vitally important scholarship on Frankism has appeared in the last fifteen years from Paweł Maciejko, whose comprehensive history of the Frankist movement, *The Mixed Multitude: Jacob Frank and the Frankist Movement*, has transformed our understanding of it, as well as from Rachel Elior, Ada Rapoport-Albert, Jan Doktór, Cengiz Sisman, Matt Goldish, Jonatan Meir, Michael Fagenblat, Harris Lenowitz, and others. A review of this scholarship is contained in the Appendix.[6] There have also been several literary and artistic treatments of Frank, including two novels by Isaac Bashevis Singer, a play by Sholem Asch, the aforementioned (and 912-page) novel by Olga Tokarczuk, various colorful presentations of Frank's life, and even a 2011 film by Adrian Panek.[7] With this growing awareness of Frank, the moment is ripe

---

[5] See Maciejko, "Portrait," 522–23.
[6] This work includes Maciejko, *Mixed Multitude*; Elior, "Jacob Frank and His Book *The Sayings of the Lord*"; and Rapoport-Albert, *Women and the Messianic Heresy of Sabbatai Zevi*. All these build upon (even as they revise) the pioneering studies by Gershom Scholem such as "Redemption through Sin" (*The Messianic Idea*, 78–141), which, despite having been based on a limited number of Frankist texts, probably remains the best-known source for the movement. The Appendix also provides a quantitative analysis of *Words of the Lord*, as well as notes on the organization and recension of the text.
[7] See Shmeruk, "The Frankist Novels"; Naor, "Post-Sabbatean," 95–103; Tokarczuk, *The Books of Jacob*; Panek, *Daas*; Mandel, *Militant Messiah*; Lenowitz, *The Jewish Messiahs*.

for an investigation and perhaps reassessment of his fascinating, complex, and often convoluted teachings.

Chapter 1 introduces two Jacob Franks: one historical, one almost entirely fictional. The first was born Yankiev Liebowicz/Yaakov Yosef ben Leib, in Korolówka, Podolia (today part of Ukraine), in 1726, to a family with known Sabbatean affiliations. Frank's family moved from place to place in the Ottoman Empire and in Poland, perhaps due to accusations of heresy; in Ottoman territories, the name "Frank" designated someone or something European.[8] After working for several years as a trader, in 1753 Frank made his way to Salonica, the center of Sabbatean activity, where he became a charismatic leader after entering in a trance in which the soul of the second messianic leader of the sect, Baruchiah Russo, was said to have entered his body.[9] Frank returned north in 1755; there, in Yiddish, the term *Frenk* designated a Sephardic or Mizrachi ("Eastern" or "Oriental") Jew, as Frank indeed appeared, in the "exotic" Turkish garb he would wear for the rest of his life. The name "Jacob Frank" thus denotes him as an outsider in both Polish and Ottoman contexts.[10] Frank was one of many heretical, charismatic preachers at the time, before becoming, inadvertently, the most notorious Jewish apostate of his day in 1759, and a prisoner for twelve years thereafter, as discussed above. Following his release, for the remaining nineteen years of his life, Frank lived as a kind of faux-noble charlatan, attaining social mobility and status through a combination of grift, mystery, quasi-Kabbalistic lore, esoteric networks, political connections, ostentatious displays of wealth, exotic dress, and rumors of hedonistic excess.[11] This Jacob Frank, the one who actually existed, died a failure in 1791, and when his daughter Eve passed away thirty years later, his sect ended as well.

The second Jacob Frank, however, is quite different: He is a semifictional character presented in ZSP, which Rachel Elior has aptly described as Frank's "auto-hagiography."[12] This figure is at once boor and prophet, frustrated failure and world-historic figure. He boasts of his sexual prowess, spins yarns about his strength and audacity, and oscillates between openness and

---

[8] Doktór, *Księga Słów Pańskich*, 586; Sisman, *Burden of Silence*, 151.
[9] See Goldish, *Sabbatean Prophets*, 130–61; Goldish, "Toward a Reevaluation," 398–405; Garb, *Shamanic Trance*, 15.
[10] Maciejko, *Mixed Multitude*, 13–19.
[11] Others of this ilk included Wolf Eibeschütz, son of the secretly Sabbatean Rabbi Jonathan Eibeschütz, Dr. Samuel Jacob Falk, Comte de Saint-Germain, and "Count" Cagliostro. Maciejko, *Mixed Multitude*, 199–231; Meir, "Jacob Frank: The Wondrous Charlatan"; Lenowitz, "The Charlatan at the *Gottes Haus*."
[12] Elior, "Jacob Frank," 476.

concealment, directness and obfuscation. His life is more myth than history, and his teachings are clothed in contradiction and misdirection. Thus, chapter 1 grapples with the question of how to read this strange text, offering methodological principles for assessing tales of Frank's "holy madness" and trickster wisdom.

Chapters 2–5 present close readings of four central elements of Frankist teaching: antinomianism, magical materialism, the quest for immortality, and eros. Chapter 2 discusses Frank's antinomianism: his rejection of traditional religion and its norms. Frank's critique is neither Kabbalistic nor Sabbatean in nature but based on quasi-reformist positions that might seem quite familiar today: skepticism, theodicy, a humanistic hedonism, and a surprising universalism, critiquing the particularity and hypocrisy of specific religious traditions. And Frank replaces religious restrictions with a celebration of sexuality, sensuality, and power. He tells his backsliding followers in §988:

> Your way is not my way, because you fasted for your gods and lay prostrate in mourning because mourning is their due, as it is written: "Rachel weeps over her children."[13] But this is not my way. When my aid [*pomoc*] arrives, I will furnish my court and keep it in festive garments. I will provide all comfort in food and drink, I will have my own music, my own theater, my own actors, and everyone will rejoice and dance together, young and old alike, and that which is written will be fulfilled: "When he came to play before Saul, the Spirit of God rested upon him,"[14] because my God does not rest just anywhere, but only where joy and merriment reside.

Joy and merriment, for Frank, are prerequisites for the Divine, and markers of the sacred. Mourning, fasting, and self-abnegation are from the "side of death." For this reason, Frank has utter contempt for the strictures of traditional religion. "All the teachings up until now have been like that dog

---

[13] Jeremiah 31:15.
[14] 1 Samuel 16:23. Frank here departs from the usual understanding of the biblical passage, in which David plays the harp to soothe Saul's spirits. The passage reads, "And it came to pass, when the spirit from/of God [*ruach Elohim*] was upon Saul, that David took the harp, and played with his hand: so Saul was relieved and was well, and the evil spirit departed from him." This is generally interpreted as meaning that Saul had a "foul spirit" placed upon him by God, and David's music caused it to depart. In Frank's rendition, music does not merely cause a foul spirit to depart but also causes the Spirit of God [*Duch Boży*—the same term for "Holy Spirit" in Christianity] to rest upon him. This reading thus supports Frank's claim that God only resides where there is "joy and merriment."

that kept vomiting, then swallowing," he says in §232, citing Proverbs 26:11 ("As a dog returns to its vomit, so a fool repeats his folly"). Rather like a contemporary "prosperity gospel" preacher, Frank says that material advancement is what God wants for the chosen. In §1292 he says the goal is lands, not laws: "All of these who are godless, let them learn the laws. God told Abraham: 'To you and your children I will give all this land.' He did not say that he would give them laws." Frank speaks of doing, not praying; the "masculine" Esau, not the "effeminate" Jacob; the physical, not the spiritual. As he says in §1089, "I do not look to heaven for aid to come from there. I only look at what God does here on earth, in this world."

Materialism is also the defining feature of Frank's theology, which we explore in chapter 3. Frank's world is an entirely material and physical one, but it is populated by beings with magical superpowers, and is but the shadow of the world of immortality and abundance. For example, Częstochowa, where Frank was imprisoned, is understood not as a site of spiritual pilgrimage but as a site located atop a physical cave filled with physical gold. Redemption is not spiritual or otherworldly but entirely this-worldly, with abundant food and drink, and gilded carriages and clothing. Frank himself puts it best in §1001:

> How greatly you misunderstood my words! I told you that there is one tower where the Lady is hiding, and if she sees somebody she desires with all her might, she throws them down a portrait of herself. . . . I did not tell you about this in spirit, or in heaven. Instead, I said everything in plain view, on earth: that there is a Lady and a tower, and there is a painting they call a portrait.

This materialism even applies, to some extent, to God: "Shaddai," normally a name of God, is, says Frank, actually a *shed*—a demon (or perhaps, in Frank's mythology, simply a being with magical powers). And the world is maintained not by the monotheistic God but by three flawed gods associated with the Nephilim, the mythical giants of the book of Genesis. Our realm, according to Frank, is but one one-thousandth of the total universe. The vast majority of the world is on the other side of the curtain, inhabited by immortal beings, chiefly the Big Brother, a kind of demigod in need of human aid but also in possession of the secrets of immortality. Frank insists that this other world, too, is a physical one: In §1299, he says that while our world takes four to five years to travel across, the other world would take five hundred to traverse. Yet the world of the Big Brother is, in contrast to our own, good and uncursed. Our world is directed by three evil gods and is filled with mortality and corruption. The other world is blessed with material goods like wonderful food, abundant wealth, and most of all, immortality.

The Frankist quest, discussed in chapter 4, is for Frank's inner circle of "Brothers" and "Sisters" to access this other world and learn the secrets of immortality. This journey, from baptism to Edom to *Das*—Frank's term for his new religion, which should be understood as gnosis, also the primary goal of Western esotericism—is a multistaged process involving the Brethren obtaining secret keys, wearing new attire, ruling over animals, enlisting mythical creatures drawn from Kabbalistic traditions, uniting with the Maiden, and then finally passing through the "curtain" to meet the Big Brother. It is bewildering and baroque, but is also utterly material in nature. It is a quest that will happen in this world and yield this-worldly rewards which are often comic (if not pathetic) in their detail—Frank even describes the menus the disciples will enjoy after their transformations. This quest is both heroic and tragic: Frank's questing tales sometimes have happy endings, but often they explain the failure of Frank's initial mission, which he endlessly blames on his followers. Chapter 4 engages with this material in the context of scholarship on failed prophecy, following in the wake of Leon Festinger's classic study *When Prophecy Fails*, and its many critics. Preached by a failed leader in a borrowed castle in 1784, Frank's myths promise power, immortality, and life.

A proleptic enaction of this redemptive liberation is found in sexuality. Chapter 5 discusses how Frank understands sexual liberation as devotion to the Maiden—the syncretic, messianic figure who is a perennial, feminine incarnation of sensuality itself. This liberation was both symbolic and real, accompanied by women (including, first and foremost, Eve Frank) taking leadership roles within Frankist communities, as they had in Sabbatean ones. It may also have been expressed in sexual liberation, as well as rare, choreographed instances of sexual ritual. There has been an unfortunate tendency in some scholarship of Frankism to magnify the scandal and frequency of sexual ritual (including accusations of incest derived from Frank's persecutors) while simultaneously reducing its meaningfulness in the context of heretical religious practice. In contrast, and drawing on the insights of feminist and queer readings of religious text and doctrine, chapter 5 explores five meanings of sexual praxis within the Frankist system: the construction of sexuality as worldly ecstasy, the queer remasculinization of the Jewish hero, the rupture of antinomian sexuality as enacting a redemptive performance, the liberation of the "feminine," and the transgressing of boundaries in a carnival grotesque. Religion has subordinated material to spiritual, female to male, sexual expression to virtuous restraint—but Frank ascribes these repressive impulses to the "Foreign Woman," literally the demonic. Perhaps drawing on existing *doenmeh* rituals, and, I suggest, analogous to contemporaneous Hasidic innovations in eroticized ecstatic prayer, Frankist sexual practice offers a "neutralized," privatized, and displaced messianic experience,[15] though in this case opposed to traditional, patriarchal religious hierarchies: a liberationist recorporealization of the eros that religion sublimates into mysticism.

Finally, chapters 6–8 set these doctrines and ideas into their wider contexts. Chapter 6 shows that Jacob Frank in the period of *ZSP*'s dictation is not a false messiah in any traditional sense, and no longer either a Kabbalist or a Sabbatean. Frank's apocalypticism does not have any of the themes of traditional or Sabbatean Jewish messianism. Frank does not declare himself the messiah, though he predicted imminent (very imminent—within two years) apocalypse and predicted that he would gain temporal power. The Maiden is the Messiah; at most, Frank may be analogized to the *Mashiach ben Yosef*, who prepares the way for the final Messiah, though he never claims this role either. Rather, Frank is in search of physical immortality and physical power. And uniquely, Frank's mission had already failed; Frank frequently laments in the subjunctive mood the redemption that could have happened had the disciples followed him more closely. Ultimately, chapter 5 proposes that, in place of messianism, a more useful term for understanding Frank's prophecies is millennialism, a more expansive concept meaning, in Richard Landes's words, "the belief that at some point in the future the world that we live in will be radically transformed into one of perfection—of peace, justice, fellowship, and plenty."[16] Frank's millennialism, public and historical in 1759, had by 1784 become privatized, with the transformation now being limited to the Brethren. Chapter 6 also explores how Frank explicitly rejects Kabbalah and Sabbateanism, both of which he ridicules for their ineffectuality. Kabbalah is marginal in *ZSP*; even counting generously, explicit Kabbalistic language or symbolism appears in fewer than 50 dicta out of over 2,500 in the text. And the view that Frankism is a continuation of Sabbateanism obscures

---

[15] See Idel, *Messianic Mystics*, 212–14.
[16] Landes, *Heaven on Earth*, 20.

more than it reveals. In fact, the relationship between Frank, Sabbetai Zevi, and Baruchiah Russo is one of displacement, not continuation. Frankism operates within a Sabbatean framework yet inverts the Sabbatean emphasis on faith and the unseen; for Sabbateanism, the *Sod HaEmunah*, the hidden "mystery of the faith," is central[17]—for Frank, faith in the invisible is ridiculous, and the manifest is all he trusts.

Instead, chapter 7 situates *ZSP* and Frank in the context of eighteenth-century Western esotericism. Arthur Versluis posits two essential features of this movement: "1. Gnosis or gnostic insight, i.e., knowledge of hidden or invisible realms or aspects of existence (including both cosmological and metaphysical gnosis) and 2. esotericism, meaning that this hidden knowledge is either explicitly restricted to a relatively small group of people, or implicitly self-restricted by virtue of its complexity or subtlety."[18] Socially, mid-eighteenth-century Europe witnessed an explosion in initiatic secret societies clustered around esoteric and occult ideas, of which the Frankist sect at the time of *ZSP* was one; it was closely connected to Masonic networks, which it exploited for political gain, and Frank was in direct contact with other Western esotericist figures and charlatans. Ideologically, by 1784, Frank more closely resembles Casanova than Sabbetai Zevi, and his theology is more like Western esotericism than Kabbalah, syncretizing materialism, libertinism, folklore, and quasi-Enlightenment rationalism. The Frankist court resembles a secret society, and the teachings of *ZSP* resemble a Western esoteric theology, with equal parts tradition and modernity, rationalist critique and magical occultism.

Lastly, chapter 8 explores how late Frankism anticipates three subsequent Jewish movements: the Haskalah (and Zionism), Hasidism, and "New Age" Jewish spirituality. In each case, there are limited historical points of influence, but broader phenomenological similarities; Frank foreshadowed these developments, even as he did not actually shape them. First, after a brief historical summary of the Frankist sect after its leader's death, I revisit Gershom Scholem's largely disproven thesis that Sabbateanism brought about the Haskalah by destabilizing rabbinic authority.[19] Ada Rapoport-Albert has shown that the Prague Frankists do form a nexus point between the two movements, but that their Maskilic ideals came from non-Jewish sources,

---

[17] See Maciejko, "Coitus interruptus," xx–xxi.
[18] Versluis, *Magic and Mysticism*, 2.
[19] See Katz, "The Suggested Relationship," 504–30; Rapoport-Albert and Hamann, "Something for the Female Sex," 98–103; Maciejko, "Gershom Scholem's Dialectic," 207–20.

not Frankist ones.[20] The present study builds on that scholarship, noting how Frank's quasi-rationalistic critique of traditional theodicy foreshadowed those of the Haskalah, and notes further connections in the context of Western esotericism. Next, chapter 8 traces the historical connections and phenomenological similarities between Frankism and early Hasidism. In addition to the Baal Shem Tov's awareness of and ambivalence toward the Frankist sect, Yehuda Liebes and Joseph Weiss have adduced strong evidence linking Frank's teachings and Rabbi Nachman of Bratzlav, who described himself as being able to "sweeten" the teachings of heretics. Chapter 8 further observes phenomenological affinities between the Frankist displacement of the messianic from the historical to the personal, and the Hasidic displacement of the messianic from the historical to the personal.[21] Finally, chapter 8 explores how *ZSP* foreshadowed the cluster of Jewish movements associated with the so-called New Age, a category that, despite its vagueness and negative associations, has lately been the subject of significant scholarly study as a twentieth- and twenty-first-century religious movement.[22] Like Frank, Jewish New Age spiritualities such as Jewish Renewal (in addition to revivalist movements like neo-Hasidism, and even the very category of "spirituality" itself) attempt to extract the spiritual and personal-transformational aspects of religion from their religious contexts, and place them into a syncretic, feminist, and universalist one. And like Frank, the New Age combines skeptical, humanistic antinomianism (or anomianism) with esoteric myth. Once again, while Frank's historical influence on these currents was quite attenuated (though not zero, given Western esotericism's and Hasidism's influence on New Age Judaism), he seems to have anticipated trends that would become widespread in Jewish religious/spiritual life.

Finally, the Appendix to this book contains a review of scholarship of Frankism; a detailed, quantitative analysis of the subject matters and genres of *ZSP*; and a review of textual questions (including dates of composition and editing) in *ZSP* and other Frankist texts including *Widzenia Pańskie* ("Visions of the Lord," a compilation of Frank's visions and dreams from 1775 to 1786), *Rozmaite adnotacyie, przypadki, czynności, i anektody Pańskie* ("Various notes, occurrences, activities, and anecdotes of the lord," hereinafter *RA* or

---

[20] Rapoport-Albert and Hamann, "Something for the Female Sex," 98–103.
[21] Idel, *Messianic Mystics*, 3–16.
[22] See Magid, *American Post-Judaism*, 115–32; Salkin, "New Age Judaism"; Huss, "Spirituality," 47–49; Rothenberg & Vallely, eds., *New Age Judaism*. On the New Age more broadly, see Hanegraaff, *New Age Religion*, 324–27; Heelas and Woodhead, *Spiritual Revolution*.

"Various Notes," an incomplete narrative of Frank's career, apparently compiled in the early nineteenth century), the prophetic "Red Letters" and the "Prophecies of Isaiah," and others.

Scholem once remarked at how shocking it was that, at the same time of the French Revolution, an odd, charismatic crypto-Jew led a secret society of heretics. In fact, however, the two phenomena were not so distant from one another. Narrowly speaking, Frank's would-be heir, Moses Dobruschka, played a bit part in the French Revolution, using his Masonic connections to run guns from the Hapsburg Empire to the revolutionaries. But more broadly, the Frankism of *Words of the Lord* welds together a quasi-Enlightenment skepticism with a quasi-gnostic esotericism, promising to liberate sensuality and attain immortality to those who follow Frank faithfully. Halfway between superstition and science, Frankism is a seemingly impossible juxtaposition of a skeptical, materialist critique and a secretive cult based on magic, obedience, and control. Yet by issuing such a startling critique of normative religion, by uprooting himself and his community from any semblance of the old order, and by syncretizing multiple and intersecting spiritual pathways, Frank was a precursor of trends that would define Western religion and postreligion two centuries after his death. It is almost as if his persecutors knew what lay ahead.

1
"I tell you everything and tell you nothing"

Charlatan, Fool, Deviant, Heretic—Who Was Jacob Frank?

The Shape-Shifter

"Having come to the synagogue in Salonica," Jacob Frank tells his followers in §19 of *ZSP*, "I took the Law of Moses [i.e., the Torah scroll], put it on the ground, pulled down my pants, and I sat on it with my bare behind. The Jews, unable to do anything, had to leave."

Did this event ever happen? Probably not. The man who told it to his small circle of close followers in 1784 was looking back thirty years and boasting. Yet what could possibly motivate someone to tell such a tale? Answering that question is the subject of this chapter. Here, I will explore two Jacob Franks. First, building on the historical research of Maciejko, Sisman, and others, I will outline the life of Yaakov ben Leib himself. Second, I will introduce "Jacob Frank," the fictional character who functions in *Words of the Lord* as the hero of the Frankist myth. For our purposes, the second Jacob Frank is more important—although Frank's truths are often even stranger than his fictions.

The first Jacob Frank was born in 1726, but he was named Yankiev Leibowicz—Yakov ben Leib. Yakov was born into a family of Sabbatean believers in a small town in Podolia, at the time a region of southern Poland in what is now present-day Ukraine.[1] The family moved from place to place around the Ottoman Empire and its borders, including Czernowitz, Izmir, Istanbul, and Bucharest; indeed, many tales in *Words of the Lord* are bawdy stories from Frank's days as a trader in modern-day Romania and Bulgaria.[2] Even in this early period, Frank thrived in chaos; Bucharest had been ransacked in the 1730s and 1740s, and by the 1750s the city experienced

---

[1] Maciejko, *Mixed Multitude*, 12.
[2] Sisman, *Burden of Silence*, 151.

outbreaks of plague and economic crisis and was in a state of social and economic flux. Frank would spend most of his life in such "interzones" of disorder and lawlessness; his was to be a life of liminality, that state of in-between-ness and shape-shifting that accompanies transitions, outsiders, and boundary-crossers.[3] As noted in the introduction, even his name means "foreigner"; he was a Sephardic *frenk* in Poland and a European *frenk* in Salonica. As Frank himself says in §1110, "When one goes to see the sun, one ought to talk like the sun and dress like the sun; and when one goes to see the moon, one ought to wear what the moon wears and speak its language."

The most important context of Frank's career was the messianic heresy of Sabbetai Zevi (1626–1676), who for a brief moment (1665–1666) convinced a sizable portion of European and Ottoman Jewry that he would soon lead the Jewish people on a triumphant return to the Land of Israel (perhaps seizing the Ottoman throne from the sultan as well).[4] According to Sabbetai's chief prophet and publicist, Rabbi Nathan of Gaza, this would also usher in a new age in which the strictures of the material "Torah of the Tree of Knowledge of Good and Evil" would be relinquished in exchange for the lenient, liberated, spiritual "Torah of the Tree of Life." The Sabbatean movement spread astonishingly quickly, with the leaders of many communities not only believing in Zevi's messiahship but ostracizing those who did not. Abrogations of Jewish law—fast days turned into feasts, women taking ritual and leadership roles equal to those of men,[5] violations of dietary restrictions—became hallmarks of the movement and, as we will explore in chapter 5, powerfully decentering experiences for believers. On the surface, it is hard to see how Sabbetai, who had spent nearly thirty years as a wandering mystic, perhaps suffering from mental illness,[6] could have inspired a mass movement—although Cengiz Sisman has recently shown that the movement was likely not as massive as Scholem and others had believed.[7] Much of the credit is due to the erudition and persuasiveness of Nathan of Gaza; much to Sabbetai's wife, Sarah,

---

[3] On the concept of liminality, see Turner, *Forest of Symbols*, 94–130.

[4] Only a brief summary of the aspects of the Sabbatean movement relevant to Frankism is provided here. The most up-to-date and concise introduction to the movement is Goldish, "Sabbatai Zevi and the Sabbatean Movement," in *The Cambridge History of Judaism*, published in 2018. Gershom Scholem's massive and brilliant monograph, *Sabbatai Ṣevi: The Mystical Messiah*, remains the essential biography of Zevi and history of the movement, though many of its core theses have been heavily contested.

[5] Scholem, *Sabbatai Ṣevi*, 403–4; Rapoport-Albert, *Women and the Messianic Heresy*, 265–75; Van der Haven, *From Lowly Metaphor*, 41–45.

[6] Scholem, *Sabbatai Ṣevi*, 298–321. But see Elqayam, "Horizon of Reason" (questioning the ascription of mental illness to marginalized figures).

[7] Sisman, *Burden of Silence*, 63–69.

who led many of the innovations regarding women's leadership, became a prophetess herself, and arguably transformed the movement from asceticism to a kind of hedonism;[8] and some may be due to messianic tensions within Lurianic Kabbalah and the social conditions of the times.[9]

Sabbateanism as a mass phenomenon ended when Sabbetai converted to Islam, under duress, in September 1666.[10] But its impact on European Jewish history was profound, challenging rabbinic authority and popularizing Jewish mystical ideas—and, partly in response to Frank's own notoriety, provoking the taboos restricting the study of Kabbalah that still endure in traditional communities today. Nor did Sabbateanism, itself, disappear. On the contrary, in both European and Ottoman contexts, it exhibited a surprising resilience, enduring as a subterranean phenomenon even through the present day.[11] By the time Frank emerged, rabbinic authorities in Europe had struggled with Sabbatean sects for over half a century; they had ignored them, suppressed them, exposed their leaders, banned their books—and yet the heresy endured.[12] Further, because Sabbateanism was clustered around individual, charismatic prophet-mystics who operated outside the rabbinic hierarchy, it threatened rabbinic authority perhaps even more than it challenged normative Jewish theology.[13] The campaigns had torn Jewish communities apart; as Elisheva Carlebach has shown, lay leaders in communities often sided with their heretical local rabbis over rabbis from outside, further weakening the latter's authority.[14] Sometimes, the heretics were so well known that the rabbis sought to hush up the entire matter, as in the famous

---

[8] Van Der Haven, *From Lowly Metaphor*, 21–22, 40–45. Alas, Scholem himself repeats the heresiological and misogynistic derision of Sarah Ashkenazi, writing that "Perhaps Sarah, his beautiful wife, demanded freedom to satisfy her sensual desires, but we should be wary of attributing too much to her influence." Scholem, *Sabbatai Ṣevi*, 403.

[9] While Scholem emphasized the role of Lurianic Kabbalah, subsequent scholarship has found that diffusion of Lurianic Kabbalah was relatively limited, certainly among the masses of Jews. See Idel, "One from a Town." Further, Goldish notes that, in fact, socioeconomic conditions for many Jewish communities were relatively good in 1666. Goldish, "Sabbatai Zevi," 492–93.

[10] See Scholem, *Sabbatai Ṣevi*, 861.

[11] See Baer, "Revealing a Hidden Community" (reviewing work of Ilgaz Zorlu); Alpert, *Caught in the Crack*. One brief anecdote: When I was a graduate student in Jerusalem, I boarded a local bus with several books on Sabbateanism under my arm. The bus driver struck up a conversation with me (unusual in and of itself) and asked if I was "from Salonica," long a code word for being a member of the Sabbatean faithful.

[12] Carlebach, *Pursuit of Heresy*, 149. Carlebach notes that the shift in tactics took place from 1713 to 1715, as a result of vigorous agitation by Rabbi Moshe Hagiz. See also Kahana, "The Allure of Forbidden Knowledge," 592–99.

[13] Goldish, *Sabbatean Prophets*, 131–51; Goldish, "Toward a Reevaluation," 398–405.

[14] Carlebach, *Pursuit of Heresy*, 104–14.

case of Rabbi Jonathan Eibeschütz.[15] But over the course of the first half of the eighteenth century, the anti-Sabbatean crusade became a broad campaign against any form of "religious renewal," and, in a sense, the beginning of what would later become Orthodox Judaism.[16]

Meanwhile, in the Ottoman context, there arose several communities of *maʾaminim*, "believers" in Sabbetai Zevi, better known externally as the *doenmeh*, which had been a generic Ottoman term for "converts" but eventually came to refer solely to the Sabbatean sect.[17] Unlike most of Sabbetai's followers, the *maʾaminim* continued to believe in his messiahship, and followed him in converting outwardly to Islam, while secretly practicing some Jewish rituals and some uniquely heretical ones, such as ritual abrogation of the dietary laws and fast days, and, occasionally, of sexual mores as well. For the *doenmeh*, the antinomianism of these rituals, of Sabbetai's conversion, and of their own duplicity as crypto-Jews living as Muslims, grew into an entire worldview, in which the manifest, unredeemed world was a kind of illusion covering the true, messianic reality. There were successors to Sabbetai, each with different claims to being the messiah's true heir; there were sects with different interpretations of doctrine, community, and leadership; and there were prominent families who went on to become wealthy and famous within the Ottoman world. Astonishingly, the *doenmeh* persisted for over three centuries as an "open secret society"[18] with its own institutions, cemeteries, and social structures—all the way until the founding of modern-day Turkey in the twentieth century, which many secularizing *doenmeh* helped to bring about as leaders of the Young Turks.

From childhood, Frank was thoroughly enmeshed in the Sabbatean milieu. His family were *maʾaminim* who had relocated from the Ottoman Empire to Podolia, which was at the time "a seditious province where dissenters gathered and heterodoxy was practiced openly and publicly."[19] Frank's wife, Hannah, was most likely the daughter of the notable *doenmeh* leader Yehudah Levi Tova (also known as Dervish Effendi); they married in Nicopol (present-day Nikopol, Bulgaria) in 1752.[20] Eventually, Frank made

---

[15] Carlebach, *Pursuit of Heresy*, 177–82. R. Eibeschütz, when pressed, harshly rebuked Sabbateanism—but his very denunciation contained "dog-whistles" to fellow Sabbateans that made clear that his criticism was not sincere. Maciejko, "Coitus interruptus," v–xiv.

[16] Carlebach, *Pursuit of Heresy*, 255, 278.

[17] Sisman, *Burden of Silence*, 151.

[18] Ibid., 151. As Maurus Reinkowski has shown, the *doenmeh* were in fact one of many crypto-Jewish and crypto-Christian sects in the Islamic world. Reinkowski, "Hidden Believers," 425–26.

[19] Maciejko, *Mixed Multitude*, 10

[20] Sisman, *Burden of Silence*, 151; Maciejko, *Mixed Multitude*, 13.

his way to Salonica, the epicenter of the *doenmeh* community, where he became fully immersed in heretical Sabbateanism. The first phase of Frank's career as a heretical leader began in late 1753, when he entered a trance in front of a *doenmeh* community in Salonica and claimed that the soul of the second messianic leader of the sect, Baruchiah Russo, also known as Osman Baba, had entered his body.[21]

The Karakash sect of the *doenmeh*, to which Frank belonged and which is discussed in more detail below, was known as both the most antinomian of the three primary sects, and the most interested in winning new adherents, sending out emissaries to Sabbatean communities elsewhere. Initially, Frank appears to have been one such emissary when he returned across the border to Podolia on December 5, 1755, and became one of many heretical leaders in the area, gathering around him a small sect of followers, primarily of lower socioeconomic status. There were, at the time, many such sects, including the early Hasidim, who coalesced in the same period, and often in the same towns, as Sabbatean sects. Indeed, the accusations that the Hasidim were Sabbatean heretics might have seemed quite reasonable from the outside. As we will explore in chapter 8, both groups emphasized ecstatic practice over rote prayer, the Zohar over the Talmud. Both transmuted messianic zeal into the immediacy of "pneumatic" (Scholem's term for what today might be referred to as "spiritual") experience.[22] Both congregated around charismatic leaders outside the rabbinic hierarchy,[23] and, perhaps most importantly, both threatened the rabbinic power structure as a result. Although the accusations against the Hasidim were largely calumnies, some were reflective of reality.

But on January 27, 1756—less than two months after Frank's arrival—Frank's sect gained infamy and entered a new, second phase. That was the night Frank's sect was caught in the town of Lanckoronie (also Landskron or Lanckorona; today Zariczanka, Ukraine) allegedly performing a Sabbatean ritual. What were they really doing that night? According to the leading heresiologist of the time, Rabbi Jacob Emden, the sect was found dancing around the wife of the local rabbi, who was standing naked under a wedding

---

[21] As Goldish notes, the Sabbatean movement was in large part a movement of mass prophecy, one of the primary reasons it was opposed by rabbinic authorities. Goldish, *Sabbatean Prophets*, 130–61; Goldish, "Toward a Reevaluation," 398–405. Frank's trance thus placed him in a clear tradition of Sabbatean prophet-leaders. See also Garb, *Shamanic Trance*, 15 (noting prevalence of trance and prophecy in Sabbatean sects and contemporaneous non-Jewish sects). It is possible that the title Hakham, attached to Frank, may refer to the ability to prophesize in this way.

[22] Scholem, *Messianic Idea*, 91. See Goldish, *Sabbatean Prophets*, 89–90.

[23] On charisma and messianism, see Oakes, *Prophetic Charisma*; Goldish, "Jacob Frank's Innovations," 12–16.

canopy, wearing a Torah crown on her head.[24] While this ritual does resonate with Frank's corporealization of the spiritual and reification of the messianic, and with Sabbetai Zevi's wedding to the Torah, there is good reason to doubt it ever took place.[25] First, the account lacks documentary evidence, and similarly unsubstantiated reports appear throughout anti-Sabbatean literature, suggesting that this may have been a stock accusation rather than a report of a particular incident.[26] Second, Emden was a relentless campaigner against Sabbateanism who argued that Jewish law demanded that all Sabbateans—who, he said, routinely committed robbery and acts of sexual morality and should be considered as beasts of the forest—be killed.[27] The source of his account, the anti-Sabbatean/Frankist polemic, *Sefer Shimush*, was captioned "a special weapon for every Jew to use in order to know how to answer followers of Sabbetai Zevi," and featured a depiction of Frank as a three-headed, fire-breathing demon.[28] And as David Biale has written, Emden himself, "is a singularly dubious sociologist of his community . . . filled with inner conflicts and even pathologies. Emden was particularly obsessed with sexual transgressions."[29] Third, the Frankist claim that the sect was merely singing songs has some plausibility; it is now known that Sabbatean circles did gather for ecstatic singing and dancing,[30] and that, according to Doktór, contemporary church sources simply state that the sect was singing "mystical songs."[31] Fourth, as we will see in chapter 5, the (very rare) sexual rituals performed by the Frankist community greatly differ from this one. Fifth, accusations of sexual immorality are commonplace in the literature of heresiology and may in this case, as Ada Rapoport-Albert has suggested, in fact be responding to the active leadership of women in Sabbatean communities, from Sarah

---

[24] Emden, *Sefer Shimush*, 78b–79a.
[25] See Maciejko, *Mixed Multitude*, 22–26.
[26] Carlebach, *Pursuit of Heresy*, 152–53. As Carlebach notes, anti-Sabbatean rabbis were not careful with their accusations, and simply accused them in general of "permit[ting] the forbidden, idolatry, and promiscuity." Id. at 153. See also Sisman, *Burden of Silence*, 153–54 (noting similarities of accusations against Frankist and *doenmeh*); Schacter, "Jacob Emden."
[27] Schacter, "Jacob Emden," 381.
[28] Emden, *Sefer Shimush*, frontispiece.
[29] Biale, "Secularism and Sabbateans." Biale reports that Emden also recycled accounts of Sabbatean transgression. For example, Emden claimed that Wolf Eibeschütz traveled with a "whore" disguised as a male servant. Biale notes that this is "a shocking story about the son of a distinguished rabbi, except that Emden relates a similar story from an inn in which another male guest suspected of Sabbateanism was also said to sleep with his 'male' servant who, when spied on through a keyhole, turned out to be a girl. Emden's repeated use of this theme of sex with a girl servant disguised as a male arouses the suspicion that he manufactured such cases to suit his image of heresy if not his own sexual fantasies."
[30] See Samet, "Ottoman Songs in Sabbatian Manuscripts."
[31] Doktór, "The History of Jacob Frank," 264. See also Doktór, "Lanckoroń in 1756."

Ashkenazi through Chaya Shorr and Eve Frank. In her words, "the sexual depravity imputed to [Sabbatean] women was inextricably linked to their full engagement with the failed messianic project. It was an untimely eruption of female spirituality—a powerful force prematurely unleashed which was now to be stowed away, kept out of sight, and securely contained."[32] (Unsurprisingly, Emden called Schöndl Dobruschka, a wealthy patroness of Sabbatean sects, "the whore of Brünn."[33]) Given the lack of evidence and the unreliability of the primary reporter of this incident, we will likely never know what happened on the night of January 27, 1756, though I lend little credence to an unsubstantiated pro forma charge that deviates from what we know of the Frankists but conforms to what we know about calumnious accusations made at the time.

Yet whether the ritual actually happened or not is, in a way, secondary. For a number of reasons, the "Lanckoronie Affair" was a bridge too far: it was, at least as reported, an open defiance of rabbinic norms, rather than furtive and clandestine. Further, Maciejko speculates that the sect's alleged wearing of crucifixes in the Lanckronie ritual, rather than its alleged sexual elements, may have most troubled the rabbis who, uncharacteristically, joined Emden's campaign.[34] From the perspective of the rabbinic Council of the Four Lands, the long-simmering Sabbatean heresy now appeared to be boiling over into open rebellion. Emden, whom the rabbis had largely denounced during his campaign against Eibeschütz, now gained the favor of the Council.[35] Better to cut off a limb from the "body of Israel," Emden wrote, than to allow the infection to spread.[36] (The Baal Shem Tov, the founder of Hasidism, would later bewail this decision in the same terms as the rabbis, saying that a limb of the Shechinah could always be healed, but once it is cut off, it is lost forever.[37]) And so the rabbis took two unprecedented actions. First, they publicly prosecuted Sabbateans, soliciting the testimony from Jews who had supposedly spied on them through keyholes and reported violations of

---

[32] Rapoport-Albert, *Women and the Messianic Heresy*, 296, 34–38, 84–86, 144–48. But see Maciejko, *Mixed Multitude*, 38 (discussing practice of "sexual hospitality").
[33] Cited in Maciejko, *Mixed Multitude*, 192.
[34] Ibid., 39.
[35] See Schacter, "Jacob Emden," 361–63.
[36] *Sefer Shimush*, 20a–b. See Elior, *Mystical Origins*, 177–79; Bałaban, *Le-Toledot*, 122–25; Ya'ari, "A History of the Campaign"; Maciejko, "Baruch me-Eretz Yavan," 335, n.9.
[37] The Baal Shem Tov's reversal of this metaphor is recorded in *Shivhei HaBesht*: "I heard from our rabbi that the Baal Shem Tov said that the Shechinah wails and says: as long as the limb is connected, there is hope for a remedy; but when it is amputated there is no remedy forever; for every Jew is a limb of the Shechinah." See Baer ben Samuel, *In Praise of the Baal Shem Tov*.

the Sabbath, theological heresies, and numerous sexual transgressions, including "sexual hospitality," masturbation, sex with menstruant women, and incest.[38] Sabbateans were flogged and banished, and on May 26, 1756, the rabbis excommunicated all the accused from Lanckoronie. Further, the rabbis restricted the study of Kabbalah only to men over forty, a policy still in force today.[39] Second, the rabbis reported the sect to the Christian religious authorities, who under canon law claimed jurisdiction over defending Judaism against internal heresy.[40] Ecclesiastical authorities had never before "defended" Jews in this way, and it was a violation of long-standing rabbinic law to report Jews to gentile legal authorities. Yet the Council of the Four Lands reported the Sabbateans to Christian legal authorities for "deviation from the true teachings of Mosaic Law."[41]

The move backfired. The Kamieniec diocese, which included Lanckoronie, was headed by a virulently antisemitic bishop, Mikołaj Dembowski (1680–1757), who used the controversy for his own purposes after the rabbis realized their mistake and tried unsuccessfully to withdraw the case. First, the Sabbateans were granted temporary safe passage—though Frank himself, as an Ottoman subject, was expelled (or chose to return) to Salonica in April 1756. He would not lead the sect in its most notorious period—the leader at the time was one Yehuda Leib Krysa—and it is unclear to what extent he still exercised leadership from afar; as for himself, he converted to Islam and took the name of Ahmed.[42] Next, under Bishop Dembowski's leadership, the tables were turned. The "deviant" Sabbateans were now presented as "Contra-Talmudists," and they acted as plaintiffs against the Jews and the Talmud in a public disputation held in Kamieniec in June 1757. In October, Bishop Dembowski issued a horrifying ruling that declared the Contra-Talmudists victorious and ordered the burning of the Talmud and other books (ironically, including the Zohar), an edict that tragically was carried out in many Polish towns.

But then Bishop Dembowski died. His sudden death, after a stroke on November 9, 1757, was regarded by Christians and Jews alike an act of divine intervention, and the tables turned immediately. The burnings of the Talmud stopped. "Contra-Talmudists" went into hiding, many fleeing across

---

[38] Maciejko, *Mixed Multitude*, 32–33.
[39] Ibid., 78–79.
[40] Ibid., 29–30.
[41] Ibid., 30.
[42] Sisman, *Burden of Silence*, 152.

the Danube to join Frank. Krysa was beaten. It seemed that the rabbinic authorities had prevailed due to divine intervention, and that the Sabbatean-Frankist-Krysist period in Poland had come to an end.

And then the tables turned yet again. In July 1758, most likely, as Maciejko suggests, under the influence of a notoriously antisemitic, corrupt, and vicious bishop, Kajetan Sołtyk, King Augustus III of Poland issued a writ of safe passage enabling the "Contra-Talmudists" who had fled to the Ottoman Empire and had subsequently gathered around the exiled Jacob/Ahmed Frank to return to Poland. The reason became clear: they were to be tools in proving the blood libel, the notorious accusation that Jews required Christian blood for their rituals (which Sołtyk himself had prosecuted in 1753, most likely to extort Jews to pay his gambling debts[43]). Now the Frankists presented themselves as candidates for conversion to Christianity (Frank having buried the evidence of his conversion to Islam), professing belief in the Trinity and announcing that they sought to be baptized. They also confirmed the truth of the blood libel. A second series of disputations took place, this time in Lwów, between July and September 1759. As Maciejko describes in detail, the 1759 disputation was at the confluence of a complicated set of Catholic and Jewish political and social currents, which are beyond the scope of the present study.[44] Fortunately, the blood libel was rejected in this case—but the damage had been done. Though it was not the first time that Jews had invoked the blood libel against their fellow Jews, the Frankists' active participation in the blood libel accusation has earned them a place of infamy within Jewish history. The Frankist sect had already stated their intention to become Christians, and on September 17, 1759, both Frank and Krysa were baptized in Lwów.

As Maciejko conclusively establishes, the idea of converting originated neither from the Frankists nor with the Catholic clergy but from the rabbinic authorities.[45] Following the 1757 disputation, when Contra-Talmudism had been recognized as a legitimate form of Judaism, the Council of the Four Lands appealed to the papal nuncio, denounced the heretical sect, and asked that they "either fully embrace Roman Catholicism, or fully accept our Jewish religion, or [be recognized] as heretics."[46] Since the third option would necessitate a death sentence, the rabbinic position was that the Frankists

---

[43] Maciejko, *Mixed Multitude*, 103.
[44] Ibid., 107–26.
[45] Ibid., 131–45.
[46] Ibid., 133.

should either repent, convert, or die—with the 1757 persecutions making clear that repentance was no longer a viable option. Indeed, as Emden said, the heretical community had become a limb that needed to be amputated.[47] It is estimated that approximately 2,000 Jews converted in those months, mostly in Lwów, with an additional 1,000 in the following few years. (Some estimates run as high as 15,000, though that is extremely unlikely.) Many Frankists-Sabbateans did not convert, remaining heretics within the Jewish community—we will touch on their histories in chapter 8. But an enormous number did. To get a sense of the massive scope of this event, Lwów itself, the second-largest Jewish community in Poland at the time, had a Jewish population of around 7,400 people.[48] Never before, and never since, has such a mass conversion taken place, with over one quarter of a city's Jewish population leaving the fold. The Frankist mass apostasy was an astonishing, shocking event.

Indeed, this entire series of events, which unfolded over a remarkably short period of time, is rather stunning. An itinerant merchant becomes a charismatic figure in an antinomian heretical sect in Salonica (1753–1755), contesting the leadership of the entire sect. Perhaps under duress, he returns to Polish territory, acquires followers mostly from marginalized and impoverished outcasts from Jewish society (but with a few wealthy benefactors), and becomes a notorious heretic, undermining rabbinic authority and changing Jewish history before being exiled in disgrace and formally converting to Islam (1755–1757). Then, after several twists of fortune, he regains his followers, returns to Poland, allies himself with antisemites, and converts to Catholicism in the largest mass apostasy in Jewish history (1758–1759). As to his followers, some seem to have been caught up in currents beyond their control, some were perhaps motivated by messianic zeal and Frank's charisma, and some likely had economic motives, as conversion offered social mobility and freedom.[49]

But the edifice soon collapsed. For a brief time, the neophyte Frank enjoyed a moment of celebrity; he was baptized in the Royal Chapel of

---

[47] Ibid., 161.
[48] Ibid., 129. The exact numbers of converts differ depending on the source. Kraushar quotes the Primate in Lwów as reporting that Frank had fifteen thousand followers, and Maciejko cites an eyewitness source with the same figure. Kraushar, *Jacob Frank*, 131; Maciejko, "Development," 43. Catholic priests stated that between one and two thousand Jews converted after the Lwów disputation. In their abortive 1766 negotiations with Russia, the Frankists boasted that twenty thousand Jews would convert to Orthodoxy if the Russians would liberate Frank from captivity. Maciejko, "Development," 58.
[49] See Levine, "Frankism as Worldly Messianism," 290.

Warsaw with King Augustus III serving as his godfather. He paraded around in a large chariot and lived in opulence. And, having cemented his leadership of the sect, he negotiated for some degree of territorial and political autonomy, promising that thousands of Jews would convert and join him.[50] But almost immediately, as early as November 1759, Frank appears to have been denounced by some of his more recent followers: he was still a heretic, they said, and was worshiped as a messiah, or even as God. He was arrested in January 1760, and promptly imprisoned (or sheltered) in the fortress/monastery of Częstochowa, where he would languish for twelve years until the Russians conquered it in 1772.[51] Frank's moment of greatest fame (or infamy) had come and gone, and after the arrest in 1760, Frankism ceased being a mass movement.

But it did not die. Rather, Frankism entered a fourth phase, which is the primary subject of this book. During his stay in Częstochowa, Frank lost most of his supporters, but he consolidated those who remained and, as Sabbetai Zevi had done a century prior, Frank interpreted his imprisonment as Divine providence. His religious ideas also changed, no doubt due to expediency but also due to the unique circumstances in which Frank found himself: Częstochowa was, and is, the site of Jasna Góra, the national shrine of Poland, which houses the "Black Virgin of Częstochowa," an ancient painting of the Virgin Mary that was reputed to have magical powers and is still today the object of intense pilgrimage, veneration, and devotion. And so, Frank developed a complex theology, which we will explore in more detail in chapter 5, centered around the *Panna*, or Maiden, a messianic, syncretic hybrid of the Shechinah, the Black Madonna, and Frank's own daughter, Eve.[52] Frank remained in touch with his remaining followers, and some even stayed with him in Częstochowa, remarkably, continuing to perform heretical rituals on the ramparts of the fortress.[53]

By the time of Frank's release in 1772, the Frankist sect had shrunk to a small and largely secret network, with faithful adherents supporting the Frankist court. That court itself was a kind of charade, existing from 1773 to 1786 in Brünn, Moravia (today, Brno, Czech Republic, 285 miles southwest

---

[50] Maciejko, *Mixed Multitude*, 157–60.

[51] Ibid., 163–66. Doktór argues that Frank was not imprisoned so much as sheltered and protected by Church authorities; his family, closest supporters, and even his personal chef went with him. Doktór, "Frankism: The History of Jacob Frank," 267–71.

[52] Eve is usually referred to as "Her Highness" in ZSP. RA, interestingly, often refers to her as "Hawacza," roughly equivalent to the endearment form "Chavaleh."

[53] Maciejko, *Mixed Multitude*, 169.

of Warsaw), then a loosely governed part of the Hapsburg Empire, and from 1786 until Eve Frank's death in 1816 in an unused castle in Offenbach, Germany. In this phase, the Frankist community existed in two distinct parts: the close circle at court, to whom Frank addressed the *Words of the Lord*, and the wider community of supporters, mostly in Warsaw and Prague, to whom Frank would frequently appeal for donations. At its head was the charismatic Frank, garbed in "exotic" attire, conducting alchemical experiments, connecting with networks of Freemasons and other Western esotericists, and participating in European politics. In Moravia, Frank attracted new, wealthier, and more educated followers, especially the Dobruschka family, whose matriarch at the time, Schöndl, was a patroness of the Sabbatean community; Frank settled in Brünn because of this connection, and initially passed himself off as Schöndl's brother (they may in fact have been cousins).[54] Moses Dobruschka, one of Schöndl's children, became one of Frank's leading followers and was offered the leadership of the sect when Frank died in 1791. He also, under the name Thomas von Schönfeld, was involved in running guns between the Hapsburg Court and the French revolutionaries; later, he became known as a Jacobin under the name of Junius Frey and was guillotined during the Reign of Terror.[55] Frank moved through European society in a variety of guises: (false) baron, (false) Russian nobility, spy, Kabbalist, alchemist, charlatan, proselytizer to the Jews, and leader of a strange and secretive sect with political intrigue swirling around it. Eve was rumored to have had an affair with Emperor Joseph II, and political machinations—including Joseph's preparations of war with the Ottoman Empire and the Russian annexation of Crimea in 1783[56]— may be what Frank refers to as the "beginning of the last days." (§555, 75) After Frank fell out of favor with Joseph II in 1786, his court relocated to Offenbach, borrowing a castle from Prince Wolfgang Ernst II, a Rosicrucian whom Frank likely met through Masonic networks; Frank renamed it the *Gotteshaus*, or God's house.[57] There, the sect passed themselves off as Polish (and, later, Russian) aristocrats, with "Baron von Franck" parading around in elaborately appointed coaches, dressed in "Turkish" fashion with a fur cap and yellow slippers. His disciples conducted paramilitary exercises on the

---

[54] Ibid., 192–97.
[55] Scholem, "The Career of a Frankist." See also Ascarelli, "The Unfortunate Encounters."
[56] See Maciejko, "Portrait," 555; Maciejko, *Mixed Multitude*, 211–13.
[57] See Davidowicz, "The Frankist Court at Offenbach," 29; Maciejko, *Mixed Multitude*, 233–36; Lenowitz, "The Charlatan at the *Gottes Haus*."

grounds, ostensibly to prepare for the coming war between Christians and Jews, though this was not explained to the neighbors. And Frank conducted alchemical experiments, either to discover the secret to immortality, or perhaps just for show. These later years of Frankism sound like the stuff of conspiracy theories: a mysterious leader and shadowy connections across Europe, with a court visited by czars, princes, Freemasons, and political radicals. Goethe described it as a vast masquerade, as indeed it was.[58] Yet Frank's political machinations and esoteric pursuits (or affectations) may have reinforced one another. As Levine notes,

> the outer signs of Frank's political entanglements are visible and abundant. His religion may have been as influenced by his political machinations as his politics have been recognized to be an expression of religious orientations. Without overrationalizing his actions or exaggerating his political savvy, it is safe to say that within the political context of his time it can hardly be claimed that he lived solely or even primarily in a mythological world. . . . Frank's inner world was made up of more than personal madness and Gnostic myths.[59]

Frank died in 1791, to the great disappointment of his followers. (At one point, his sons even masqueraded as Frank and rode around in his carriage to prove he was still alive.[60]) Sisman estimates that by 1791, there were at most 6,000 Frankists in Warsaw, and 24,000 in all of Poland.[61] Even that number dwindled: As we will discuss in chapter 8, the fifth phase of the movement, which lasted until Eve Frank's death in 1816, was one of decay. After Frank's death, disciples sent out apocalyptic letters warning the Jews of imminent war and urging them to convert. The letters were written in red ink (a pun on Edom, a symbol of Christianity, and *adom*, the color red) and became known as the "Red Letters"; they are dense with biblical allusions and, though their style is quite different from Frank's oral teachings, they were advertised as having been written by Frank himself—but they were also largely ignored.[62]

---

[58] Maciejko, *Mixed Multitude*, 238.
[59] Levine, "Frankism as Worldly Messianism," 295.
[60] Davidowicz, "The Frankist Court at Offenbach," 36–37.
[61] Sisman, *Burden of Silence*, 152. Even that figure may be too high, as it is in part based on anti-Frankist propaganda. Allerhand, "The Frankist Movement and Its Polish Context," 108–9.
[62] Maciejko believes these letters were written by Frank himself during his imprisonment, and were originally part of his campaign to ingratiate himself to the Polish authorities by encouraging more conversions. Maciejko, *Mixed Multitude*, 184–85.

In these later texts, the esotericist worldview of the *Words of the Lord* was set aside, replaced by a more conventional eschatology. The end of the world is nigh; Jews must convert to Christianity; Frank is a divine redeemer, the heir to Sabbetai Zevi. Meanwhile, in the real world, debts piled up, only occasionally postponed by rumors of "Her Highness" Eve Frank's (nonexistent) connections to Russian royalty.[63] Eve was placed under house arrest for unpaid bills, and when she died in 1816, there was no one to take her place. Frankism as a movement was over.

And yet, Frank's followers did not disappear. In Prague, as I discuss in chapter 8, the Sabbatean community, at least some of whom regarded Frank as an important personage, went on to become leaders of the Haskalah; one even described anti-Sabbatean persecution as having targeted at "the progressive party" within the Jewish community.[64] In Warsaw, the "neophytes" remained a distinct community throughout the nineteenth century, and included numerous prominent attorneys and members of Poland's professional class. Adam Mickiewicz, considered Poland's greatest poet, invoked Frankist themes in his work, married into a Frankist family, and advocated for a Poland inclusive of Jews, whose presence there he said was divinely ordained.[65] And over a century later, Justice Louis Brandeis had on his desk in his Supreme Court chambers a portrait of Eve Frank, an heirloom he received from his Dembitz relatives, whose ancestors were followers of Frank. It's remarkable, really, to think that a Supreme Court justice had a memento on his desk depicting someone said to be the Messiah, an incarnation of the Divine Feminine, a possible participant in sexual ritual, and a former *ingenue* who had liaisons with Hapsburg royalty. Finally, as we will see in chapter 8, Frankism anticipated important currents of subsequent Jewish thought, including the Haskalah, Hasidism, and New Age Judaism.

But the sect itself has largely faded from memory, and to the extent it remains, it is primarily associated with the blood libel, the burning of the Talmud, and allegations of sexual licentiousness. Even the Polish neophytes distanced themselves from the scandal of Frankism, writing *apologia* to explain how they had rejected their earlier antinomianism, and, it appears, censoring some Frankist records as well. For example, Alexandr Kraushar, the neophyte-appointed historian who first published excerpts from *ZSP*

---

[63] Ibid., 237–38.
[64] Ibid., 251.
[65] See Duker, "Some Cabbalistic & Frankist Elements"; Duker, "The Mystery of the Jews"; Bosak, "Mickiewicz, Frank, and the Conquest of the Land of Israel."

in the 1880s, called Frankism "a theosophical system born in the head of a boor."[66] This was likely for polemical reasons: namely, to distinguish between Frankists in the movement's early period and the blameless bourgeois citizens who were their descendants. But the characterization has stuck. The great Jewish historian Heinrich Graetz called Frankism "the impure spring that poisoned the sap of the tree of Judaism."[67] Abraham Brawer analogized Frank to a drug addict, stated that the Frankists had "blood on their hands" due to the blood libel in the Lwów disputation, and claimed that Frankism could only be understood as "sexual psychopathology."[68] Hillel Levine said, "the renewal in Sabbateanism in the second part of the eighteenth century has been the object of moral condemnation and psychological reductionism."[69] (Avraham Elqayam has observed that such pseudo-diagnoses are often applied to figures rendered marginal by history, including Sabbetai Zevi.[70]) Of course, these scholars were primarily focused on the Contra-Talmudists' collusion with Christian authorities, not the theological utterances in *ZSP*, which came decades later. Still, the threshold question of the present study is whether Frankism has anything worthy of attention as a religious phenomenon.

My claim is that it does. One cannot contest Frank's opportunism and apparent uses of sex, violence, and verbal abuse in relationship to his followers. But he also developed a coherent, materialistic, and protomodern skeptical worldview that he combined with myths and tales of startling originality. Both are true: both the charlatan and the innovator, the genius and the manipulator. As Matt Goldish has written, Frank is "highly energetic, grandiose in his self-confidence, dominant, rhetorically skilled, manipulative, demanding of conformity, disempowering of his followers, self-contained, strong, and socially insightful."[71]

Theology or Nonsense?

The "Jacob Frank" of *Words of the Lord* is as much of a shape-shifter as Jacob Frank was in real life. Sometimes he is a "holy fool" who possesses great

---

[66] Kraushar, *Jacob Frank*, 106.
[67] Graetz, *Geschichte der Juden*, 10:422, quoted in Maciejko, *Mixed Multitude*, 197.
[68] Brawer, *Studies in Galician Jewry*, 197–98.
[69] Levine, "Frankism as a 'Cargo Cult,'" 81.
[70] Elqayam, "Horizon of Reason," 23.
[71] Goldish, "Jacob Frank's Innovations," 12.

wisdom despite outward appearances to the contrary; other times he is the chosen one who, while not the messiah, will herald the coming of the messiah and an age of tumult and blood. In *ZSP*'s perplexing mythical utterances, Frank is an initiate in possession of esoteric secrets, and in communication with superhuman figures from a parallel dimension. Elsewhere, he is a scold, bitterly admonishing his followers; other times, he is a would-be prophet; still others, an embittered old man. In the next section, we will explore this character in detail, but first, we must address a threshold question: How seriously are we to take *ZSP*'s wild tales, reports of supernatural prophecy, and oracular utterances? Are these actual experiences, visions, episodes of mental illness, or mere fabrication? Is Jacob Frank a theologian, a fool, a con man, or all of the above?

Clearly, *Words of the Lord* is not a traditional collection of religious teachings; its over 1,400 dicta available to us, chronologically arranged and today contained in three manuscripts (two in the Jagiellonian library in Krakow and one in the Hieronim Łopaciński library in Lublin), span multiple genres and subject matters: exhorting Frank's followers to fulfill their mission, interpreting the Torah in radical ways similar to those of Western esotericism, ridiculing traditional religion, portraying the outlandish character of Jacob Frank, and inventing a new myth based on magic, folklore, and Frank's original materialist theology. Its recorded oral teachings include autobiographical statements, interpretations of dreams and visions, biblical exegesis, exhortations to the Frankist followers, long and short theological utterances, tales and parables, and other material. Here, I will focus on three interrelated issues: vulgarity, concealment, and the meaning of Frankist prophecy.

First, *ZSP* presents itself as a "low" work that explicitly denies the worth of traditional religious rhetoric as part of its transgressive program. If piety, boundedness, and righteousness are antithetical to the Frankist theological-religious project, they are in the literary/oral project as well, which explicitly disdains standards of taste, decorum, and learning. Particularly in the tales, which Frank himself describes as vulgar, *ZSP* consists in large part of boasting, profanity, and vulgarity. Yet Frank insists that the vulgarity conceals a deeper wisdom. Over and over again, he states that "wisdom is hidden in most debased of places" (§33). For example, in § 172, Frank states,

I have told you several times that the more precious the stone, the baser the rock it is in, scorned by all eyes, while those who are knowledgeable about such things know that here a good stone must lie. So it is with me and you. I told you base things about Bucharest, about keeping the company of women and similar things, and told you various similar things, and you scorned me. You should have understood that in all of my words, if a person receives them as humbug, he can come and find wisdom. From now on I admonish you, although you will see me do strange deeds, childish acts, stupidities, lies, you have to bear it all, listen and see, and not turn your heart away, because that is virtue and constancy.

Likewise, in §115 Frank castigates the Brethren, complaining,

You did not find any wisdom in my simple stories; you have to learn well and understand in order to comprehend what I tell you. That is why from now on I will not reveal anything to you unless you are worthy of it. . . . I told you about a few escapades in Bucharest—you should have considered whether I, who have come to lead you into religion, [would] say futile things? You should have understood that there is wisdom hidden in this foolishness and everything that looks like a deadly herb on the surface contains a life-giving herb within. I have given you a good thing but I have covered it on the surface with a veil that appears ugly to you and that is why you have not understood anything or discovered anything.

Similarly, in §302, Frank says,

I was telling you things which in your eyes were strange, boorish and meaningless. You could not drink this bitter water, but you know that when walnuts are gathered, the first husk is green, bitter and dark, and tars your hands, until you get to the kernel. How did you not surmise this?

And in §922, he states,

I tell you everything and nothing, I tell you nothing and everything, because you do not understand what I tell you. In the worst of all places, which seems to you to be full of stupidity, there is great wisdom, but you have not yet been given the heart to understand.

What seem to be bawdy tales of wild Bucharest in fact are to be read carefully for the wisdom that lies within. The "Jacob Frank" of these tales, and the way in which they are told, are ruses, literary tactics.

Even the word "simple" is not meant in a simple way. In §333, Frank says, "until you learn that all my words are simple, just as I say them, you will not reach anything," but then tells a series of short tales in which "simple" actually means hyper-literal, even to the point of absurdity. First, Frank tells someone that he heard he was "going from house to house." The other person is insulted, assuming the phrase refers to begging, but Frank means hyper-literally walking from house to house. Then Frank says he heard he was going around with intestines. The other man assumes this means that he was selling intestines, and is insulted again. But Frank means it hyper-literally: with intestines in his body. Then Frank gets a man to promise him money if he tries to cut a stone with a string. Frank runs a string over the stone and demands the money—after all, he just tried! In all these cases, "simple" does not mean "in the ordinary sense" but overly literally—a principle that also extends to Frankist mythical statements that are meant to be taken literally and physically. There is an actual well under Częstochowa. There are actual *ba'alei kaben*, quasi-magical beings living in caves, as §1259 says, in Switzerland, the Tyrol, Hungary, and Poland. They eat off physical dishes of gold. This "simple" speech is deceptively simple; it is in fact a rejection both of Kabbalistic and Sabbatean symbolism, in which the manifest world is less important than the supernal (or deeper) worlds in which redemption has already come, and of any religious speech that defers meaning and power into a spiritual realm. Frank's "simplicity" is a critique of conventional religion.

A second dynamic interplay in *ZSP* is, like that in many esoteric texts, between openness and concealment. On the one hand, as Rachel Elior has observed, *ZSP* is a brazen act of disclosure, spoken "so that everyone can see," with tales of trickery, sexuality, and violence, and with a radical contempt for traditional religion.[72] Over and over again, Frank boasts that he does things openly, where previous leaders were secretive. Linking corporealization with disclosure, Frank says "I will, in turn, reveal everything in daylight, so that what was of the spirit can remain in the body, so that nothing is hidden, the whole world will see it clearly and openly" (§552). Similarly, Frank repeatedly enjoins his followers to be open. In *RA* §20, he says, in a self-martyring vein:

---

[72] See Elior, "Jacob Frank," 471–75.

> If we know the true God and you believe in Him, why should we hide? We will go out in the open and let everyone know it. Whoever wants to sacrifice their body for the love of the faith, come with me.

And in *ZSP* §1311, Frank claims that the discovery of the secret ritual in Lanckoronie was not accidental but rather a result of his deliberate action: "When I arrived in Lanckoronie and you were singing songs, during the night, with the windows shut, I went out and opened the window so that everything would unavoidably be heard."

On the other hand, total openness, Frank says, must be deferred to the future, due to the Brethren's betrayal of Frank in 1759 (§895). Until that time when all will at last be revealed, Frank imposes *ma'asah dumah*, the "burden of silence," a phrase taken from Isaiah 21:11 that was also used frequently in *doenmeh* circles and which is mentioned in sixteen dicta in *ZSP*.[73] Carrying this burden means acting secretly, knowing secretly, and not speaking of what one knows (§746). *Das*, the esoteric gnosis that will lead to immortality, is likewise a secret, and identified with this burden (§795). In §993, Frank cites the famous passage in 1 Kings 19:10–15 that depicts God not in the fire or the earthquake but emerging as a still, small voice; for Frank, this shows that revelation is secret and quiet at first. (Frank also cites Maimonides as an example of a sage who knew to conceal his most provocative teachings, belying the claim that Frank is an unlettered boor.) Angels and faithful servants act, says Frank; they do not speak (§753). This burden must be carried, Frank states in §611, again citing Isaiah 21:11, until "they will call me from Seir," meaning, until Frank's "aid" arrives and the quest is completed. Once the Brethren put on the garments of Esau (one of the many stages in their quest, discussed in chapter 4), Frank states in §1014, then all will be revealed and the burden will be lifted. Until then, however, not only must the Brethren keep secrets, but *ZSP* does as well. It is an esoteric text, a secret disclosure given over only to Frank's inner circle of disciples, and it constantly speaks of the need to be quiet, careful, and even duplicitous.

Of course, perhaps the simplest explanation for the tension between openness and concealment is that it enables Frank to manipulate his followers. By endlessly saying that the tales are only the surface of the matter—and yet the Brethren are not perceiving the "simple" meaning—Frank may endlessly postpone disclosure, and gain the frisson of secrecy and esoteric knowledge.

---

[73] See Sisman, *Burden of Silence*, 148–50.

The tension may also reflect the necessary shift in Frank's career. Until 1759, Frank advocated greater openness. When that ended in catastrophe, he shifted direction and advocated skillful silence. Frank preaches openness, but demands silence; says he is speaking simply, but says that his words are more complicated than they appear. Not surprisingly, in §115, Frank quotes Ecclesiastes 3:7 that there is "a time to speak, a time to be silent."

A third puzzle of *ZSP* is how to understand Frank's outrageous, fantastic prophecies, conversations with supernatural beings, and visions—or, more precisely, how to understand what Frank wants us to believe about them. It is certainly possible that Frank actually experienced elaborate visions of the "world behind the screen" with the Big Brother and his retinue, of magical beings, and of apocalyptic prophecies. Perhaps these occurred as dreams, or as mystical experiences, or trance states or as hallucinations.[74] But with the exception of the forty-two dicta in *ZSP* proper that specifically recount dreams (mostly of Frank, though some of Eve Frank and some of leading disciple, and possible transcriber of *ZSP*, Mateusz Matuszewski), the only clear statements of this phenomenon are in the semidistinct text, *Visions of the Lord*, comprising dicta 2189–2286. Most of those dicta include Frank saying "I saw" (*widziałem*), but except for those that are dreams (e.g., §§2189, 2191) there are no clues as to what kind of vision this refers to: an experience of actual sight, hallucination, trance, prophetic vision, dream, or otherwise. *ZSP* proper is even less clear. A handful of dicta suggest that they were, in part, likely derived from trancelike altered-consciousness experiences ("visions"), auditory hallucination ("I was told . . . "), and other mind-states that often are characterized as "prophecy." For example, in §978, Frank says he was "shown those places" and goes on to describe the other world behind the curtain in great detail. If this represents an actual visionary experience, it is surely among the most colorful and expansive mystical visualizations in the Western corpus. But in §990, Frank implies that "see" may be in dreams; referring to the Big Brother, he says, "When I am worthy of seeing him, if only in my dream, I will already have eternal life." §1097 suggests that Frank's religious/prophetic experiences are based on hearing voices: "I have a leader who leads me everywhere, telling me: Jacob, go there, look this way, do this, and he never turns away from me." These glimpses of reports of religious/mystical/prophetic/auditory experiences suggest that there may have been

---

[74] See Garb, *Shamanic Trance*, 65–71, 123–26. Trance-prophetic states were present throughout the Sabbatean movement and other spiritual movements at the time. Id. at 15; Goldish, *Sabbatean Prophets*, 130–61; Goldish, "Toward a Reevaluation," 398–405.

some experiential basis for Frank's statements. Notably, however, while we noted earlier that Frank's career began with a trance in which he allegedly inherited the soul of Baruchiah Russo, there are no direct reports of prophetic trance in ZSP.[75]

It is certainly possible that Frank was simply making these claims up, using his evident charisma as a way to deflect attention from his manifest failures and maintain control over the Brethren. This, too, has precedent in Sabbateanism; Matt Goldish notes that the Sabbatean prophet Nathan of Gaza once forged an "ancient" manuscript and distressed the paper on which it was written to make it look old.[76] And there is no denying Frank's constant, endless dissembling. In perhaps the reductio ad absurdum of Frank's lies, the Brethren are literally not allowed in Frank's physical room: "You cannot be in my room, and it is all for your good; and when you see, you will understand and thank God for it" (§617; see also §§476, 554) In §447, Frank says,

> Truly I tell you, there is a thing in my room that walks from one door to another, and when I see that this thing covers its eyes and shields them from you with its hands, I, too, grow angry with this man, and this thing's actions are surely not in vain. I do not know [what] this [means], perhaps it is showing me that when assistance comes, you will not be in my room, or perhaps it is telling me that you have a certain flaw.

Such remarks are the ultimate, ridiculous postponement: Even in the innermost circle of the Brethren, even in Frank's house, there is still something magical supposedly happening in his very room, which only he can enter. (Then again, it may accord with reports of Frank conducting alchemical experiments, which did apparently take place in a sealed room,[77] or, if they report an actual experience, signs of mental distress.) Once Frank had ambitions to rule part of Poland; now his territory is literally his bedroom. Perhaps all of Frank's fantastic claims are simply made up.

A third possibility is that Frank's supposed prophecies are not meant to be taken entirely seriously. Did Frank really think that his inner circle would believe that one of their number was to be made thirty cubits tall, and that another would get ten billion ducats? The grotesque nature of these promises

---

[75] Maciejko, *Mixed Multitude*, 15.
[76] Goldish, "Messianism and Ethics," 166–67.
[77] Maciejko, *Mixed Multitude*, 233. This report is from Offenbach, rather than Brünn, however.

makes them seem almost parodic—as if Frank is saying they'd get a zillion dollars and run a million miles. Likewise in §317, where Frank says that underneath Częstochowa there are secret caves from which the Brethren would obtain fifty or sixty carriages decorated in precious stones. Perhaps Frank is speaking on multiple levels, duping the people who take such absurdities seriously, while winking at those who do not. Frank is, after all, a self-conscious charlatan; conning the credulous is part of the game.[78]

Functionally speaking, the fantastic material serves as an "inner myth" that differentiates the Brethren/elect/elite from the masses. This is a common feature in emerging religions and new religious movements, which often have elaborate cosmologies reserved for small elites, alongside more accessible teachings for the wider community of followers. Examples include Mormonism, where secret cosmological teachings about the afterlife and immortality were long reserved for the few; Jehovah's Witnesses; and Scientology, with exoteric teachings on psychological insight and esoteric ones on intergalactic warfare.[79] These secret doctrines construct an elite identity and perpetuate an air of mystery and revelation; the inner circle is able to preserve the aspect of novelty and mystery by continuing to have revealed to them newer and more abstruse legends and myths. In the case of Frankism, most Frankists may have believed they were still following Sabbetai Zevi, or converting to Christianity, or creating some new religion combining Judaism and Christianity, or even, as Hillel Levine proposed, following a useful "cargo cult" that enabled them to progress economically.[80] And yet the inner circle had *Das*, a secret *gnosis* of supernatural beings and immortality. Conceivably, whether the Brethren believed in these secret myths may have been less important than the fact that they possessed them.

Chosen Fool and Wise-Mad Trickster: The Characters of "Jacob Frank"

The "Jacob Frank" within the tales is a character, not an author. The tales, after all, are made up. Did Frank really leave footprints when he walked on oak wood, as he boasts in §25? Presumably not. Did he really sit bare-bottom

---

[78] See Casanova, *History of My Life*, in which Casanova revels in using real and fake wisdom to obtain material benefit from higher-rank people who would ordinarily have excluded him.
[79] See Urban, *Church of Scientology*, 64–86.
[80] Levine, "Frankism as a 'Cargo Cult,'" 87–93.

on a Torah scroll, as he says in §19? Also probably not. These are the actions of a constructed literary character, not records of history. And that means we can inquire as to the pedagogical and literary purpose of Frank's tales, and set them in historical context, which in this case includes the eighteenth-century libertines with whom Frank was in contact. Like them, Frank tells bawdy tales to highlight the absurdity of conventional morality, and creates a seemingly mad protagonist to depict the madness of society. The prophet Hosea wrote that as the end of days draws near, "the prophet is a fool, the man of spirit is mad" (Hosea 9:7). Here, I will explore these two aspects of the "Jacob Frank" of the tales: a "holy fool" on a divine mission, and a trickster who engages in outrageous acts to satirize his opponents.

In numerous tales, Frank presents himself as an idiot protected by Divine providence and chosen for a Divine mission. In many of the tales, he describes himself as a *prostak*, which roughly means simpleton, moron, or fool—I render it as "idiot" here since it includes negative, even offensive, connotations of both low intelligence and boorishness. This parodic mystical antihero is an almost comical failure, nearly killed a number of times by angry mobs (often as a result of grotesque and vulgar displays) and bumbling through one adventure after another. The Frank character is indeed "unlettered," as Scholem once described him, even though Frank himself, educated within a highly sophisticated heretical kabbalistic milieu, was not. Certainly, Frank himself is not the fool of the tales. In fact, several dicta relate how Frank and his companions are quite knowledgeable, and defeat wise sages at their own game. In §46, for example, Frank's companion Jakubowski wins multiple disputations with learned rabbis, and Frank reveals that he, too, knows the intricacies of the laws of Shabbat. In §443, Frank quizzes the Brethren about the Bible and Zohar. Nor are such dicta mere boasts; Frank clearly has a high degree of facility with Jewish textual traditions (see, e.g., §§166, 374) and Kabbalah (§1267). The *prostak* act is a put-on, but one with several functions in the construction of the Frankist myth.

First, Frank's foolishness proves that he is the chosen one: Clearly, he did not earn his status by merit, since he is utterly devoid of that. Therefore, he must be chosen by God. (Remarkably, this theme reappeared in American Evangelicals' defenses of former President Donald Trump, whose "imperfection" and evident faithlessness were seen as signs that he had been chosen by God, not come to power by his own merits.[81]) In a series of dicta early in *ZSP*,

---

[81] Burton, "The Biblical Story"; Scott, "Comparing Trump to Jesus."

Frank explains how he is at once foolish and chosen. In §34, for example, a female astrologer wants to have sex with Frank not because he's attractive or smart but because she recognizes that he is chosen. In §37, Frank jumps, on horseback, back and forth over a deep pit, and says "from this, consider how simple and thoughtless my deeds were, yet I was chosen regardless, because I was so upright and God-fearing." And §49 describes the paradoxical nature of Frank's journey to Poland. On the one hand, he is unprepared and unwilling to go. On the other hand, he must "do what is necessary," because he is "chosen by God" and is thus told, "you may do whatever touches your heart." These motifs occur time and again: Frank is an anti-hero, ill-equipped for the task before him, and yet, he is granted divine protection and power. "What kind of artfulness would it be for God to lead the world with the wise and the learned?" Frank asks Eve Frank in §34, continuing,

> God intentionally wants to appear to the world among the lowliest and the basest, so that his power might be shown from such a place. Pay heed and look at me, there has been no greater simpleton than me, a person who would seem completely devoid of reason. But wisdom, as I have said, emerges out of nothing.

This doctrine rests on, and transforms, a Sabbatean myth. Sabbetai Zevi's "strange acts" and varying moods were seen as evidence of his messianic status: The redeemer must descend to the depths to release the fallen sparks there. In Frankism, however, the Frank character really is among the lowliest and basest. He is not descending; he is already there.

Second, the idiot is the ideal vessel for the Frankist mission because he is too dumb, or mad, to hesitate. In §57, Frank tells a parable of a man with a precious pearl who cannot convince expert artisans to drill a hole through it because the pearl is so valuable the experts are afraid of damaging it. But the man brings the pearl to an ignorant apprentice who, unaware of the pearl's value, simply drills through it and succeeds. The full text reads as follows:

> In Iwanie the Lord said in year [17]59: There was a certain man who had a priceless pearl. It had not been drilled, and he went from one big city to another looking for an artisan who could drill a hole in it, promising him an excellent sum, if only he would endeavor not to cause the slightest damage. None of the greatest artisans would endeavor to do so. At last, he was offering 1000#, but no one would dare do it. Being at a loss about what to do

with this pearl, the man went to see an apprentice whose master was absent at that point, and without warning him about the danger of damaging the pearl, said: Take this pearl and pierce it for me, I will pay you well. This apprentice was the first one to take the pearl, and he drilled it well without fear, and the man paid him well and, full of contentment, went on his way. In the same fashion, many wise men here wanted to drill and could not, because they were afraid, but I was chosen because I am a simpleton who, with the help of my God, will drill through everything and lead to everything.

As the proverb says, fools rush in where angels fear to tread, and in the Frankist project, that is an advantage. Only Frank is stupid, incautious, and rash enough to do what God requires of him. God does not want hairsplitting, caution, or prudence; God favors the bold, incautious, and imprudent. No one sane could do it, which is why Frank can do it.

Third, the fool is often wiser than the wise. For example, in §688, Frank, as a child, thinks that the loaves of challah, baked for him by a local woman, actually are the Sabbath, and so when the woman falls ill and doesn't bake the challah, Frank assumes the Sabbath has been canceled and goes to work in his shop. Other merchants "gave me to understand that it is not the bread that is the Sabbath," Frank continues, "but that a certain secret thing comes, which is the Sabbath. I told my father about this incident, and this is how he replied: 'Do not distress over it, because sometimes the Sabbath leaves and goes in hiding.'" Again, on the surface, §688 is about Frank being a fool; but beneath the surface, it is a critique of *halacha*, with its invisible demarcations and restrictive laws. Frank sees what is real: the material, the challah, the baker. He has no idea that these real, material things are but the symbol of some fictive, "spiritual" realities, and thus actually understands reality better than the adults around him. This theme echoes not only the Zoharic tropes of the child who possesses great wisdom—in the Zohar, the young child (*yanuqa*) often has the most sublime mystical insights—but once again, Sabbetai Zevi, who would sometimes append to his statements "thus spake the utter fool."[82] It is also interesting to compare this utterance with nearly contemporaneous Hasidic stories of the prayers of illiterate but sincere shepherds being more favorable to God than those of wise sages. There, too, wisdom is more an obstacle than an aid, and a certain amount of ignorance is valuable. In addition to Jewish precedents, the "foolish" Frank is

---

[82] See Maciejko, *Sabbatean Heresy*, 142. On the *yanuqa*, see Benarroch, *Sava and Yanuka*.

similar to Christian traditions of the holy fool. The Apostle Paul also refers to himself as a fool (*mōros*) in the New Testament: "if anyone among you thinks that he is wise in this age, let him become a fool so that he may become wise" (1 Cor. 3:18). Like Paul, however, Frank's "foolishness" is really a form of wisdom. And in Orthodox traditions, the holy fool exposes false wisdom among the supposedly pious, and shocks with his extreme behavior while ultimately acting as a "fool for Christ's sake."[83] It is possible that Frank became aware of these traditions, given that he borrowed heavily from Christian doctrines and imagery even prior to his imprisonment at Częstochowa.[84] One is reminded here of William Blake, heavily influenced by Western esotericism (and perhaps, in a secondhand way, Sabbateanism, by way of the Moravian Church of London), who wrote in his "Proverbs of Hell" that "[i]f the fool would persist in his folly he would become wise."[85]

Finally, and in a more sinister key, by casting himself as merely the foolish instrument of the Divine, Frank is able to be at once egomaniacal and self-effacing. Frank demands total obedience from his followers—yet, since Frank himself is simply a tool in the hands of God, it's really God who demands such subservience. This, too, has a long, dark lineage among leaders of fringe sects and new religious movements, as charismatic leaders demand subservience yet disclaim responsibility.

In addition to being God's chosen fool, Frank as a prophet is a wise-mad trickster. Frank sees a religious world that he judges to be insane: sacrificing pleasure and power for a nonexistent "spiritual" benefit, setting up arbitrary lines distinguishing permitted and forbidden, and cutting itself off from worldly reality. In response, Frank makes himself appear insane to them. His "madness" is, itself, a critique—and also pedagogy. As the old saw (often incorrectly attributed to Kurt Vonnegut) holds, "a sane person to an insane society must appear insane."[86] Indeed, §986 of *ZSP* contains one of the most famous Jewish examples of this kind of madness, because the tale it

---

[83] Ware, "The Holy Fool as Prophet and Apostle"; Ivanov, *Holy Fools in Byzantium and Beyond.*
[84] See Maciejko, "Christian Elements."
[85] Blake, "The Marriage of Heaven and Hell." See Schuchard, "From Poland to London."
[86] There are numerous variations of this sentiment, none apparently by Vonnegut. George Bernard Shaw wrote to Maxim Gorki in 1915, "When all the world goes mad, one must accept madness as sanity, since sanity is, in the last analysis, nothing but the madness on which the whole world happens to agree." Laurence, ed., *Bernard Shaw: Collected Letters*, 341. Erich Fromm wrote in 1973 that "it is the fully sane person who feels isolated in the insane society—and he may suffer so much from the incapacity to communicate that it is he who may become psychotic." Fromm, *Anatomy of Human Destructiveness*, 356. And Jiddu Krishnamurti may or may not have said, in a quotation often replicated but never sourced, "It is no measure of health to be well adjusted to a profoundly sick society."

contains was subsequently retold by Rabbi Nachman of Bratzlav (discussed in chapter 8). In Frank's version of the tale, a merchant goes mad after his ship fails to come in, and begins acting like a rooster, running around naked and eating on the floor. A "wise man" cures him by likewise pretending to be a rooster but then convincing the merchant that roosters can wear clothes, eat at table, and so forth. What would appear to be madness—a wise man chatting naked with a lunatic—is in fact the sage's skillful means of curing the lunatic of his lunacy.[87] Frank's holy madness is pedagogy, because one must feign madness in order to communicate with the mad—namely, most people, who are still somehow entrapped by the insanity of religion.

That being said, Frank's trickster tales are also bawdy, vulgar, funny, and crude, at times like the *Canterbury Tales* or *Decameron*. In §953, Frank heals a girl who farts unceasingly, a circumstance that Frank analogizes to Jews who talk too much about the law. Elior has described Frankism as a "carnival of the grotesque in total contravention of the existing order,"[88] citing Mikhail Bakhtin in his famous study of Rabelais. There, Bakhtin states that in a carnival "order is destroyed and an abyss opened where we thought to rest on firm ground. . . . [T]he grotesque totally destroys the order and deprives us of our foothold."[89] Significantly, the grotesque transgresses the boundary between the body and the rest of the world:

> The main events in the life of the grotesque body, the acts of the bodily drama, take place in this sphere. Eating, drinking, defecation and other elimination (sweating, blowing of the nose, sneezing), as well as copulation, pregnancy, dismemberment, swallowing up by another body—all these acts are performed on the confines of the body and the outer world, or on the confines of the old and new body.[90]

ZSP, which describes all of the foregoing excretory and reproductive functions, often with Chaucerian detail and impropriety, exemplifies this phenomenon. Frank scandalizes traditional society with his penis (which, he says, is so large that small children can climb up on it, §579), his mouth

---

[87] On the similarities and differences between Frank's madness and Rabbi Nachman's, see Mark, *Mysticism and Madness*, 205–11.
[88] Elior, *Mystical Origins*, 191. See also Elior, "Jacob Frank," 502–5.
[89] Bakhtin, *Rabelais and His World*, 59. For a recent application of Bakhtin's carnival grotesque to Frank, see Kantner and Aleksandrowicz, "Olga Tokarczuk's *The Books of Jacob*: The Revolution in Language."
[90] Bakhtin, *Rabelais and His World*, 317.

(eating twelve Cornish hens for money, §300), and his strong arms and brute strength (§§11, 20, 26, 272, 291, 528, 579, 1234). The Frankist libertine-carnival does not simply happen to take place on the physical body; it is specifically an exaggeration of the carnal, the worldly. Boundaries are defied, taboos are transgressed, and the (permeable) body is the primary site of the crossing-over—an effect heightened if we situate this praxis in the context of Jewish body-taboos, which seek to refine exactly those distinctions which Frank seems intent on effacing. Bakhtin again: "Nearly all the rituals of the feast of fools are a grotesque degradation of various church rituals and symbols and their transfer to the material bodily level: gluttony and drunken orgies on the altar table, indecent gestures, disrobing."[91] Likewise here.

The "grotesque carnival" of which Frank is a part is a deliberately vulgar undermining of established order.[92] The grotesque aspects of Frank's antinomianism are of a piece with his overall critique of societal mores, discussed in the next chapter, and project of personal transcendence of them. Religion, says Frank, is oppressive and ineffectual—and then, like his libertine contemporaries, he spits in its face. Frank insists, in numerous dicta, that his disgust-inducing stories have a purpose—that within their rough stone is a pearl of wisdom (§§115, 172, 201, 302, 334, 340, 423, 1290). One such purpose, I suggest, is to challenge the boundaries around eros constructed by patriarchal civilization—a challenge mythologized as liberating the Maiden from her exile, as we will discuss in chapter 5. Civilization is founded on the subjugation of embodied, animal-human instincts, chiefly sexual instincts—in Frankist terms, the subjugation of the Maiden.[93] Repression and domination thus are at the center of the enterprise of civilization, and the marking of that power begins on the sexual-animal body. This is particularly true in Jewish and Christian contexts, wherein the drawing of boundaries around sexuality was a constitutive act of erecting boundaries between Israelite and Other, and, later, Christian and "Pagan."[94] In this context, the Frankist antinomian grotesque is an expression of radical critique.

Unsurprisingly, many of Frank's provocations have to do with transgressing the boundaries between or within religions. In one series of tales early on in the text, Frank harasses believers, mocking their piety and belief. After bribing a peasant who works in a synagogue, Frank controls

---

[91] Ibid., 74.
[92] See Koepping, "Absurdity and Hidden Truth," 191–214.
[93] Marcuse, *Eros and Civilization*, 55–105; Martin, *Art, Messianism and Crime*.
[94] Michaelson, "Chaos, Law and God," 81–84.

the ovens heating the sanctuary, and then overheats it to the point where attendees faint (§282). He bribes another peasant to give him the bell to wake people for services and then wakes people for morning prayers at midnight (§283). In another tale, Frank even replaces the spices in the Havdalah ceremony with excrement (§295). He shouts "go to shul" to Christians on Saturday (§284) and forces Muslims to shake the lulav and etrog (§285). As a youth, he sneaks a Christian boy in to be the "tenth man" in a minyan (§289) and brings Catholic children to pray for women giving birth (§290). Or consider §42, set in the town of Dziurdziów during Ramadan. Frank relates,

> I went up to a Greek man, who offered me some dumplings and a pipe. I was eating and smoking. Some Turks came up . . . and one said: "Happy is the nation which is ruled by a free king." Nevertheless, if they ran into one of his people like that, he would surely not get away with it alive.

Because Frank is not Muslim, eating and smoking on Ramadan is perfectly fine; were he a Muslim, it would be a capital offense. The same material action, but forbidden to one person and permitted to another. And for what? Why not enjoy the pipe? Yet even as Frank transgresses religious boundaries, he often takes a triumphalist attitude when it comes to Christianity, both in numerous apocalyptic statements and in the tales. In the outrageous §762, for example, Frank recounts being in a Christian village. A farmer taunts Frank by telling a story of the Christian God punching the Jewish God in the snout, invoking an old antisemitic belief that the eating of pig is forbidden to Jews because the pig was actually a god of the Jews.[95] But Frank outdoes his interlocutor by telling an obscene story of Mohammed raping St. Peter, "like the Turks do" until St. Peter relents and accepts the "sanctity" of Islam. Frank here invokes an anti-Muslim belief that homosexuality is prevalent among Muslims, and turns it against those who espouse it.[96] The village farmers sheepishly reply, "We won't make fun of your God and don't you say anything against our St. Peter." Many themes are present in this short tale: Frank's ability to shock, his professed success at out-insulting Christians, his transgressions of religious taboos, and his critique of particularism, as Frank exploits one nasty stereotype in order to outdo another. Frank's choice

---

[95] Felsenstein, *Anti-Semitic Stereotypes*, 127–32; Shachar, *Judensau*. This motif, known as the *judensau* (Jew-pig) was widespread in Germany in the eighteenth century.
[96] Boswell, *Christianity, Social Tolerance, and Homosexuality*, 279.

of image also alludes to his frequently gendered rhetorical violence toward Christianity; as we discuss in chapter 5, Frank, in contrast to supposedly "effeminate" Jews and Sabbateans, presents an assertive, militaristic, and hypermasculine hero who will overthrow Christian dominion and bring about worldly redemption.

In these tales, "Jacob Frank" the trickster exposes the ineffectual nature of religion and the hypocrisy of conventional morality. (In some cases, other characters fill the role of "Jacob Frank"—for example in §985, a drunkard defecates on the bimah on Yom Kippur because, he says, actually Yom Kippur is two weeks later; like Frank's sitting naked on the Torah scroll, this causes everyone to leave the synagogue.) In Frank's theological utterances, he proclaims that the traditional pieties of religion are empty of meaning; in these pranks, he mocks them. He is a trickster deflating the pretensions of the solemn. Let us explore just a few more examples. In §278, a poor widow asks a rabbi for advice, and Frank advises her to pretend to be a doctor and take money from sick people, then recite the *Adon Olam* (among the most common and familiar of prayers) for them. A witty satire on how religion is a fraud—but then the story takes a turn: The woman's patients are healed. Finally, the rabbi himself has a fish bone stuck in his throat, and the miraculous healer is called in to pray over him, at which point the rabbi laughs so hard that the fishbone is dislodged and he recovers too. The story is thus about the falsity of religion, the power of the unlettered *prostak*, the power of faith, and what we would today call the psychosomatic efficacy of religious belief, a shell-game that the rabbi himself recognizes when it is revealed. (Indeed, the same lesson is taught in the next dictum, §2789, wherein Frank "prescribes" eating a poppy seed on one foot in order to cure a fever, and the remedy works.) Even the rabbi, who taught the widow to be fraudulent, is healed when he sees through the con of traditional religion. In his laughter—in that seeing through artifice and pretense—he is able to be healed. Traditional religionists believe, and cynics laugh at them, but laughter itself brings a kind of salvation. Seeing through belief is as efficacious as belief itself.

Frank's hyperliteralism is also a kind of skepticism, as we will explore more fully in the next chapter. For example, in §1074, Frank meets a red-haired Jew nicknamed the "lion." He spreads a rumor to twelve children that there is a lion outside Bucharest. The rumor spreads all the way up to the nobles, who are terrified, until it is revealed that the "lion" is just a red-headed Jew. The characters laugh at the trick—happy to be duped, and also relieved that the Jewish lion (perhaps a satirical reference to the "Lion of Judah"?) doesn't actually roar. In part, this short tale is a dig at Jewish weakness—the "lion" is hardly a lion. But it is also one of many Frankist tales in which the Frank character satirizes religious claims and language by taking them far too literally, not unlike the "simple" passages discussed above. As we will discuss in the next chapter, he even beats up the beadle of a synagogue named after the prophet Elijah when Elijah is not to be found within it (§18).

The lion story in §1074 is also one of many tales in which those duped by Frank laugh at the end of the tale. In another, §709, Frank is traveling with a *Frenk* merchant (the coincidence is unstated yet clearly intentional) whose son brags that he is not afraid of robbers. Dubious, that night Frank makes noises that sound like he is being robbed and beaten, and everyone flees. Having tricked the merchants and exposed the son's false braggadocio, Frank then steals valuable jams that the merchants were carrying (Frank's love of fruit jam figures in numerous dicta: §§709, 812, 838, 886, 1053, 1090, 1092, 1276, and 1311), and stuffs cheese into the merchants' guns. The merchants return the next day, and much later, they recognize their jams in the marketplace, which Frank has obviously stolen and sold. The rich *Frenk* tries to shoot Frank but finds his gun stuffed with cheese—and laughs. Frank has shown the hollowness of the merchant's son's boasting, has outwitted the group, and has shown them their own folly. Throughout the tales, many kings, rich people, princesses, and noblemen approve of the schemes of the Frankist heroes. They laugh, give their daughters for marriage, and give promotions to these schemers because they appreciate a good con and a good joke, even if it's on them. The nobleman wants his fruits to be stolen; the king wants his treasure to be taken. Likewise, as we will explore more in the next chapter, Frank's God favors the crafty individual who schemes, plots, and wins. His theology is quasi-Nietzschean: God helps those who help themselves at other people's expense. Traditional religion doesn't show people how to win the game of life, but convinces them to lose it. Frank's jokes win.

In one tale, the Frank character even tricks the angel of death. In §484, Frank tells of a butcher who, unable to feed his children, attempts to drown them. The angel of death sees this, and, rather than allow the children to be killed, offers the butcher a magic herb which can cure diseases—which, the angel says, will surely make him rich. The angel puts only one condition on the use of the herb: when the butcher sees him at the head of a sickbed, he is to know that the patient is beyond hope and not attempt to heal them. Sure enough, the butcher becomes famed as a healer and becomes rich. Eventually, the king himself becomes ill and sends for the butcher/healer.

The butcher sees the angel at the head of the bed, but rather than give up, he orders the king's bed be turned around, so that the angel is now at the foot of the bed. Quickly, before the angel can adjust, the butcher cures the king! The angel of death accepts the trick (but just this once, he says) and with that, the tale ends. The butcher here is a stand-in for Frank, utterly undeserving, yet favored by a divine/angelic being nonetheless, who he subsequently tricks, with the supernatural being's approval. As we have seen, the Frankist tales praise those too bold, or simply too stupid, to hesitate—and they also take a humorously literalistic approach to their subject matter (as if it matters that the angel of death is at the foot, rather than the head, of a bed!).

What are we to make of such tales? Frank's tales are remarkable in their daring, vulgarity, and ability to shock, even over two centuries later. Yet the madness of the literary character Jacob Frank is not without precedent. First, it is quite similar to nearly contemporaneous writing by the Libertines of the eighteenth century, such as the Marquis de Sade (1740–1814), imprisoned at Miolans in the same year Frank was set free from Częstochowa, and the writings of Giacomo Casanova (1725–1798), with whom Frank was acquainted.[97] Frank was in contact with many of his Libertine contemporaries, and like them, he mocks in order to undermine, to show the contingency of that which is presumed to be absolute, to highlight the hypocrisy of those who seem pious.[98] He constantly undermines any pretension to sincerity or ethics on the part of someone who, we know, is ultimately a hypocrite. Frank's outrageous, often grotesque behavior offers a satirical commentary on the hypocrisy of traditional values.

Second, Frank's tales of playing tricks on the pious and mocking their religious devotion is similar to the "trickster" motif found in a number of religious and cultural traditions, including the Hebrew Bible.[99] As Carl Jung put it, the trickster "is both subhuman and superhuman, a bestial and divine being."[100] Georg Feuerstein describes the figure as

---

[97] Maciejko, *Mixed Multitude*, 222–25.
[98] See generally Feher, "Libertinisms"; Cryle and O'Connell, eds., *Libertine Enlightenment*.
[99] See Jung, "On the Psychology of the Trickster-Figure"; Radin, *The Trickster*; Mollenkott, "Reading the Bible from Low and Outside;" Nichols, *The Trickster Revisited*; Niditch, *Underdogs and Tricksters*; Koepping, "Absurdity and Hidden Truth." For an excellent analysis of trickster tales in Jewish thought, see Belser, "Rabbinic Trickster Tales." Applying queer and feminist theoretical critiques to Talmudic trickster tales, Belser notices that female tricksters are viewed as dangerous, whereas male ones are seen as playful.
[100] Jung, "On the Psychology of the Trickster-Figure," 261.

a being who is very clever but unprincipled, delighting in the irrational. There is an element of malice in many trickster figures, though they are never entirely demonic. They are out to best their adversaries and spare no cunning to achieve their goal. As part of their duplicity, they often pretend to be stupid. . . . The trickster is, moreover, depicted as having a voracious sexual appetite, which is often indicated by a huge penis. His character is a juxtaposition of carnality and spirituality. More than any other mythological figure, the trickster celebrates bodily existence, which includes all the many functions that civilization seeks to suppress or control.[101]

While Feuerstein cites figures from non-Western traditions such as Wakdjunkaga, the Winnebago trickster who scatters creatures across the earth with a huge fart, or Edshu, trickster-god of Yoruba, who says that "spreading strife is my greatest joy," these characteristics are also found in Jacob Frank of Podolia, who pretends to be a fool while outwitting his rabbinic opponents, who indulges every physical appetite while dispensing spiritual teachings, and who likewise boasts of his priapic anatomy.[102] The trickster mocks in order to undermine, to show the contingency of that which is presumed to be absolute, to highlight the hypocrisy, or at least overseriousness, of those who seem pious.

Here, unlike the persona of the fool, the character of Jacob Frank resembles his creator. Arguably, the entire character of "Jacob Frank" is the creation of Jacob Frank the trickster. Throughout the over 175 tales contained in *ZSP*, this character is an unlettered *prostak*, even as Jacob Frank is not; "Jacob Frank" is able to do miracles, even as we assume Jacob Frank could not; "Jacob Frank" is a divine messenger, which Jacob Frank only dreamed about. Perhaps Jacob Frank's greatest act of spiritual tricksterism was the creation of "Jacob Frank" as a literary character. Indeed, in some ways, the latter was invented to conceal the former.

---

[101] Feuerstein, *Holy Madness*, 3.
[102] Ibid., 3–6.

2
"I do not look to heaven but at what God does here on Earth"
Frankist Antinomianism as Materialist Skepticism

In §62 of *ZSP*, Jacob Frank states,

> All religions, all laws, all books of old, if one reads them, it's like turning your face backwards and examining words which have long gone extinct. All this originated from the side of death.

This is among the best-known aspects of Frankism: antinomianism, the deliberate transgression of ritual and moral law. But what is the reason that Frank casts aside "all religions, all laws, all books"? Frank provides a hint in this dictum: that they are "from the side of death." But what does that mean?

In fact, Frank's critique of religion is a surprisingly modern one, albeit one framed within a premodern mythic framework, which we will explore in chapters 3 and 4. As we will see in this chapter, Frank espouses a skeptical materialism, grounded in the belief that the supernatural claims of religion are false and that only the material is real.[1] Religion is at best ineffectual, at worst, actively evil, insofar as it holds people back from living a full life; Frank's replacement for it is a materialistic quest with the goal of attaining this-worldly immortality and power, both in this world (in terms of power and sexual liberation) and in the world behind the screen. For Frank, traditional religion is, in Hobbes's words, "feare of power invisible, feigned by the mind, or imagined from tales publiquely allowed."[2] Sometimes, this critique is quite ordinary: In §292, a very young Frank confounds a rabbi by asking how

---

[1] To an extent, this materialism extends even to Frankist messianism. Rapoport-Albert observes that one aspect of the Maiden, the female messiah, is the longtime (and problematic) association of the feminine with the earthly and material. See Rapoport-Albert, *Women and the Messianic Heresy*, 225–28.

[2] Hobbes, *Leviathan*, 124 (Part I, Chapter 6).

Passover could be a *leil shimurim* ("guarded night") when so many attacks against Jews have taken place during it, and how Elijah could drink from all the Elijah's cups in the world. But Frank also brought this skeptical attitude to Sabbateanism. In §1013, he tells the Brethren that he is unimpressed with them because they lack "the wisdom [*mądrości*] of making gold" and that he told his first Sabbatean teachers, "I will not believe that you are chosen unless I see that wisdom from you." Frank demands proof in the material world; indeed, he says that his commitment to materialism took hold when he visited the grave of Nathan of Gaza,[3] perhaps struck by the failure of the Sabbatean prophet to defeat death after all.

A useful symbol for Frank's materialist critique of religion is found early on in *ZSP*, in §18. There, Frank tells a tale of visiting a synagogue in Salonica known as *kahal eliyahu hanavi*, the congregation of the prophet Elijah. Frank asks the *shamash* (beadle) why it is known as Elijah's congregation, and the *shamash* replies that an ancestor of his once found the prophet Elijah sitting in a chair. Frank knocks down the *shamash* and demands to see Elijah himself. The *shamash* shouts for help, and the Turkish authorities arrive. Frank says to them, "Admit it yourselves, you will not believe it until you see Elijah the Prophet with your own eyes. Why shouldn't I ask to be shown him?" The authorities agree and cheer Frank on as he beats the *shamash*. On a superficial level, this tale is one of many in which Frank ridicules religion and piety, often with violence or the threat of violence. It also draws on Sabbatean precedent: Sabbetai himself had allegedly smashed the gates of a synagogue that had shut him out.[4] But the tale is also about Frank's this-worldly orientation more generally. If a synagogue is "the congregation of Elijah," then Elijah had better well be there. And if Elijah is not there, the representatives of the synagogue should be beaten for lying about it. This materialist skepticism gives rise to Frank's contempt for religion.

Part of the challenge for understanding Frankist antinomianism is establishing an adequate framework for understanding antinomianism in general. Over time, the term has become used quite loosely to refer to any religious or philosophical view that opposes obedience to the law. Yet not all antinomianisms are the same; they have different rationales, different manifestations, and different intended effects on the individual or even the cosmos. This chapter thus begins by briefly tracing the history of the concept

---

[3] Maciejko, *Mixed Multitude*, 27.
[4] Scholem, *Sabbatai Ṣevi*, 398.

of antinomianism and setting forth a four-part taxonomy for understanding it. Then I will apply this taxonomy to the case of Frank, in whose work three of the four types are found. As already noted in the previous chapter, none of this analysis is intended to somehow rescue Frank, who remains, based on the textual evidence available to us, a manipulative, violent, and cruel individual who extorted his followers for material gain. Yet he also developed a coherent antinomian philosophy; moral venality and theological innovation are not mutually exclusive. And Frank paid a price for his heresy; again, if mere advancement were Frank's only agenda, he did not simply pursue it. As noted in the previous chapter, Frank's early rival for leadership, Yehuda Leib Krysa, converted in 1759, assimilated into Polish society, and was never heard from again.[5] Why did Frank not do the same?

Antinomianism as Religious Ideology

The term "antinomianism," referring to the rejection or transgression of law as a religious or moral value, was coined by Martin Luther in the 1530s, most famously in his 1539 treatise *Against the Antinomians*, written in response to fellow reformers who rejected religious law even more than Luther himself had done. For Luther, as for Paul, the coming of Christ had obviated the need to obey the details of the biblical law.[6] Yet others were more radical: Johann Agricola, Luther's primary target, argued that preaching any of the Old Testament law (including the moral law) was actively misleading to Christians and that it should be totally set aside. In response, Luther set forth three specific uses of the law—"curb, mirror, and guide" in the now-classic Protestant formulation—and said that only the first had been abrogated by the coming of Christ.[7] His fellow reformers, Luther argued, had gone too far in discarding the law altogether. Luther thus entered "antinomianism" into the lexicon as a term of derogation.

Since Luther, the term has been projected backward and forward across historical and cultural boundaries. Within Christian contexts, there have been antinomian outbreaks such as the seventeenth-century Massachusetts case of the radical reformer Anne Hutchinson; the sixteenth-century

---

[5] Maciejko, *Mixed Multitude*, 157.
[6] The extent to which Luther was himself antinomian has been controversial for centuries. See Baker, "Sola Fide, Sola Gratia"; Sproul, *Essential Truths*, 3.
[7] See Sproul, *Essential Truths*, 3.

Anabaptists, who were accused by Calvin of antinomianism and immorality; the medieval Brethren of the Free Spirit; and various waves of American antilegalism.[8] But conceptualizing antinomianism in a rigorous way has proven challenging even within the boundaries of Christianity. In his discussion of the Antinomian Controversy in Massachusetts, David Hall defines antinomianism as the view that "the moral law is not binding upon Christians, who are under the law of grace."[9] Yet the term often has far more wide-ranging meanings: The Evangelical theologian J. I. Packer defines five different strains of Christian antinomianism,[10] and the term is often used to describe all manners of heresy, from the Cathars and Bogomils of the twelfth century to American Evangelicals in the twenty-first. It is sometimes deployed in non-Western contexts, for phenomena such as Left-Hand Tantra, in which traditional Hindu taboos are ritually transgressed as a means to transcending identification with the dualistic world.[11] It is sometimes used casually to refer to any nonnormative religious practice.[12] And in secular contexts, it may refer to the general idea that the law is unreliable or unimportant.[13]

This wide scope of usage indicates the need for a more rigorous understanding of antinomianism as a religious phenomenon. First, antinomianism is, by definition, principled. It is not antinomian when a driver runs a red light simply because she thinks she can get away with it or is running late for an appointment. Only if the driver runs the light precisely because she thinks it is morally or religiously better to defy traffic laws is it properly antinomian.

---

[8] On Hutchison, see Hall, ed., *The Antinomian Controversy*; Winthrop, *Antinomianism in the Colony of Massachusetts*; Lang, *Prophetic Woman*, 4–5; Battis, *Saints and Sectaries*. On the anabaptists, see Michel Feher, "Libertinisms," 11–12. On the Brethren of the Free Spirit, see Lerner, *The Heresy of the Free Spirit in the Later Middle Ages*, 10–34. On American antilegalism, see Michaelson, "Hating the Law"; Galanter, *Lowering the Bar*; Michaelson, "In Praise of the Pound of Flesh"; Kennedy, "A Semiotics of Critique," 1158.

[9] Hall, *Antinomian Controversy*, 3.

[10] Packer, *Concise Theology*, 178–80. Packer's five strains are dualistic/dialectical (salvation is of the spirit, the body is irrelevant), Spirit-centered (trust the Holy Spirit; the law is irrelevant as a guide as well as a means to salvation), Christ-centered (belief is really all that matters), dispensational (biblical law is not God's direct command but meant only to inspire the spirit), and situationist (love is what matters, and the specific law may be set aside when love dictates otherwise).

[11] See Govinda, "Principles of Tantric Buddhism"; Urban, "The Omnipotent OOM." Although Tantra is iconoclastic toward social conventions, it prescribes its own rigid rules for the performance of meditation, sexual rituals, and other spiritual practices. See Rawson, *The Art of Tantra*, 14–16.

[12] See Braiterman, "Critical Reflections." With regard to Frankism, see, e.g., Feiner, *The Origins of Jewish Secularization*, 73–74. Feiner describes Frank's statement that "I will trample on all the laws" as "antinomianism and libertinism," without defining either term. See Feher, "Libertinisms," 11–12 (noting similar confusion regarding Anabaptists).

[13] Kennedy, "Semiotics of Critique," 1158. See, e.g., Hartigan, "Unlaw"; Galanter, "The Three-Legged Pig."

To take another example, contrast a formerly Orthodox Jew eating *treif* (non-kosher) food because she has concluded the law is meaningless with another person, who has never heard of kashrut, eating the same food. The former may be a type of antinomianism, but the latter is simply anomian, with no particular meaning attached to the food in question.

In the Jewish context, Shaul Magid has provided a useful taxonomy of antinomianism in a study of R. Mordechai Lainer of Izbica.[14] Magid defines historical antinomianism as "the denial of the relevance of the moral law to the Christians because of the ability claimed for the Holy Spirit to separate persons directly and radically from the obligations of ordinary worldly existence."[15] Conceptually, he proposes a continuum from libertinism ("the performance of licentious or immoral acts, often but not always buttressed by antinomian or fatalistic ideologies") to antinomianism ("a belief in the ability to be released from the constraints of the moral law while still being assured of salvation)" to neonomianism, which holds that "the law is not abolished but transformed, requiring behavior that previously had been forbidden."[16] Magid's case in point is Izbica Hasidism, which is selectively antinomianism, because of the radical determinism that "all is in the hands of heaven, even the fear of heaven."[17] Obedience to the law is not a meaningful act if everything is determined by God.[18]

This schema is extremely helpful, but I wish to go further. Magid's libertinism is quite broad: A "libertine" mob breaking windows may be anomian, nihilistic, or principled (as in a political protest). And Magid's iteration of antinomianism includes ideologies that are quite different from one another. Thus, based on how the phenomenon manifests in Frankism, I propose the following four-part taxonomy of antinomianism:

1. Nihilism: The law should be disobeyed because life is without value or meaning. (Some libertines hold this view.)
2. Skeptical/humanistic antinomianism: The law should be disobeyed because it is valueless and thwarts human flourishing. (Many libertines hold this view.)

---

[14] Magid, *Hasidism on the Margins*, 208–15. See also Garb, *Chosen*, 83.
[15] Magid, *Hasidism on the Margins*, 208.
[16] Ibid., 201, 208–12.
[17] Ibid., 209.
[18] On panentheistic Hasidism and the problems of quietism and free will, see Schatz Uffenheimer, *Hasidism as Mysticism*; Michaelson, *Everything Is God*, 210–13; Gellman, "Hasidic Mysticism as an Activism."

3. Religious antinomianism: The law should be disobeyed because of another positive religious value. (This was predominant in Sabbateanism, but nearly absent in Frankism.)
4. Experiential antinomianism: The law should be disobeyed because the act of disobedience has its own value, such as a psychological or social rupture. (Apparently present in both Sabbateanism and Frankism.)

In the next section, we will explore how the antinomianism of Jacob Frank reflects types 2 and 4 primarily and 3 secondarily, and how this conceptualization of antinomianism helps address issues in the scholarship regarding him.

Antinomianism in the Frankist Corpus

Nihilism

Nihilism is a philosophical position that argues that life is without meaning, purpose, or intrinsic value and that, as a result, any code of conduct is likewise meaningless. More specifically, the *Routledge Encyclopedia of Philosophy* defines it as "a philosophy of negation, rejection, or denial of some or all aspects of thought or life."[19] Morality, in this view, is simply a sham to disguise personal preferences; epistemology is a delusion; and political institutions have no value (though the nihilist has no plan for replacing them).

The term has often been applied to Frank, but as we will see, with a variety of different meanings. Gershom Scholem calls Frankism "a veritable myth of religious nihilism, the work of a man who did not live at all in the world of rational argument and discussion, but inhabited a realm entirely made up of mythological entities."[20] Similarly, Rachel Elior writes that Frank "undermine[d] the foundations of the traditional world. His nihilistic approach fostered anomie and anarchy."[21] Elior elsewhere states that Frank preaches "nihilism and destruction . . . in the name of an anarchic messianic vision, following a blend of wrathful prophecies in the style of the Zohar and

---

[19] Donald Crosby, "Nihilism."
[20] Scholem, *Messianic Idea*, 132. See also Scholem, "Der Nihilismus." Of course, neither irrationality nor inhabiting a mythic realm can be synonymous with nihilism—otherwise much of Kabbalistic literature would have to be considered nihilistic.
[21] Elior, *Mystical Origins*, 187.

Shabatean antinomian traditions," noting that Frank's "followers were completely subjugated to him, a socially isolated group subject to abasement and alienation in an atmosphere of secrecy, sinfulness, reproof, dashed expectations, betrayal, punishment, and guilt."[22] Maciejko claims that, "there is no place for redemption in ZSP. The bawdy and grotesque content of Frank's teaching cloaks a fateful vision. The true God remains distant and unknown, the tradition does not carry any meaning, the only legitimate activity is destruction."[23]

My claim is different. To the extent that some of Frank's pronouncements are solely intended to cement his own power, then indeed they may be said to be nihilistic. However, Frankist antinomianism is not only a means of control; it also, as discussed below, has a number of other stated purposes, including the accretion of power, a mythic esoteric quest, and a skeptical critique of religious piety. These aspects of Frankism are not nihilism but a principled, skeptical materialist libertinism that rejects meaningless religion in favor of sensual life. It is actually a rejection of nihilism.

Having said that, Scholem's assessment of Frankism as nihilistic itself has different qualitative valences. On the one hand, Scholem states that the Frankist mission is to "cast off the domination of these laws, which are laws of death and harmful to mankind" and "entering the abyss." This seems quite negative, and is at odds with what Frank actually says in §130: "The only reason I came to Poland was to wipe out all laws and all religions, *and my desire is to bring life to the world*"[24] (emphasis added). The first act is for the purpose of the latter; by erasing religion, human beings can truly live. A hedonically defined life of riches and sensuality, not the "abyss," is the goal. On the other hand, in Scholem's last reflection on Frankism, in 1974, he spoke of its nihilistic aspect approvingly; there, Frankists are like anarchists who "struggle for individual freedom against tyrannical and hypocritical institutions and in favor of free association of communities helping each other."[25] As Michael Fagenblat recently put it, "Scholem's pronouncements of Frank's degeneracy do not then amount to a denunciation. On the contrary, Frank's 'anarchist rebellion [. . .] within the world of Law" was, in many respects, just what Judaism needed."[26] And according to Meir and Yamamoto, Scholem believed

---

[22] Ibid., 187.
[23] Maciejko, *Mixed Multitude*, 215.
[24] Scholem, *Messianic Idea*, 132.
[25] Scholem, "Der Nihilismus," 49.
[26] Fagenblat, "Frankism," 37.

that "the nihilism of the Sabbatian and Frankist movements, with its doctrine so profoundly shocking to the Jewish conception of things that the violation of the Torah could become its true fulfillment (*bittulah shel torah zehu kiyyumah*), was a dialectical outgrowth of the belief in the Messiahship of Sabbatai Zevi, and that this nihilism, in turn, helped pave the way for the Haskalah."[27]

We will discuss Scholem's theory (largely discredited) about the relationship between Frankism and the Haskalah in chapter 8; for now, the point is simply that the term "nihilism" can have many different meanings. If nihilism has the more rigorous philosophical meaning of rejecting any meaning whatsoever, then it does not apply to Frank or to Scholem. But if nihilism simply means the rejection of traditional authority, then the term may be applied to Frank, and one can understand how Scholem might have used it approvingly. Indeed, it may also apply to Scholem himself.[28] While David Biale has said that Scholem was "not a nihilist, that is, someone who rejects all authority," but a "religious anarchist" for whom "tradition still has authority, even if it does not speak with one voice and even if the modern Jew need not obey the laws the tradition attributes to divine revelation,"[29] Maciejko argues that Scholem was a nihilist because "every form of Jewish religious practice is, in the last analysis, unsatisfactory and only provisional; that every interpretation of Revelation is ultimately a misreading; or that any attempt to create a successful structure of Jewish life is futile."[30]

For Frank, there are loci of meaning and value in the world—the trouble is that religion does not possess them. Frank rejects religion not out of philosophical nihilism but out of a positive, skeptical belief that religion is false. Consider the metaphor of wine, which Frank invokes dozens of times in ZSP. First, Frank uses the Talmudic idiom (used in the context of God telling Satan to destroy Job's body but not to kill him): "Break the barrel but keep the wine" (§224), in this case, break the old forms of religion but maintain their secret wisdom.[31] This is an almost Reformist utterance from Frank: There is a valuable essence within religion, but its container has become corrupted and must be discarded. Second, seven times in ZSP Frank cites Isaiah 63:3 for the principle that he comes to tread, like treading wine in a vineyard (§§69, 186,

---

[27] Meir and Yamamoto, *Gershom Scholem*, 24–25.
[28] See Meir and Yamamoto, *Gershom Scholem*, 24, n.5, citing Biale, "Shabbtai Zvi"; and Maciejko, "Gershom Scholem's Dialectic."
[29] Biale, "Gershom Scholem on Nihilism and Anarchism," 9.
[30] Maciejko, "Gershom Scholem's Dialectic," 217.
[31] BT Bava Batra 16a.

275, 615, 1061, 1066A, 1151). Frank's point here is that treading wine involves strong, forceful action that crushes many grapes, not mere speech or careful, studious reverence: action, not words. But it leads not to an abyss—but to wine. Or consider two dicta on the *sefirah* of Tiferet. In §1210, Frank rejects the Kabbalistic notion that Tiferet is the seat of providence, saying no one has ever seen it actually work. And when, as Frank recounts in §527, his teacher Rabbi Mardocheusz tells him a secret of Sabbatean Kabbalah—that God is found in Tiferet, instantiated in the messiah—Frank asks how he knows that and then mocks him with a reference to the prophet Elijah mocking the prophets of Baal. What is the difference between the faith in the invisible God in Tiferet, and the faith in the invisible Baal who, in 1 Kings 18:26–28, does not answer the prayers of his prophets? Both are faith in the invisible (Elijah absent in his congregation again), and both are equally unjustified. Frank's vulgarity is also his this-worldliness, and even his outlandish myths of transfiguration and immortality are expressed in very real, this-worldly terms. His braggadocio about being strong (he even boasts of his swimming ability in §528), his promises of meat and wealth—on the one hand, all of these are quite vulgar. On the other, they are a refutation of the world-negating tendency in religious faith.

As Ada Rapoport-Albert put it, Frankist transgressions "bore the hallmarks of antinomian activity—meaningful precisely because it recognizes the authority of the laws it sets out to violate."[32] As we will see in the next section, Frank's complaint is not that nothing has value; it is that religious observance, in particular, is without value. In this regard, Frank is no more "nihilistic" than the Holocaust survivor who rejects God because of the experience of radical evil or the contemporary unbeliever who cannot square the notion of a just God with plagues or natural disasters. In part, such critiques may be understood as an explicit and direct rejection of the Kabbalistic and Sabbatean emphases on faith, on unseen powers, and on the connection between human ritual action and divine realms. Yet they have even more in common with the early Modern European skepticism of Montaigne, Pierre Bayle, François de La Mothe Le Vayer, and even David Hume, all of whom sought to use reason and empirical evidence to undermine religious claims.[33] Of course, *ZSP* also contains many bawdy, outrageous tales of Frank disrespecting taboos, tricking business opponents, engaging in violent acts,

---

[32] Rapoport-Albert, *Women and the Messianic Heresy*, 166–67.
[33] See Popkin and Neto, *Skepticism*, 19–29.

and generally undermining all sense of propriety.[34] Yet the character of Jacob Frank in these tales (as distinct from Frank the historical figure) plays quite specific teaching roles, as we saw in the previous chapter.

As for Frankist sexuality, it cannot seriously be maintained that sexuality is itself the goal of the Frankist enterprise. Had Frank simply been interested in having sex with his disciples, he could have, as it were, left Israel for Edom and enjoyed an opulent life in Warsaw, where he landed following the 1759 apostasy. Many Jews, of course, have done precisely that over the centuries. Yet Frank clung to his heretical beliefs, at great personal cost—his twelve-year imprisonment (1759–1772) resulted from the discovery on the part of Christian authorities that Frank and his followers were not "neophytes" at all but were secretly maintaining elements of their old faith.[35] There are far easier ways to enjoy the pleasures of the flesh than maintaining a secret sect for decades and engaging in bizarre rites certain to attract the condemnation of secular authorities. On the contrary, as we will see in chapter 5, the few accounts of Frankist sexual antinomianism imbue transgression with symbolic and even eschatological meaning. Intentional transgression is not nihilism; on the contrary, it is the ultimate act of signification because it undermines the boundaries it transgresses.[36] It is to these richer meanings of antinomianism that I now turn.

Skeptical-Humanistic Antinomianism

Skeptical/humanistic antinomianism is the view that the law should be transgressed because it needlessly restricts human freedom. Historical examples include reflective Epicureanism, principled hedonism, and several ideologies in Frank's own milieu: libertinism in its eighteenth-century formations; radical skepticism; and scientific materialism. For example, chief among the libertine's values is that the expression of human pleasure and potential is a positive good, and the law is negative insofar as it restricts them; the libertine delights in exposing the hypocrisy of the pious and in taking advantage of the foolish. Casanova, for example, takes a principled stand against propriety because it is foolish, hypocritical, meaningless, needlessly

---

[34] See Elior, "Jacob Frank," 471–541.
[35] See Brawer, *Studies in Galician Jewry*, 267; Maciejko, *Mixed Multitude*, 50–54, n.50–54; Elior, *Mystical Origins*, 183.
[36] Rapoport-Albert, *Women and the Messianic Heresy*, 166–67.

restrictive, and antithetical to human flourishing. Masonic texts such as the notorious *Traité des Trois Imposteurs* (1711) radically questioned the divinity of the Bible and its restrictions on human freedom.[37] As Frank himself says in §1282, mocking the notion both of ritual observance and Kabbalistic *tikkun*, "You would have been better off eating dirt than pronouncing laws in this place, as laws are given for accountability and responsibility, and thus weaken the power of man. What have you 'repaired' with your futile speeches? Did you think that with your silly chatter you would come closer to your country or heaven?"

In Frank's skeptical antinomianism, religion is not merely unfounded and incorrect—it is also that which holds us back from sensual enjoyment and material wealth and health. If religion were a pointless diversion, one might just leave it alone. But no, Frank insists, it cuts us off from life, power, and pleasure. This is the "humanistic" aspect of skeptical humanistic antinomianism: that religious observance reduces human flourishing and pleasure. For example, in the tale recorded in §694, Frank steals string meant for memorial candle wicks and makes a bowstring out of them. In doing so, Frank is not only scandalously disrespecting the sanctity of the memorial candle but also converting it from uselessness to usefulness: specifically, to prevail in an act of violence rather than continue to say inefficacious and impotent prayers. In a sense, Frank is beating a useless spiritual plowshare into a useful material sword. Actions, not words; violence, not mourning; Frank's followers are meant to leave behind the religion of wailing for a future that is in part militaristic, in part sensualistic. As he tells the Brethren in §988, which we quoted in the introduction:

> Your way is not my way, because you fasted for your gods and lay prostrate in mourning because mourning is their due, as it is written: "Rachel weeps over her children."[38] But this is not my way. When my aid arrives, I will furnish my court and keep it in festive garments. I will provide all comfort in food and drink, I will have my own music, my own theater, my own actors, and everyone will rejoice and dance together, young and old alike, and that which is written will be fulfilled: "When he came to play before Saul, the

---

[37] Most likely written by the Freemason Rousset de Missy, the *Traité des Trois Imposteurs*—said imposters being Moses, Jesus, and Mohammed—was among the most notorious atheist tracts of the eighteenth century. See Jacob, *Radical Enlightenment*, 185–90. Rousset was banished in 1749 and later became a spy for the Austrian government, as did members of the Frankist court. Jacob, *Radical Enlightenment*, 205.

[38] Jeremiah 31:15.

Spirit of God rested upon him,"³⁹ because my God does not rest just anywhere, but only where joy and merriment reside.

This highly materialistic, mundane vision of redemption stands in contrast to the laws of religion. Jews mourn and fast; Frank is on a quest to joy and riches.

Frank is a skeptic, not a nihilist. In §1210, having rejected the cosmology of Tiferet, Frank says he once saw someone eating on Yom Kippur, but nothing happened to him: "Good or evil, it was all the same." And in §1066 he states,

> it astonishes me when the world prays and begs for places they have heard about but have not seen with their own eyes. Maybe they are begging and praying for a place that is worst of all!

Elsewhere, Frank belittles the arbitrary rules of religion in terms that might sound familiar today. In §616, Frank tells of a German youth accompanying a Jewish merchant to an inn. A pot of kosher stew is cooking, but the German throws in a bit of pork. The Jews argue about whether the pork is less than 1/60 of the total amount and thus whether they can eat the stew. Frank finds this legalism ludicrous: "those who do not hold firm eat it; those who hold firm do not eat it." There is no sense to these designations—they are simply conceptual distinctions with no meaning. And those who are lenient get to eat. Perhaps the most audacious of Frank's defiance of taboos is the story in §15; Frank says that while in Salonica,

> I received an order to conduct opposing acts.⁴⁰ So when I met a Turk on a Greek street, I drew my sword and forced him to speak the names of the First and the Second [i.e., Sabbetai Zevi and Baruchiah Russo] and to make the sign of the cross, and then I did not let him go until, like it or not, he made it. Likewise, when I met a Greek on a Turkish street, I forced him to say *Mahomet Surullah*, i.e., Mahomet is the true prophet, and also the names of the First and the Second.

---

³⁹ See note 8, *supra*.
⁴⁰ The Polish *przeciwne* commonly means "opposite" but may also mean "antagonistic" or "against." Lenowitz renders it "contrary." Frank's usage here may refer to Sabbatean *ma'asim zarim* ("strange acts" or "foreign acts") or may refer to the confrontational nature of the actions in question.

Frank adds that he would compel a Jew to make the sign of the cross on a Greek street and raise one finger upward, "according to the Mahometan custom" on a Turkish street. "I performed these acts every day," Frank concludes. This tale is a remarkable story of transgression and relativism. In each case, Frank forces the believer to take on the religion of his location: Islam and Sabbateanism on a Muslim street, Christianity and Sabbateanism on a Christian street. (The Sabbateanism of the *doenmeh*, of course, was both Jewish and Muslim.) This is a radical illustration of Frank's own ethos (or perhaps post hoc rationalization) of the sect's apostasy. As discussed below, it is also a deconstruction of taboo: What is forbidden to one is permitted to another, but nothing happens in any case. The skies do not part, the earth does not open up. Only the believer's sense of identity, perhaps, is shaken. The tale also illustrates the perpetual liminality of "Jacob the Outsider," who has himself been Jewish, Sabbatean, Muslim, and Christian, and has seen the emptiness of these taboos and divisions. And it, too, has Sabbatean precursors: Sabbetai reportedly forced his own followers to pronounce the Tetragrammaton, which is strictly forbidden by Jewish law.[41] Of course, Frank is not preaching a multicultural universalism in this story of force and violence; these are victims forced to sin at knifepoint. But as a trickster figure, which we described in the previous chapter, he is shining a harsh light on the ineffectual, unreal nature of religion's prohibitions and taboos, which he is out to transgress.

Frank's rejection of religion is based on basic theodicy: It just isn't true that righteous people are rewarded and wicked ones punished. For example, in a disturbing tale in §820, Cossacks attack a Jew, who begins to pray and confess his sins—but they only beat him more. Finally, a Jewish woman takes his prayer book away, causing him to flee and perhaps saving his life. The Cossacks say, "We're beating him and he recites the confession. We wanted to see if his prayers would help him to escape from our hands." This basic refutation of religion may seem familiar or even trite today, but is remarkable in its temporal and cultural context. Does praying help stop the Cossack attack? Obviously not.

And yet, Frank observes, religious people keep on following the rules. "All the teachings up until now have been like that dog that kept vomiting, then swallowing," Frank says in §232, citing Proverbs 26:11. Despite abundant evidence that religious observance does not yield any rewards, the dog

---

[41] Scholem, *Sabbatai Ṣevi*, 402–3.

keeps reswallowing the same vomit. In §1318, Frank tells a tale of a priest abandoning the priesthood and subsequently having a successful material life; abandoning religion is a step toward personal flourishing. Indeed, when a king, defrocking the priest, asks if he is ashamed because of his decision, the priest says no; on the contrary, if he regrets anything it was joining the priesthood at the age of fifteen, when his judgment was unclear—just like, one might add, that of thirteen-year-olds who become *b'nai mitzvah*. Similarly, the peculiar, short tale in §872 tells of a general who divines cards and foretells his own death; when it does not come to pass, rather than rejoicing, he curses death for defying the cards; his magical-religious beliefs are more important to him than his own life—though in an amusing coda, Frank says his anger did not last long: "Despite this, he continued to live and ordered his wife to bake him a good turkey and give it to him to eat." Oh well, supernatural predictions are wrong, my entire religious worldview is shattered; time to eat turkey. Perhaps spiritual matters are not such a big deal after all.

Frank is indeed largely "without shame and free of guilt," as Elior has written.[42] But that is because, if we may translate from the Frankist idiom to a contemporary one, he believes he has liberated himself from systems of shame and guilt that needlessly repress human potential. Indeed, given that shame is a cultural construction, dependent on societal consensus for its substantive content, the shamelessness of Frank, while it may of course be attributable to personal characteristics, is a theological as well as psychological position. Shamelessness is a mark of liberation. Frankist antinomianism is a deliberate "treading"—the metaphor discussed above, which appears in over two hundred dicta—upon the strictures of traditional religious and sexual morality. Each transgression affirms the freedom of the individual from oppressive religious norms. One of the recurring metaphors for this idea is the theme of stealing and eating fruit—with its attendant connotations of the Garden of Eden and of sexuality. In §556, Frank is challenged by a lord to break into his walled garden and steal the pears inside, and through a stratagem, Frank does so. The pears are forbidden fruit, but forbidden so that the hero can obtain them. In §692, Frank steals fruit from a Christian's garden and whips the Christian's children, a reference to the Frankist myth of displacing Christianity. Unpicked fruit is bitter, while fruit that can be eaten is sweet, Frank remarks in §622. The "fruit" of sexuality is meant to be picked—not merely looked at, or limited, or left to rot, as in the lives of religious people

---

[42] Elior, "Jacob Frank," 471.

who deny themselves sensual enjoyment. "Jacob Frank" here is the trickster who is meant to trick the pious.

As we noted above, Frank's ethos here is quite similar to those of his contemporary charlatans and libertines. Maciejko has drawn persuasive social parallels between Jacob Frank (and Wolf Eibeschütz) and principled charlatans like Cagliostro, Casanova, and Saint-Germain.[43] Frank and Eibeschütz in particular exploited the enthusiasm for new converts to Christianity, the mystique of Kabbalah, the patronage of elites (both Frank and Eibeschütz lived in borrowed palaces at the end of their lives), and new conditions of social and geographical mobility to assume false titles and advance through European society. Both were connected to the burgeoning secret societies of Western esotericism, dabbling in alchemy and exploiting the new Christian/esoteric fascination with Kabbalah. And both made use of the interstitial status of Sabbatean subcultures, exploiting networks of protosecularists for whom moving between worlds was a fact of life and of ideology.[44] In literary forms, the essence of the libertine tale is the individual will of the emancipated protagonist triumphing over the hypocritical niceties of bourgeois society. This, too, is not nihilism but a principled opposition to piety, an outsider's "seeing through" the affectations of the majority culture. Really, the libertine says, all of us are self-interested; the difference is that the pious are deluded or hypocritical about it. In a sense, the charlatan is the most honest man in the world, since he is truthful about his selfishness.

Similarly, as we noted in chapter 1, many libertine tales, like Frankist ones, depict traditional morality as ridiculous, even absurd. Moralizing characters are routinely dispatched by the cruel hand of fate or the crueler hands of cunning schemers. But libertinism is not nihilism. In the seventeenth century, the term referred to a Montaigne-inspired "small group of freethinkers who shared an aversion to dogma; seeking to demystify superstition and to dismantle baseless beliefs and preconceived ideas, they contested both political and religious authority."[45] And in the eighteenth century, particularly from 1715 until 1789 (i.e., the reigns of Louis XV and XVI), libertinism arose again as a cynical movement that denied the truth of moral claims, particularly those about love, led by the Marquis de Sade, Crébillon *fils*, Vivant Denon, Choderlos de Laclos (author of *Dangerous Liaisons*), and the Abbé Prévost. Libertinism seeks to liberate human beings from their constraints; libertine

---

[43] Maciejko, "Sabbatean Charlatans," 373. See also Lenowitz, "The Charlatan at the *Gottes Haus*."
[44] Maciejko, *Mixed Multitude*, 212–18.
[45] Feher, "Libertinisms," 12. See also Cryle and O'Connell, eds., *Libertine Enlightenment*.

heroes practice hypocrisy to expose it and show through their actions the emptiness of conventional pieties. As Feher writes, "those lusts condemned by the Christian world... are in reality the closest to the desires of nature."[46] Likewise in Frank's many tales in which naked ambition and lust triumph over propriety and piety.

Unlike the libertines, Frank devotes most of his attention to Jewish law, ultimately arriving at an ambivalent position in which normative Judaism comes "from the side of death" but the Jews will still be the first to recognize the Redemption. In §977, Frank says,

> This is what Abraham was also told: *Go, leave your country*, and so have you been told. It means that you need to leave behind the customs you kept while you were in the Jewish state, such as: fasts, mournings, condemnations, pretense, beating one another, because all of these things belong to the mortal side.... I led you to Esau, but (at his place) all the kings and their children are among delights and pay no heed to mourning. I led you to life.

As we will discuss more in the next chapter, Esau/Edom/Christianity stands for worldly power and riches; power, not prayer, will stop the Cossacks from beating up the Jews. As Frank says in §1292, "All those who don't have God, let them learn laws. God gave lands to Abraham, not laws." Lands—material success, power, and property—not laws. The Torah/Law is "from the side of death" (§805) and given by Samael (§980). Indeed, Frank says in §2142, "Just as Christ, as you know, said that he came to free the world from the hands of Satan, I came to free the world from all laws and statutes of yore, because this was all work of the hands of Satan, and because of this, everyone fell into his hands. I need to destroy it all, and erase entirely all that is black on white. At that time the good God will reveal himself." This stark rejection of religion is not nihilism, for Frank maintains a sense of right and wrong; it's just that traditional religion is profoundly wrong. For example, he says in §450, "You were in the Jewish religion, and although you were *ma'aminim*, you had to keep those customs of other Jews. When I came out from there and pulled you from that left side, you should have discarded all teaching, all religions, all that is wicked, so that you would be able to go to the right." Left and right, evil and good, do exist—it is just that Judaism is on the side of evil. To come to the right is to be like Abraham, that is, leave Judaism and its ways behind.

---

[46] Feher, "Libertinisms," 33.

Frank is quite clear on this point. Law is "from the side of death" (§805). Samael gave the Torah (§980). Interestingly, Frank does not deny the potential efficacy of religious practices; like other Western esotericists, he regards them as magical powers that are misconstrued by religion. In §1180, Frank observes that the Jews fast to mourn the destruction of the Temple. But, he continues, this is pointless; the Temple is gone. King David fasted when a child was alive, to save him—that is the use of fasting, here understood as a magical (perhaps theurgical) practice. Fasting does work—but not when the child is already dead.

Frank's vocabulary here is worthy of note. Frank generally uses the term *praw*, the ordinary Polish word for "law," to denote the Torah—not "teaching," or "Torah," or other terms (see, e.g., §§19, 286). When Frank refers to the Torah specifically, he uses the term *Praw Mojżeszowe*, or Law of Moses (capitalized in the manuscript). When he refers to the physical Torah, he uses terms for scroll or commandments (*przykazania*, § 286). This terminology is noteworthy for several reasons. First, that Frank uses the term "law" rather than "Torah" shows a Christian influence, as the term is not generally used by traditional Jews to refer to the Torah. Second, it sheds light on Frank's essentialization of the Torah as legal. Torah is essentially law: a restrictive, governing, and legalistic avenue to salvation, all of which Frank rejects. This is certainly not the mystical approach to Torah that contemporary Kabbalists or Hasidim would understand. Nor is there any hint that Frank is making use here of the Sabbatean-Zoharic distinction between the Torah of the Tree of Life and the Torah of the Tree of Knowledge of Good and Evil, or the Torah of *Atzilut* and Torah of *Asiyah*. None of these terms are used in ZSP. Third and finally, to not name the Torah as such, but rather refer to it simply as the "Law of Moses," is itself a form of denigration or marginalization. This is not Torah, essential to the religious life; this is simply law, a superseded method of religious life.

Still, at the same time as Frank issues a radical critique of Jewish religion, he remains, perhaps opportunistically, focused on the Jewish people. As he says in §439, "my highest expectation is with the Jews." On the one hand, the Jews are to be transcended—the brethren need to get over their Jewishness, and the Jewish religion is a limitation on human potential and a wrongheaded particularism. On the other hand, Jews play a crucial role in the unfolding of Frankist millennialism: they will come to Frank first, then other nations will follow (§§260, 262). Indeed, Frank adds, "My eyes and my heart are always turned toward them" (439).

In Frank's skeptical antinomianism, it is not that life is empty of meaning; it is that specific kinds of religious law are—in particular, those which restrain sensuality, which as we will see in chapter 5, turns out to be part of the messianic impulse itself.

Religious Antinomianism

Religious antinomianism condemns the law because obedience to the law is religiously wrong, often because the law has been supplanted by some new religious value. (What Magid terms "neonomianism" is a subset of this form.[47]) Perhaps the most famous example of religious antinomianism can be found within the writings of the apostle Paul. For Paul, obedience to the written biblical law—as opposed to the spirit of the law—is literally soul-killing. "The letter kills, but the Spirit gives life," Paul writes in 2 Corinthians 3:6. And in Galatians 5:7–8, he says, concerning circumcision, "You who want to be justified by the law have cut yourselves off from Christ; you have fallen away from grace."[48] It is not simply that the law no longer is binding; it is that it is deadly: "Now we are discharged from the law, dead to that which held us captive, so that we are slaves not under the old written code but in the new life of the Spirit."[49] For Paul, to obey the literal, physical law (physical circumcision, physical dietary laws) is to privilege the body over the soul.[50] And "if you live according to the flesh, you will die; but if by the Spirit you put to death the deeds of the body, you will live."[51] Being free from the law is thus a religious requirement.

More relevant for these purposes, religious antinomianism is predominant in Sabbateanism. As noted earlier, Sabbateans, primarily Nathan of Gaza, expanded on the Zoharic notion of two Torahs to distinguish between the legalistic, materialistic, and dualistic "Torah of the Tree of Good and Evil" and the spiritual, permissive "Torah of the Tree of Life," which would replace it in the messianic age.[52] "Freedom is the secret of the spiritual Torah," the *doenmeh* leader Dervish Effendi—Frank's father-in-law—reportedly said.[53]

---

[47] Magid, *Hasidism on the Margins*, 211–12.
[48] See Boyarin, *A Radical Jew*, 78ff.
[49] Romans 7:6
[50] See Michaelson, "Hating the Law."
[51] Romans 8:13.
[52] See Scholem, *Sabbatai Ṣevi*, 11–12; Elior, "Jacob Frank," 487–94; Scholem, *Messianic Idea*, 176–78.
[53] Sisman, *Burden of Silence*, 185.

(Nathan of Gaza wrote that continued observance of the Torah of the Tree of Good and Evil was still required in the liminal period of the 1650s–1670s because the souls of the generation still contained an admixture of materiality, but that the souls of the believers would eventually be purified of all materiality and would only adhere to the spiritual Torah.[54]) The myths of Sabbatean antinomianism likely exceeded the reality: Sisman has shown that the only documented antinomian acts of the initial phase of the Sabbatean movement were disregarding some of the rules of sexual morality, pronouncing the tetragrammaton, eating forbidden foods, reading Torah from a printed copy rather than a scroll, turning fast days into feast days, and calling women to the Torah.[55] Nevertheless, these ritual abrogations signified that the old Torah had been replaced by a new one. They signified the onset of the messianic age.

Frankist religious antinomianism is quite different. The law is to be transgressed not because there is a new Torah but because *all* religion is antithetical to true service of God. The famous antinomian statement quoted earlier that "all religions, all laws, all books of old . . . originated from the side of death," is actually just the first part of §62. Frank then continues, quoting Ecclesiastes 2:14:

> "A wise man has eyes in his head," that is, one should look at the one who walks ahead of him, not to the right, nor to the left nor backwards, but fix him with his gaze, and follow him closely.

In other words, real religion—pure obedience to God (and Frank)—replaces traditional religion. "To serve another God is one thing; to take the path you are led onto, is another," Frank states in §1156. And when it comes to qualities like constancy and virtue, Frank often sounds like a traditional moralist. For example, in §66, he states, "Whoever wants to be attached to the living God has to be virtuous, and display all kinds of good qualities toward God and man, and do good by everyone as much as possible. Similar statements are found in §§114, 133, 590, 916, 975, and throughout ZSP, as Frank warns his followers to be good and steadfast (§66) and not to be distracted by hedonistic pleasures (§71). Frank even complains that the Brethren got waylaid from their mission by "eating and drinking" (§1127). Frank does not cast off

---

[54] See Scholem, *Sabbatai Ṣevi*, 323–25.
[55] Sisman, *Burden of Silence*, 47.

the ritual law out of nihilistic anomie, but, he says, in order to serve God, liberate the Maiden, reach the Big Brother, and triumph over the fallen world that was not created by God at all.

The figure of Abraham recurs in Frankist religious antinomianism as a figure who is obedient to God and transgressive of religious boundaries. Abraham "stays to the right" (§§450, 869, 871, 941); he is ethical, but he leaves his father's house and religion behind (§§403, 1072). Frank says to the Brethren in §871, "you should have compared yourself with Abraham and not followed simple folk" and holds Abraham as a model for them in §§214, 217, 438, 450, 869, 871, 941, 957, and 1097. God promises Abraham lands, not mere laws (§1292). Abraham's sexual "sharing" of Sarah with Abimelech and Pharaoh is seen, in §§848 and 871, as a supreme act of simultaneous faithfulness and transgression. Frank even fundraises on the basis of Abraham's example, noting that Abraham had to pay money for the cave of Machpelah, just as the Frankists must now pay money to Frank (§581).

One area in which Frank builds on, rather than rejects Sabbateanism, is in the rejection of particularism. The Karakash sect of the *doenmeh*, of which Frank was a member, was known for its syncretic beliefs and practices—adherents were dubbed *on yollular*, or the "men of ten tricks."[56] The notion that multiple religions might point to the same truth (esoteric or otherwise) could well have been nurtured in that context. Yet Frank's iteration of this principle is still remarkable in its quasi-modernity. As Frank states in §413, the term *ma'asim zarim* (foreign, strange acts) really just means going to foreign places, because there these same things are *ma'asim yofim*, beautiful acts. (Notably, Frank's universalism is negative as well as positive. As well as the "beautiful acts" of other religions, Frank notes in §525 a book that listed various awful foreign customs, such as Pharaoh bathing in the blood of children.) A striking metaphor for Frankist universalism is the three-branched tree, representing the three Western religions. In §§102, 228, 321, and 470, Frank relates the parable of the tree surrounded by a high wall. Because of the way it branches, it looks like three trees, though in reality it is only one. Once more making use of the long-standing Kabbalistic trope of the orchard, which we have already encountered in the context of stealing from it, Frank says in §470 that he wanted to lead the company into the orchard, where they would have "been free from everything and feared nothing." The meaning here is clear: what appears to be three religions, Judaism, Christianity, and

---

[56] Sisman, *Burden of Silence*, 142.

Islam, is actually one religion. Frank's universalist statement in §102 is even more clearly developed. He says,

> There is a tree whose broad branches spread behind the wall that surrounds it. Those who stand on the outside think that there are plenty of trees, but the one who is inside can see that there is only one tree. So should we know and pursue only one tree, instead of searching for many.

Or as he states in §321, "you are still standing on the outside and are not worthy of seeing that instead of many trees, there is only one tree here." Like his contemporaries in esoteric circles who sought to identify the universal roots of all religions, Frank says here that there is, in fact, one tree—one true religion of which the manifest religions are but bare approximations. Similarly, in §740, Frank uses the roots and branches of a tree as a symbol of transgressing religion's manifestation while keeping its roots; citing Daniel 4:20 and Isaiah 52:2, Frank notes that the branches of a tree may be cut, or the tree itself cut down, "but the roots may not be cut out." And in §708, Frank states, "if you cut down a tree, the foundation of its roots remains in the ground. This means that all the religions that have been till now, even the First and the Second who you had, have only been temporary." In fact, the branches are from the "tree of death" while Frank "wanted to take hold of the foundation of the root."

Frank's universalism surely reflects his own liminal career, moving from culture to culture, sometimes by choice, other times by coercion. As his fellow skeptic de La Mothe Le Vayer observed in the mid-seventeenth century, "In this infinity of religions there is hardly anyone who does not believe that he possesses the true religion, and who does not condemn all the others."[57] Obviously, all of the claims of all religious communities cannot all be right, which gives strong support to the view that none of them are. Yet in ordinary circumstances, the absurdity of religious triumphalism may be concealed by a social environment in which like-minded believers agree with one another, and separate themselves from unbelievers. In extraordinary circumstances such as those of Frank's life, however, spent among Ottoman Turks, Polish monks, Jewish heretics, and secularist politicians, the absurdity of competing religious claims is made apparent. Frank's universalism and his marginality thus reinforce one another. As Frank remarks in §2184:

---

[57] De La Mothe Le Vayer, "Of Divinity," 142.

Hold on to it tight, and do not let go of it. For if a man holds on to something with one hand, even if he holds on to it for several years, his hand must faint in the end and let go. But if a man holds on to two places with both hands, when one faints, the other holds on; when this one also faints, the other one will grab it again. That is why many people fell, because they did not pay attention and only held on to one place. These two were Ishmael and Esau. Solomon also only held on to one place, and that is partial wisdom; but even through that wisdom he did not come to complete wisdom, and said: *I recognized that I was wise already, but the other one was not within reach*. The one, however, who will attain both kinds of wisdom, will reach and attain God himself.

To "reach God" cannot be accomplished through a single religious system of knowledge. Ultimately each individual system will "become tired." Consequently, the only effective way to "reach God himself" is to be have multiple viewpoints, multiple paths, even multiple identities. Likewise, in §421, Frank states a universalist claim for his mission (or perhaps for religious truth generally): "to him peoples will gather"—not Israel, but everyone. From this Frank reminds his audience how he forced the Brethren to sell all their old Jewish books "for a pittance" because "all books and laws will be broken like a potsherd. For when a man passes from one place to another, he should drop all the rites of one place and abide by those in which he enters."

Now, Frank's view may simply be a matter of expediency; Hillel Levine called it "a safety measure as well as a religious orientation."[58] As quoted earlier, Frank himself states in §1110, "When ones goes to see the sun, one ought to talk like the sun and dress like the sun; and when one goes to see the moon, one ought to wear what the moon wears and speak its language." This does suggest a highly accommodationist position that accords with Levine's assessment. Yet again, surely the "safer route" would have been to discard the Jewish "hand" and simply adopt Christianity, a path Frank opted not to take. As we will explore in chapter 8, I propose that we read Frankist universalism in the context of eighteenth-century Western esotericism, combining a skeptical rationalism with an esoteric, materialistic understanding of the universal religion. Ironically, though Scholem's view that Frankism was a stepping stone to the Haskalah has not been borne out by subsequent scholarship, Western esotericism offered a different path to some of the same values,

---

[58] Levine, "Frankism as Worldly Messianism," 293.

including a humanistic critique of normative law, a materialist rereading of religiomagical concepts, and an incipient syncretic universalism. In this context, the rejection of otherworldly and particularist religion was the pathway to God, or power, or both.

Experiential Antinomianism

Finally, antinomian acts may bring about a decentering, perhaps traumatic, experience that can bring about a break from conventional nomic reality. This rupture has many aspects. First, the experience may be associated with messianism or prophecy; it is possible that the sexual antinomianism of the *doenmeh* sought to confirm and enact an embodied, messianic reality. The traumatic nature of the transgressing of fundamental sexual boundaries may, itself, have provided a cognitively dissonant rupture that confirmed the alternate reality of the believer. Second, antinomianism may be social in nature, dividing inside and outside. In Emden's accounts of the Sabbatean persecutions, for example, he describes how Chaya Shorr, a close associate of Frank, tested the loyalty of one person by demanding that he eat the unkosher animal fat in a piece of candle wax.[59] Eating the unkosher wax is a test of which nomic community an individual is a part of; it is a test that divides inside and outside, and one that cannot be faked. Third, and conversely, the experience of antinomianism might also have the effect of shaking one's prior faith: The forbidden word is said, the taboo action is taken, and yet the world does not end, God does not mete out punishment, the sin goes unpunished.

So, for example, when Sabbetai Zevi forced his followers to pronounce the Ineffable Name,[60] the antinomian act may be traumatic for the practitioner, or it may be liberating; certainly, she or he is in a new religious reality than previously. Or consider when Frank forces (or says he forced) Jews, Muslims, and Christians to pronounce the sacred phrases of other religions ($15, discussed above) this could engender an experience of transgression without punishment. It is not only mockery; by forcing religious people to transgress, it may unmoor them from their faith. Indeed, arguably the antinomian experience is one of the central "spiritual" (Scholem's term is

---

[59] See Feiner, *Origins of Jewish Secularization*, 74–75.
[60] Scholem, *Sabbatai Ṣevi*, 402–3.

"pneumatic") experiences of Frankism.[61] Radical antinomian experience represents a significant, decentering rupture from conventional life. The Frankist inner circle, despite coming from a Sabbatean ancestry, was, after all, still Jewish in its origin and thus imbued with a millennia-old sense of taboo, boundary, and law. Again and again, Frank castigates the Brethren for remaining attached to their old ways of restriction, piety, and taboo. In this light, antinomian activity is a kind of pedagogical initiation ritual that pries the practitioner away from their former nomic universe.

Transgressive sexuality, in particular, is often found in antinomian millennial and postmillennial movements, with eroticism enacting what Dominic Pettman calls the "rupture of discontinuity" that the millennial sect either predicts or is continuing to experience.[62] As we will discuss in detail in chapter 5, evidence of antinomian sexual ritual is, in fact, quite limited in the Frankist corpus, yet one such account is an excellent example of the phenomenon Pettman examines. In one of the very few sexual rituals discussed explicitly in the Frankist corpus, in *RA* §46, Frank conducts a remarkable sexual ritual among the Brethren involving disrobing, lighting candles, waving a cross in the four directions, and then engaging in sexual relations at Frank's command. "With this deed we go to the naked thing," Frank is recorded as saying, "therefore it is necessary to go naked." This ritual, in and of itself, is bizarre. Yet its meaning becomes clearer in context: it is said to have taken place in July 1759, on the eve of the sect's baptism. The antinomian ritual is thus a kind of initiation rite, in which the Brethren confirm that they are not becoming Christian, but entering into some new, heretical sect, bound to one another and to Frank. The text in *Various Notes* does not describe the Brethren's responses to the rite, so we can only speculate as to the psychological, experiential impact it may have had on them. The antinomian experience here confirms the group identity, marks a sharp break from conventional nomic reality, and perhaps evokes a shocking and decentering "pneumatic" experience of its own. There is no going back; the bridge has been crossed and burned.

This analysis of antinomianism, in its many varieties, demonstrates that the phenomenon is not reducible to nihilism, hedonism, or sensual expression. It can be a critique of religion, an enactment of messianic reality, or

---

[61] Scholem, *Messianic Idea*, 91. Sabbateanism in general was largely a "pneumatic," that is to say, charismatic, prophetic, mystical, trance-ecstatic-spiritual movement. See Goldish, *Sabbatean Prophets*, 89–129.
[62] Pettman, *After the Orgy*, 51. Frankist millennialism will be discussed in chapter 6.

a defiance of ineffectual religious strictures. It can be a protest of freedom raised against the strictures of religious norms. Frank transgresses the law for skeptical/humanistic reasons (because the law needlessly restricts human potential), for religious reasons (because the true God does not want obedience, but personal flourishing), and for experiential reasons (because transgression is decentering and "pneumatic"). And Frank's followers are exhorted to abjure pointless religious norms, venerate the Maiden through sexual expression, obey Frank's commands, pursue this-worldly life and immortality, and fulfill the Frankist quest of libertine self-assertion and personal fulfillment in the face of repressive religious norms. This is critique, not nihilism. And it is bound up with Frankist materialism. As Rapoport-Albert has proposed,

> Frank had turned on its head the long-standing eschatological tradition ... whereby the messianic future would be experienced as a refinement of every aspect of corporeal existence—a spiritualization or intellectualization of material reality, including the sublimation of the body and its physical appetites. By contrast, Frank's vision of the redeemed world entailed the concrete substantiation of the spirit, including the full physical materialization of the divine.[63]

As Frank says in §1089, quoted earlier, "I do not look to heaven for aid to come from there. I only look at what God does here on earth, in this world." It is to that materialist theology that we now turn.

---

[63] Rapoport-Albert and Hamann, "Something for the Female Sex," 119, n.2.

3

"Everything that is of the spirit has to be turned into flesh"

Magic, Myth, and the Material *Imaginaire*

An (A)Theology of Material Magic

The religious world of Jacob Frank is a bizarre hybrid of materialism, gnosticism, and myth even more fantastic than the religion Frank seeks to displace. It is populated by "real" physical beings with magical superpowers, ruled over not by the monotheistic God but by three flawed gods identified by Frank with the Nephilim; indeed, the God of the Bible did not even create it. It exists together with a parallel universe "behind the curtain," where Frank's counterpart, the Big Brother, leads a sect that has gained the secret of immortality. Yet all this is said to be physically real. We already noted Frank's insistence in §1001 regarding stories of the Maiden that "I did not tell you about this in spirit, or in heaven. Instead, I said everything in broad daylight, on earth: that there is a Lady and a tower, and there is a painting they call a portrait." A real maiden, a real tower, a real portrait—not a symbol, a spiritual maiden, a metaphor, or a Shechinah disincarnate. Whereas the prophet Zechariah wrote, "Not by might, nor by power, but by my spirit, says the Lord" (Zech. 4:6), Frank argues the exact opposite. By might and power, not by some invisible spirit, are the truths of religion known. Or as Frank states in §548, "I say that even in this world everything that is of the spirit has to be turned into flesh, just like our own, so that everyone will see as clearly as you see something that is apparent."[1] Frank's world is not a spiritual or imaginal domain but a concrete, mytho-folkloric one in which demons and black magicians are running rampant and there is another realm on the other side of a partition, filled with godlike superhumans who may or may not have our best interests at heart. It has more in common with the scraps of practical

---

[1] See Maciejko, *Mixed Multitude*, 16.

Kabbalah, folklore, and demonology that became integrated into Masonic orders, and, later, the theosophical society and Crowleian "magickal" circles, than with the philosophical expositions of Sabbatean thinkers like Nathan of Gaza or Abraham Miguel Cardoso.[2] Frank's heroes are Balaam, the black magician (who "lives today, and is essentially a man," Frank says in §2157); the Queen of Sheba, who was a visitor from the "other realm"; and others who are aware of the hidden worlds and magical beings which inhabit them.

This combination of myth and materialism is perhaps an unusual juxtaposition—but it is not without precedent. For example, one hundred years before Frank, the British skeptic Joseph Glanvill attacked metaphysical philosophy while at the same time attempting to prove the existence of witches, spirits, and a "natural religion."[3] And as we will discuss in more detail in chapter 7, the juxtaposition of skepticism and magic is at the heart of many Western esotericist rereadings of biblical themes including the Temple, the story of King Solomon, and so forth, which are reinterpreted from being about God to being about secret, but worldly, magical powers. Religion may be false in Frank's world; but magical objects are not.

Frankist eschatology, or perhaps soteriology, is likewise entirely material; in §1161, he predicts that the faithful will gain fat and lovely faces, and as noted earlier in §988, he says that in the future, he will furnish his court in splendid dress. Even prophetic utterances that once were understood metaphorically should be understood literally; in §1294, he says, "Take heed, Daniel said to Nebuchadnezzar: 'Your head is golden.' But his head was just like anyone else's. However, it must be the case that there is a man who has a golden head." In §966, Frank describes a precious stone but is at pains to point out that it is not a metaphor but an actual precious stone. The angel described in the book of Daniel is actually a man with divine protection (§324). Jews and Kabbalists live on an actual magical island (§320). And the notion of "spiritual" power is mistaken. For example, in §831 Frank castigates the followers who "did not know what to make of this thing, so you turned it into spiritual power; but here everything will be done in daylight, and your eyes will see it." The worldly is what matters, not the otherworldly. In place of divine, heavenly realms, Frank conceives of magical, earthly

---

[2] On Cardoso, see Liebes, "On a Jewish-Christian Sect," 221–25; Maciejko, "Christian Elements," 21–25; Goldish, "Sabbatai Zevi," 515–17; Scholem, *Messianic Idea*, 106–7; Wolfson, "Constructions of the Shekhinah." To be sure, the boundaries between Kabbalah and magic were always porous and contested. Harari, "Practical Kabbalah," 40–57.

[3] See Glanvill, "Essays," 165–68.

realms populated by fallible, material beings who await redemption just as we humans do. These beings—the Big Brother and his brothers and sisters, demigods, *shedim*, *baʿalei kaben*—are all physical material beings like us.[4] As Frank states in §138, at the end of a long parable, "the wise look to heaven, though they see nothing there. But all nourishment springs from the dirt and so it is to the dirt we should look."

Such a position is a refutation of religious metaphysics generally—but also of Sabbateanism specifically. Rachel Elior writes in *The Mystical Origins of Hasidism* that

> for Shabateans, the revealed world is devoid of all meaning.... Moreover, if daily life is to be lived according to a conceptual world that pertains to messianic reality, then nothing is forbidden and everything is permitted. If the real world is meaningless, then concepts of commandment and sin are meaningless.[5]

The Frankism of *ZSP* is a rejection of this position. The "real world," which is to say the material world, is of paramount importance to Frank. Unlike his Sabbatean forebears, Frank rejects the view that this world is illusory or unimportant, and insists on this-worldly evidence for religious truth. Frank explicitly rejects the otherworldliness of Sabbateanism in §1199. In that tale, Frank's father is visited by Nahman ben Levi, who after conversion takes the name Piotr Jakubowski, coming from Salonica.[6] Yet Frank's father is uninterested in the Kabbalistic secrets Jakubowski has learned. The conversation continues:

> Jakubowski said to my father: "I came from such a precious place, and I am surprised that you, such a respected man, are not questioning me about the teachings, and similar information, which I acquired there." He answered him: "Truly I tell you that I will not benefit from it even if you reveal to me that it is Market Day in Heaven. What can I take from this and what wisdom can I gain from it? In my eyes this is all foolishness. Rather than that, tell me

---

[4] One is once again reminded of new religious movements that teach about magical-material entities that "really" exist in the world, such as UFOs. These include not only numerous "UFO cults" but Scientology's cosmology of alien warfare, and the Nation of Islam's teaching that there is a UFO called the Great Wheel on the dark side of the moon. Lieb, *Children of Ezekiel*, 129–97; Allison, "Ezekiel, UFOs, and the Nation of Islam."
[5] Elior, *Mystical Origins*, 184.
[6] See also §§46 and 47.

about what will happen here, in this world, so that my own eyes can see all the things that God will do in this world. That would make me happy."

There can be no clearer rejection of Sabbatean spiritualization than this, and no clearer exposition of Frankist materialist religion.

Perhaps the most shocking example of Frank's materialist rereading of Torah is that "God appeared to Abraham as El Shaddai to indicate he is a *shed*" (§1266), a term that normally means "demon" but which Frank defines in the next dictum as a quasi-divine powerful being: "there are *shedim* of a higher degree, like kings and lords. They do nothing evil—in fact, they do good."[7] This is a redefinition not only of the concept of the *shed* but also, of course, of the God spoken of in the Torah. Later in §1266, Frank says that the power of El Shaddai is exactly like the power of the unicorn. This is beyond the gnosticism of Sabbateanism, which we will discuss shortly; here the El Shaddai of the Bible is nothing more than a powerful being. Moreover, as discussed in the next chapter, these *shedim* are but an early stage in the Frankist quest; they will bring the Brethren "across the curtain" to the Big Brother and the other brothers. As with the Big Brother, the *shedim* will help the Frankist company in exchange for the Frankist company helping them. In §1267, Frank says that he will redeem the fallen *shedim* and unite them with the good *shedim*. Speaking to the Brethren of the *shedim*'s relationship to the Big Brother, Frank states,

> You would be the middle men between me and them, and through you all would end. For you must know that they cannot approach the King of All Kings who is before God, even though he is their God and he is with them like these two trees that stand opposite each other with a river between them; so is the Big Brother with them.

Here, the fallen *shedim* rely on Frank and the Brethren to redeem them; together the Frankist Brethren and the *shedim*, led by El Shaddai, would in turn lead the Brethren to the Big Brother and the other brothers, who would welcome them. Frank continues:

> The name *El Shaddai* is very respectable, but they need us to repair them and we need them to serve us so that they can lead us to distant lands

---

[7] See Ben-Amos, "On Demons," 29–34.

without exhaustion or labor. They have the power in their hands to give us a curtain that will make us invisible in certain places, wherever we would need it. All that I have revealed to you is but a drop in the sea compared to all that exists where I want to go with the power of my God.

Frank's mythic theology is really an atheology here, thoroughly magical in orientation. El Shaddai is not God, but a mortal figure who gives the sect invisibility cloaks like those in the Harry Potter books. El Shaddai may be more powerful than a sorcerer or a wizard, but he is not different in kind from them; he is a magical being possessed of power. As we have already remarked, this rereading of Scriptural subjects is similar to those in some forms of Western esotericism, which redefined King Solomon and the Temple in terms of magic and sorcery, and redefined Egypt as the place of ancient material magic. In §85, for example, Frank cites his prophecy that Edom/Poland would be given as an inheritance to Israel[8] and analogizes the Israelites deriving power from their "powerful thing," the Temple in Jerusalem, to Poland deriving its power from Częstochowa.[9] He understands both the Temple and the portrait not as sacred spaces for prayer and spirituality but in technological terms, as "powerful things" that maintain kingdoms. As discussed in chapter 7, this doctrine resembles those of eighteenth-century Freemasonry, which understood the power of the Temple in Jerusalem as being technological in nature,[10] and to early Mormonism, likewise influenced by Western esotericism, which held that the Garden of Eden was a real, physical place located in Independence, Missouri, and that the faithful would live forever in transformed but still-physical bodies.[11] Indeed, while in his exhortations to the Brethren, Frank frequently speaks of faith in God, the agencies that will grant power to the sect have nothing to do with God. They are occultic-mythic-magical in nature: various beings, powerful angels and demons, and an entire parallel world of superhumans, led by the Big Brother. Frank's promised transformation is neither a redemption nor an apocalypse but the transformation of humans into superhumans, with power and wealth at their disposal.

---

[8] On the linkage between Esau/Edom and Poland, see Maciejko, *Mixed Multitude*, 162. Maciejko notes that this was not a Frankist innovation but was present in earlier Sabbatean sources.

[9] Frank cites Proverbs 30:23—"the servant-girl has inherited the property of her mistress"—which often refers in Kabbalistic sources to Lilith taking he power of the Shechinah. As discussed in chapter 5, this suggests that the portrait in Częstochowa may be the "husk before the fruit," rather than the Shechinah incarnate.

[10] Faivre, *Access to Western Esotericism*, 163–76.

[11] See Buck, *Religious Myths and Visions of America*, 93–94. On the relationship between Western esotericism and Mormonism, see Katz, *Occult Tradition*, 98–109.

Of course, the boundaries between magic and religion are always porous in nature, from biblical Israelite religion, in which prophets perform supernatural acts and witches and sorcerers possess actual magical abilities,[12] to the highly permeable boundaries between magic, practical Kabbalah, and theoretical or theosophical Kabbalah.[13] Frank's material-magical rereading of Scripture also has ample precedent within Jewish traditions, which themselves existed in dialogue with traditions of magic, esotericism, astrology, and myth. It resembles Elior's account of the cosmos-maintaining function of the Temple in Jerusalem,[14] for example, and the notion of the Temple as quasi-astrological tool, a theme which occurs in Ibn Ezra.[15] The Temple is not powerful because God chose it; it is powerful because it exists at a particularly auspicious astrological location, and has specific magical potency. More broadly, within practical Kabbalah, in the words of Chajes and Harari,

> Jewish intellectuals in Italy created a sizable body of magical literature that had much in common with the better-known works by figures including Marsilio Ficino (1433–1499) and Giovanni Pico della Mirandola (1463–1494). These rabbinic authors construed Judaism as a system of perfected magical words and hermetic vessels, and shared the view of their Renaissance contemporaries that magic was the highest actualization of human potential.[16]

This is Frank's conception as well. In ZSP, as in these other ideologies, the "power" that Frank and his cohort seek is not abstract; it is physically instantiated in the portrait in Częstochowa, in Poland generally, and in the physical entities whom Frank will enlist for support in his quest. In contrast to the synagogue that is the "house of Elijah" but which lacks Elijah's actual presence, Częstochowa does possess the actual portrait of the actual Maiden. Yet the Christian guardians of Częstochowa do not know what it is they possess. Frank's mission is to bring the two halves together.[17]

---

[12] See Dolansky, *Now You See It, Now You Don't*; Janowitz, *Icons of Power*.
[13] See Harari, "Practical Kabbalah," 40–57; Idel, "On Judaism, Jewish Mysticism, and Magic."
[14] See Elior, *The Three Temples*.
[15] See Halbertal, *Concealment and Revelation*, 34–48.
[16] Chajes and Harari, "Practical Kabbalah," 2. As Harari points out, "magic" is more of a scholarly category than a Kabbalistic one; in fact, magic and Kabbalah were always intertwined one with the other. Harari, "Practical Kabbalah," 40–48, 53–57.
[17] These themes build on earlier Sabbatean conceptions of Christianity such as those of Cardoso and Eibeschütz, as well as on the earlier phase of the Frankist career in which Christian syncretism was primary. See Maciejko, "Coitus interruptus," xxxvi–xli; Maciejko, "Christian Elements."

From Jacob to Esau

A frequently recurring symbol for this polarity, which Frank seeks to resolve in *Das*, esoteric gnosis, is that of Jacob and Esau, which appears in eighty-six dicta in *ZSP*. As we have noted already, Jacob represents the incomplete, ineffectual, particularistic, and feminized Judaism that, by rejecting Esau and his worldly, physical power, ultimately failed. In refusing to admit the power and reality of Rachel's *terafim* (household gods), which she took from Laban, Jacob also represents the pitfalls of Jewish particularism, which we discuss in more detail below. But Jacob Frank will succeed where Jacob the patriarch failed. As Frank says in §219,

> Jacob worshipped his lord in a foreign god. So should we worship our lord, but how? This is how: abandon all laws, religion, etc., and follow me step by step.[18]

This inversion of Jacob's particularism, monotheism, and piety will ultimately not only integrate Jacob and Esau but also displace Christian domination (§§69, 92, 155, 185, 263, 275, 404, 598, 1227, 1254, 1261, 1288). Frank says, "the story of Jacob and Laban, and of Jacob and Esau, is the beginning of the world and the end of the world" (§§65, 187).

Rachel Elior has noted that Frank ascribed traditional appellatives regarding Jacob—the God of Jacob, Camp of Jacob, Messiah of the God of Jacob—to himself and his world, but saw himself as needing to leave the confines of that identity to walk the path of Esau and gain "the knowledge [*da'at*] of Esau."[19] In Elior's view, Frank saw himself as unifying Jacob and Esau, which correspond not only to Judaism and Christianity but also, in Elior's view, Tiferet and Samael, the Tree of Life and the Serpent.[20] And while Frank does not use these Kabbalistic terms to describe the Jacob/Esau relationship (and, as we will explore in chapter 6, mocks Kabbalistic symbolism in general, and the doctrine of the sefirot in particular),[21] clearly

---

[18] In his translation of *ZSP*, Lenowitz inserts "at the place of" in the first clause, rendering it "Jacob honored his Lord at the [place of] a foreign god."

[19] Elior, "Jacob Frank," 496, citing §§185, 188, 202, 500, 535, 584.

[20] Ibid., 495, citing Zohar I: 146a. In his early work on Frank, which was not included in *The Mixed Multitude*, Maciejko described the myth of Jacob and Esau as "the Frankist equivalent of the Christian doctrine of the Original Sin or of the kabbalistic idea of breaking of the vessels." Maciejko, "Development of the Frankist Movement," 207–10.

[21] See §707 (mocking Tiferet), §521, and §585 (mocking Yesod).

Jacob represents both the model for Jacob Frank, and the failure that he will now correct. Frank often interprets the Jacob narrative in terms of his own career—for example, §208 states, "Jacob came out from Beersheba—that means the same as my coming out was from Dziurdziów." Frank takes on Jacob's mystical status for his own (§§400, 623) and refers to his quest in terms of Jacob's (§981). Jacob's faithful service to Laban is used by Frank to exhort the Brethren to be faithful to him (§§135, 1071). He began with nothing, but became rich at the court of Laban, just as the Frankist company is to rise from poverty to power in Edom—that is, Poland (§73, 134). Jacob, too, is a trickster, as is Frank.

Yet Jacob failed, a failure that represents a lack of will, a fearfulness in the face of the heroic quest. "Jacob saw a ladder . . . and he did not step even on the first rung, because he was afraid," says Frank in §164 (see also §148). When Jacob fearfully said *mah norah hamakom hazeh* (how terrifying is this place), Frank said he should have known that the place of God is without fear (§§74, 765). In §84, Frank recounts how during the wrestling match with the angel, Jacob said he was going to the fields of Edom (which Frank again glosses as Poland). The angel tells Jacob what must be done, and "at that time a great fear fell on Jacob and he fainted." Because Jacob was unable to gather the courage to do the work necessary in Edom, the angel renamed him Israel. "Not Jacob is your name, but Israel. Another Jacob will come and carry out these deeds in Poland." In other words, what is regarded in Jewish tradition as Jacob's successful rite of passage and renaming as the progenitor of Israel is here transvalued as a failure. Jacob is here *constricted* into Israel, a particularistic and limited version of his prior identity.[22] Jacob Frank will toil in the fields of Edom and complete the work that the patriarch Jacob feared.

Unsurprisingly, this failure is understood in the context of material, magical power. Frank reinterprets the purpose of Jacob's sojourn with Laban: He is not there to win Rachel as a wife, or hide from his brother Esau, but rather to pursue the Maiden, embodied in Rachel, in order to obtain the magical objects in Laban's possession, the *terafim* (§§92, 107). Here, Jacob's quest was the right one, but he failed in achieving it, as only Rachel/the Maiden was able to obtain the *terafim* (§67) while Jacob was not. In the context of the material-magical theology discussed in this chapter, the *terafim* of Laban are magical power objects, physical items which, unlike the symbols of conventional religion, have true efficacy (§1005). They are talismanic objects with

---

[22] See Maciejko, "Development of the Frankist Movement," 208–10.

this-worldly magical power, which Frank likens to the image of the pope in Rome and the image of the Maiden in Częstochowa (§67).

Another recurring motif in Frank's reinterpretation of the Jacob/Esau story is that of the "garments of Esau," which recurs in dozens of dicta (e.g., §§122, 222, 404, 505, 535, 628, 859, 869, 1288). These garments are not merely a stratagem to deceive Isaac, as in the biblical story, but, like the *terafim*, magical objects that grant great power, such as the power to have children, triumph in battle, and attain immortal life. Indeed, Frank suggests that it was the attire, not divine wish or Isaac's own efficacy, that enabled the blessing to flow from Isaac to Jacob (§68). Jacob's quest is thus the Frankist one—it is one for the Maiden, power, and magical objects that enable the hero to attain this-worldly goals. As discussed in the next chapter, the receiving of these garments becomes one in a series of redemptive steps toward the transformation of the Frankist sect. Just as Rebecca gave the garments to her son Jacob, so will the Maiden give the magical attire to Frank and the company.

In Frank's reconstruction of the Jacob/Esau myth, Esau/Edom represents Christianity, of course, but a Christianity of a very particular construction: materiality, externality, and power.[23] In §946, Esau is identified with the ark that holds the Torah. The Torah is internal, the ark external. Esau is also worldly power as against spiritual impotence: Frank notes that Esau, a "man of the field," gets things done, but Jacob initially goes simply to pray, which accomplishes nothing (§562). This accords with Frank's overall view, discussed above, of Christianity as possessing the Maiden while not knowing who She is, while Judaism as knowing who She is but not possessing Her. In Maciejko's words, "the Frankists did seem to believe that there is a mystery in Christianity, but they doubted that Christians knew this mystery. . . . [T]he Frankists seemed to believe that they understood Christianity better than the Christians."[24] Indeed, as Maciejko has also discussed, Frank's relationship to Christianity was not one of syncretism or assimilation, but of conquest. Frank states that he will bring about the rule of Jacob over Esau, whose dominion is only temporary (§§69, 155, 166, 188, 658). For this to happen, the messiah must "really enter" Esau, unlike Jacob, who never truly entered Haran (§1261), where Laban resided, because of his fearful encounters with dark foreign forces, all fraught with danger (§1105). Yet where Jacob cowered from his confrontation with power, Jacob Frank promises triumph—not

---

[23] See Levine, "Frankism as Worldly Messianism," 293–94.
[24] Maciejko, *Mixed Multitude*, 42–43.

by joining with Christianity, but by defeating it. Notably, this overthrow of temporal power does not come from divine dispensation or from an otherworldly messiah, nor, by the time of *ZSP*, through the pragmatic territorial program that the Frankist sect had pursued earlier in its history, but from this-worldly "technology": magical attire and powerful objects. God is virtually absent. The triumph of transformed Judaism over Christianity—in yet another audacious rereading of Scriptural text, the "voice of Jacob but the hands of Esau" (§1254)—takes place not through otherworldly intervention but this-worldly, material, heroic, sexual, and magical action on the part of Frank himself.

Finally, Jacob's failure is also gendered, in Frank's simultaneously misogynistic and protofeminist reading. On the one hand, building on the biblical gendering of Jacob as feminine (high voice, smooth skin, cooks at home rather than hunts, favored by the mother, alienated from the father),[25] Frank depicts Jacob as insufficiently masculine. On the other hand, when Jacob hides Rachel at the time of his reunion with Esau, rather than acting, as Frank does, audaciously and out in the open, he forces women and sexuality (the two being linked, as we explore in chapter 5) into hiding and concealment (§§63, 149). As Ada Rapoport-Albert described in depth, Sabbatean protofeminism, which apparently continued in the Frankist circle, regarded the emancipation of women as a sign of the messianic age.[26] The biblical Jacob, in contrast, concealed women/sexuality because, paradoxically, he himself was too "feminine" to allow it to be expressed. As we will see in more detail in chapter 5, Frank's hypermasculinity is necessary for femininity *qua* sexuality to be fully expressed, as it will be in the messianic age. One might say that for Frank, a "real man" encourages rather than represses women.

In Frank's interpretations of Scripture, Jacob may be understood as someone who, in a sense, got the question right, but the answer wrong: He frames the quest properly, but simply cannot achieve it. Jacob pursues the this-worldly Maiden, obtains the this-worldly garments, seeks the magical *terafim*, and even knows of the existence of the Big Brother (§1280). His company of twelve sons prefigures the Frankist company of twelve brothers (§1280). And yet, having come the closest to attaining power, Jacob was particularistic, was afraid, and failed. He is the Jewish hero given the opportunity

---

[25] See Michaelson, "Kabbalah and Queer Theology," 8.
[26] Rapoport-Albert, *Women and the Messianic Heresy of Sabbatai Zevi*, 208–9.

to seize the magical-material power of Edom, yet he is not bold or masculine enough to do so.

Magical Materialism in the Tales

The world of Frank's narrative utterances is one suffused by magic, conniving, danger, and fortune. It is like an epic fantasy film, filled with extraordinary events, demons, witches, evil men who plot harm for one another, and, throughout, a sense that Frank is blessed, or just lucky—a "chosen one" not unlike the heroes of familiar fantastic tales. Frank's tales refer to medicinal herbs (e.g., §280), magical roses (§204), herbs that drive people insane (§389), acidic water (§53), dervishes skilled in the black arts (§593) and alchemy (§1013).[27] God, however, is quite absent, and on the rare occasions when God does appear in the tales, it is often merely as a powerful entity who provides material benefits. For example, in §99, Frank tells the following story:

> A certain witch, who had enormous palaces under water, said to a prince, a tiny dwarf, after she healed him and made him incredibly tall from a potion she gave him, "See how great my powers are, yet we do not compare to the might of God. The power he will give to people will be greater than resurrection of the dead in terms of beauty, height, healing and everything else."

God here is troped as nothing more than an exceptionally good sorcerer, able to provide even more material benefits—beauty, height, healing—than the witch can. Nor is theosophical Kabbalah or conventional mystical wisdom a significant factor in the tales. *ZSP* as a whole contains thirty-eight dicta with direct references to Kabbalah—many of those, as discussed in chapter 6, are negative. Yet it contains 233 dicta focused on magic and folklore, including twenty-one dicta on demons in general, thirteen on Asmodeus in particular,[28] twenty-three on the *ba'alei kaben* (discussed below), sixteen on the

---

[27] See Lenowitz, "Jacob Frank Fabricates a Golem," 421; Maciejko, *Mixed Multitude*, 217–18.
[28] Asmodeus/Ashmedai is, in talmudic literature, essentially the false Solomon and originates as a Babylonian elaboration of the Palestinian Haggadah concerning Solomon's punishment for his sins: having his throne taken over by an angel, whereas Solomon must wander about as a beggar. See Jerusalem Talmud Sanhedrin 2.6; Pesahim 169a; Ta'anit 3.55; Ecclesiastes Rabbah 2.2. Frank greatly elaborates on the myth of Asmodeus stealing King Solomon's ring and the Sabbatean myth of Benayahu stealing it back.

land of Egypt's magical properties (discussed in chapter 7), eleven on the concept of the "golden thread," twenty-two on the Queen of Sheba, and twenty-six on King Solomon, most of which treat him as a magical folk hero.[29]

Consider, for example, §53, in which Frank meets six peasants who have a magical drill that, like a divining rod, can find and extract metal. They ask Frank to dig for treasure in a mountain with them, due to his superhuman strength, and he agrees. After a day's work, however, he decides to poison the peasants rather than share the treasure with them, only to learn that they are plotting to kill him as well. The next day, Frank and the peasants are set upon by a "certain Turk" whom Frank recognizes as a demon, and as Frank flees, the mountain where they had been digging is magically filled in. What does a story such as §53 "mean"? Perhaps a better question is what such a story *does*; that is, what functions it serves for Frank to tell it and for his followers to preserve it. First, as we discussed in chapter 1, it elevates the person of Frank, even as it denigrates him: Frank is amoral, greedy, and not terribly bright, but he is also magical, strong, and extremely fortunate. Second, these magical tales implicitly denigrate establishments and institutions that pretend to authority. Not unlike like contemporary fantasy books and films such as the *Harry Potter* series, there is an entire hidden world in Frank's *imaginaire* that the self-important rabbis, rulers, and rich men know nothing about; they are mere Muggles.[30] But worse than that: They are Muggles who believe that there is an order to this fallen world, that God is protecting the righteous. But as we will explore below, the true God did not create and does not govern this world. In this world, it's everyone for themselves, with a lot of luck involved.

At the same time as Frank's *imaginaire* is filled with magical creatures, he brings to it the same skepticism brought to bear on religion. In §1166, Frank tells a tale of a castle taken over by "the black ones." Everyone believes they are demons, but when a prince spends the night in the castle, he discovers that the "black ones" are simply men who wear black, not demons—and they possess a huge treasure. Just as Frank exposed the con of religion, so he exposes the con of superstition—and the prince gets fifteen million ducats because he keeps the secret. And in §55, Frank is accosted by a Sabbatean woman who "began to scold me because I had brought everything out into the open." Frank does not deny this charge but instead, a bit like a mentalist, states that the woman is in possession of a counterfeit coin and that "you

---

[29] See Scholem, *Messianic Idea*, 263–67.
[30] See Hallett, ed., *Scholarly Studies in Harry Potter*; Whited, ed., *The Ivory Tower and Harry Potter*.

got it this morning from a nobleman who whored with you." Suddenly the woman realizes that Frank is indeed possessed of magical power, and says, "[Y]ou are right and your words are true." Perhaps this tale is satirizing the credulity of the Sabbatean, or perhaps it is praising Frank's magical abilities, or praising his abilities as a con man. Perhaps all of the above.

The combination of Frankist materialism and mythology is perhaps best reflected in the twenty-three dicta in *ZSP* that speak of the *ba'alei kaben*, literally "those with prostheses." As discussed by Scholem and Elior, this topos has a long history in Jewish myth and mysticism.[31] It derives, ultimately, from an elaboration in the Tikkunei Zohar on Mishnah Shabbat 6:8, which states that an amputee may go out on the Sabbath with his prosthesis (*kab*). Tikkunei Zohar 69 tells a tale of two wise men who visit a "Cave of Wonders" (*me'arat pela'im*) inhabited by a *ba'al kab* who divests himself of one body and inhabits another, and who offers a discourse on Ecclesiastes. A second strand of the *ba'alei kaben* myth is a Sabbatean gematria on *kab*, which equals 102, the same gematria as *tzvi*. On that basis, Sabbatean texts create a wholly different myth of the *ba'alei kaben*, this time referring to the 102 secret, faithful disciples of Sabbetai Zevi who were charged by Baruchiah Russo with maintaining only thirty-six of the *mitzvot* and otherwise leading a secret antinomian existence on a "closed street" in Salonica.[32] These *ba'alei kaben* function rather like the Kabbalistic myth of the thirty-six hidden righteous people (*lamed vav tzaddikim*) who sustain the world; they maintain the Sabbatean antinomian messianic freedom in secret. According to Scholem, the Frankists in Lwów adopted this myth upon their conversion, stating that just as 102 faithful disciples of Sabbetai Zevi had to convert to Islam to perform a *tikkun* on the *kelipot* in Islam, so too must 102 sages (*gedolei Torah*) convert with Jacob Frank to Christianity to perform a similar *tikkun* on Christianity.[33] The theme was well known enough to be adopted even by the Sabbateans' arch-nemesis Jacob Emden, who in the *Sefer Hitavkut* uses it to describe the *doenmeh* as a whole, who in his view are deformed wanderers who have no contact with anyone else.[34]

---

[31] Scholem, "Baruchiah," 196–99; Elior, "Jacob Frank," 507–8, 542. See also Lenowitz, "The Struggle over Images," 123.

[32] Scholem, "Baruchiah," 196–97.

[33] Ibid., 197–98.

[34] See Lenowitz, "The Struggle over Images," 123. Lenowitz also suggests that the image of them may be included in the "woodcut at the end of R. Y. Emden's *sefer shimush* incorporating the proverb 'lies have no feet.'" Id.

In *ZSP*, Frank blends these two myths to create a characteristic hybrid of supernaturalism and naturalism. On the one hand, Frank returns to the Tikkunei Zohar's supernaturalist version of the *ba'alei kaben* myth—in Scholem's words, they are "part humans, part demons, part gods"—and embellishes it further, adding details about their three bodies (§§679, 1302) and their power over the *shedim* (§745) and about how they came to lose their legs (§§1196, 1259, 1273).[35] These embellishments appear to be original to Frank. On the other hand, Frank insists that the *ba'alei kaben* are real people, living in the real world. In §806, Frank describes how ten thousand *ba'alei kaben* live in the mountains and how they would have given the Frankist company one million ducats, plus servants and spies.[36] In §§1023 and 1241, Frank indicates that they are located close to Brünn; in §1122, they are said to be living in the mountains of Bohemia. In other words, the *ba'alei kaben* are the quintessential Frankist trope: at once magical and (purportedly) real, possessed of otherworldly powers but this-worldly riches and strength.

As Elior notes, the hybridity of the *ba'alei kaben*—part human, part demonic, part godly—places them in a liminal position, not quite of this world and not quite of the other world.[37] They are also quite like Frank himself: Though hobbled in this world, they possess immense secret power and can help the Frankist Brethren reach the world behind the screen. These intersecting liminalities are related. We have already remarked at some length about Frank's own liminal status in terms of nationality, language, and religion. The *ba'alei kaben* dicta suggest that the liminality is ontological as well. Frank and the *ba'alei kaben* stand between this fallen human realm and the more exalted domain—still part of the material world, but separated from the world we know—that belongs to the Big Brother and his retinue.

Frank's is a hybrid brew of mystification and demystification. He tells his disciples that he is speaking simply and regales them with tales of swindling dupes by taking advantage of their credulity and faith in the unseen. Yet then he tells us fantastic tales himself, all the while insisting that angels and demons are actually real beings with real flaws and concocting a mythology of demythology. Most important, as we will discuss in the next chapter, he

---

[35] Scholem, "Baruchiah," 199.
[36] Frank's elaboration of the *ba'alei kaben* myth to include hoards of buried treasure has some antecedent in Jewish folklore. See Trachtenberg, *Jewish Magic and Superstition*, 224–27. Interestingly, most of Trachtenberg's examples include divining arts, which appear only briefly in *ZSP*.
[37] Elior, "Jacob Frank," 507–8.

creates a wholly new quest for the Brethren: to leave this fallen world, unite with the Big Brother and his parallel brothers and sisters to the Frankist circle, and gain immortal life and power.

Frankist "Gnosticism"

"The whole world is the true God's enemy," Frank says in §555. This quasi-gnosticism can seem quite shocking. As Scholem remarks,

> to anyone familiar with the history of religion it might seem . . . he was dealing here with an antinomian myth from the second century composed by such nihilistic gnostics as Carpocrates and his followers than that all this was actually taught and believed by Polish Jews living on the eve of the French Revolution.[38]

Yet Frank's "gnosticism" is actually of its time and place: Both the Sabbatean theologian Abraham Miguel Cardoso (1630–1706), who held that the true God did not create the world,[39] and contemporary Western esoteric societies drew similar distinctions between the Creator of the universe and the God of the Bible, though rarely is that God demoted to the rank of mortal but powerful sorcerer. As with many other aspects of Frankist doctrine, however, Frank transforms and combines existing themes with his own innovation.

In *ZSP*, the main reason for Frank's gnosticism is clear: theodicy. For Frank, injustice, the fallenness of the world, and human mortality are incompatible with the traditional view of God as creator. In §578, Frank says,

> No man has yet had a soul in this world, even the First or Second [i.e., Sabbetai Zevi or Baruchiah Russo]. None of the patriarchs, or the pillars of the world, have had a soul. Because a soul can only come from God himself or from one other place. At that point will the world be permanent and the one who has a soul will likewise be eternally permanent and will be able

---

[38] Scholem, *Messianic Idea*, 132. As David Biale describes, Scholem saw the gnostic myth as residing at the core of Jewish mysticism for centuries, with antinomian and heretical impulses barely contained, until they finally exploded in the Sabbatean heresy. Biale, *Gershom Scholem*, 71–72.

[39] On the gnosticism of Cardoso, see Cardoso, *Selected Writings*, 228–42; Scholem, *Messianic Idea*, 129; Elior, "Jacob Frank," 492; Maciejko, "Development," 205; Carlebach, *Pursuit of Heresy*, 98; Liebes, "On a Jewish-Christian Sect," 221–25; Maciejko, "Christian Elements," 21–25; Goldish, "Sabbatai Zevi," 515–17.

to see the world from one end to the other, increasingly more and higher, as I have said above. For there were three things missing at Adam's creation, and wherever there is a deficiency, there is no permanency. And as it is written: *asher bara Elohim la'asot* [literally, God created so he could make], which means, so that he could make a man without deficiency. We see this clearly: when a child asks his father for bread, does the latter give him a stone instead? We also see that there are people who are honest, God-fearing, who ask God for bread and still don't receive it. Where is the mercy of the father for his own children? Also, is it proper for a father to kill his own children? From this it follows that the true God has had no part in the current creation. That is why all vessels have been broken until now, because the one who created them broke them himself so they would be re-created as purer and more beautiful each time.

God cannot possibly be responsible for the world as it appears; there is too much evil and death for that to be true. Thus the true God has no part in the present creation, and the vessels have all been broken (one of the very few uses of this image in *ZSP*). §586 has an even more succinct summation of the "gnostic" theology based on theodicy:

How could the true God have created this world, where you have to die, separate, and where so many things are deficient? This would go against his dignity. It follows that, undoubtedly, the one who created this world was not the true God who is going to fix everything to bring about complete wholeness.

And similarly in §205:

God himself has not yet created anything, and everything to this date has been rotten, and the whole world has been deficient; there is nothing permanent. For it is only when they become worthy of being created by God himself that the worthy ones will receive from him a new soul. In an instant, man will become as eternal as God himself.

As we have observed, there is a gnostic character to the Sabbatean theology of Abraham Miguel Cardoso, with which Frank was likely familiar, though the endpoint is quite different. Cardoso argued that Jews and Christians alike had confused the God of the Bible with the Creator, who he described in

Maimonidean terms.[40] In Cardoso, as Scholem states, "here we have a typically gnostic scheme, only inverted: the good God is no longer the *deus absconditus*, who has now become the deity of the philosophers for whom there is no room in religion proper, but rather the God of Israel who created the world and presented it with His Torah."[41] Similarly, Nehemiah Hayon, suspected of Sabbateanism in 1713, drew a distinction between the *Ein Sof* and the God of Israel and suggested that the First Cause does not descend into the world.[42] These "gnostic" ideas were at the center of the investigation into Hayon's suspected Sabbateanism by Moshe Hagiz in his crusades against the Sabbateans.[43]

Though originating from the same Sabbatean roots as Cardoso and Hayon, Frank's presentation is closer to gnostic Christian heresies that denied the divine origin of the Hebrew Bible. In *ZSP*, the Torah, with its restrictions and ineffectual rules, is not a gift from God but "from the side of death," obstructing the individual from experiencing personal transformation and thus fulfilling God's intention that human beings become immortal. Frank in §452 recounts a dream in which he is asked whether he acknowledges God as the Creator. Frank says no, he only thanks God for Shavuot, the holiday of receiving the Torah. This suggests that the God of the Torah is not the God of Creation—again, one of the heretical Christian Gnostics' central claims, but the opposite of Cardoso's. For Frank, the remedy for this state of affairs is, as the alchemists had it, to refine the soul from its current, base, mortal form into a refined, immortal or at least one. Frank continues in §578, "That is why it cannot be that a soul is in such a dense and vile body as the present on. I wanted to lead you to a certain place to bathe you, to first cleanse you so you would have the strength to receive the soul." We will discuss this mission in the next chapter.

Notwithstanding all the foregoing, Frank does refer to "God" many times, often in traditional ways. He advises the Brethren to follow God and be faithful to God and says that God has favored him, perhaps even chosen him. Yet God is not an active agent in *ZSP*; though God seems to have a plan for human history, God does very little. Even when Frank speaks of receiving messages and prophecies early on in *ZSP*, he does not state who sent them. The language in those early passages is not "And the Lord said to Moses" but

---

[40] Scholem, *Messianic Idea*, 106–7; Maciejko, *Mixed Multitude*, 51, 76.
[41] Scholem, *Messianic Idea*, 106.
[42] Feiner, *Origins of Jewish Secularization*, 67.
[43] Carlebach, *Pursuit of Heresy*, 75–194.

"I received a message." Indeed, Frank says in §866, "I have not yet revealed a single word to you that pertains to God himself. Because specific things that pertain to God himself cannot be written even in black ink, for fear of great danger." Notice once again the emphasis on magic; it is not that God is ineffable or the name unpronounceable, but that there is a danger in writing about the Divine. Whatever the reason, it is remarkable that in a text with so much theology, Frank says he has never spoken of "God himself."

The tale recorded in §1096 explores these quasi-gnostic themes, with two "great and learned men debating whether there was a God who kept watch over this world." Since they were masters of Kabbalah, "they summoned the angels so they could give them the proper answer to this question." But even the angels don't know the answer, and they tell the Kabbalists that they must go on a quest to find out—rather like the Frankist company itself. So the two men go on a long journey, finally arriving at a special mountain made of "rocks as pure as glass and marble." There,

> it was revealed to them in a dream that no man should push, seek, or even think about finding God himself. And the more he tries, the more confused and lost he will become. A man can only try to find and seek the one who is before God. Therefore, when I tell you that I will show you God, I mean the one who is before God.

In other words, one cannot find God—only the Big Brother, the "one who is before God," as we discuss in the next chapter. And neither the Kabbalah nor an angel summoned by means of Kabbalistic magic has the answer as to whether God is watching over the world or not.

Who is governing the world, if not God? Ruling this world are three "gods," discussed by Frank in §§98, 163, 204, 303, 337, 350, 361, 721, and 891.[44] Despite being gods, Frank says in §2157 that "they are in human bodies and here in this world." Whatever these entities are, they are malevolent. They distract and tempt human beings so that we do not seek immortality (§721). They are unaware of the Big Brother (§346). They obstruct human efforts to gain power (§350), are responsible for the confusion at the Tower of Babel (§891), and Jacob went down to Egypt to escape them (§891). Unsurprisingly, they actively oppose the Frankist mission. In §337, Frank says that they feared that they would lose their power when the company

---

[44] See Scholem, *Messianic Idea*, 129.

entered baptism, and "they tried with their tricks to upset that thing." Frank notes in §98 that the Egyptians know one of the Three and that they derive their magical power and ability; we will return to this subject in chapter 7, as it is a core feature of Western esotericism as well.

While this quasi-Gnosticism is indeed surprising, in fact there is Kabbalistic precedent not only for Gnosticism generally but also for the Three specifically. In particular, Frank may be making use of an existing Kabbalistic tradition of the three (or four) *memunim*, angels appointed to rule over the world, discussed in Zohar 3:236b–237a, and alluded to in a story in the Midrash HaNe'elam, contained in Zohar 2:6b–7a.[45] In that story, R. Yose sees a bird flying three times upward and once downward, and R. Elazar explains that this refers to the three *memunim* who rule the world, plus a fourth one: "Three nation-rules stand over the earth, and they will impose decrees upon Israel on the part of the Romans." Ronit Meroz interprets this text as essentially apocalyptic, predicting three rulers of the world, followed by Israel's rule of the world. These traditions themselves build on the earlier mystical conception of the seventy *memunim* (guardians) of the world with the notion in the book of Daniel that four empires would have sway over Israel: the Babylonians, the Medes, the Persians, and the Greeks, each of which would rise and fall like the angels on Jacob's ladder.[46] Note that by the time of the Zohar, the original mythology had been transformed into three nations working on behalf of the Romans; Meroz suggests this may be a reference to the Crusades, although it may also refer to European Christian powers. There is insufficient direct evidence to link *ZSP*'s three who rule the world to the Zohar's three who rule the world. Yet the two concepts are obviously similar, although Frank extends the ruling of the world beyond the political into the cosmological. The Zohar, after all, does not propose that these three truly rule over the entire physical world; they are empires ruling over the political one. Yet in Frank, they function like gnostic demiurges, ruling over the world, and malevolently.

The defining feature of this world, ruled over by the Three, is death. And the heroic quest that Frank describes, and to which we will turn next, is aimed at overthrowing it. It is less a messianic quest than an esoteric, alchemical one. While not promising collective transformation, let alone the

---

[45] I am grateful to Ronit Meroz for bringing these texts to my attention. I refer here to her presentation "The Bird and the Children," at the Academy of Jewish Studies in December 2011.
[46] Daniel 2:31–45, 7:1–28. See Leviticus Rabbah 29.2; Kugel, *Traditions of the Bible*, 374.

redemption of Israel, the Frankist heroes will be personally transformed into immortal beings with temporal power and riches. They will open the "gate which has been closed since the beginning of the world" (§206)—namely, the condition of mortality. In this world, created not by God but by malevolent forces, magical beings vie for power and control, and chaos reigns. In the other world, there is eternal life. But Frank's "world to come" is not reached after death; it is reached in order to defeat death entirely.

4

"To make a man in wholeness, stable and possessing eternal life"

The Occult Quest for Immortality

The Goal: Staged Transformation into Superhuman Beings

Just as Frank's critique of religion is that it is not materially effective (chapter 2) and just as Frank's mythic-theological replacement for religion is a corporealization of religious themes (chapter 3), so too is the Frankist quest, both in terms of individual transformation and collective apocalyptic messianism, rendered in explicitly material terms that, unlike earlier iterations of Frankist thought, are redolent of Western esotericism. It has almost nothing to do with the typical Jewish messianic narrative involving redemption and restoration of Israel. Rather, its goal is the same as that of much of eighteenth-century Illuminism and early nineteenth-century theosophy: wealth, health, spiritual perfection, and eternal life.[1] In Frank's own words, the project is "to make a man in wholeness, stable and possessing eternal life" (§238).

This is a quest of deeds, not words; to be pursued, not merely spoken of; it is action to be taken. As noted earlier, Frank's favorite biblical quotation, in terms of sheer numbers of citations, is Isaiah 63:3: "I have tread the winepress alone, and of the nations there was no man with Me; I trod them in My anger, and trampled them in My fury, and their lifeblood is dashed against My garments, and I have stained all My raiment" (§§69, 186, 275, 615, 1061, 1066A, 1151, 1191). For Frank, both the triumphalist and the activist aspects of the verse are important: to make wine, one must tread, not merely speak

---

[1] Versluis, *Magic and Mysticism*, 15–16, 85–87 (discussing the *Chymical Wedding of Christian Rosencreutz*); Faivre, *Access to Western Esotericism*, 163–75; Snoek, "On the Creation of Masonic Degrees." Interestingly, Frank's greatest Jewish opponent, Rabbi Jacob Emden, was also interested in alchemy. See Kahana, "An Esoteric Path to Modernity"; Scholem, *Alchemy and Kabbalah*. See discussion *infra*, chapter 7.

or pray. Similarly, as Frank interprets Genesis in §1191, the phrase *asher bara elohim la'asot* means "God created for doing." Again, actions rather than words; worldly work rather than spiritual work.

But what actions, exactly? The answer varies as Frankism evolves through its various permutations. From 1757 to 1759, the "actions" are conquering, or being given, lands and gaining an autonomous region within Poland.[2] In other Frankist texts such as the "Red Letters," they refer to immanent eschatological events and wars. But in *Words of the Lord*, with the failure of these prophecies apparent, the "actions" have to do with personal transformation, not unlike contemporaneous Hasidim transformed historical messianism into personal experience, as discussed in chapter 8. Of course, Frank's actions are not spiritual in nature, which leads to the Frankist quest being a peculiar hybrid of interiorization and corporeality. On the one hand, the Frankist quest in *Words of the Lord* is a personal one that remaps messianism from the historical realm to the personal one. The "world to come" is experienced not because of historical transformation but because of personal transformation and quasi-mystical experience. On the other hand, the Frankist quest remains physical and material; the Brethren are seeking immortality, union with the Big Brother and his retinue, and worldly power. All of this, Frank says, is real, albeit occulted. Even within different sections of *ZSP*, the Frankist myths shift in emphasis, though with the same basic structure of a heroic quest to gain worldly power. The recurring theme in the quest and prophetic passages is a new religious knowledge (*Das*) leading to worldly power, strength and/or immortality. But that process is a convoluted one with many phases and intermediaries. At times, the quest is mostly about trying to liberate the Maiden, discussed in the next chapter. Other times, the primary emphasis is on the failure of the initial Frankist project and on striving to retrieve some of what would have happened had the Brethren been faithful. Still other times, Frank focuses on the Big Brother and the sect's transformation into new people with superpowers. Yet others, it is about gaining magical attire that will cause fear in animals, and then moving on to further degrees. These different areas of emphasis are, in general, found in different sections of *ZSP*, suggesting that, given the chronological nature of the text, that Frank simply told different stories at different periods in 1784, and again in 1789–1790.

---

[2] See Maciejko, *Mixed Multitude*, 160.

That being said, based on a close review of the quest dicta of *ZSP*, I believe we can synthesize an overall staged model of the Frankist quest, which is roughly as follows. First, the inner Frankist circle of Brothers and Sisters is constituted and designated as such. Second, the Brethren will enter baptism and "come to Edom." These first two steps have already been completed. Third, the sect will unite (and thus transcend) Jacob and Esau, Judaism and Christianity, with the secret, new religion/gnosis called *Das*. This will bring about the first step of transformation, which entails receiving new clothing (sometimes linked with the clothing of Esau) that will give them magical powers, including power over animals (§§185, 222, 245, 518, 535, 859, 900, 1050, 1275). Fourth, they will encounter the Maiden, who like the Shechinah is the gateway to the "other world." Fifth, with the assistance of the Maiden and other powerful beings, they will meet the Big Brother and the sect's other counterparts in the other world. And finally, in gratitude (or, sometimes, equal exchange) the Big Brother will transform them into beings like he is: gigantic, powerful, and immortal. We will assess each of these steps in order.

The first stage is the designation of the inner circle of twenty-four followers as Brothers and Sisters.[3] At the end of §1118, Frank indicates why the faith of the Brethren is so important: as he says in numerous other dicta (including §§6, 358, 372, 469, 703, 847, 1047, and 1086), there is a burden that must be lifted, that requires everyone to work together.[4] Frank tells the Maiden, "I will lift the burden," but she answers, "That cannot be." According to *ZSP*, Frank designated the Brethren in this way for several reasons. First, they exist for mutual aid and protection and so that the close circle of disciples would keep watch on one another (§§168, 1140, 1214). But the designation is also described as a test (§234); at another moment, as a necessary criterion for founding a new religion (§1244). The creation of the Brethren ensures a magical protection as well and gives the group strength that, Frank says, will exceed that of nations (§§120, 565, 1101). Second, the twelve Brothers parallel the brothers of the Big Brother, and, clearly, the disciples of Jesus (§§261, 305, 446, 768). In a rare positive use of Kabbalistic symbolism, Frank refers to the *sefirot*, sometimes also referred to as brothers and sisters (§§7, 236, 305) and even to the Zoharic circle of R. Simeon bar Yochai (§701). Additionally, one of Frank's most straightforward statements regarding Jesus comes in this context, where in §1290, he states that the Brothers were to be given the names

---

[3] See Rapoport-Albert, *Women and the Messianic Heresy*, 158–63.
[4] See Lenowitz, "*Me'ayin yavo 'ezri?*," 284.

of the apostles, Frank was to be Jesus, and the world would thus see that Jesus was not the messiah and that Frank would "smash everything." These mythic parallels between the earthly Brethren and the brothers of the Big Brother, the *sefirot*, and the apostles of Jesus, reflect the Frankist syncretic impulse. Frank's company is the culmination of the sefirotic drama, the realization and supercession of the circle of Jesus, and the parallel of an otherworldly family of which these other myths are merely vague approximations.

Finally, there is an undeniable sexual theme to the appellation of Brothers and Sisters, as Frank alludes to the incestuous connotation of the terms multiple times. In §375, Frank states that, when he was interrogated in Warsaw, "I was asked during an interrogation in Warsaw: 'If you call them sisters, how can you be intimate with them?' Because I did not conceal anything from them, I did this purposely in the open, in front of the whole world, so that when I come to the place where I need to be, it will be known that you are Brothers and Sisters." (I discuss this text in relationship to charges of incest levied against the Frankist community in chapter 5.) Further, Frank notes that Abraham and Sarah called one another brother and sister (§392) when they visit the land of Egypt, one of Frank's primary examples of a biblical hero contravening sexual prohibitions for a higher purpose. And Frank states that Brothers are not to be judged like other people, making specific reference to the *prima nocte* right of the king to have sexual relations with new brides. Just as a (nonconsensual) sexual act forbidden to ordinary people is permitted to royalty, so too the Brothers and Sisters are to be above sexual convention and prohibition. Curiously, Frank does not refer to Kabbalistic conceptions of incest as the example par excellence of something forbidden to most people to but permitted to royalty.

Alas, Frank laments many times, the grand plan for the Brethren did not come to pass. In §428, he says, "If you had followed my advice in this state [i.e., Christianity] and cherished this state, went to church in the morning and in the evening, loved one another, respected one another, rejected all teachings and foundational laws, you would have known that even their leader would have cherished you and the lords would have even bestowed riches and gifts upon you." But since this did not take place, Frank states that he has not yet truly designated the Brethren as such (§§582, 895), that he has revoked the designation due to their betrayal (§631), or that the betrayal itself undid the special relationship (§§735, 779). Due to their betrayal, Frank says, he must try to lift the burden alone, even though he knows that is impossible (§§1061, 1067A). The Brethren were meant to be coequals, Brothers and Sisters with

Frank himself. But because they failed, this status, which affords this-worldly protection and otherworldly significance, has been revoked (or unearned). The apotheosis of the Brethren now may be impossible; only picking up the pieces remains.

The second stage of the Frankist quest is the baptism that the sect underwent back in 1759, and its entry into Edom—both Christianity and Poland specifically and, more generally, the domain of worldly power.[5] This is the unification of Jacob and Esau, which we discussed in the previous chapter: the bringing together of Jewish knowledge with Christian power. Frank states that Christians are not true servants of the Maiden—she is alone "with nobody to serve her"—even though they are in physical possession of one of her incarnations, the portrait in Częstochowa. The sect's baptism and entry into Edom are but a transitional phase, a necessary prerequisite to attaining power—as stated above, no longer overthrowing Christianity or even gaining some autonomy from it, but attaining *Das* and personal immortality. In *ZSP*, baptism is only the gateway to *Das*.

What is *Das*? Scholars have debated whether this term refers to knowledge (*da'at*—*daas* in Ashkenazi pronunciation), or religion (*dat*—*das* in Ashkenazi pronunciation), or the quasi-*sefirah* of *Da'at*, or even to *das*, the German word for "this."[6] My view is that Frank intended the term to be polysemous, and that it is a deliberate conflation of gnosis, the new religion into which Frank is to bring the Brethren, and the occulted *sefirah* of *da'at*. Above all, *das* means "gnosis," specifically the gnosis of Western esotericism: the secret knowledge that will enable the Brethren to proceed on their journey toward immortality. In §110, Frank states, "*Das* is that hidden *Das* and the explication of the word *Das* means knowledge, that is, 'Know before whom you stand.'" In §1303, Frank says that just as *da'at* is outside the *sefirot*, so too *Das* is outside of traditional religion.[7] *Das* is also a secret that can only be revealed esoterically, if at all: "I must enter *Das*, which is called the burden of silence," Frank says in §894; recall from chapter 1 that this term (*ma'asah dumah*) had been central to Sabbatean communities;[8] now it refers to the secrecy of esoteric wisdom. *Das* is not mere knowledge but gnosis that is a means to the end: the this-worldly empowerment of Frank and his followers.

---

[5] Maciejko, *Mixed Multitude*, 162.
[6] See Elior, "Jacob Frank," 500; Lenowitz, *The Jewish Messiahs*, 190. Hillel Levine called *Das* Frank's "syncretic messianism." Levine, "Frankism as Worldly Messianism," 293.
[7] See Elior, "Jacob Frank," 516.
[8] See Sisman, *Burden of Silence*, 148–50.

Accordingly, once attaining *Das*, the Brethren are to be transformed. First, they are to be given supernatural powers and supernatural clothing that bestow (or perhaps reflect) immortality (§§120, 185, 245, 1014, 1050, 1058, 2165). Frank here draws on the rabbinic midrash that the animal skins that Rebecca puts on Jacob's smooth arms—to fool Isaac into thinking they are Esau's hairy ones[9]—were, in fact, entire garments,[10] and have a complex lineage, which he describes in §1014:

> Nothing needs to be said, except the burden of silence, that is, be silent and proceed from one level to the next, until you become worthy of donning respectable robes [*szat powabnych*]. Nimrod wore that attire [*strój*] and was therefore a powerful hunter before God. But he missed once, and that is why it was taken away from him. Jacob sought them, but he received them from the mother, rather than the father; he had to receive a blessing from Isaac. He was afraid and fretted after putting them on, saying: "How will my father feel me," etc., etc. These were not the true robes [*szaty*] yet, because if they were, then Jacob and Esau, after putting them on, would live forever, just as we hope to do.

Frank here makes use of an additional midrashic tradition that the biblical Nimrod, great-grandson of Noah and, in rabbinic legend, responsible for the building of the Tower of Babel,[11] was in possession of the original coats of skin that God made for Adam and Eve.[12] These garments were, in turn, stolen by Esau,[13] and then taken from Esau by Rebecca, who gave them to Jacob. Yet Frank puts his own twist on the midrashic stories, adding that these robes were actually not the true robes, because Nimrod and Jacob each failed in their missions, and the true robes confer immortality. A similar deferral of the "real robes" occurs within the Frankist community. The Brethren have already donned the "robes from the nations"—specifically, the *żupan*, the traditional robe worn by Polish nobility which became the Frankists' attire of choice after their conversion.[14] But now these robes, representing Christianity/Edom, will be exchanged for magical robes, symbolic of *Das*/

---

[9] Genesis 27:1–19.
[10] See Genesis Rabbah 75.11 and Zohar 1.142b.
[11] BT Chullin 89a, BT Pesahim 94b, BT Eruvin 53a, and BT Avodah Zarah 53b.
[12] Pirkei de Rabbi Eliezer xxiv; Sefer ha-Yashar, 9a; Bereshit Rabbah 45:12.
[13] BT Bava Batra 16b; Bereshit Rabbah 65:12.
[14] Maciejko, "Sabbatean Charlatans," 367. Frank mentions the *żupan* in a dream in §793 with no apparent connection to the magical attire.

Western esotericism. (Notably, freemasons and other esoteric organizations wore special robes for their rituals.[15]) The Brethren will wear theirs as they live forever, as powerful superhumans. The initial robes of Esau, i.e., the robes of the nations, provide temporal power, which was the goal of the preconversion Frankist quest. But they are but a foreshadowing of these new robes, which provide eternal life, the goal of the revised Frankist quest in ZSP. As §1050 states that "the robes that the Brethren put on from the nations will be the robes from the Brethren of the Big Brother," Frank's own attire—he wore "Turkish" garb and, in the few engravings of him, is pictured thus attired—is similarly provisional. He says in §245 that were he to wear the "robe of Esau," he would confirm an esoteric Polish prophecy "that a Jew will be born in Poland, and convert to Christianity . . . and that soon the Day of Judgment will be fulfilled in Poland." However, "when we shall be worthy to come to the secret *Das*, we will don a robe that will attract everyone's attention." So, the Brethren have taken on the robes of Esau, namely the dress of the gentiles, but these are not the final robes; Frank is wearing Turkish robes, but they are not the final robes either; and even the Biblical robes of Esau, passed down from Adam and Eve, were not the final robes, because the final robes confer immortality. For now, the final robes, Esau's true robes, remain hidden. In §120, Frank remarks, "be whole, be worthy of knowing and seeing Esau's robe. His robe is hidden in this world, not anywhere else."

Having donned their new, magical attire, the next step is for the Brethren to meet the Maiden, who will bring them to the Big Brother. I discuss the character of the Maiden (*Panna*) in depth in the next chapter; in the quest narrative, She serves as a kind of gateway to the other world, not unlike how the Shechinah is the gateway to the *sefirot* and the Virgin Mary is the gateway to God. Here, as in the Christological, Kabbalistic, and esotericist formulations, the Maiden is an intermediary before the Big Brother, who in turn is a kind of intermediary before the *deus absconditus*, much as Christ is an intermediary before God the Father.

The quest culminates in the meeting with the Big Brother and his retinue. The figure of the Big Brother combines traits of multiple mythical figures, mostly Jesus, but like the Maiden, is ultimately Frank's original, syncretic creation. The Big Brother is the "one before God" who lives in the pure, undefiled world where God may be found and known and who exercises many powers people wrongly ascribe to God (not unlike El Shaddai, whom we

---

[15] See Faivre, *Access to Western Esotericism*, 182–83.

discussed above). In §1151, Frank states, "There is one place where no living man has ever been, from the beginning of time, and never will be. And since I, a simpleton, accepted you as brothers and sisters, I would have guided you and you would have followed me to the place where God himself resides," in other words, the hidden world. The Big Brother would have gained great strength had the Frankist enterprise succeeded, just as the Brethren would have gained strength from him. He is not God—but he is *a* god. He is half a mile tall and "a fearful god" who was to give the land of Poland to Frank (§384). In §338, Frank refers to "the one who stands before God" with "the royal seal of God in his hands" as a kind of demigod and the "king of kings over kings." The Big Brother is a demiurgical stand-in for God, fulfilling many of God's providential functions and interceding on behalf of those who merit grace.

The Big Brother acts as a kind of salvific, Jesus-like figure who saves some people from the fallen world ruled by the Three, as described in the last chapter. Frank says in §418, "these three that lead the world proceed according to their arrangement. But the one who is the lord of death intends to force the whole world out of their hands. Without their knowledge, this Big Brother has providence over this world; he saves as many as is needed to keep the world going." And Frank says in §600, "Although this thing is in this world, it is hidden and concealed even from these three, for great darkness is the border between this and the other world. They are separated by a dark cloud, and one kingdom cannot enter the other." At the same time, the Big Brother is in as much distress as Frank is. Frank states, "I need him and he me. If we, having become united, would perform a certain thing . . . God would have consented to it Himself" (§418). In §1296, Frank states the Big Brother is "divine, but has greater troubles than I do. He is very upset over you, and his brothers all the more so." In §1302 he states that the Big Brother is in difficulty, just as Frank is. "Despite the fact that he is in the divine, he still does not know in what way or by what means and power he can step over the border so that he may be here among us; because that partition is from the beginning," Frank says in §410.

The relationship between the Big Brother and Jesus is complex. In §964, the Big Brother seems clearly to be Jesus: a "king of kings" who has his own set of disciples. And in §1290, Frank states that the twelve brothers were meant to be a new version of the twelve apostles. Like Jesus, the Big Brother is both human and divine. Like Jesus, he is accessible to people in this world (or at least to Frank) and bestows favor on them—unlike "God" who is remote.

And on a symbolic level, if the biblical Jacob's big brother was Esau, then it stands to reason that Jacob Frank's Big Brother is the true Esau, or Jesus. Yet as Maciejko has noted, when it comes to Jesus himself, Frank is generally disparaging (see §§729, 504, 614).[16] Moreover, to whatever extent the Maiden is to be identified with the Virgin Mary, or the portrait of her, as I discuss in the next chapter, the Big Brother is clearly not the Maiden's son. And while Jesus had twelve disciples, the Big Brother is the leader of a group of twelve quasi-immortal transfigured humans who now live forever but await their ultimate redemption, which was to be obtained together with the Brethren. This obviously is a rather different myth. Frank clearly patterned some of the Big Brother's attributes after Jesus and the Christian relationship to Jesus, but he inserted this Christlike figure into a mythological world of his own. As Maciejko has observed, this is Christian messianism reframed, even as Christ himself is rejected.

The Big Brother and his retinue are set in roughly parallel structure to Frank and his, including, it seems, the intermingling of mystical and sexual union. "I have Brothers and Sisters, as he does," says Frank in §410. Yet while Frank has twelve Brethren in total, the Big Brother has twelve brothers, seven maidens, and seven wives (§338). He gives each of these seven maidens a ring with his seal, which is itself the seal of God. These seven maidens can then cross the boundary into our world; indeed, says Frank in §338, they "have a great desire to unite with people in this world." Most intriguingly, the Queen of Sheba is identified as one of the seven maidens, and when she heard of King Solomon, she apparently fell in love with him, and obtained permission from the Big Brother to cross into our world to "unite" with him, even giving her ring to King Solomon, who wielded it for magical power. Often, in Kabbalistic contexts, the term "uniting" (*yichud*) has a sexual and/or erotic-theurgical meaning, and clearly that is present here. Citing 2 Chronicles 9:12, Frank says that King Solomon satisfied all of the Queen of Sheba's desires, and that is what is meant by "unite." Later in the passage, however, Frank states, "I cannot unite with this king [Solomon] now," because Solomon gave up the ring and died. And Frank says, he can "unite" with the Big Brother with the help of Brothers and Sisters.[17] It seems unlikely that Frank's "uniting" with King Solomon or the Big Brother is meant in sexual terms, given Frank's voracious heterosexuality, as discussed in the next chapter. Perhaps it means

---

[16] See Maciejko, "Jacob Frank and Jesus Christ."
[17] On "help" potentially referring to sexual coercion, see Elior, "Jacob Frank," 514–36.

something akin to the Lurianic "unitings" (*yichudim*) wherein the mystic would enter a trance or meditative state to unite (psychologically/spiritually, not sexually) with a long-dead figure. Perhaps Frank's relationship with the Big Brother is similarly nonphysical, perhaps occurring within a state of trance.[18] Or perhaps Frank's *yichud* with the Big Brother takes place when he unites physically with the 'Sisters' and enables a boundary crossing similar to the Queen of Sheba's. On the other hand, Frank is so insistent on the materiality of the Big Brother and the world behind the screen, and so explicit about defining what is meant by "union" in §338 that one cannot dismiss the homoerotic valence of these phrases, even if only psychologized or displaced. At the very least, Frank is playing on the multiple layers of the term "unite" with their shifting connotations of mystical and erotic union, like centuries of mystics before and after him.

The Big Brother, together with his brothers, wives, and maidens, including the Queen of Sheba, lives in a hidden world that is real, physical, and much larger than our own. Our world, according to *ZSP*, is but one one-thousandth of the total universe (§265). In §265, Frank says,

> There are hidden countries of which the whole world has no knowledge. And the world that we are in is one thousandth part of these hidden countries. These countries have not been cursed. Therefore, Queen Sheba who was at Solomon's, came to see him but he could not come to her because one kingdom cannot enter another, and her country is hidden from this world. To this day she lives alone. Her land is golden, it is neither ploughed nor sown. The land alone gives rise to all that is good, that is why their wisdom and knowledge is great, for the land and air there are pure for the good of the country, which is not under a curse, unlike this world, which is cursed. That is why we have no knowledge among us, so that you would not understand that it is deficient, that the earth is cursed now. Indeed, because it is necessary that light be revealed from darkness, and God will be revealed in this world.

Frank insists that this other world is a physical one: in §1299, he says that while our world takes four to five years to travel, including the other world brings the total to five hundred years' travel time (see also §265). The world

---

[18] As noted earlier, the cultivation of trance states was frequent in the Sabbatean movement and other spiritual movements at the time. See Garb, *Shamanic Trance*, 15; Goldish, *Sabbatean Prophets*, 130–61.

of the Big Brother and Queen Sheba is, in contrast to our own, good and uncursed, yet its blessings are material in nature. As Frank says in §410:

> I tell you that all good is kept with the Big Brother, who I told you about earlier. From the initial creation, all good has been residing in his bounds, because there the earth is not cursed and it is in between worlds which remain cursed, it is a fence and a shield against them. Everything that a man's heart desires to try is there: fat fowl, white bread, the earth generates everything of its own in the blink of an eye. It is always his desire to see and unite with those who live in this world. He knows about me, and that I have arisen in this world, and knows that I am alone in my efforts to pursue something good. He also knows that I have brothers and sisters like him. However, despite that he is godly, he still does not know in what manner and with what power to cross the boundary, so he could be here among us, because this fence has been here since the beginning.

On just the other side of a nearly impassable cosmic partition: fat fowl and white bread. Not completely impassable: the Queen of Sheba crossed over, one of her lords crossed over, and, we learn in §418, the Big Brother has some "oversight in this world as well."

Just as the hidden world is defined by its material opulence, so too will be Frank's rewards in this world. In §418, Frank states that the Big Brother will give him (Frank) a large estate in Poland, a proper house, and access to good food. And in §432, Frank says the Maiden will grant eternal life, rejuvenation to the age of twenty years, and a face as bright as the sun. Similarly, in §655, Frank describes the interior decorating of the rooms he will build "when my aid comes," right down to the red damask and silver braids.

To be sure, materialism is not the same as realism. In §308, Frank says that one member of the Brethren would grow to thirty cubits tall and another would receive ten billion ducats, and in §317, Frank says that underneath Częstochowa there are secret caves where there are fifty or sixty carriages decorated in precious stones. But even these are worldly rewards, almost comically (or perhaps tragically) so. On the one hand, the transfiguration Frank promises is fantastic; but on the other, it is entirely material. And in §1042, Frank states that he "wanted to send you to that place where the body can be transformed and you can fly 1,000 miles; yet your bodies would have not been transformed, you only would have been given power in your limbs, so you would have height and power." Then again, in §1274, Frank says that "we are the water, and they are the fire, and from great fervor, unity would be achieved. For they desire human bodies, and we need them." If the other Brothers and Sisters are made of fire and lack human bodies, how does the Big Brother live in a six-story palace with walls of gold (§309) and eat meat and bread (§410)? It is possible that this contradiction must remain unresolved.

As we have noted, this privatized redemption replaces the more public, communal messianism that, by 1784, had clearly failed. Yet even this quest is often described in the subjunctive, as something that would have happened if only the Brethren had been faithful. For example, in §309, Frank relates that his close disciples Jędrzej Dębowski (formerly Yerucham ben Lippman of Czarnokozienice) and Mateusz Matuszewski (formerly Chaim) were going to be given a secret word and secret pass (another possible Illuminist influence) and sent to a secret place. There, they would experience the personal transformation that Frank promises to the followers in general: They would grow to thirty cubits high, would be made young again, and would be exceedingly strong and rich. Both would then obtain for Frank all the riches he desired. But this prophecy is tinged with failure, as Frank indicates that it now can no longer come to pass. Similarly, §1118 contains the most sustained subjunctive prophecy in *ZSP* and encapsulates the materialist nature of the Frankist promise. In it, Frank gives Dębowski a long list of what would have happened had he been faithful: Frank would have taken him to prison with him and tested him three or four times, Dębowski would have had the power of invisibility, the Maiden would have giving him a new name, he would have spoken with her directly, they would have learned of a hidden treasure of six hundred million ducats in the mountain of Częstochowa and another one in Olsztyn, he would have been sent to a cave under Częstochowa where six hundred tailors were sewing precious gold garments for Frank, Frank would have ordered five coaches of silver and gold (with matching harnesses), they would have ridden off with the Maiden and the gold but the Maiden would be invisible to others, in Warsaw the gold would have spilled out and Frank would be anointed king while the current king is thrown into the river, every place Frank walked would yield treasure, and the Russians would fear him. This lengthy, rather absurd laundry list is entirely material and combines motifs of overthrowing Christian authority with fantastic claims of treasure, transformation, and wealth. Częstochowa is not some spiritual Eden; it is where the literal gold treasure is buried. Frank is not to be made some spiritual king; he is to be king of Poland, riding around in a golden carriage. As with Frank's theology, his eschatology is entirely worldly and material.

It is also interesting to observe how closely the prophecy in §1118 echoes the actual circumstances of Frank's brief career between the conversions of 1759 and his imprisonment. Then, as Maciejko records, Frank did in fact ride around in a gilded carriage and was, for a short time, held in high regard.[19] It may well have seemed to his followers that he was about to ascend to the throne, or at least to some high status. The prophecy in §1118 echoes many details of the 1759 period, suggesting that the visit to Częstochowa was intended to be a kind of errand to rescue the Maiden and obtain the treasure (and robes) that was hidden there. But because the Brethren lost faith, what was meant to be the final act in Frank's ascension to kingship instead became the beginning of the end. Indeed, the initial failure of the quest has disappointed parties on both sides of the "fence"; in §964, Frank says that the Queen of Sheba has already tasted of the "other world" together with Solomon and is thus especially angry with the Brethren that their opportunity to enter it has been ruined.

Is this quest messianism? Not in any conventional or historical sense, nor even in the quasi-secularized sense of Early Frankism, with its goal of geographical sovereignty. As we will explore in chapter 6, the Frankist quest may be described as a kind of privatized millennialism: Even if the world will not be transformed, the Brethren will be, and they will presumably usher in some kind of new era for humankind. But even those aspirations are often secondary to more mundane promises. When Frank and the Brethren come to *Das* and cross the "curtain" to contact the Big Brother, they will receive this-worldly rewards, including immortal life, power, land, beauty, and even abundant meat and lavish homes, not with any collective messianic expectation, but for the seekers' apotheoses.

Motifs of the Frankist Quest as Expressed in the Tales

ZSP contains 176 tales and parables (not counting the *Visions of the Lord*). Of these, 99 are about the Frankist mission. This statistical fact bears attention: most of Frank's tales are allegories for the Frankist quest, or, more broadly, the qualities of the chivalric hero. They only rarely contain specific elements of the staged transformation we have just explored; those details are conveyed in direct statements by Frank, as are Frank's apocalyptic

---

[19] Maciejko, *Mixed Multitude*, 158–59.

statements, many of which are quite brief. Rather, like contemporaneous tales of eighteenth-century Western esoteric initiatic societies,[20] the majority of these "quest tales" are presented in the form of chivalric knight's tales, albeit with some very unlikely knights or other heroes, usually hidden, pursuing a maiden, eventually showing his true worth and emerging victorious. We will explore a representative sample of them here.

Numerous tales describe heroes in unusual circumstances who, by a combination of fortune and fortitude, win military victories, the favor of kings, and the hands of fair princesses. In §171, Frank tells the tale of a prince who wants to woo a princess. His teacher says that far greater and richer kings and princes have already failed, but the prince responds, "If God wishes it, then even without riches she will come into my hands." Thus far, the tale is a straightforward parable for Frank's own self-presentation as a fool who is nonetheless chosen by God and thus destined to succeed. When the prince reaches the princess's court, he succeeds because he devotedly serves the princess's father, the king (familiar Frankist themes of faithfulness and constancy). Finally, the prince is promoted to the rank of field marshal and, because he is lucky on the battlefield, he wins various battles and eventually the hand of the princess, who was "inflamed with a secret love for him." The success of the quest is due to a combination of God's/the king's grace and Frank's/the prince's faithfulness and devotion—even though his devotion to the king is really out of desire for the Maiden/princess. Just as the prince is seemingly devoted to the king, and through a combination of devotion and fortune, he wins the princess's hand, so Frank serves God—but ultimately for the rewards he will receive from the Maiden. Without even saying so explicitly, this apparently simple tale is also quite cynical. Sincere devotion is assumed to be, in part, self-interested. Similar patterns occur in §180 (where a prince who has no fortune becomes the gardener to a king and labors for eleven years; despite many setbacks, eventually the prince prospers and wins the hand of the princess) and §246 (where the princess's love for the prince gains him Divine favor). An interesting twist on this theme is in §976, wherein a queen has a favorite servant girl whom she sends to the forest to get silk from a woman there—to get it by force, in fact, as the servant has to beat the woman to obtain it. (Magic objects are often taken by force; in §968, Frank says the Brethren will take something from Solomon—not be given it). Meanwhile, a prince traveling incognito (a motif seen again and again—see

---

[20] On the Masonic use of these tropes, see Faivre, *Access to Western Esotericism*, 177–200.

§§705, 739) buys fabric for an outfit, but no one can find the silk to match it. The servant girl is found with the silk, which not only matches but also is magical and heavy in weight. The prince is smitten, and because of the magical silk, realizes this is the girl whom God has chosen. Notice here the inversion of gender; the servant girl, not the prince, is the stand-in for Frank, and again a combination of will and grace enables her to "win" the prince.

In §97, a royal family with recurring sickness is told by a sorcerer that the cause of their sickness dates back to "ancient times" when a different sorcerer, in love with a maiden princess in their family, was rejected and in revenge turned her into a tree and set her on an inaccessible mountain surrounded by wild animals. The king promptly dispatches his forty-eight sons to redeem her; most fail, twelve make it to the mountain but are repelled, and the youngest, attacked by a tiger, kills the tiger with his spear. Since the young prince is now unarmed, he blows a trumpet, causing all the beasts to flee, and makes his way to the cursed princess, who turns back into human form. The prince takes her home and the royal family's sickness is cured. Several aspects of the Frankist quest are alluded to in this tale: the princess trapped in a tree (like the Maiden trapped in the wooden portrait of the Virgin), the twelve Brethren, the young prince (obviously a stand-in for Frank) gaining power over animals (the theme recurs in §§518, 531, and 845), and the healthy (if not immortal) life that is the reward for redeeming the Maiden. The tale is also one of twenty-two dicta in *ZSP* concerned with illness and healing; Frank himself was frequently ill, and frequently complained about it. But the tale is not simply an encoded doctrine; its creativity and complexity are also remarkable literary creations. They echo familiar tropes of chivalric tales—it is not known what written or oral sources Frank may have drawn from—but is also distinctively Frankist in its themes. Indeed, so elaborate are some of the tales, that one wonders whether the tales are allegories for the Frankist quest, or whether the quest was itself derived from folkloric and literary material.

A second recurring theme in the "quest tales" is the replacement of religion by magic and sorcery. As Frank says in §868, "It would be better for you if you had been taught the wisdom of sorcery; you would have known a great deal." In a tale told in §1219, people in a village speak of a bogeyman in the mountains, so the thirteen-year-old Frank goes to investigate. The reader perhaps expects Frank to debunk the myth and see that there is no bogeyman. But in fact, Frank says, he found the bogeyman: "It was like a little naked man; he was all red as blood, burning eyes like torches; he had red hair which fell down over his arms." Contrast this real being with the absent Elijah from the Congregation of Elijah the Prophet; magical beings are real, even if religious ones are not. §1005 is a story of a flying portrait, a magic statue of a woman that gives immortality, and other magical objects that Frank links to the *terafim* discussed in the previous chapter. The *terafim* weren't gods, Frank says, but magical talismans. So too in §1011, a tale of a sorcerer able to summon demons from a magic book now lost. In §1013, "wisdom" means not textual learning but the ability to make gold, i.e., alchemical, magical wisdom, and Frank demands that two of his followers show that they possess it. In §1246, a foolish prince is sent to another country to "learn wisdom," but all he actually learns is the parlor trick of divining what someone is holding in their hand. When the prince returns, the king, delighted, holds a banquet to show off his son's talents, but one lord, knowing the prince is still a fool, comes bearing a ring in his closed hand. The prince sees the shape, but not knowing what a ring is, he says it is a millstone, and is ridiculed. And in several dicta, including §§908 and 1002, Egypt is referred to not as the place where the Israelites were enslaved, but as a magical place. This, too, shows the influence of Western esotericism on Frank; Egypt is the mythical seat of the Hermetic tradition as well, as we will explore in chapter 7.[21] And of course, magical themes appear in the stories of the *ba'alei kaben* described in the previous chapter, who appear in §§307, 639, 647, 656, 679, and 806, occasionally having a triple body (one legless and crawling, one with wings, and one in normal human form—the last suggesting that they may be in this form among us), and possessed of great power and wealth.[22]

A third theme in the quest tales is that of transgression. One of the most quintessentially Frankist tales is recounted in §96 tells of a princess "of lesser rank" who seeks to marry a prince, whose father, the king, disapproves. Hoping to deceive the princess, the king sends his gardener instead of his son, but the princess sets traps: She covers the road in rich cloth and plants trees the wrong way and turns over the flower pots. The gardener carefully steps around the cloth and notices the mistakes in the plants; recognizing that a true prince would not care about such things, the princess rejects him. Next the king sends his chef, who again avoids the cloth on the road, and notices various problems in the princess's kitchen. Now the princess threatens war. The king relents and sends his son the prince, who heedlessly tramples on

---

[21] See Faivre, *Access to Western Esotericism*, 17; Faivre, *The Eternal Hermes*, 127.
[22] Scholem, "Baruchiah." See also Lenowitz, "The Struggle over Images," 113, 123.

the fine cloth, does not complain about any flaws, and is thus clearly the true prince. Transgression here is the sign of nobility; the true prince doesn't care about how the garden should look or the value of the rich cloth. He tramples, he disregards, and he "unites" with the princess. The gardener and the chef are like law-abiding Jews with their commandments, as well as those Brethren who are unable to cast aside their social mores. They think it matters that a kitchen is one way (say, kosher) and not another. But the hero disregards the norms and thus is recognized as noble. Notice, too, that the princess/Maiden is controlling the entire quest and is able to threaten the king with war. In fact, it is the Maiden who is in control of everything.

Perhaps the most shocking and transgressive tale of a heroic/antiheroic prince is contained in §712. That tale concerns a prince expert in "the art of theft" who, not in line to inherit the throne, goes to a foreign city whose king has a beautiful daughter and two small children. The prince-thief stays with an old man, and together they plot to rob the king. Their first effort is successful, but on the second, the king lays a trap: a vat of pitch. Anticipating such a trap, the prince has the old man go first, and he falls into the pitch. Promising to help the old man, the prince instead cuts off his head and leaves the corpse there—Frank tells this tale without a hint of judgment of the prince's conduct. But it continues: The prince tells the old man's widow (who, Frank notes, is beautiful) of his death and proposes marriage, and she accepts. Meanwhile, the king decides to parade the headless corpse around the city, in order to provoke the thief's widow to cry and thus expose his identity. To prevent this from happening, the prince spills boiling water on the widow's (now his wife's) children, causing them and the widow to cry—and thus avoid detection by the king. The tale continues still further: At one point the prince gets the king's guards drunk, dresses them in priests' garments, and cuts off their arms. Finally, at the end of the tale, the king recognizes that this prince is motivated not by greed but by art, and offers his daughter to him in marriage. The prince marries the princess (no mention is made of the old man's widow) and inherits the kingdom. Needless to say, §712 is shocking in its violence and amorality. In addition to its familiar themes of a prince being above ordinary morality and being rewarded for his amoral actions by "winning" a princess, it also serves, in its length and absurdity, as a reflection of the twists and turns of the Frankist career. It seems unlikely that the specific details have any particular symbolic meanings; rather, the tale stands as a reductio ad absurdum of tales featuring the thief who is really a prince, the deceived king/god who celebrates the art of deception, and the preposterous happy ending promised at the end of the antinomian quest. Just the act of telling such a tale defies conventional propriety.

A fourth recurring theme is that of unquestioning faithfulness even in the face of challenging circumstances, an obvious reflection of the situation in which the Brethren find themselves. Frank is here at his most transparently manipulative.[23] In §544, for example, Frank tells a parable of a prince who marries a goddess, who demands that he not question any of her actions. She subsequently bears two children, one of whom she throws into a fire and second of whom she throws to a wolf. (Perhaps this is a reference to the Maiden having rejected Sabbetai Zevi and Baruchiah Russo—or perhaps it is simply another shocking story.) Finally, the prince questions her, and she separates from him for ten years. After all that time, seeing that he still pines for her, the goddess reunites and reveals that the children are alive and well. This harrowing story is, of course, about a test of faith, which Frank demands—to the Maiden, but by extension to her chosen representative—no matter what. §553 is also about total obedience; Frank says everything in the world happens through his power and that it is within Frank's power to give and take away. In §181, the same qualities of transgression which seemed so important elsewhere are here repaid with punishment. A prince is given forty keys to forty rooms filled with treasure but told not to open the fortieth one. Disregarding the instructions, he opens the fortieth door, but unlike tales in which transgression is rewarded, here, the prince loses everything. Frank's conclusion: "You must obey." In §204, a long parable seemingly made up of two independent stories, the hero is told by a princess/witch that in order to obtain a magical rose that will give everlasting life, he must "do only what I command you—do not deviate right or left"—orders which include flying blindly and sifting through brambles. The Brethren are to practice bold antinomian transgression toward the conventional world, and yet total obedience to the Maiden and her representative.

Finally, it is difficult to ascribe a clear meaning to many quest tales; I will provide an example of one of them by way of illustration. §141 tells of a man with "the gift of supernatural vision" who sets out to ask the sun a question. Along the way, he meets with four beings, each of whom asks *him* a question, all having to do with forms of barrenness. First, a man asks why his field is barren when his neighbor's is rich. Second, a river asks why it cannot produce fish while others can. Third, a barren tree asks why she cannot bear

---

[23] See Elior, "Jacob Frank," 497–502.

fruit while others do. And fourth, a thirty-year-old virgin woman asks why she can have no "happiness." The man reaches the sun, "asks for the things he needed" (which Frank does not specify), and then asks the sun these four questions. The sun replies that the man with the fallow field had been inhospitable and stingy; his sin is being rewarded tit for tat, *midah k'neged midah*. Regarding the river, the sun says that someone must first drown in the river first in order for it to yield fish. With the tree, the sun says that the problem is unrequited love: the tree is longing for another tree across the stream and must be replanted near it in order to bear fruit. And about the virgin, the sun says that she complains too much, and that is why she is single. One searches in vain for a philosophy that unifies the sun's responses: One is conventionally ethical, the second magical, the third quasi-romantic, and the fourth perhaps a jibe at the complaining of the Brethren. Perhaps the sun's situational responses perhaps reflect Frank's shifting, even contradictory, instructions, and this is yet another tale about power and obedience—or perhaps it is about how Frank, the man with supernatural vision, mediates between the world of magic and the world of the Brethren. It is difficult to resolve the meaning of this and many other such tales, and perhaps contrary to their spirit; as with some tales of Rabbi Nachman of Bratzlav, who, as we explore in chapter 8, was apparently familiar with ZSP, the inscrutability of such tales is part of their value. The world of the tales is askew, oblique. It resists easy interpretation. Or perhaps, as Frank says in §912, "it is necessary to employ a ruse at every turn."

Failure of the Quest and Berating of the Brethren

One of the striking aspects of the Frankist project is that, by the time of the dictation of ZSP, it had already failed. Indeed, it had failed several times. The sect of the "Contra-Talmudists" had not been granted autonomous status in the 1750s; Frank had not seized temporal power after converting in 1759; and even the quest for personal transformation, which may well have begun as a post hoc rationale for the failure of these more public missions, was itself regarded as a failure by Frank. Consequently, the motif of failure is an important one in ZSP, as Frank frequently laments in the subjunctive mood what could have happened had only the disciples followed him more closely, or what could have been a redemptive moment. To take but one of literally hundreds of examples, Frank states in §130,

> If only all of you had walked and not a single person had left; but when I saw your misconduct and that not a single person stayed whom I could give life to, I had to let go of my power.

Here, as elsewhere, the blame for the failure lies squarely with the Brethren and their lack of faith. Specifically, as described in §§60, 371, 409, and 456, the defining betrayal was when Frank was sent to prison in Częstochowa. Unlike Sabbetai Zevi's followers, who interpreted his imprisonment as a sign of his messianic mission (they even called the fortress where he was jailed the "Fortress of Strength"), most of Frank's followers deserted him when he went to prison. This, Frank says, was because they failed to understand that the period of imprisonment was intended to bring Frank together with the Maiden, incarnated in the Portrait of the Black Virgin. As Frank states in §1088, "Who led me to Edom? God did. Who led me to Poland? God did. Who led me to prison in Częstochowa? God did. Who released me from prison? God did. And so it will be forever." But the Brethren did not understand this. During a long series of dicta about the Maiden (§§200–260), Frank repeatedly berates the group for unfaithfulness during his period of imprisonment. For twelve years, he was with the Maiden, and yet most of his close followers abandoned him. Had they only been faithful during that period—in §258, Frank suggests that the group should have gone to prison with him—the Maiden would have raised them up. But because the group didn't have faith that this was the mission, the revelation of the Maiden was for him alone. Indeed, Frank suggests that his followers abandoned him just prior to his imprisonment, which was at just the wrong time. In §896, he states,

> If you had waited at least until I went to jail, and if you had been attached to it then, no wind of the world would have been able to displace you. However, already in Warsaw you turned the other way, and I went a different way.

Such endless harangues—over 330 in *ZSP*—vacillate between the demonic and the pathetic. They conjure up images of latter-day leaders of new religious movements, abusing their followers and demanding ever-greater levels of fealty in the face of increasingly obvious defeats. Particularly in these endless exhortations, Maciejko is not off the mark when he describes Frank as a "rather pitiful character . . . a little pathetic."[24]

---

[24] Maciejko, *Mixed Multitude*, 214.

Here, it is instructive to make use of the theories of failed prophecy initially put forward by Leon Festinger in his classic 1956 study *When Prophecy Fails*, and subsequently critiqued and modified by fifty years of scholarship.[25] Festinger's theory was that the failure of prophecy would not lead close adherents to abandon the faith; on the contrary, if certain conditions were met, it would lead to a heightening of faith and proselytization. Festinger coined the phrase "cognitive dissonance" in the 1956 study to explain the psychological phenomenon of a disconfirmed prophecy and the motivation for close adherents to reaffirm their faith in the face of contrary evidence rather than doubt their closely held beliefs.[26] "When people with strongly held beliefs are confronted by evidence clearly at odds with their beliefs," Festinger wrote, "they will seek to resolve the discomfort caused by the discrepancy by convincing others to support their views rather than abandoning their commitments."[27] Festinger's case study was a small UFO cult, the leader of which—interestingly, like Frank, she said she was receiving messages from an entity called "Elder Brother"—predicted a massive flood in the winter of 1953, which did not come to pass. But instead of abandoning their leader, her closest followers reaffirmed their faith, claimed that the non-flood was a result of their actions, and began to proselytize more assertively.[28] Festinger set out five conditions under which his thesis would prove true: (1) A deep conviction is held with relevance to action, (2) commitment, (3) enough specificity to be clearly refuted, (4) undeniable disconfirmatory evidence, and (5) social support.[29] Subsequent research has shown that while most millennial groups do indeed respond the way Festinger predicted in terms of reaffirmation of faith, only a minority engage in proselytization.[30] Further, scholars have observed that a bifurcation tends to take place between the most committed followers, who increase their intensity of faith, and less committed ones, who tend to drop off.

Applying this model to Frank, conditions (1), (2), and (5) are all present: a deep conviction that has caused dramatic actions to be taken (conversion),

---

[25] See, e.g., Stone, ed., *Expecting Armageddon*; van Fossen, "How Do Movements Survive?"; Stone, "Prophecy and Dissonance"; Dawson, "When Prophecy Fails and Faith Persists" (surveying subsequent studies); Melton, "Spiritualization and Reaffirmation"; Dein, "What Really Happens When Prophecy Fails"; Bader, "When Prophecy Passes Unnoticed." Articles upholding Festinger's thesis include Hardyck and Braden, "Prophecy Fails Again."
[26] See Stone, "Introduction," 5–6.
[27] Dawson, "When Prophecy Fails and Faith Persists," 60.
[28] Festinger, *When Prophecy Fails*, 10–11, 169.
[29] Ibid., 31–32.
[30] See Stone, "Introduction," 8–10.

a commitment to follow Frank into baptism, and a social support system for the inner circle of the Brethren in particular—by necessity, really, since they had left behind their entire former community. And, in *ZSP*, Frank's failed prophecy is squarely blamed on the insufficient faith of the faithful—just as, for example, the inner circle of Jehovah's Witnesses (who, incidentally, also called one another Brother and Sister) blamed the failure of the 1975 prophecy on the insufficient faith of the community.[31] As in Festinger's model, the followers take the blame for the failed prophecy. This theme echoes throughout *ZSP*, when Frank admonishes the Brethren for falling to the left, disobeying his commands, and being seduced by the "Dark Mother," who, as we will explore in the next chapter, represents repression and religion; in other words, the Frankists had not severed their ties with traditional religion enough. (Indeed, one wonders why the inner circle remained faithful to Frank at all after 1759; though Frank berates the Brethren for faithlessness, to the outside observer, it is surprising how faithful they remain.) The hundreds of dicta on the Frankist mission—the largest single subject area of *ZSP*—are mostly about the need for faithfulness and obedience, using the Brethren's past failure as a bludgeon.

But much is different from Festinger's model as well. It is unclear in the Frankist case whether the third and fourth conditions were met, i.e., whether there was a clear enough prophecy that was definitively disproven. On the one hand, it seems clear that in 1759, Frank's followers expected him to seize some kind of power, and Frank's brief period of fame indicated that his fortunes were rising until he was thrown into prison. On the other hand, there was not as much specificity as, say, Festinger's case study in 1953 or the failed Jehovah's Witnesses' prophecy of the millennium in 1975. What exactly was to have happened? The Frankist case (and, for that matter, the Sabbatean one) is less pellucid than Festinger's. Further, there is no evidence that the Brethren increased their proselytizing fervor after the imprisonment.[32] That would only take place after Frank's death in 1791, when his closest confidantes circulated the "Red Letters," an act that hews closely to Festinger's model, though it may have been motivated more by financial than cognitive dissonance.

Moreover, one of the common tactics of a postdisconfirmation prophet was unavailable to Frank: the spiritualization of prophecy.[33] This rhetorical

---

[31] Singelenberg, "It Separated the Wheat from the Chaff," 202.
[32] Maciejko, *Mixed Multitude*, 167.
[33] See Melton, "Spiritualization and Reaffirmation."

tactic—claiming that, for example, the disappeared leader-messiah is still alive but on some spiritual plane or that the world transformation has occurred but only in a spiritual sense—is common in failed messianic movements. Susan Dein has shown, for example, that in the case of the Chabad-Lubavitch Hasidic sect, the seventh rebbe's messianic mission was turned from a conventional messianic redemption to a "spiritual" redemption that is still being effected despite his physical demise.[34] Some Lubavitch Hasidim even maintain that the rebbe is not dead but alive on a spiritual level. Yet for Frank, this tactic is unavailable, given his antispiritual cosmology. What Frank does instead is rewrite the entire prophecy itself. Clearly, neither the Maiden myth nor the esoteric quest for personal transformation was even known (or preached) in 1759; Frank developed it over time, first between 1759 and 1772 under the influence of the cult of the Black Virgin and then between 1772 and 1784, under the influence of Western esotericism. But retroactively—Frank often says that a particular teaching was said "even in Iwanie" or at some other earlier period—Frank personalizes the promised (material) transformation, away from gaining territorial autonomy and toward personal immortality. Even as Frank continues to prophesy the coming war, the coming plague, and the coming doom—in over 10 percent of the dicta in ZSP—his actual activities had turned inward, away from public dissidence and toward personal transformation in an alchemical-esoteric model.

As we will see in chapter 8, it was Frank's Hasidic contemporaries who managed to "spiritualize" the messianic redemption, redefining it in terms of personal spiritual experience rather than historical restoration. Hasidism, too, may be understood through a Festingerian lens, except that their redefinition of the messianic mission was based on erasing and vilifying Sabbetai Zevi and everything he was alleged to have represented, even as the Hasidim channeled Sabbatean messianic fervor into (mostly) normative Jewish practice.[35] Most importantly, Hasidism succeeded where Frankism failed. Because of his materialism and skepticism, Frank's attempt to displace historical messianism into the personal realm could not be as radical as the Baal Shem Tov's. It left him in a liminal, often ridiculous zone of godlike superbeings with great strength and wealth; a curious hybrid of materialism and myth, prophecy and postponement.

---

[34] Dein, "What Really Happens When Prophecy Fails."
[35] Rapoport-Albert, *Women and the Messianic Heresy*, 264–86.

5

"With this deed we go to the naked thing"

Sexual Antinomianism as Mystical Messianism

> It is in the area of sex that we must search for the most secret and profound truths about the individual, that it is there that we can best discover what he is and what determines him.
>
> —Michel Foucault[1]

Theorizing Sexual Transgression

Allegations of sexual transgression lie at the center of Jacob Frank's public and scholarly reputations. From the outset, Frank's opponents accused him—like other Sabbateans—of sexual immorality, including incest.[2] Even today, sexual antinomianism—that is, the deliberate and perhaps ritualized transgression of established sexual mores[3]—is probably the predominant theme in scholarly and popular accounts of the Frankist movement.[4] But what do we really know about Frankist sexual practices? Were they wildly orgiastic or rigidly controlled? Were they frequent or rare? Did they have some theological meaning, or was the theology mere pretext for licentiousness or for Frank's exertion of power over his followers? Did Frank really commit incest with his daughter Eve?

In fact, we know very little. Apart from the accounts of Frank's accusers, unusual sexual practices are directly mentioned in only five episodes of *Various Notes* and a handful of oblique references in *ZSP*. There is no evidence

---

[1] Foucault, *Herculine Barbin*, quoted in Kripal, *Roads of Excess*, 15.
[2] See Carlebach, *Pursuit of Heresy*, 152–53, 184.
[3] As discussed in Chapter 2, an act must be deliberate to be properly considered antinomian. At the same time, any sexual expression, even very "tame" ones, may thus be antinomian if it intentionally transgresses a norm, so this chapter will include not only ritual acts but Frank's broader disregard for sexual mores as well.
[4] See Elior, "Jacob Frank," 524–32; Shmeruk, "The Frankist Novels"; Mandel, *The Militant Messiah*, 39–44.

of Frank committing incest with his daughter (when Frank discusses incest, it is because he calls his female disciples Sisters and his male disciples Brothers, as noted in chapter 1 and further discussed below). Indeed, the gulf between information and innuendo is so vast in this case that it invites a broader reflection into how scholars wittingly or unwittingly engage in a kind of quasi-theological moralization, repeating the claims of orthodox heresiologists.

This chapter explores the meanings of sexual praxis as reflected in the Frankist sources. It begins by assessing what we can and cannot know about Frankist sexual praxis, and by providing close readings of what little textual evidence we possess. Next, this chapter explores the figure of the Maiden, a messianic figure who I propose is best understood as the principle of material, embodied sensuality, incarnated in many women over time. The Maiden is an original Frankist figure with elements of the Shechinah, Frank's daughter Eve, Jewish conceptions of the messiah, and the Black Virgin of Częstochowa, where Frank had been imprisoned.

Finally, this chapter situates Frankist antinomian sexual practices in the context of the Frankist theology discussed in previous chapters. Not unlike Hasidic prayer, which "neutralized" historical messianism (Scholem) or "displaced" it (Idel) to the personal/experiential, Frankist sexual antinomianism is an act of realizing messianic consciousness, specifically the rejection of repressive religion and the liberation of the Maiden, the principle of embodied sensuality—in the here and now.[5] As Ada Rapoport-Albert put it,

> The apparent licentiousness of the Frankist court should not be viewed as wanton anarchy, unregulated and unchecked. On the contrary, the sexual contraventions practiced there, which Frank endowed with symbolic, sacramental meanings, were always performed at his own dictate, in carefully prescribed manners, and at particular times and places. They bore the hallmarks of antinomian activity—meaningful precisely because it recognizes the authority of the laws it sets out to violate.[6]

Specifically, I explore four ways in which sexual antinomianism functions within this program:

---

[5] Idel, *Messianic Mystics*, 3–16, 212–14 (critiquing the concept of "neutralization").
[6] Rapoport-Albert, *Women and the Messianic Heresy*, 166–67.

1. The rejection of repression is troped by Frank as rejecting the "Foreign Woman" who stands before the Maiden like the husk before the fruit. Frank reverses the usual association of the Foreign Woman with licentiousness and here associates her with sexual repression.
2. The liberation of the Maiden in sexual expression is a this-worldly enactment of the messianic reality. The decentering experience of sexual transgression is a psychological rupture between conventional reality and messianic reality.
3. Sexual experience brings power. The Maiden is the expression of and gateway to worldly power. For Frank, this is a gendered phenomenon and is a queer remasculinization of the Jewish hero.
4. Finally, the liberation of sexuality/the Maiden is described as the liberation of the feminine, both in terms of the actual liberation of women and symbolically as the victory of sensuality over repression, female over male. It is at once protofeminist (associating women's liberation with the messianic age, and accompanied by actual empowerment of women) and misogynistic (essentializing, and part of the longtime association of women with bodies, sexuality, and carnality).

In contrast to the "effeminate" Sabbetai Zevi, Frank sets himself up as a powerful, priapic male hero who can "capture" the Maiden. Paradoxically, this masculine quest is undertaken so that the feminine—the Maiden—can rule over the masculine, i.e., so that desire, eros, and the body dominates repression, spirit, and the intellect. This is neither true feminism nor true sexual liberation, yet it may also be seen as presaging a more authentic liberation of embodiment and sensuality, so briefly I engage with one such program, that of the theologian Audre Lorde, as a point of comparison and perhaps as a point of departure.

What Do We Actually Know about Frankist Sexual Practice?

I begin with a methodological note regarding what it is possible to know of the Frankist sect's behavior. In terms of primary Frankist documents, we have only five remarks in *RA* and four dicta in *ZSP* that speak directly about unusual sexual practices—and only two total that discuss sexual ritual specifically. However, due to the Frankist corpus having been censored (it appears) by the sect's descendants, the estimate for how often sexual antinomianism occurred in the Frankist community ranges from hardly ever to all of the time. At one extreme, sexual antinomianism may have been almost completely absent. Heretics are always accused of sexual deviance, even when they were in fact ascetic, such as the medieval heresies of the Bogomils, the Cathars, or the Brethren of the Free Spirit.[7] For example, the historian Robert Lerner describes how the Brethren of the Free Spirit were portrayed as possessing "religious doctrines that are merely pretenses for fornication."[8] Compare that to how one contemporary scholar has proposed that in Frankism, "libertine behavior was justified by the claim that the transgressions have a secret religious meaning."[9] Now as then, heresies are sexualized, just as liberated sexuality is often turned into heresy by orthodoxies. In the case of the Frankists, it is quite possible that the sensationalistic descriptions of Frankist sexual ritual were the inventions of the sect's prosecutors. Rapoport-Albert has already pointed out that in general, Sabbatean women were apparently quite chaste, their "loose" morality being a calumny of their opponents who were disturbed by women's visibility and leadership within the movement.[10] As we discussed in Chapter 1, even the famous incident at Lanckoronie, wherein the Frankists allegedly danced around a naked young girl and kissed her breasts, may never have happened. As discussed in more detail there, I do not share Maciejko's being "inclined to accept the basic veracity of Jacob Emden's description" of the incident, given Emden's zealous persecution of Sabbateans and the fact that the ritual is a stock accusation used against them.[11] Clearly, something went on that evening—Frank himself mentions it, and perhaps his description of it as "singing songs" is a euphemism or excuse. Notably, a similar term—"singing the psalms, with the company of 'women and wine'"—was used in conjunction with the first arrest of Sabbateans for allegedly conducting a sexual orgy, in 1672, although recent research has shown that the *doenmeh* did, in fact, conduct rituals of actual singing of songs; the term was not an excuse or pretext.[12] In principle, I am not inclined to

---

[7] See Urban, *Magia Sexualis*, 33–35; Versluis, *Secret History*, 57–58; Cohn, *Pursuit of the Millennium*, 150–51; Lerner, *Heresy of the Free Spirit*, 20–22, 239–40.

[8] Lerner, *Heresy of the Free Spirit*, 12. Some scholars have questioned whether the sect even existed at all, or was instead the product of an anti-heretical imagination. See Cohn, *Pursuit of the Millennium*, 149; Versluis, *Secret History*, 69.

[9] Feiner, *Origins of Jewish Secularization*, 74, 78.

[10] Rapoport-Albert, *Women and the Messianic Heresy*, 41–47, 259–61; Carlebach, *Pursuit of Heresy*, 152–53.

[11] Maciejko, *Mixed Multitude*, 22–26.

[12] Sisman, *Burden of Silence*, 106.

accept the account that the leading prosecutor/persecutor of Sabbateanism provides of a Sabbatean antinomian ritual, especially without evidence, and especially in the context of hundreds of years of similar accusations of other heretical groups, and half a century of accusations made against Sabbateans in particular.[13]

At the other extreme, it is possible that sexual antinomianism was more prevalent among the Frankist sect than the extant records suggest, given that those texts were "cleansed" by descendants of the sect who were scandalized by its excesses and persecuted in their own right. The manuscripts of ZSP show signs of redaction and editing, and scandalous passages may have been edited out (though, given the passages we will explore, clearly incompletely). Our discussion of Frankist sexual antinomianism is thus bookended between unknowns: Perhaps there was less than we think, perhaps there was more.

It is also important to situate Frank in the context of his Sabbatean forebears, at least some of whom did engage in sexual antinomian ritual, though the rumors and calumnies against the Sabbateans seem to have been far more capacious than the realities. Sabbetai Zevi famously annulled sexual prohibitions as part of his overall antinomian-messianic project, and admitted to fathering a child with the wife of a follower.[14] Sexual symbolism and imagery ran throughout the Sabbatean movement, including in explicit (even today) texts such as *And I Came This Day unto the Fountain*.[15] Ritualized sexual antinomianism did exist among the *doenmeh*, particularly among the Karakash sect, with which Frank became affiliated.[16] Karakash sexual antinomianism was confined to specific times and places: primarily, as part of the *doenmeh's* Festival of the Lamb, observed on the twenty-second of Adar (later, on the vernal equinox), the sect practiced the "Putting out of the Lights," at which, after the festive lamb meal, the lights were extinguished and sect members had sexual relations with one another.[17] It is not known

---

[13] Shmuel Feiner accepts Emden's account of "free sexual relations, exchanging wives, incest, sexual intercourse with menstruating women and Christians, and masturbation." Feiner, *Origins of Jewish Secularization*, 73. But there is absolutely no evidence for these stock accusations, which are generally part of heresiology, not scholarship.

[14] Scholem, *Sabbatai Ṣevi*, 879; Sisman, *Burden of Silence*, 105.

[15] See Maciejko, "Coitus interruptus," xxv–xxxii (discussing the text's descriptions of "supernal" masturbation, homosexuality, anal sex, and oral sex).

[16] See Sisman, *Burden of Silence*, 150–88; Shai, "Antinomian Tendencies," 21–42; Yamamoto, "The Last Step." The *doenmeh* drew on much older Kabbalistic notions that the laws of incest and sexual propriety generally were the "scepter of the king" that would be annulled in the messianic era. See Idel, "Interpretations of the 'Secret of Incest'"; Tikkunei Zohar, 69 (stating that "above there are no laws of incest"). At least in the texts available to us, Frank does not make use of these concepts.

[17] See Shai, "Antinomian Tendencies," xi–xii.

whence this custom was derived, and there is no record of it being practiced among the Frankist circle.[18]

Yet it was likely part of Frank's early experiences in the Sabbatean movement. More broadly, the link between heresy and sexuality was drawn by the *doenmeh* themselves. Early on in *ZSP* §4, Frank refers to his *doenmeh* past by recalling,

> Rabbi Leib, when I, in my youth, asked him to reveal the secret faith to me, said to me: "My son, you will not learn of it until you are worthy of taking a wife. At that time, during the wedding itself, the secret will be revealed to you."

It is surely not a coincidence that the *doenmeh* reveal the "secret faith" of Sabbateanism to adherents on the eve of their weddings, and Frank clearly indicates that he had been thus initiated. It is also interesting that Frank says here that the secret would be revealed during the wedding itself—perhaps during the consummation of the marriage. More broadly, the *doenmeh*, at least in the first century of the sect's existence, did reject traditional customs of modesty and sexual propriety.[19] This we find in abundance in Frank.

And yet, within Sabbatean communities, attitudes toward sexuality had varied since the inception of the movement. As much as Sabbateanism became associated with liberated sexuality, in fact, as Alexander van der Haven has shown, there were internal debates about sexual ethics from Sabbateanism's earliest stages, reflected in the conflict between the quasi-ascetic Nathan of Gaza and Sarah Ashkenazi, who rejected asceticism in favor of a kind of hedonism, and who, van der Haven suggests, may be the individual most responsible for Sabbatean libertinism.[20] At the same time, Sarah was also the target of slanders and attacks by her adversaries. She was rumored to have formerly been a prostitute, which was almost certainly not true.[21] R. Jacob Emden alleged that she tried to seduce the teenage son of a well-known physician, which is also likely not true,[22] allegations

---

[18] Sisman, *Burden of Silence*, 184–85.
[19] See Rapoport-Albert, *Women and the Messianic Heresy*, 85–89; Shai, "Antinomian Tendencies," iii–vi.
[20] Van der Haven, *From Lowly Metaphor*, 9–11, 38.
[21] Ibid., 29–32; Scholem, *Sabbatai Sevi*, 403.
[22] Goldish, "Messianism and Ethics," 168. Goldish says he finds the accusation "credible." On the relationship of Sarah Ashkenazi to the Sabbatean movement, and the slanders against her, see Van Der Haven, *From Lowly Metaphor*, 21–22, 38–45.

which suggest that Rapoport-Albert's position is the correct one.[23] In sum, establishing the Sabbatean context for Frankist sexual antinomianism is fraught with uncertainties and may depend on which sources one is more inclined to believe.

Turning, then, to the Frankist texts themselves, we can identify three types of sexual antinomianism within Frankist texts: sexual ritual, sexual liaisons commanded by Frank (which may follow the Sabbatean model) among the twelve Brethren, and the abrogation of restrictions on sexuality in general. We will proceed chronologically.

First, §17 of *ZSP*, which recounts the arrest in Lanckoronie, only states that "the *ma'aminim* sang, danced, and there they were jailed with the lord." There is no discussion of the alleged choreography of this "dance" involving a topless adolescent girl standing in the center of the circle and being kissed on the breasts, and, as we stated above, this stock accusation was leveled many times against Sabbateans, who in fact did engage in ecstatic singing and dancing that was not sexual in nature, as Hadar Feldman Samet's scholarship of Sabbatean hymns has shown.[24] "Danced" may be a euphemism, or a lie, or this note may have been censored—but we do not really know.

Second, in *RA* §46, titled "A Secret Act," the text states that on July 3, 1759, on the eve of a number of baptisms of sect members,[25]

> The lord set up a guard made up of our people in the courtyard, so that no one could see through a window, and he went inside with the Brothers and Sisters and Her Highness, may her memory be for a blessing.[26] He stripped naked and ordered all those gathered [to do likewise]. Then he took a small bench, drove a nail into the center and set two burning candles on it and hung his cross from the nail. He kneeled before it, and took the cross, bowed in four directions, and kissed it. Then he ordered Her Highness and everyone else to do likewise. After that, sexual relations took place according to his determination. At that point, one of the women laughed, and the lord ordered the candles put out, saying: "If they would have let the candles

---

[23] Rapoport-Albert, *Women and the Messianic Heresy*, 41–47, 259–61; Carlebach, *Pursuit of Heresy*, 152–53.
[24] See Samet, "Ottoman Songs in Sabbatian Manuscripts."
[25] The text actually states 1758, but as Lenowitz observes, this and many other dates in the *RA* are inaccurate. As the text itself relates, it takes place after the sect's conversion, which took place in 1759. Frank, *Collection of the Words of the Lord*, 403, n.1713.
[26] This refers to Frank's wife Hannah.

burn, they would see what would happen." And then he said, "With this deed we go to the naked thing, therefore it is necessary to go naked."

Unlike the fantastical events in *ZSP*, most (though not all[27]) of the events in *RA* are realistically described, and it is reasonable to believe that they actually took place. This episode follows a sequence of rites in which Frank gives the Brethren their new names and identities, and it appears as a kind of parodic-sexual refutation of their recent conversion: The cross is appropriated into a heretical sexual ritual. As discussed below, the ritual appears to be a kind of initiation rite. The temporal context here is central. This was the period of the Lwów disputations, which rabbinic and church authorities forced on the sect, newly led by Frank, in order to force them to convert to Christianity.[28] The first baptisms took place on August 19, 1759; Frank himself was baptized on September 17 (the *RA* states this took place on September 24). In other words, this rite of passage—a kind of heretical counterbaptism, if you will—takes place just as the sect is about to engage in actual baptism. (It is also interesting to note Frank's disapproval of the woman laughing. The text does not indicate whether it was laughter of ecstasy, mockery, embarrassment, or joy, but it apparently interrupted the ritual before it reached full culmination.) This is a fascinating, provocative description of a sexual ritual—but it is the only one of its type in the entire Frankist corpus.

Third, *RA* §104, titled "A Very Secret Act," relates a planned sexual ritual that did not take place. It states that when the fourteen "Sisters" visited Frank in prison for the first time, he said, "I need to bring forth a great thing," and said that after one Sister would be chosen, "I will take her to myself, I will arrange for her to eat and drink well; I will have sexual relations with her seven times every night and six times in the daytime. That woman will become pregnant with a daughter." Hannah Frank volunteered, but Frank said, "[T]hat is not for you for you must have sons." However, "that thing did not come to fruition," the text relates. Indeed, when one disciple is chosen, another is said to have objected, "wanting to be chosen herself." §104, in sum, relates an event that did not take place and that seems to be a mythological origin story for the birth of Eve Frank (who was, as far as we know, the daughter of Hannah Frank, not another disciple). Given Eve's status as an incarnation of the Messiah, she, like other messiahs, must have unusual circumstances

[27] §106, for example, states that Frank flew over the ramparts of Częstochowa.
[28] Maciejko, *Mixed Multitude*, 127–31.

surrounding her birth—in this case, she was to have been the product of copious sexual activity between Frank and a disciple who volunteered for the task. Ironically, as with many of Frank's plans, this never came to fruition, and Eve was born of Frank's wife.

Fourth, *ZSP* §74, dated to February 24, 1769, also takes place on the eve of baptism, though in this case the baptism of a single follower. At this point, Frank had been imprisoned in Częstochowa for nearly a decade and was being visited by several of the Brethren. The text then relates,

> At that time [March 4, 1769], the lord ordered [Mateusz] Matuszewski z"l, Pawłowski z"l, and Matuszewski of Nadworno z"l to have sexual relations with the wife of Henryk Wołowski. The second night he ordered Henryk, Michał Wołowski, Dębowski and Jasser to have sex with Wittel [Matuszewski]. And on [March] 7, Pawłowski, Matuszewski, Matuszewski of Nadworno with the wife of Jakubowski z"l. On the 8th, Matuszewski of Nadworno was baptized, and the Lord and Her Highness held him at the baptism.

As recorded elsewhere in *RA*, these individuals made up the inner circle of Frank's inner circle. The question is whether §74 is recording one of many such events, or whether this particular event was special in some way. On the one hand, it was recorded, suggesting that these events were not frequent, but were rare and thus deserving of mention. Moreover, the final sentence suggests that the sexual acts were in some way connected to the baptism, as they were in *RA* §46. On the other hand, the text simply records Frank ordering these sexual relations without any commentary at all, suggesting that there was nothing particularly unusual about three Frankist women having sex with three Frankist men each, on three successive nights. Maybe this sort of thing happened all the time. But then, why were other occasions not mentioned?

Quantitatively, compare these four texts on sexuality with six *Various Notes* entries about food (§§47, 68, 69, 71, 104, 106), three about beating the disciples (§§81, 88, 93), and two about Frank's hemorrhoids (§§68, 93). At least eight entries record strange ritual acts that do not involve sexuality (§§7, 11, 30, 31, 43, 44, 99, 105). The lacuna regarding sexual antinomian practice is particularly striking given that *ZSP* frequently discusses violence, desire, disrespect for religion, braggadocio, and castigation. In over two thousand dicta of *ZSP*, Frank has no problem bragging about (allegedly) defecating on a Torah scroll, (allegedly) beating up pious religious observers, and (allegedly) having a large penis. In nine dicta, he confesses his love of fruit jam (§§709, 812, 838, 886, 1053, 1090, 1092, 1276, 1311; see also *RA* §20). In forty-eight dicta he brags about his physical strength. In over two hundred dicta he abjures his followers to disrespect all religious law. Yet *ZSP* contains just fifty or so dicta on sexual topics (and 110 dicta on the Maiden, discussed below), and most of them do not discuss sexual activity in detail, merely bragging about sexuality or the beauty of various women Frank encounters. Only one refers to the sexual "secret deeds" that are recorded in *RA*, in §397.

Not coincidentally, §397 also contains the longest sustained discussion of the Maiden, the Foreign Woman, and sexuality, and I will analyze it in greater detail below. For now, let us only look at the sexual deed recounted in that dictum:

> What did I do? I ordered two among you to perform this base thing. The first among her great servants ran away with a lot of noise, with all of his company. I ordered them to perform such a deed that that one cannot go back to his first place anymore, because they were shoved out of their place.

What the "base thing" is here is unclear, but there is good reason to understand it as some form of compelled sexual act.[29] First, it comes in the context of Frank abjuring his followers to abandon conventional sexual morality. Second, as we have discussed already, the vague term "thing" is often used to indicate topics of a sexual nature. For example, §693 uses the term "one other thing" to refer to sexuality—in this case, Ham's rape of Noah, as recorded in midrashic and talmudic sources. And just a few dicta later, in §698, Frank refers to "that thing" as something which he orders the Brethren to do—perhaps sexual in nature, perhaps not. Third, as discussed in the next section of this chapter, whatever was commanded represents a rupture: "one cannot go back to his first place anymore." This suggests some kind of break that decenters and unmoors the devotee.

Notably, in these dicta, Frank makes no use of Kabbalistic tropes regarding incestuous erotic union such as the Tikkunei Zohar's statement that "above

---

[29] Lenowitz translates *podłą* as "vile thing." However, while *podłą* does mean "vile" in contemporary Polish, it did not have the same negative connotation in eighteenth-century Polish. For example, a sexual, excretory or alimentary act may be *podłą*—physical, base, perhaps even disgusting, — without being "vile." Cognates of the word *podłą* occur several times in *ZSP*, including §§33, 172, and 578.

there are no laws of incest," or the notion that incest is the "scepter of the king."[30] Nor does Frank discuss Sabbatean sexual antinomianism in theory or practice. Indeed, it is remarkable that the handful of explicit sexual accounts in *RA* and *ZSP* are utterly devoid of theorization. The Brethren have sex; that is all; next dictum.

In addition to these four explicit texts, other texts in the Frankist corpus do suggest a libertine attitude toward sexuality generally. Frank intimates several times that he has sexual relations with his female followers. In *ZSP* §375, which is a post hoc rationale for why Frank was arrested, Frank states that, when he was interrogated in Warsaw,

> I was asked during an interrogation in Warsaw: "If you call them sisters, how can you be intimate with them?" Because I did not conceal anything from them, I did this purposely in the open, in front of the whole world, so that when I come to the place where I need to be, it will be known that you are Brothers and Sisters.

This openness, Frank says, differentiates him from the "Second" Sabbatean messianic leader, Baruchiah Russo, who kept everything secret. §395 is the sole reference to Frank committing incest, and it refers not to Frank having sexual relations with his actual daughter but to Frank having sexual relations with the devotees known as "Sisters." The allegations of incest came from Frank's adversaries. And it is a boast, after all, not a record of what Frank actually said to his Polish interlocutors. Nonetheless, if we take it at face value, it is an admission that Frank had sexual relations (with an unknown degree of consent or coercion) with the "Sisters."

Similarly, in §614, Frank retells the notorious episode of Abraham and Sarah in Egypt. In the biblical story, Abraham orders Sarah to say she is his sister, so that if Pharaoh desires to have sex with her, he will not kill Abraham in order to do so. The biblical story is, of course, shocking: Abraham is essentially making Sarah available (again, with consent not even mentioned) to be another man's sexual slave. Frank, though, reverses the meaning of the story, shifting Abraham's motive from saving his own life to permitting Sarah to engage in sexual activity: "If she were known as [his] wife, none would have been able to take her from him. He ordered her to call herself his sister

---

[30] Tikkunei Zohar 69. See Idel, "Interpretations of the 'Secret of Incest'"; Maciejko, "Development," 133.

precisely so that he could permit her to consort with others." In other words, the term "Sister," which Sarah shares with Frank's female followers and with the lover in the Song of Songs, is almost a kind of license; it makes the woman who bears the identification eligible for (possibly) consensual sexual relations. And just as Sarah could now "consort" with Pharaoh, so the Sisters may with Frank. Or so it seems; Frank does not say this explicitly, and the dictum moves on to criticizing the Brethren for their lack of faith in him.

More broadly, Frank's attitude toward sexual morality in the tales and autobiographical passages of *RA* and *ZSP* is generally boastful and libertine. *RA* §64 relates how Hannah Frank had sexual intercourse with Jacob Frank (presumably visiting him during his confinement) on Yom Kippur, a clear violation of Jewish law. And *RA* §67 relates how the two had intercourse "in broad daylight, and everyone there was aware of it." In *ZSP* §34, a woman wants to have sex with Frank because she is an astrologer and recognizes his good fortune. Frank dreams of deflowering a virgin in *ZSP* §823. And in *Visions of the Lord* §2248, Frank recalls a vision he had on June 22, 1784, wherein

> Two Polish maidens, daughters, prepared for bed and were about to lie down. I wanted to have intercourse with them, but then a nun came, undressed herself, and also lay down on the bed. I lay down in the bed. The nun said to me: "Lord Frank, what are you doing? After all, I have professed my vows." I answered: "So what?"

Once again, the emphasis is on openness and shamelessness. The nun lays down on the bed presumably to protect the young virgins' virtue, but Frank doesn't care if she watches, or perhaps even participates. But then the text goes further, saying that the Brethren should have sexual relations with nuns "in the public squares, in town, and in streets" with priests becoming their servants. Many familiar themes are present: Frank's triumphalist attitude toward Christianity, his quasi-prophetic vision of sensual antireligion triumphing over repressive religion, and of course, the scandalousness of the original "vision" and the even more outrageous "meaning" ascribed to it.

Another erotic vision is recounted in *Visions* §2254. There, Frank recounts, in near-pornographic detail, that on July 14, 1784:

> I saw myself gliding through a hall. A maiden of exceptional beauty came to me. She was wearing a common robe, not an expensive one, [and]

her breasts were exposed. I fondled her, she pretended to be shy. She did not say much. I felt her breasts and they were as hard as rocks. I say to her: "Are you still a virgin?" She answers: "I was a virgin and I still am a pure virgin." I spoke to her about a few things and each time she responded well, word for word. I went to my bedroom. In the room in front of my bedroom I see another maiden following her. This one was a bit larger than the first one, of fatter flesh; her neck was like a tower, shining like the sun. She was dressed in expensive and rich robes, her breasts were also exposed, and she spoke openly, without shyness. I felt her breasts with my hands as well and fondled her, they were also hard as a rock. I ask her as well: "Are you still a virgin?" She replied: "I was and am a pure virgin." I ask her if she will have intercourse with me. She responds: "Others certainly cannot do this, but since we fell into your hands, you are allowed to do what pleases your eyes, because we came under your shadow."

Here once again are two maidens, sexualized and objectified by Frank, but with important differences between them. One is reticent, the other forthright. One is beautiful, the other even more beautiful. This passage seems to refer to dichotomy between the visible Maiden (sometimes Eve Frank, sometimes the Portrait of the Black Virgin) and the "other Maiden" who will, finally, come to the Brethren's aid; this will be discussed in detail in the next section. The initial maiden appears to be the summit of erotic perfection—yet, Frank maintains, even she is just the husk before the fruit, the prelude to the ultimate erotic-mystical experience which Frank alone can penetrate.

The tales of *ZSP* contain numerous references to sexuality, often in quasi-chivalric contexts: knights pursuing princesses, queens in love with forbidden men, and so on. For example, in §545, a prince is in love with a princess, even when she disguises herself as a gypsy dancer; this seems like a reference to Frank's devotion to the Maiden, though the tale includes a moral that Frank demands the same kind of love from the Brethren. In §1268, a princess helps a prince sneak into her chamber; just as the Maiden wants Frank to transgress societal norms and reach her. In §140, a king marries a slave girl, distressing his wife the queen, who then falls very ill, until a "faithful servant" makes sexual advances on her in order to rouse her to the point where she is willing to take medicine. Once again, this seems to be a reference to Frank (the faithful servant) engaging in sexual ritual to rouse the dormant Maiden who is dismayed and in need.[31] In the most ornate and shocking such tale, in §722, the king of the "Children of the Sun" requires that every "beautiful girl child" be "consecrated" by living in a kind of harem for a time before having sexual relations with the king, only after which would she be able to marry. One of the king's sons bribes the matron in charge of the harem and manages to have sex with one such girl, who reports to the king, "your son has dishonored me." The king has the matron burned alive, but the king's family says that "the prince cannot be tried like common men . . . for he is the heir, and you are old already." Thus the prince is spared, and Frank approvingly analogizes him to the Brethren who "could not be judged as other people." This and other tales scandalously cast aside morality and ethics, but note that in §722, that morality is already depraved; the king is committing institutionalized rape, after all. The prince is amoral, even evil—the tale is not a love story—but so is the system of law which he rebels against.

Finally, in addition to textual references to libertine sexuality, there were rumors, noted in the introduction, that Eve Frank had an affair with Emperor Joseph II, during the period in 1777 when Frank attempted to be ennobled by the Hapsburg Court and was granted several audiences with the emperor.[32] (It is likely that these connections were later used by Moses Dobruschka/Junius Frey for the smuggling of weapons, as discussed in chapter 1.) While these rumors may or may not have been based in fact, Frank did attempt to marry Eve off to a number of European noblemen and bragged of nearly doing so. These slivers of information suggest that, at this phase of Frankist history, Eve's own sexual conduct could be considered libertine, even if it was unremarkable among European royalty at the time. For Frank, it was following in the footsteps of Abraham, as well as a sign of the fulfillment of his prophecy that (former) Jews would ascend to the heights of secular power, libertine sexuality included.

---

[31] The "moral" at the end of the parable states that just as the servant had to agitate the queen in order to save her, so Frank must agitate the Brethren. This seems to miss the point of the parable itself. In the Appendix, I discuss the possibility that these tacked-on morals (which almost always have to do with the faithfulness of the Brethren) represent a later editorial hand redacting the text and simplifying (or sanitizing) the complex erotic tales of *ZSP* into simple exhortations to faithfulness.

[32] Maciejko, *Mixed Multitude*, 211–13.

The Maiden-Messiah with a Thousand Faces

A central figure in understanding Frankist discourse on sexuality is the Maiden (*Panna*), a syncretic, messianic entity who is the gateway to the world of the Big Brother. This figure plays a central role in Frankist theology and myth, and appears directly in over one hundred dicta in *ZSP*—more than the Big Brother (40), Jacob and Esau (86), Eve Frank (16), or any other figure save Frank himself.[33] The Maiden, not Frank, is the messiah (§1051), and Frank states in §124 that "all of our forefathers' efforts were aimed at pursuing the Maiden, upon whom all life depends and who protects from all evil. No weapon could harm a man thanks to her aid." The Maiden, thus, is the indispensable figure for Frankist messianism.

And yet, she is perpetually deferred. Thematically, the ever-postponed encounter with the Maiden functions as a post hoc justification for the many twists and turns of the Frankist story. In §258, the Maiden is given as the reason why the sect entered baptism in the first place (no mention of lost disputations and charges of heresy) and why Frank went to Częstochowa (no mention of Frank's false pretenses being discovered). In no synagogue in the world, Frank says, could the Brethren learn of the Maiden, but Christianity teaches that "the whole world is filled with her," perhaps a reference to Isaiah 6:3's utterance that the whole world is full of the divine *kavod*, understood in Kabbalistic literature as referring to the Shechinah. Yet in §1194, Frank says it is improper to use the term "Shechinah"; one should use *Panna*, which is not only the term for "maiden" but also, as Maciejko points out, is the standard Polish appellation for the Virgin Mary.[34] Drawing on long-standing conceptions of the Shechinah as going into exile with Israel, Frank says that the Maiden was imprisoned just as Frank was, and the place of her imprisonment is the portrait in Częstochowa. Yet because of their betrayal, the Brethren are still not able to meet the Maiden because they are not in "wholeness," again deferring the redemptive moment to some point in the undetermined future. Still, Frank promises that the day is coming when they shall reside beneath the wings of the Maiden, again an allusion to the righteous dwelling under the wings of the Shechinah. In §232, after rejecting "all teachings up to now" as worthless, Frank says, "there is nothing left to do other than walk in lockstep and surrender yourselves under her wings."

[33] Rapoport-Albert, *Women and the Messianic Heresy*, 175–236; Maciejko, *Mixed Multitude*, 171–77; Elior, "Jacob Frank," 514–20.
[34] Maciejko, *Mixed Multitude*, 174–75.

The figure of the Maiden includes aspects of the Shechinah, Eve Frank, and the Black Virgin of Częstochowa, and, I suggest, should be seen as encompassing these figures within Her.[35] She is, to paraphrase Joseph Campbell, a "goddess with a thousand faces," a feminine principle of embodied sensuality who incarnates many times and whose liberation may be experienced in the liberation of sexuality. In §609, the Maiden seems to be identical to the sexual inclination itself. "Without her no building can be," Frank says, quoting the Midrash that suggests that without the evil inclination, no building would be built.[36] The Maiden is also life eternal (§232). Quoting Tikkunei Zohar 1.17b (in one of the relatively rare direct quotes from the Zoharic corpus), Frank says that when the Maiden departs from us, we are like bodies without souls (§758). Ada Rapoport-Albert has suggested that these shifting emphases reflect a shift in Frank's conception of the mission following his experiences in Częstochowa:

> From the time when the Maiden was first revealed to him at Częstochowa, a transformation occurred in Jacob Frank's conception of his messianic mission. Only then did it become clear to him that the embodiment of the divinity in flesh and blood ... could come about only by way of the manifestation of the feminine powers of the divine in a human female.[37]

At the same time, no single manifestation *is* the Maiden. As Frank says in §173,

> You have heard of the Maiden of Israel and the Daughter of Edom, the Daughter of Egypt, but there is one more that is still dormant and no one in the world has heard of her, or knows where she is.

Even when the Maiden is found and liberated, she is less a single, discrete figure than a transformation that will be understood differently by different people. §173 continues,

> But when the gate opens for us, the one in which we have hope, we will raise that thing up: the whole world will see it without knowing what it is. And

---

[35] See Lenowitz, "Me'ayin yavo 'ezri?," 294–95 (understanding Rachel and the Black Virgin of Częstochowa as "hypostases" of the Maiden).
[36] Genesis Rabbah 9.7.
[37] Rapoport-Albert, *Women and the Messianic Heresy*, 208–9.

like a school teacher, I will ask each one of you separately what it is that you see, because each of you will be worthy of seeing only as much as your degree permits.

Each person will experience the Maiden, or the principle she embodies, in a different way, says Frank; some will experience it even without knowing what it is—much as Frank understands Christianity as venerating the Virgin without knowing Her true identity. Frank continues in §190,

> When we are worthy of seeing her and of hiding beneath her wings, we will attain eternal life, and she will reveal herself in even greater glory every day. Each will see her according to one's degree. The worthier one is, the more beautiful she will appear, and each will see her following one's own heart.

Clearly, then, while Frank insists that the Maiden is a physical entity, she is somehow perceived differently by different people. Further, in §410, Frank states, "there are several maidens: When you had only entered baptism one maiden was given to you to protect you, but she is not the one we pursue."[38]

As we have already seen, the Shechinah is the most obvious influence on the conception of the Maiden, as Frank uses many symbols of the Shechinah to refer to the *Panna*: As just noted, the Brethren seek shelter under her wings (§1052); she is identified as a *shoshanah*, a lily, a common cognomen of the Shechinah (§410); and she is the "entry point" to the other world, much as the *sefirah* of Malchut is the gateway to the world of the *sefirot*. In the many myths of Jacob and Esau, the Maiden is clearly associated with Rachel, who is herself traditionally associated with the Shechinah. For example, in §240, Frank states that Jacob lived forever because at the well he saw an image of Rachel. This, amid a sequence of dicta about the Maiden, links the symbolism of the Maiden (eternal life, gazing at her image) with the character of Rachel.[39] Frank may also be influenced by Sabbetai Zevi's own love of the song "Meliselda," which describes a nude princess emerging from her bath, and which Zevi sang as a hymn to the messiah. More subtly, Frank is also drawing on Sabbatean notions that the messiah would be heralded by a woman, a concept that Rapoport-Albert, following Scholem, traces to

---

[38] See also §145, where Frank states that "there are four maidens and another four."
[39] See Elior, "Jacob Frank," 518.

Cardoso.[40] In these constructions, the female herald of the messiah plays a role roughly analogous to that of Elijah in Zoharic literature. It is perhaps ironic that in following this tradition, Frank, who may seem here to be at his most innovative, was in fact at his most conservative.

Second, Frank draws heavily on the figure of the Virgin Mary in general and the portrait of the Black Virgin of Częstochowa in particular. At one point, Frank refers to the Maiden as a "portrait" (§193), and in §190 he observes "how people try to paint her so she is never out of sight and the whole world may look at her." Just as the Virgin Mary is an intermediary between the Christian and God, so the Maiden is an intermediary between the Brethren and God: "And being worthy of seeing her and flooded by love for her, you will then be able to reach the love of God, through her" (§195).[41] Elsewhere Frank remarks, "when I said to you, I will show you God, but the Maiden must be revealed first. Because she is before God, and she is the gate to God. It is only through her that you can come to God and to reach Him" (§620). The parallels to Marianism are clear enough, but it bears noting that the Christian theological system in which Frank was operating was not a conventional one; the cult of the Black Virgin of Częstochowa, the famous portrait (and symbol of Polish national-religious identity) housed in the monastery of the same name where Frank was imprisoned for twelve years,[42] does not venerate the Virgin Mary and regard the portrait as a rendition of her, but rather, as clearly stated in numerous hymns and prayers, it venerates the portrait *itself*.[43] The portrait, not the subject it represents, possesses magical powers and divine energies. Likewise for Frank, the Maiden is *in* the portrait, not depicted by it. In §614, Frank asks, "[W]hy did you not ask me what it means that the Maiden was in Częstochowa, and was hidden in a portrait? It certainly would not have been futile." But even the Black Virgin is not the ultimate Maiden. In §917, Frank states,

---

[40] Rapoport-Albert, *Women and the Messianic Heresy*, 50–52, citing Scholem, *Studies and Texts*, 427. Rapoport-Albert notes that there are isolated precedents for this idea, but that they are few and far between, and that Cardoso should be understood as the primary source for it, as Scholem had first proposed. Rapoport-Albert, *Women and the Messianic Heresy*, 52.

[41] On Mary as intermediary, see Ludwig Ott, *Fundamentals of Catholic Theology*, 211–18.

[42] Scholem, "Jacob Frank and the Frankists," 302; Doktór, "Jakub Frank," 64–67; Maciejko, *Mixed Multitude*, 169–70; Maciejko, "Development," 212–13. On the cult of the Black Virgin of Częstochowa, see Begg, *The Cult of the Black Virgin*; Moss and Cappannari, "In Quest of the Black Virgin." The Black Virgin has been a symbol of Polish nationalism for hundreds of years, and was even the patron of the Solidarity movement. Galland, *Longing for Darkness*, 245.

[43] See, e.g., sources cited in Pasierb, *The Shrine of the Black Madonna*; Shrine of Częstochowa Association, *History of the Painting of the Blessed Mother of Częstochowa*.

It is always the case that the husk precedes the fruit. You see for yourself that everyone calls her: Eternal Lady. They say that she is the Queen of Heaven. All kneel before her and bow to her. They call her the Lady of Perpetual Help. At first, she suffered with him and had no rest, she went wandering with him and ran away with him to Egypt. She is the one who precedes the fruit which will come into this world, and before which all kings of the world will kneel openly.

Here, Frank makes use of the well-established metaphor of husk and fruit to analogize the Virgin Mary to the actual Maiden, the messiah to come. Both the Christian influence and the anti-Christian supersessionism are present. On the one hand, Maciejko observes that the word *wspomożycielka*, the "Lady of Perpetual Help," is a technical theological word, which confirms that Frank took it directly from Catholic liturgy.[44] On the other hand, the use of "Queen of Heaven" is both a Marian reference—Mary is known as the *Regina Coelis*—and possibly a reference to the demonic, by way of Jeremiah's complaint that the Israelites are baking cakes for the goddess Anat (Jer. 7:18). After all, the Virgin Mary is the husk before the fruit—that which is ultimately to be discarded.

For Frank, the Jews have known who the Maiden is (i.e., the Shechinah) but have not "possessed" her; the Christians have possessed her (i.e., the Virgin) but not known who she is. In §315 he says, "All Jews seek and desire something, but they do not know what that thing is. It is their custom each Saturday to say: *Go friend and face the bride* and to the lady they say: *Come in peace*. All this is only in speech and song, but we pursue her and try to see her in broad daylight." The Jews err in precisely a complementary way to how Christians err. Jews have the right words, greeting the Shechinah on the Sabbath, but they are words without actions. The Christians have the Maiden but lack the vocabulary to understand her.

Third, the Maiden is also incarnated in Eve Frank, who was treated as royalty in the late Frankist court (referred to as "Her Highness") and perhaps regarded as the messiah incarnate. Maciejko states that "the final and complete revelation of Frankism amounts to the true incarnation of the divine Maiden in a true human maiden: Eve Frank."[45] Yet Eve is only one manifestation of the Maiden. She is not in captivity, or in a portrait, or venerated by

---

[44] Maciejko, *Mixed Multitude*, 176.
[45] Maciejko, *Mixed Multitude*, 177.

Christians; those are aspects of the Black Virgin. Moreover, as the Frankist myth becomes embellished, it becomes clear that to reach the Maiden will be the culmination of a long series of steps, so perhaps Eve is not the final incarnation of the Maiden either. That being said, Eve is *an* incarnation of the Maiden, and clearly, Frank sets up numerous parallels between Eve and the Black Virgin of Częstochowa, from the processes of adoration described earlier to the veneration of her portrait, a tradition which lasted for generations after her death.[46] And Rapoport-Albert makes a convincing case that the emphasis on the Maiden in general only really began after Frank's wife Hannah's death in 1770 and the shift of the focus onto Eve.[47] In her formulation, Frank sought the "assimilation of his daughter in the figure of the supernal Maiden."[48]

Finally, the Maiden is a messianic figure of Frank's own devising with elements of the sexual inclination as well as numerous other sources, synthesized into something quite original. For example, in §609, he states,

> Without her no building can exist. Unlike what you have said before, that the Shechinah goes out at night and collects nourishment for the God-fearing, now everything will be out in the open. Therefore, I would need people for her convoy. And the place where she is to bathe is in this world and those who bathe there will be rejuvenated like an eagle. They would know all languages and would learn the customs of the royal state. She herself and those around her would shine like sun rays.

As noted earlier, "without her no building can exist" is a reference to the Talmudic phrase that describes the "evil" inclination, and the peculiar reference to the place where the Maiden will bathe (which we will return to below) seems to be an eros-laden reference. The reference to the Shechinah going out at night and collecting nourishment appears to be a reference to Zohar III: 249a–b, in which the Shechinah is figured as a gazelle who hunts at night and shares her food with other animals. Here, Frank seems to be using the reference only to make his familiar point (discussed in chapter 1) that all that was secret will now be done out in the open. And, as we should now come to expect from Frank, the messianic vision is of a worldly queen

---

[46] See Rapoport-Albert, *Women and the Messianic Heresy*, 199.
[47] Ibid., 197, 183–84.
[48] Ibid., 203.

who will require all the trappings of worldly royalty. Despite the Maiden not being a single personage but an entity that manifests in different ways at different times and to different people, Frank insists that each incarnation of the Maiden is a material, physical woman. As Frank says in §1001, "I did not tell you about this in spirit, or in heaven. Instead, I said everything in daylight, on earth: that there is a Maiden and a tower, and there is a painting they call a portrait." And yet, the Maiden appears even where she is least expected. In §325, Frank relates, "in Częstochowa a few Polish lords went to a chapel. Upon returning from the chapel, they came to see me. One of them was very respectable. He looked her Highness in the eye and said to his companions: 'I would find it easier to believe that this is the Holy Mother and the true Virgin.'" Frank adds, "they understood that he was saying it in jest," but as far as Frank was concerned, they had no idea how correct they were.

The Meanings of Frankist Sexual Antinomianism

Having described what we know about Frankist sexual praxis on the one hand, and the figure of the Maiden on the other, it is now possible to assess the multiple meanings of Frankist sexual antinomianism. Here, I will address four of them: casting off of laws that come from "the side of death"; enacting the messianic reality; gaining worldly power; and liberating the feminine.

Repression as the "Foreign Woman"

As we noted in chapter 2, Frankist antinomianism is, in large part, a proto-rationalistic rejection of normative religion's needless constraints on human flourishing. In that context, sexual liberation, symbolized by the liberation of the Maiden, is a kind of declaration of independence from repressive religion. Unlike religion, sexuality is part of having a "share in this world" (§383). Sexual pleasure is thus a positive religious value, because it affirms the reality of worldly life as against the illusion of spiritual pursuits. Unpicked fruit is bitter, while fruit that can be eaten is sweet, Frank remarks in §622, one dictum after recalling how as a child he would eat off of both milk and meat dishes deliberately, as if to openly mock the meaninglessness of the laws of kashrut. For Frank, both food and sex are dishes meant to be enjoyed. As one character in Oscar Wilde's *The Picture of Dorian Gray* remarks, "Pleasure is Nature's test, her sign of approval."[49]

Amazingly, Frank describes repression as the temptress, the Foreign Woman. Indeed, precisely the Kabbalistic tropes once associated with sexual transgression are repurposed by Frank to refer to sexual repression. The Foreign Woman—sometimes the "Mother of the Other Side" or "Mother of the Mixed Multitude"—represents lapsing into traditional religion, with its asceticism and denial, and a rejection of the sensuality the Maiden embodies. She pursues the Frankist circle and occasionally causes their downfall (§§196, 396, 780, 1192). "He who, God forbid, turns to the wrong path, is shrouded by the shadow of the mother of the evil side," Frank says in §396. Let us now look at §397 in more detail:

> But when a man turns away from the right path, then immediately they hunt for his life, and she leads him into her chamber. There, there are different chambers; in some, they drink; in others, they fast; in others still, they dance. And she tried to persuade you to fast in that state and to study the law.

Frank here makes the startling claim that fasting and studying Torah are the demoness's enchantments, no different from drinking and dancing. Frank continues, citing Proverbs 30:23:

> And through the deference that she possesses, she entices all people to come to her, and later she herself becomes the beating they receive as punishment. She is the servant that inherited the possessions of her lady. And that is what I have said before, that even the true Maiden is in distress. She is sheltering and hiding while the other one takes power.... The servant knows well that when the other takes power, she will fall.... God created them against each other.

Repressive religion becomes its own punishment, and Frank, citing the Zohar's interpretation of Proverbs 30:23 as referring to Lilith,[50] says she only has power because it has "inherited the possessions" of the Maiden. Frank then continues his ethical critique of normative religion:

---

[49] Wilde, *The Picture of Dorian Gray*, 56.
[50] Zohar 2:118a–118b, 2:17, 3:69a, 3:97a.

> All arms from the beginning of the world have been handed to her. And all distress, pain, troubles have their beginning with her, and all who have fallen, even the First one, who made a good deed by disobeying the laws of Moses and establishing the state, even though he thought he would escape her net in so doing. But in the country where he was, this thing could not have been done, because there is no mention of the Maiden there.

Sabbetai Zevi, Frank says, did a "good deed" by rejecting the laws of Moses, but could not complete his mission in a Muslim context because there is no veneration of the Maiden there; in other words, because Muslim society represses women and sexuality, and has no comparable figure to the Virgin Mary. Thus even Sabbetai fell into "her net." Frank continues, now situating the "Mother from the Other Side" into his quasi-gnostic mythology:

> From the beginning, she has been the beloved of the tree of death, which is one of the three gods that rule the world. His love for her has no limits. He chose her and placed her above all pain, worries and all forms of death that happen on earth, for all of his arms had been handed to her. She is called that alien woman, that evil woman who is worse than death. She is the depth of the abyss; nonetheless, there is something very great and good hidden inside of her, and no one can come close to this thing except by entering her. She is the good door, the sphere of baptism, that is why all great people who knew that there was a great thing hidden inside of her came close to her, but they did not enter her because she is like the husk that protects the fruit.

Once again, Frank uses a familiar Kabbalistic symbol of husk and fruit, here meaning that the Maiden/sensuality/life is hidden within the Unholy Mother/repression/death; after all, the Portrait is located in a Church, the Maiden is garbed as the Virgin. Thus one must pass through Christianity in order to reach the Maiden. Notice, as §397 continues, how Frank at once explains and denigrates Jewish and Christian religious observance:

> What did she do? She led all the righteous hermits and the God-fearing into great love and fear of herself. She inspired them with the holy spirit and revealed all secrets of the law to them. But she did it all through fasting so that

they would fall into the net she had set for them and that she would strangle them with that foul fear. Her name is Esther. It is thanks to her that a miracle happened for the Israelites but through the three-day fast they fell into her hands and into her net. Therefore, she enticed you to fast for three days as well, and that is why you fell.

Just as the Maiden incarnates in various forms, the Unholy Mother appeared as the biblical Esther, who indeed calls a three-day fast in the Purim story, and again as a temptress who caused the Frankist company to repent and return to religious observance. It is the Unholy Mother who inspires "righteous hermits" and "the God-fearing" toward greater piety and study of the "secrets of the law." Once again, Frank is boldly inverting the notion of the demonic female from one who leads away from restraint toward sensuality, to one who leads away from sensuality to restraint. The Unholy Mother is also identified here with the weeping Rachel and with the inspiration for the building of the biblical Temples:

> But our hope is that, "even if we walk into the shadow of death, we will not fear because you are with us," for I am meant to accept baptism so that I can break and destroy all laws that have existed until now. Until now she was called the queen of everything, because all is in her hands. Her name is Rachel, the one about whom it is written: "The one who weeps over children." She persuaded you to build the two temples, the first and the second one, and she destroyed them herself. If Solomon had destroyed his own creation, he would have been freed from her net and reached the good thing, and he would have lived. Repeatedly I led you by that good thing that is hidden in her, and that power has saved you from her hands and you did not fall with everything into her.

The Foreign Woman is the one who weeps, who creates temples of antilife religion only to destroy them and create a religion of mourning and penitence. Astonishingly, Frank has here taken most of normative Judaism's central images and depicted them as Satanic in nature; they were instituted by the Foreign Woman, part of the fallen world, ruled over by three malevolent demigods and saturated with death and suffering. And the threat continues, as She tempted the company as well. It is at this point in §397 that Frank recounts commanding sexual transgression in the passage quoted in the first section of this chapter. To repeat:

What did I do? I ordered two among you to perform this base thing. The first among her great servants ran away with a lot of noise, with all of his company. I ordered them to perform such a deed that one cannot go back to his first place anymore, because they were shoved out of their place. And whatever I do to afflict and slander you, I do it only to purify you and rid you of her, which subdues her power.

Now, situating that passage in the context of §397 as a whole, we can see that Frank required the Brethren to transgress sexually to fully break from traditional, repressive religion. The "base thing" acts "to purify you and rid you of her," i.e., the Mother of the Unholy Side, the embodiment of sexual and personal repression. To fully cast off the "net" of repressive religion, one must perform a deed so great that "one cannot go back" to how one was before. For the Brethren to defeat the Foreign Woman, their tether to conventional morality must be broken. Antinomian sexual activity is undertaken to throw off the yoke of the Foreign Woman and to embrace the Maiden.

Sexual Transgression as Messianic Enactment

What might that "embrace" have felt like experientially? Here, we are limited by the sparse Frankist sources at our disposal, which only fleetingly describe the interior experiences of Frank (let alone the Brethren) in the context of sexual antinomianism. Clearly, Frank is demanding a traumatic break: In his words, to "perform such a deed that that one cannot go back to his first place anymore." Building on the analysis we began in chapter 2, as well as the work of Idel, Rapoport-Albert, and others, I suggest that the transgression of a sexual taboo is an enactive messianic performance that ruptures the practitioner's connection to traditional society and creates a different, messianic world apart from it.[51] Recall that the most elaborate record of Frankist sexual ritual dates from the eve of the sect's baptism. There, sexual transgression is a dividing line, demarcating "in" and "out." It is an initiation rite, cementing the bonds of the inner circle and separating them from the world outside. Like Chaya Shorr testing the loyalty of a professed Sabbatean by demanding that they eat (unkosher) candle wax, sexual transgression is a

---

[51] See Idel, "Mystical Union," 35–44; Idel, "Sexual Metaphors and Praxis;" Hellner-Eshed, *A River Flows from Eden*, 200–202, 218–22; Kripal, *Roads of Excess*, 17–23.

kind of experiential Rubicon that, once crossed, cannot be uncrossed—or, in Frank's words, such that "one cannot go back to his first place anymore." To be sure, such acts also enforce a cult-like devotion to Frank himself, not unlike in contemporary new religious movements. Though some Frankist texts describe a willingness among Frank's followers to participate in them, we obviously have no way of knowing what they were really thinking.

In the context of Sabbateanism, sexual antinomianism also inculcates messianic consciousness. There is precedent for this understanding of antinomian sexuality in the *doenmeh* communities from which Frank sprung. Conceptually, messianism had already been sexualized in Lurianic Kabbalah, which saw *yesod*, the locus of sexuality, as the root of the Messiah, who would unify masculine and feminine within the Godhead.[52] Sabbateanism had asserted that the transgression of sexual restrictions (*arayot*) and the spilling of seed (*shituf haraglayim* or *shichvat zera*) were signs of the messianic age.[53] As Sisman describes,

> Such "strange acts" were justified by the postmessianic Dönme Kabbalah, which professed that the messiah had already come and abolished the rulings of the Torah of Beri'ah (this world) and initiated the Torah of the 'Azilut (world-to-come) in its place. In order to penetrate into the 'Azilut world fully, a believer was supposed to transgress the rulings belonging to this world.[54]

But it would be a mistake to reduce the significance of this practice to purely intellectual, conceptual, or symbolic meaning. Surely, in practice, the transgressive sexual experience may also be understood as a corporeal, this-worldly messianic/spiritual experience—an example of what Rapoport-Albert called "the concrete substantiation of the spirit, including the full physical materialization of the divine"[55] and what Idel described as the Sabbateans' "realistic" and "non-metaphorical" interpretations of Kabbalistic understandings of eros.[56] Eli Shai speculates that rituals such as the "Putting Out of the Lights" "gave them the sensual taste of the paradisical redemptive state in their own lifetime . . . the only area in which the Shabbatean underground could have

---

[52] See Wolfson, "Tiqqun ha-Shekhinah," 289–92.
[53] Ibid., 292–99.
[54] Sisman, "The Redemptive Power of Sexual Anarchy."
[55] Rapoport-Albert and Hamánn, "Something for the Female Sex," 119.
[56] Idel, *Kabbalah and Eros*, 202.

a given a meaningful experience of redemption was the sexual dimension."[57] Just as the Hasidic masters brought the messianic *pneuma* out of history and into spiritually eroticized ritual, so the *doenmeh* and Frank brought it into sexually eroticized ritual. Moreover, Shai continues, "the sexual dimension offered, therefore, a real compensation to a major trauma, and the near total frustration in its wake. It gave the selected few a feeling that not all was lost after the conversion, exile and death of the humiliated Savior."[58] As with the *doenmeh*, the postimprisonment Frankist community had failed, its messianic dreams deferred, as Frank bemoans in over 150 dicta in *ZSP*. Yet here was an arena in which they had not failed, in which the dream of a new world could be experienced. That the sexual initiation ritual takes place during the period of the Frankist conversion lends credence to this interpretation; while it may seem to the world outside that the community had capitulated, in fact they had "doubled down" on their heresy. Sexuality is material mystical messianism.

Though there is no known or likely historical connection, it is interesting to juxtapose Frank's commanded sexual practices with the antinomianism of Tantra, which, in Hugh Urban's felicitous definition, "refers historically to esoteric and guarded practices in Hinduism which express and seek Divinity not through renunciation but through the expression of that Divinity in the world."[59] Frank's theology is different, but the emphasis on experiencing "what God does here on Earth" is similar. And as Kripal puts it, "one of the first things needful for the initiate into Tantrism is for him to be weaned as soon as possible from the traditional standards of morality. He must first learn to be indifferent to the traditional taboos. He must then positively reject them. And finally, he must become actively hostile to them."[60] With that break made, sexual ritual may generate magical power. Thus the Tantric practitioner "intentionally, systematically, and secretly engages in transgressive rituals, the use of impure substances, and illicit acts (often of a sexual nature) in an attempt to accumulate power."[61] (Similar notions are found in the rituals of Aleister Crowley and other practitioners of occult magic/magick,

---

[57] Shai, "Antinomian Tendencies," xxii–xxiii.
[58] Ibid., xxiii.
[59] Urban, *Tantra*, 272. See also Kripal, *Roads of Excess*, 223. For a comparison of Tantra and Kabbalah, see Mopsik, "Union and Unity in Kabbalah," 223–42.
[60] Kripal, *Roads of Excess*, 31.
[61] Ibid., 23; Feuerstein, *Holy Madness*, 62; Urban, "The Cult of Ecstasy," 281–91. For a comparison of Tantra and Kabbalah, see Mopsik, "Union and Unity in Kabbalah."

who, among other sources, drew on Kabbalah.[62]) It is to this link between transgressive sexuality and worldly power that we now turn.

The Remasculinization of the Jewish Hero

Symbolically, the Maiden is at once the Messiah and the gateway to the hidden world whence will be derived worldly power and immortality. Yet even before such transformations take place, sexuality brings power in the world and is a kind of metonym for it. In numerous tales, Frank describes how "winning" the princess or other female figure is part of the heroic quest for worldly power and success (§§97, 180, 246, 593, 739, 1142). Sexuality brings about magical power in the first visionary experience recorded in *ZSP*: "There we were approached by the Maiden, whose beauty was indescribable. She was clad in a Polish blouse and her breasts were exposed. As soon as I saw this, I could see from one end of the world to the other" (§2). Though this may be mere hyperbole, it is echoed in numerous other texts. §116 states that the Turkish state's power rests on sexuality. In the bizarrely polymorphous §145, Frank refers to a "certain rock. . . . He who could have intercourse with the rock and bear it, could live for a thousand years." And when the Brethren are to finally meet the Maiden, Frank says in §314, they will each see her in a different way, but each will follow a choreography imbued with biblical allusion, royal symbolism and sexual tension:

> She will ask, what do you desire? You will answer: "Until now I have worked to serve God and to be allowed to see you, because without you I cannot reach God. Now I ask you to lead me on my way to God." Upon hearing this she will say: "Come closer." You will come closer and kiss her feet, but not her hands. Then she will say: "Rise," and she will rise as well. Stand on the side, not facing her, eyes looking down, hands folded on your heart, one on the other, and lift your eyes a little, but do not look at her face. Then she will tell you: "*Kardasz!* Brother!" At that point you can already kiss her hands. She will command you to sit next to her and ask again, "What do you desire?" Then you will ask her with these words, "*Open for me, my sister! My*

---

[62] See Feuerstein, *Holy Madness*, 59–63; Martin, *Art, Messianism, and Crime*, 74–75; Versluis, *Magic and Mysticism*, 138–39; Urban, "The Beast with Two Backs"; Hanegraaf, "The Beginnings of Occultist Kabbalah"; Segol, *Kabbalah and Sex Magic*.

friend!" She will then open the tall gates and will feel your eyes and face with her right hand, saying: Up until now you were blind, you did not see anything, from now on open your eyes and see. You will then start to see and will behold what your forefathers and fore-forefathers did not see.

This remarkable, highly eroticized passage, citing Song of Songs 5:2, culminates in a kind of esoteric-prophetic vision. It is almost as if the power of the sexual tension building throughout the passage reflects the power of the prophetic sight that is granted.

This power is also heavily gendered. The quest to "unite" with the Maiden is a metonym for the will of the male hero confronting a hostile world, and succeeding where others have failed. Frank is quite explicit that his masculinity is superior to that of other would-be heroes. Frank tropes the patriarch Jacob's failure as a failure to be masculine. He boasts of the size and strength of his penis (§579), and says that his enemies want to wound him in his genitals (§591). Such machismo is today often referred to as "toxic masculinity," and is rightly criticized for its brutishness, its tendency to objectify and subjugate of women, and its propensity to violence. Yet in the context of normative Judaism and especially Sabbateanism, Frank's masculine is a striking inversion of norms. As Daniel Boyarin has described, certain currents in rabbinic Judaism often put forth surprisingly feminine-gendered constructions of Jewish masculinity, generally disfavoring brute strength, which was associated with Christianity, and favoring the bookish, even "effeminate," ideal Jewish male, whose knowledge gives him power.[63] Frank generally agrees with this dichotomy (later taken to its extreme conclusion by Otto Weininger[64]) but turns it on its head. Anticipating the gendered critique of diaspora Judaism by the early Zionists, Frank demands that his followers reject the "effeminate" Jacob for the "masculine" Esau, i.e., reject powerless Judaism for powerful Christianity. As Frank repeatedly boasts of his sexual prowess, he sets himself up as the sexual-typological opposite of the rabbinic ideal of Jacob, and the embodiment of the powerful man of Esau. As such, deploying here some of the analysis of queer theory, with its recurring interest in the social construction of sex and gender,[65] Frank's hyperbolic

---

[63] Boyarin, *Unheroic Conduct*, 31–150. For critiques of Boyarin, see Baader, ed., *Jewish Masculinities*; Belser, "Rabbinic Trickster Tales"; Dahan-Kalev, "Gender, Sexuality, and Queer."
[64] Weininger, *Sex and Character*.
[65] See generally Butler, *Gender Trouble*; Sedgwick, *Epistemology of the Closet*; Halperin, *One Hundred Years of Homosexuality*; Sullivan, *A Critical Introduction to Queer Theory*; Corber and Valocchi, eds., *Queer Studies*; Campbell, *Arguing with the Phallus*. Applications of queer theory

masculinity may be seen as "queering" rabbinic Jewish conceptions of Jewish masculinity.

Frank's masculine Esau-ness is particularly radical in the context of mystical Judaism in general, and Sabbateanism in particular. First, as Jeffrey Kripal, Elliot Wolfson, and Howard Eilberg-Schwartz have pointed out, monotheistic mysticism is intrinsically and problematically homoerotic, since it involves the male mystic seeking to unite with the male God, often by means of the mystic's female-gendered soul.[66] Indeed, even when the male mystic is uniting with the Shechinah, he is often doing so in order to arouse the male energies above or reconstitute the divine male *anthrōpos*.[67] In Wolfson's words, "heterosexuality is transformed by kabbalistic symbolism into a homoeroticism because the union of male and female is a reconstitution of the male."[68] Frank, in practically banishing the male God from the world and pursuing, physically and sexually, the female Maiden, radically rejects even the symbolic homoeroticism of Kabbalah, replacing it with a voracious masculine heterosexuality.

Frank's masculinity is also a departure from Sabbateanism, which was perhaps the most homoerotic movement in Jewish history.[69] Frank provocatively states, on numerous occasions, that Sabbetai Zevi was a woman in the guise of a man—"secretly a woman" (§§552, 609, 725, 982).[70] This was not Frank's invention; it draws on several sources, including the *doenmeh*'s homoerotic liturgy praising the beauty of Sabbetai and Baruchiah Russo; accounts of Sabbetai having a number of young male servants whom he lavished with affection; stories of Sabbetai's sexual dysfunction, including a story of having his penis wounded by fire at age six, years of nonmarriage and

---

to Jewish studies include Boyarin et al., eds., *Queer Theory and the Jewish Question*; Stone, *Queer Commentary*; Rosen, ed., *Unveiling Eve*; Michaelson, "Kabbalah and Queer Theology"; Watts Belser, "Rabbinic Trickster Tales."; Kann, "Yichud Rachel and Leah."

[66] Kripal, *Roads of Excess*, 223; Eilberg-Schwartz, *God's Phallus*, 99; Wolfson, *Through a Speculum That Shines*, 79. But see Garb, "Gender and Power in Kabbalah," 101–3.

[67] See Garb, "Gender and Power in Kabbalah," 101–3; Idel, *Kabbalah and Eros*, 70–71, 97–101, 129–24; Idel, "Sexual Metaphors and Praxis in the Kabbalah," 217–44; Hellner-Eshed, *A River Flows from Eden*, 202; Michaelson, "Queering Kabbalistic Gender Play," 58–59; Garb, "Gender and Power in Kabbalah," 93–96.

[68] Wolfson, *Through a Speculum That Shines*, 396. See also Wolfson, "Engenderment," 213: "There is a unity wherein the female is contained in the male and the male in the female, a unity, that is, wherein the gender dimorphism is transcended through the constitution of the one, male androgyne."

[69] See Sisman, *Burden of Silence*, 80 (noting widespread homoeroticism in Ottoman Empire at the time); Rapoport-Albert, *Women and the Messianic Heresy*, 190; Michaelson, "Kabbalah and Queer Theology," 54; Idel, *Kabbalah and Eros*, 232–33.

[70] See Elior, *Mystical Origins*, 189–90; Elior, "Jacob Frank," 534.

two marriages annulled prior to his meeting Sarah Ashkenazi; and Sabbatai's own identification with the divine androgyne and with the biblical Esther.[71] Frank was also surely aware of rumors that the son of Baruchiah Russo/Osman Baba—"the Second" in Frank's terminology—worked for a time as a male prostitute before assuming leadership of the Karakash sect, of which Frank was a member.[72] In the uniquely homoerotic context of the *doenmeh*, Frank's aggressively masculine, priapically endowed, and violently sexual male figure is a radical disruption of conventional mystical homoerotic rhetoric; it is a queering of the queer.[73] In §58, Frank says (in German) that he is Esther's brother—a reference to Sabbetai that would be clear to a Sabbatean audience. Where Sabbetai/Esther was cagey and secretive (recall, too, that Esther is troped as a manifestation of the Foreign Woman), Frank would now be audacious and open. Sabbetai was a secret woman, but the messiah, that is, the Maiden, has to be an actual woman (§609) and Frank will be her uniter and redeemer, her revealer, her "man."

Returning to §609, the passage, discussed above, about the public bathing of the Maiden, we find a similar dynamic. Frank states that the seven Sisters would help the Maiden bathe, but then adds that seven Brothers would be present as well, stating, "just as it was said of the First, that he was secretly of female sex, so must it be of you; you would have served Her and the whole world would have understood that you are women." This may mean that the Brothers must neuter their sexual urges and be like eunuchs in the Maiden's court; the mystic as eunuch a common trope in Kabbalistic literature.[74] But in the context of *ZSP* and its association of femininity with sexuality, it seems more likely that all the Brethren, male and female, now partake of the sensuality that is normally only the provenance of the feminine. Becoming "women" means becoming embodied erotic beings. The Maiden will make women out of men: that is, liberated sexuality will transform men into sexual beings who express, rather than repress, eroticism. Frank presents himself as

---

[71] Idel, *Kabbalah and Eros*, 232–33; Liebes, *The Secret of the Sabbatean Faith*, 107–9; Elqayam, "To Know the Messiah," 637–70; Shai, *Messiah of Incest*, 138–39, 260–61; Elior, "Jacob Frank," 471–547; Scholem, *Sabbatai Ṣevi*, 434; Van der Haven, *From Lowly Metaphor*, 34; Wolfson, "Engenderment," 246.

[72] Shai, "Antinomian Tendencies," xiv.

[73] To be clear, there is no assumption here that male mystics were homosexual or sexually active with males. As Mark Jordan has said, these are "rhetorical positions, not copulatory ones." Jordan, *The Silence of Sodom*, 198. See also Kripal, *Roads of Excess*, 18; Wolfson, *Through a Speculum That Shines*, 223.

[74] See Zohar 2:89a; Wolfson, *Language Eros Being*, 296–332. This symbolic act of neutering is often accomplished in circumcision. Michaelson, "Kabbalah and Queer Theology," 59–63.

hypermasculine, which really is feminine, because sexual expression is feminine, and that masculinity will arouse the feminine to liberate the masculine by turning them into feminine beings, i.e., sexually liberated beings. Thus the Maiden can rule over Israel, and allow men who have been repressed by the Foreign Women to become properly "feminized," which is to say, sexually liberated. Frank remarks that "Israel is chosen for that because no people pursue the Maiden as the Israelites do, and in the end, She will lead them" (§169). The male hero acts as masculine sexual agent in order to be transformed into a feminine sexual agent, which is to say, an embodied one. Israel pursues the Maiden so that she may lead them.

The Liberation of the "Feminine"

Finally, the liberation of sexuality is understood as the liberation of the Maiden, and thus the feminine more generally, as part of the messianic redemption. In §2183—perhaps drawing on Zohar 3:83b—Frank says that the "concealment" of Eve, hidden behind veils of modesty and subjugation, was due to Adam's sin, which is to be rectified through the liberation of the "feminine" principle of sensuality.[75] Sexual shame has caused this concealment; sexual freedom will end it. Frank here is likely building on the Sabbatean emphasis on liberating women from the "curse of Eve," which includes not only the pain of childbirth but also the subjugation to men in general.[76] Both women's liberation and sexual liberation are part of the essence of the messianic age, and in particular the repair of the primordial, Edenic sin.

It is also possible that Frank is drawing on the gendered Sabbatean/Kabbalistic messianism described by Elliot Wolfson. Examining several Lurianic and Sabbatean sources, Wolfson notes that the "crowning" of the messiah should be understood in terms of circumcision, the inscription of the "feminine" onto the phallus.[77] "In the messianic period," Wolfson writes, "the feminine rises from the submissive position characteristic of the state of exile to her restoration in the realm of emanation."[78] As usual, we do not find in Frank the level of conceptual sophistication found in the Lurianic texts Wolfson adduces. Yet the general move is similar: The messianic period will

[75] See Lenowitz, "Me'ayin yavo 'ezri?," 285.
[76] Rapoport-Albert, *Women and the Messianic Heresy*, 258–60.
[77] Wolfson, "Engenderment," 214–23; Michaelson, "Kabbalah and Queer Theology," 50–57.
[78] Wolfson, "Engenderment," 241.

be the time of feminine liberation and sexual liberation, with feminine dominance over the masculine. As Fagenblat put it, "if the Kabbalistic dogma of divine bisexuality was for the most part used to reinforce gender inequality and exclusion, in messianic utopian circles it motivated an egalitarian agenda driven by these very theological considerations."[79]

What did this mean in practice? Is it to be understood as an early form of women's liberation (not uniquely early, given that Mary Wollstonecraft's *Vindication of the Rights of Woman* appeared in 1792, and ZSP was dictated in 1784 and 1789–1790), or is that too much to ascribe to Frank? On the one hand, there was indeed some actual liberation of women in the Sabbatean and Frankist worlds, beginning with Sabbetai's own pronouncement, perhaps at the urging of Sarah Ashkenazi, that the liberation of women would be part of the messianic age, and his then-radical act of calling women up to the Torah.[80] Women led Sabbatean communities and participated in ritual in ways that would not appear in mainstream Judaism for three hundred years. At first, women within heretical circles primarily acted as ecstatic prophets, speaking in tongues, uttering passages from the Zohar when they did not even know a word of Hebrew (let alone Aramaic), practicing divination, and so on. (This may have evolved under the influence of from Bektashi Sufism in the Ottoman empire, which likewise regarded women as specially attuned to the Divine spirit.[81]) But women's roles gradually expanded beyond that. According to Rapoport-Albert,

> women continued to be drawn to the [Sabbatean] sectarian fellowships not only as messianic prophetesses . . . but also as full-fledged members in their own right, personally and even prominently engaged in all the fellowships' activities alongside or together with the men.[82]

Chaya Shorr is mentioned, for example, as a leading Sabbatean figure in her own right. In the Frankist inner circle, women participated in armed guards, unheard of in its day. And Eve Frank's dreams and visions, particularly in the latter days of the movement, were accorded respect and situated within the Sabbatean framework of prophecy and messianic theology.[83] Frankist sexual

---

[79] Fagenblat, "Frankism," 40.
[80] See Scholem, *Sabbatai Ṣevi*, 403–5; Rapoport-Albert, *Women and the Messianic Heresy*, 15–56, 80–107. On women in Frankist communities, see Rapoport-Albert, *Women and the Messianic Heresy*, 157–236.
[81] See Fagenblat, "Frankism," 72.
[82] Rapoport-Albert, *Women and the Messianic Heresy*, 107.
[83] Ibid., 171–74.

liberation is not only a liberation of the symbolic feminine; it included the actual liberation of actual women.

On the other hand, Frank was no feminist. First, Frank makes numerous misogynistic statements, such as §561, in which Frank states, "nothing can be done with a woman because a woman brought death to this world, whereas I want to lead and guide to eternal life on earth." §93 rehashes the familiar trope of women being devious while men are more direct; that dictum criticizes Jacob for following Rebecca's "woman's advice" of engaging in a "scheme." Second, even when Frank praises sexuality, he adopts the long-standing misogynistic and essentialist equation of the feminine with the sexual and with the body; he just valorizes the sexual, and thus the "feminine."[84] This is a very old patriarchal association, found in classical Greek thought, the Talmud, the New Testament, Maimonides, and many other sources, and usually it is deployed as part of a program of the denigration and suppression of women.[85] A similar ambivalence occurs in the late Frankist text "Something for the Female Sex," most likely written by the Prague Frankist Löw Enoch Hönig Von Hönigsberg. As Ada Rapoport-Albert has shown, this unusual text seeks the liberation of women's sensual, sexual natures from "shame," "modesty," or "captivity" (all synonyms) as part of an emancipatory redemption.[86] In that text, sexuality, gendered feminine, is troped as a source of "creative vitality" with transformative power. In Rapoport-Albert's characterization of this idea,

> the unleashed innate sensuality of the females will in turn revitalize the sensuality of the males, which has been dormant or reduced to base lust in the "corrupt nature" of this world, but is bound to revert to the full glory of its true nature at the time of the Redemption.[87]

This is liberation, but only of a narrowly, essentialistically, and problematically defined category of women.

Third, the women in Frank's texts, from the princesses of the tales to the Maiden herself, are primarily the objects of Frank's pursuit, and often described in primarily physical terms. The princess is always beautiful and

---

[84] Rapoport-Albert and Hamann, "Something for the Female Sex," 100–102; Maciejko, "Development," 242.

[85] See Rapoport-Albert, *Women and the Messianic Heresy*, 85; Boyarin, *Carnal Israel*, 58–60.

[86] Rapoport-Albert and Hamann, "Something for the Female Sex," 102–3; Fagenblat, "Frankism," 41–43.

[87] Rapoport-Albert and Hamann, "Something for the Female Sex," 102.

desirable—she is a sexual object, something to be "won." The princesses do have some power: the power to accept or refuse suitors and sometimes a prophetic ability to discern who is worthy. Still, they are generally receptive figures. For example, in §739, the princess recognizes the nobility of the incognito prince, but the prince carries the action of the story. In §551, the Maiden gives a prince magical objects to test his fitness; she tests him, but again he performs the actions. In §545, a prince falls in love with a princess, even though she disguises herself as a dark gypsy dancer; here, the princess dons the disguise on her own (perhaps a metaphor for the Maiden disguised as the "Mother from the Unholy Side") but primarily exists as something to be unmasked by Frank. There are some counterexamples; in §1142, the princess disguises herself as a prince and proves to be a valiant hero. But in general, the power of these feminine figures is primarily to test and admit worthy men.

Finally, the evidence is mixed as to whether the women in the Frankist company had the opportunity to resist Frank's orders. As we observed earlier, *RA* §104 records the fourteen Sisters trying to choose among themselves who would perform a sexual ritual with Frank, and being unable to do so: "When the lord strongly urged them, they discussed amongst themselves and chose [the wife of] Henryk Wołowski, but Ewa Jezierańska did not consent to that, wanting to be chosen herself." In the same section, Frank's wife Hannah also sought to participate in the ritual, though Frank refused her. And yet, when in *RA* §74, Frank orders various male disciples to have sex with one another's wives, neither the men's nor the women's responses are recorded. To whatever extent *RA* can be trusted as a source, it documents some instances when consent was essential and other instances when consent was not mentioned at all.

Is this liberation then a kind of feminism? Only in certain respects. Frank presented a female messiah, embodying sexuality and vitality, as the doorway to worldly redemption and eternal life. The communities around him empowered women to an extent without precedent in Jewish history. Yet Frank also essentialized women in a way redolent of two millennia of patriarchal discourse, instrumentalized women's liberation as ultimately for the benefit of men, and coerced the women and men in his community into sexual activity. Perhaps Frank is not the villain contemporary scholarship has depicted, but he is not a hero either. Such a conclusion is consonant with our overall assessment of Frankist sexual praxis. Throughout, this chapter has sought to show that Frankist sexual antinomianism is not reducible to mere pleasure-seeking or lascivious conduct but has several specific theological meanings within the context of Frankist texts and teachings. This is not, however, to absolve Frank of culpability for the physical and emotional abuse of his followers or to hold Frank up as some sort of paragon of sexual liberation. Frank's discourses on sexuality are obviously vulgar and replicate the patriarchal power dynamics from the same society he seeks to undermine. His coercion, abuse, and manipulation of his followers perhaps deserves the condemnation that has been heaped upon him, albeit for mistaken reasons. Simply because Frankist sexual antinomianism is theologically grounded does not mean it is ethically defensible—no more or less than conservative sexual repression, likewise grounded in theology.

In any case, the immediate response to Sabbateanism-Frankism was to reject all of the proto-feminist aspects of the movement. In a passage partially quoted in the Introduction, Rapoport-Albert argues that the leadership of women was, for Sabbateanism's critics, a critical aspect of the movement's reputation for licentiousness:

> For the Sabbatean heretics had left behind a profound dread above all of the breached halachic boundaries of sexual propriety. The sexual depravity imputed to their women was inextricably linked to their full engagement with the failed messianic project. It was an untimely eruption of female spirituality—a powerful force prematurely unleashed which was now to be stowed away, kept out of sight, and securely contained until the appointed time for its discharge, which was not to be until some unknown point in the distant messianic future.[88]

Traditional rabbinic communities blamed this short experiment in women's leadership for the reputed licentiousness of the Sabbatean and Frankist movements, and in response extinguished most of the ways in which women could exercise religious leadership, such as prophecy (with only isolated exceptions such as the Maid of Ludmir). They variously associated women with materiality, thus subjugating both, or symbologized or spiritualized the feminine into the Shechinah, a safer partner for men's prayerful ecstasy and sexual intercourse.[89]

---

[88] Rapoport-Albert, *Women and the Messianic Heresy*, 296.
[89] Ibid., 265–75. See also Idel, *Kabbalah and Eros*, 202.

Still, despite its rejection by history, and despite its deep inadequacy, it is interesting to reflect on the possibility of how Frankist liberated sexuality (and even, perhaps, quasi-feminism) might be adumbrated by more contemporary and liberating voices, and so I conclude this chapter with a brief remark along those lines. After all, Frank's principled rejection of sexual repression anticipates by more than a century the modern and postmodern critiques of those same ethical norms, both for the potential-thwarting reasons that Frank alludes to and because of all their attendant marginalizations of women, queer people, and others. Hopefully, one would not seek to replace traditional sexual morality with Frankist sexual amorality, but Frank's critiques of the former may be prescient even if his replacement for it was not. More specifically, Frank's difference-feminism, which associates femininity with long-repressed sensuality, has been replicated (for all its problematic essentialisms) by several iterations of third-wave feminism, including ecofeminism, as well by the New Age spiritual movements described in chapter 8. Perhaps Frank's insistence on the positive value of sexual expression may, in the potent metaphor of Adrienne Rich, be retrieved from the wreck of his failed messianic enterprise.[90] Audre Lorde, the pioneering feminist, queer, Black scholar-activist, describes in her landmark essay "The Uses of the Erotic: The Erotic as Power" a connection between liberated sexuality on the one hand and liberated personhood on the other. For Lorde, as in a very different way for Frank, the liberation of the erotic has potential for the liberation of the human (and especially female) subject more broadly. She writes:

> The erotic is a resource within each of us . . . firmly rooted in the power of our unexpressed or unrecognized feeling. In order to perpetuate itself, every oppression must corrupt or distort those various sources of power within the culture of the oppressed that can provide energy for change. For women, this has meant a suppression of the erotic as a considered source of power and information within our lives. . . . But the erotic offers a well of replenishing and provocative force to the woman who does not fear its revelation, nor succumb to the belief that sensation is enough. . . . The erotic is a measure between our sense of self and the chaos of our strongest feelings. It is an internal sense of satisfaction to which, once we have experienced it, we know we can aspire. For having experienced the fullness of this depth of

---

[90] Rich, *Diving into the Wreck*.

feeling and recognizing its power, in honor and self-respect we can require no less of ourselves.[91]

Frank's myth of the redemption of the Maiden is not a Lordean liberation of the feminine erotic—but it did, in a way, prefigure it. Within its many limitations, Frankist sexual antinomianism argued for the liberation of sexuality and materiality, and an enaction of that liberation. In the normative religion of Frank's time, as in our own, material has been subordinated to spiritual, female to male, sexual to religious. Frankist sexual antinomianism embodies the inversion of these priorities. His practice is the recorporealization of that which religion sublimates into spirit.

---

[91] Lorde, "The Use of the Erotic," 75–76.

6
"We don't need the books of Kabbalah"
Rejecting Kabbalah and Sabbateanism

Having completed our analysis of four major themes of *ZSP*—antinomianism, materiality, the quest for immortality, and sexuality—we turn in the final three chapters to situate Frankism in historical and phenomenological contexts. Taken together, these three chapters argue for a reassessment of the place of Frank in Jewish and European religious history.

First, in this chapter, I will address, and largely refute, the scholarly conception of Frank as a Sabbatean, Kabbalistic messiah. As much as Frankism is historically continuous with Sabbateanism, Frank rejected Sabbatean theology and the Kabbalistic foundations upon which it was built. Nor did Frank claim the title of messiah in any usual sense; while in the early phases of the Frankist career, he hoped to head an autonomous region within Poland, and was seen as some sort of redeeming figure, the Frank of *ZSP* is more of an alchemist, at most the harbinger of a messiah or the herald of an apocalyptic age. There is no theurgical or Kabbalistic significance to Frank's violation of the law; rather, the law is to be disobeyed because it is meaningless, ineffectual, and contrary to human fulfillment. The goal of the Frankist quest is not a Sabbatean messianism, nor a Kabbalistic *tikkun*, but the Frankist company's transformation into semi-immortal beings who will ride in gilded chariots, own huge mansions, and eat gourmet meals. This is not "redemption through sin" in a Sabbatean mode but transcendence of the limitations of human mortality by transgressing the conventional religion that pointlessly restrains human potential.

Next, in chapter 7, I will situate the Frankism of *ZSP* in the context of Western esotericism. Philosophically, the magical materialism and quasi-gnosticism typical of eighteenth-century Western esotericism is at the center of Frank's theological worldview, and historical sources confirm several touch-points between the Frankist court and contemporary esoteric circles. Moreover, as we will see, it is no coincidence that the Frankist court was, on the one hand, enthralled by preposterous myths of magic and sorcery, and, on the other, active in revolutionary politics in Austria, France, and elsewhere. Perhaps shockingly, some of the most outrageously antisemitic claims of a "Jewish-Masonic conspiracy" behind the French Revolution have a slender basis in fact, centered on the Frankist court in general and Moses Dobruschka, memorably rendered in a biographical essay by Scholem, in particular.[1] Finally, in chapter 8, I will explore how Frankism's juxtaposition of myth and secularity, as well as its extraction of messianic 'spirituality' from its religious container, prefigured certain aspects of the Haskalah, liberal Judaism, Zionism, Hasidism, and New Age Judaism.

Displacing Sabbateanism

Scholem once stated that Sabbateanism and Frankism form "a single continuous development which retained its identity in the eyes of its adherents"[2] and that "there is no basic difference between Sabbateanism and Frankism."[3] In accord with scholars including Maciejko and Shinichi Yamamoto, I will propose here that while the first sentence is true historically, the second one is not. Although it ultimately failed to do so, Frankism as explicated in ZSP sought to displace Sabbateanism, not continue it.[4]

Historically, Frank came out of the Sabbatean movement, and many of his followers remained part of it and understood Frank in its context. Following his death, many of those still within the Jewish community returned to it; indeed, it is not known whether the wider communities in Prague and Warsaw even knew of ZSP until long after Frank's death.[5]

---

[1] Scholem, "The Career of a Frankist."
[2] Scholem, *Messianic Idea*, 84.
[3] Ibid., 355, n.4.
[4] When Scholem wrote "Redemption from Sin," he was not yet familiar with ZSP. As discussed in the Appendix, I am inclined to agree with Maciejko that "Redemption through Sin" is "unquestionably the most influential, arguably the most original, and ... also the most misleading interpretation of Frankism." Maciejko, "Development," 198. See also Yamamoto, "The Last Step."
[5] It seems likely that ZSP was known to the Prague Frankist elites, though not widely. First, Löw Enoch Hönig von Hönigsberg, the probable author of "Something for the Female Sex," discussed in chapter 5, cites the "words of the holy father" on numerous occasions, a likely reference to ZSP in some form. Rapoport-Albert and Hamann, "Something for the Female Sex," 131. And Scholem notes that von Hönigsberg "was several times in Offenbach." Scholem, "A Frankist Document," 788. Second, one would also presume that Jonas Wehle, a Prague Frankist who spent time in Offenbach and was taught "the mysteries of the Frankist esoteric doctrine," would have been acquainted at least partially with ZSP. These references suggest to me that at least some parts of ZSP were known to Wehle and von Hönigsberg at least.

On the contrary, after Frank's death in 1794, the Frankist court in Offenbach and the Frankist community in Prague reverted to the mainstream of Sabbateanism, incorporating Frank into the very system he sought to displace,[6] and as time went by, Frank indeed became seen as one more in a line of Sabbatean leaders. (Interestingly, a similar pattern took place within Sabbateanism itself, where Nathan of Gaza incorporated Sabbetai Zevi into Lurianic Kabbalistic frames absent from Zevi's own teaching, and set aside the innovations and self-conceptions that may have been derived from Zevi's own mystical experiences.[7]) Thus, Scholem may be correct that Frankism is "continuous" with Sabbatean in a very broad sense, since, as Elior says in the context of Hasidism's relationship to Sabbateanism, assertions of "continuity" may

> not refer to direct theological continuity, nor do they mean to establish a causal connection between the phenomena . . . [b]ut rather, these remarks concern the need to evaluate the meaning of the Hasidic phenomenon, which grew up contiguously in time and place with controversial manifestations of Sabbateanism, in light of the continuity of Kabbalistic thought with its historical manifestations, on the one hand, and in the light of the essential change which took place in spiritual and social reality in the wake of the Sabbatean crisis, on the other.[8]

In the stronger sense of "continuous," however, there are major thematic and theological discontinuities between Sabbateanism and the Frankism of *ZSP*. Here, we will explore differences in theology, language, and worldview.

First, let us consider theology. Whereas for Sabbatean theology, transgression enacts the messianic redemption (ontologically and psychologically), in Frankist theology, transgression is an affirmation of the material and this-worldly as against otherworldly religion. Sabbatean antinomianism is a transcendence of the apparent; Frankism is an embrace of it. Sabbatean antinomianism recognizes the theurgical power of the *mitzvot*, whereas Frankist antinomianism ridicules it. Frank explicitly rejects the Kabbalistic and Sabbatean emphases on faith in unseen powers. In §527, Frank rebukes his Sabbatean teacher Rabbi Mordechai for believing a particular secret of

---

[6] Maciejko, *Mixed Multitude*, 247.
[7] Sisman, *Burden of Silence*, 39–42, 123–24; Elqayam, "Sabbetai Zevi's Holy Zohar"; Idel, "One from a Town and Two from a Clan"; Idel, *Messianic Mystics*, 184–85.
[8] Elior, "Hasidism: Historical Continuity and Spiritual Change," 310.

Kabbalah, mocking him as Elijah mocks the prophets of Baal (1 Kings 18:26–28), which is notably one of the rare biblical cases in which empirical evidence is provided for God.

Of Scholem's five characteristics of Sabbatean theology, only one holds true for Frankism. Scholem enumerated those characteristics as:

1. The belief in the necessary apostasy of the messiah and in the sacramental nature of the descent into the realm of the *kelipot*. (Not present in Frank. Frank does not claim he is the messiah; the Maiden is. And he never describes his apostasy in terms of the *kelipot*.)
2. The belief that the "believer" must not appear to be as he really is. (Present in Frankism, though also contradicted by Frank's exhortations to "openness.")
3. The belief that the Torah of *Atzilut* must be observed through the violation of the Torah of *Beriah*.[9] (Not found anywhere in the Frankist corpus. As discussed in chapter 2, in the Frankist schema, the law is cast aside in favor not of a new, spiritual Torah but of the pursuit of power and immortality. Sabbetai Zevi could abrogate the Torah because the Messiah's soul is higher than that of Moses; Frank abrogates the law because he believes it to be nonsense.[10])
4. The belief that the First Cause and the God of Israel are not the same, the former being the God of rational philosophy, the latter the God of religion. (Not present in Frank.)
5. The belief in three hypostases of the Godhead, all of which have been or will be incarnated in human form.[11] (Not present in *ZSP* but present in earlier Frankism. There is no evidence to connect the Sabbatean "three knots of faith" with the Frankist "Good God," "Big Brother," and "Virgin," as Scholem hypothesized,[12] although Maciejko has shown that a syncretic form of Sabbatean trinitarianism does appear in early

---

[9] Scholem, *Sabbatai Ṣevi*, 319–24. See also Maciejko, *Mixed Multitude*, 14. As discussed in chapter 2, this doctrine is itself rooted in the Raya Mehemna, which said that in the messianic days, the nonlegalistic Torah of the Tree of Life would replace the legalistic Torah of the Tree of Knowledge of Good and Evil. See Scholem, *Sabbatai Ṣevi*, 11–12; Elior, "Jacob Frank," 487–94; Scholem, *Messianic Idea*, 176–78.

[10] See Idel, *Messianic Mystics*, 191.

[11] Scholem, *Messianic Idea*, 126. The last belief combines, in Frank and perhaps in Cardoso, Christian trinitarianism with Sabbatean Kabbalistic reading of the Zohar's "three knots of faith," itself a combination of two different Zoharic notions, the *telat dragei dimehemnuta* equivalent to *hesed*, *gevurah*, and *tiferet*, and the three *partsufim*. See Liebes, "On a Jewish-Christian Sect," 221–25.

[12] Scholem, *Messianic Idea*, 134.

Frankism[13] and that the Frankists were familiar with Abraham Miguel Cardozo's trinitarianism, which may itself have been drawn from Christian sources.[14])

In sum, only one of these five theological tenets is clearly present in *ZSP*, one is present in earlier Frankist sources, and several of them are explicitly rejected.

Second is the matter of language. Nowhere does *ZSP* make use of Sabbatean terminology such as the distinction between the "light that includes thought" ('*or sheyesh bo machshavah*) and the "light without thought" ('*or she'ein bo machshavah*), or "the depth of the abyss" (*nikbat tehom rabah*) and "the redemption of the sparks" (*ge'ulat nitzotzot*). Indeed, not only the words are absent, but also their cosmology, their theology, even their tone.[15] Even those few times in which Frank does make use of Sabbatean themes, he does so to displace and transform their meanings. For example, the metaphor that Scholem says "conveys the whole of sectarian Sabbatean psychology in a nutshell" is that "just as a grain of wheat must rot in the earth before it can sprout, so the deeds of the 'believers' must be truly 'rotten' before they can germinate the redemption."[16] Yet when Frank himself quotes that Sabbatean metaphor, in *ZSP* §2123, he rereads it in terms of Frank's own aging and physical suffering: "As you know the grain will not blossom forth until it has completely rotted. . . . Similarly, I must take upon myself all the suffering and beatings such that I will have no strength. I must continue to suffer until all the beatings and pains will be experienced by me. Only then will the good God renew and make young my years." Not "rotten" sinful practices germinating into redemption—rather, Frank being beaten.

Third, Frank many times rejects the worldview of Sabbateanism both in general and in particulars. Frank regards his forebears as failures, ridiculing them for not achieving their goals, for not being masculine enough, and for not undertaking a mission like his own. In §2124, Frank says:

---

[13] For example, Frankist documents which discussed the trinity do so in Sabbatean Kabbalistic terms (e.g., using the term *oblicza*, "face," as a translation of *partzuf*) rather than Christian ones (usually *osoba*, equivalent to the Latin *persona*). Maciejko, "Christian Elements," 19, 21–25. See Liebes, "On a Jewish-Christian Sect," 221–25.

[14] Maciejko, "Christian Elements," at 21–25. Maciejko also notes the irony that arguments once used against Cardoso that he was dressing Christian doctrine in Jewish clothing were now used, by the anti-Frankist side, to show that Frankism was dressing Jewish/Kabbalistic doctrine in Christian clothing.

[15] Elior, *Jewish Mysticism*, 6.

[16] Scholem, *Messianic Idea*, 116.

It is said among you that the First[17] said: "When oil is poured from one vessel to another" et cetera. But that is false, because he was not beloved of the nations. But when my name becomes revealed in the world, it will be seen. Then you will see yourselves how I will be loved by all the nations and all will bow before me.

Consistent with the materialist worldview we discussed in chapter 3, if the messiah doesn't actually achieve worldly redemption, he has failed. This materialism upends the basic notion of Sabbateanism, which is faith in the unseen (the Sabbateans, after all, called themselves *ma'aminim*: believers),[18] with an insistence on the visible, the seen. In §48 Frank questions an article of Sabbatean faith, namely that Baruchiah died so that he could experience death. Frank asks why, if that is so he didn't also experience being a king over other people. "I don't believe it," Frank states bluntly.

Frank frequently disregards Sabbatean mystical motifs in favor of simpler ones. An excellent example of this is Frank's use of the dualities of low/high, left/right, and shell/kernel, particularly in discussing the qualities of good and evil. At first, Frank's language may seem similar to that of Sabbateanism. God will lead the world not with the wise but with the lowest (§§34, 1097, 1179). What is sought is not beautiful but ugly (§§71). The Brethren's low state mirrors that of Adam's after the Fall (§§361, 542). But Frank says that all this is temporary. Soon, the bitter will become sweet (§§162, 508, 860). Soon the powerful will be overthrown by the powerless (§367). The present darkness is just so that light can be revealed (§444). The daughter of Zion will rise from the dust (§776). In these statements, however, the good does not lie hidden within the evil like the sparks of God hidden within Islam, or forbidden acts, or some other realm of "darkness." Rather, the evil is simply transcended. Likewise, Frank states dozens of times that the herb of death is before the herb of life: the good lies beyond, not within, the evil (§§76, 83, 172, 357, 538, 685, 1290). Evil is an obstacle in the path, not the residence of the reward. In §684, Frank goes into some detail about goodness hidden in bitterness—but never makes explicit use of the Kabbalistic formulation of it:

---

[17] I.e., Sabbatai Zevi. According to Doktór, the earliest known editions of ZSP contain the names Sabbetai Zevi and Baruchiah Russo. These were subsequently censored and rendered as "The First" and "The Second." Doktór, *Księga Słów Pańskich*, vol. 2, 157.

[18] Scholem, *Sabbetai Sevi*, 283–84. See also Van der Haven, *From Lowly Metaphor*, 9.

At times, even though something appears to be good, it may be ugly inside; and at other times, it may be ugly on the outside, and full of love and goodness on the inside. For anything good and valuable is hidden inside something evil and ugly so that what is good cannot be recognized by just anyone, as it is clearly written: God hid their light from the godless. A sign of this are beautiful and precious roses. They always grow among thorns, so that whoever wants to pick them always gets pricked.

The reason for the good being hidden in evil has nothing to do with sparks, cosmology, or creation. It has to do with reserving the good for the elite few who know the secret. Given Frank's reference to the Zohar in this very dictum and what we know of his biography, he surely would have been familiar with the Kabbalistic version of this ontology. He chooses not to use it, returning to a more conventional map of good and evil.

Frank's conception of redemption is similar. In §126, Frank states, "Ever since the time of Adam the world has been falling and thereby it is constantly breaking so that it can be built anew." Here again, it is not that sparks within the zone of evil are uplifted; rather, the world falls apart and then is built again. Kabbalistic doctrines that were important in the Sabbatean discussion of these themes are absent in these discussions.[19] His cosmology is different. As Frank says in §542:

the Jews are in great contempt and disdain among all nations, and the *ma'aminim* are disdained even more than the Jews are. And ever since the sin of Adam, the world has been falling lower and lower, and will continue to do so until it reaches the place that is vile and most despicable of all. When you reach this last place where there is nothing more despicable, only then will you start to rise up with no end. And that is the ladder that Jacob saw, and which God's angels climbed up and down, but he himself has not yet climbed. But when he starts to climb up, he will never again climb down.

This is less a Sabbatean "descent for the sake of ascent"[20] than a conventional promise that who is last now will later be first, and a millennial prophecy

---

[19] See, e.g., the homily by Nehemiah Hayon quoted in "Redemption through Sin," which describes "filling the *kelipah* with holiness," which "rais[es] up many sparks from the *kelipah*." Scholem, *Messianic Idea*, 119–20. Such a formulation is not found in ZSP.

[20] See Elior, *Jacob Frank*, 492–500. The doctrine predates Sabbateanism; see Zohar 2:244a–45a.

that the world falls to the lowest point before redemption. The entire world is falling, not just the messianic hero or messianic sect; the millennial narrative here is more like contemporary Christian premillennialism than Sabbatean messianism. And the redemptive turn will take place not because of messianic activity, but simply because the world cannot fall any lower.

This pattern repeats in numerous dicta. In §514, the Brethren being in the dark is described as a temporary condition, again not because of a heroic descent for the sake of ascent, but because they made a mistake. In §78, he says, "Before the herb of life there appears the herb of death. But there is no death there; only in people's eyes does it seem as though there is death." This, too, suggests a temporal aspect: death lies before the "herb of life" but it is only a temporary appearance, not reality. In §522, Frank's debased state is only a temporary one—soon he will have many followers. §1116 states,

> It is written: *A star will step forth from Jacob.* Since the beginning of time, this star has followed its practice of going lower and lower. All things despised and vile, all of it is in the power of this star. And if you do not enter the star, you cannot attain anything; for it is the gate. I wanted to lead you into this star, in which I am myself. You pulled yourselves out of this star, which is why this road is hard for you. Therefore, it is my desire to lead you into the gate, and when the time has come for the star to ascend, it will never cease to ascend, and will forever keep ascending with no end.

Once more, the hero enters the fallen star not to uplift the sparks of divinity found there. Rather, as Frank says many times, redemption is not up to individual effort—the star will rise "when the time has come for the star to ascend."

As with descent and ascent, so too with left and right.[21] Over and over again, Frank abjures the Brethren to abandon the left and come to the right: "Be among the chosen. Leave Left behind completely" (§450); "All of your deeds strengthened the left over the right. However, the right should always be strengthened over the left, for no one can lift the left, except God

---

[21] On the dynamic of the evil "left side" and its integration within the "right side," see Berman, *Divine and Demonic*; Wolfson, "Left Contained in the Right."

Himself." (§690; see also §§524, 573, 821, 869, 941, 969) This is a departure from the Sabbatean myth and an embrace of more conventional symbolism that the right must be preferred to left. Frank rejects the idea that the hero can travel into the realm of evil and rescue it, instead saying that only God can "lift the left." In §573, Frank says:

> Even if it is necessary to turn left, it should only be done by the one who can smash [it] and strengthen the right hand into the left. Even though I will pull you out of the left side, since you fell, in the right side there is also a left side.

The first sentence rejects the Sabbatean justification for "going to the left" and replaces it with a more conventional one: to smash it and strengthen the right. Likewise the first half of the second sentence, which underscores the point: that the fallenness onto the left side is only a temporary failure, not a cosmological/heroic mission. The second clause of the second sentence complicates matters, since "in the right side there is also a left side" may refer to the Sabbatean principle that evil exists even in the godhead, but overall §573 says that one goes to the left to smash it, not to uplift what is there. On the other hand, in §447, Frank states:

> Therefore, always make sure that you have attachment to the true God and to myself. My endeavor is, and has been, to lead all of you to the right, but you leaned towards the left. What we should do, however, is to make left part of right.

Here, Frank does seem to be making use of the Kabbalistic concept that, ultimately, the left should be reintegrated into the right, the feminine reintegrated into the "masculine androgyne," and evil reintegrated into the good. And in §730, Frank says,

> You fell to the left. It is true that the left is grand and valuable; but it is also two-sided; one is before the fruit, the other is good.

In these dicta, Frank seems to be attempting to reconcile his own more left/right cosmology with the Sabbatean one, essentially saying the left doesn't mean the left and ultimately the followers must keep to the right—in other words, to follow him.

Abandoning Messianism

A second common association with Frank is that he was a false messiah. As with Sabbateanism, this association began with the Frankists themselves. In Moses Porges's memoir, Frank was clearly regarded, in 1794 at least, as the messiah.[22] And the "Red Letters," circulated in 1800, prophesy an imminent apocalyptic conflict that will usher in the messianic age, presumably with the eight-years-deceased Frank at its head.

But the complete picture is more complicated. At various stages of his career, Frank sought an autonomous territory for his sect, wealth and power, and the secret of immortality, which he would learn from his supernatural counterpart, a figure known as the Big Brother. He did sometimes promise that a massive war was coming and that Christianity would be overthrown. And in ZSP, Frank himself makes numerous, often outrageous claims about his divine mission. He is God's chosen messenger, he foretells the imminent apocalypse, he will succeed where Sabbetai Zevi failed. Is this messianism, let alone Jewish messianism? Nowhere does Frank seek the restoration of Jewish autonomy in the Land of Israel, or promise a cosmic *tikkun*, or do any of the things Jewish messiahs are supposed to do.[23] Now, some of these changes in the messianic role were already present in Sabbateanism, which, in Yehuda Liebes's words was "not concerned with the redemption of the people but rather with the redemption of religion and faith, the redemption of God, and the redemption of the Messiah."[24] But Frank is more explicit. He never refers to himself as a messiah in ZSP,[25] and insists that the messiah would be a woman: perhaps the Maiden incarnated as Eve Frank, or in some other form. For example, in §639, Frank goes away on a quest and returns adorned with rainbow lights that all can see. The world goes into tumult, and then the messiah arrives. And §1117 indicates that Frank will crown the messiah, who will be the Maiden. At most, Frank is John the Baptist to the Maiden's Jesus—or perhaps *Mashiach ben Yosef* rather than *Mashiach ben David*. But he does not use these terms in ZSP.

Rather than "messianism," a more useful term for understanding Frankism is "millennialism." Originally, "millennialism" took its name from the Christian belief that Christ will return to Earth and rule for one thousand

---

[22] See Porges, *Memoirs*; Duker, "Frankism as a Movement," 133.
[23] See Goldish, "Jacob Frank's Innovations," 25–27.
[24] Liebes, *Studies in Jewish Myth and Messianism*, 99.
[25] See Maciejko, *Mixed Multitude*, 167, 247.

years; indeed, a defining religious-political question in the contemporary United States is whether Christ will arrive after the world has been redeemed ("postmillennialism," which necessitates worldly action to bring redemption about) or before ("premillennialism," in which, on the contrary, the world will fall to its lowest ebb before Christ redeems it; this latter view is ascendant among American Evangelicals). In scholarly discourse, though, the term has a broader meaning, referring, in Richard Landes's words, to "the belief that at some point in the future the world that we live in will be radically transformed into one of perfection—of peace, justice, fellowship, and plenty."[26] Millennialism thus includes not just traditional messianism but a variety of forms of secular "perfectionist thinking"—Landes discusses Marxism and radical Islamism as species of millennialism, for example.[27] Millennialism is not a view of heaven or the afterlife, however; it is a this-worldly affair, promising, for example, that "the just will live free in this world."[28] Millennialism may be either hierarchical or demotic in nature; it may promise one nation/God/leader triumphing over all others (Christian millennialism, Nazism) or, on the contrary, that people will be transformed such that they will live without the need for a ruler at all (Marxism, Blake's utopian vision, the pop idealism of the Sixties).[29] Finally, and recalling the analysis of Festinger in chapter 4, Landes notes that millennialisms frequently lead to a set of "apocalyptic expectations," namely, that

> the inspired "prophet"; the receptive community that, in the expectation of an imminent and radical transformation of the world, "burns bridges" to the "normal" future and "goes for broke"; the disastrous results of the error; and the retrospective and disapproving voice of the narrator writing after the failure of the expectations.[30]

Does the Frankism of *ZSP* fit this definition? Partially, though not entirely. Often, Frank prophesizes that a "radical transformation of the world" is about to take place, a prophecy that appears in 156 dicta. For example, in §367, Frank states, "when the dawn rises and the morning of Abraham comes, no power will remain in the hands of those who wield it now." In

---

[26] Landes, *Heaven on Earth*, 20. See also Popkin, "Introduction."
[27] Landes, *Heaven on Earth*, 318–52, 421–66.
[28] Ibid., 13.
[29] Ibid., 23–27.
[30] Ibid., 4.

§429, the partition of Poland is a sign of this prophecy coming true. Because of Poland's mythological status as Edom, its partition was both a political upheaval of the sort that frequently leads to apocalyptic speculation, and a religious revolution. In §1097, the immediacy of the prophecy is striking: "Truly I tell you that we can lift up one more thing so that we can come to power and life in four weeks." §861 indicates that the timeline for redemption is twenty-five years of wandering, and a year and a half of cleansing. The years 1759–1784 are the twenty-five years of wandering, meaning the years of "cleansing" (i.e., war and suffering) was to begin imminently. Many dicta are purely subjunctive, with Frank bemoaning what would have happened had the Brethren been faithful. To take one of many examples, in §1301, Frank states, "Had you been in wholeness, I would've been the king of Poland, and you would have been twelve rich lords." (§384 contains the same conditional prediction.)

In other dicta, however, ZSP focuses on the transformation of the Brethren into superhuman beings. In these texts, the Frankists themselves will be given all that they desire—strength, wealth, sensual pleasures—but it is not clear whether the world itself will be transformed. Other prophecies have a mixture of elements. In §177 and §194, for example, Frank reveals his plan for a new religion, headquartered in Częstochowa (§177). Frank says that the twelve male disciples would have resided in twelve different countries, outwardly appearing as converts but secretly remaining faithful to Frank and periodically coming to Częstochowa, where they would have to fast for three days and recite a prayer to the Portrait of the Black Virgin, stand waiting for six hours without moving, and only then gain admission to see Frank and the magical "thing" he would reveal to them. The result of this arduous and ascetic practice, Frank says, "would have been" that the Maiden would impart power and speak directly to the twelve, as she does with Frank. In this prophecy, Frank combines several different millennial themes. It is somewhat historical in nature, although it is not clear how much the world order is supposed to change, unlike in some of Frank's predictions of imminent violence and chaos. Frank is in charge of Częstochowa, but at least twelve countries have retained their existing religious structures, which is why the disciples must appear to adopt them. Contrast that with the messianism of contemporary Sabbateans, who interpreted, for example, the 1781–1783 clashes between the Ottoman Empire and the Hapsburg Empire as evidence that Islam was soon to be overthrown and Sabbetai Zevi to return as messiah,[31] prophecies echoed in Frank's own statement that 1783 was the beginning of the "last days" (§75). Nor is it clear what messianic role the Maiden plays in this prophecy. She is incarnated in and speaks through the Portrait (not, incidentally, Eve Frank), but Frank retains his special role as her gatekeeper, and she is not revealed for all the world to see. And unlike in some other prophecies, here there is no suggestion that the Brethren have transformed into immortal beings; they are more like they are now, secret members of a clandestine sect. Indeed, Frank's messianic prediction reads like a conspiracy theory.

Ultimately, there is no single Frankist millennialism. Different dicta promise different things: transformation into superbeings, apocalyptic violence, fine coaches, world recognition, or perhaps just a private revelation of the Maiden. The simplest explanation is that these varying millennial prophecies reflect different pretexts and promises that changed along with external circumstances. As Frank's worldly circumstances changed (usually for the worse), so did his prophecy. Ironically, the messianism for which Frank is known may be among the least original, least consistent, and most expedient aspects of his teaching.

Ridiculing Kabbalah

Finally, while Frank is often included in the history of Kabbalah, he offers hardly any original Kabbalistic teaching, and often ridicules Kabbalah entirely. He is not ignorant of Kabbalah—as we have seen, there are abstruse Zoharic, Lurianic, and Sabbatean references in the text. But he is dismissive of it. Kabbalistic references in *ZSP* are few and far between; explicit Kabbalistic language or symbolism appears in only 38 dicta in *ZSP*. Compare this figure with 86 dicta about Jacob and Esau, 233 dicta discussing magic or folklore, 415 on the Frankist myth in general, and, for that matter, 66 dicta about money. And those references to Kabbalah tend to ridicule theosophy,[32] focusing instead on magical and folkloric elements, with several dicta on Asmodeus, Benayahu, demons, the Golden Thread, and similar material. Frank's few references to Baruchiah and to Nathan of Gaza are mythic-historical, not theoretical; he does not expound on Nathan of Gaza's

---

[31] See Maciejko, "Portrait of a Kabbalist," 555.
[32] See Rapoport-Albert, *Women and the Messianic Heresy*, 189 n.64 and 226 n.240.

Kabbalistic doctrines but talks of Nathan's failed heroic status. And as we just saw in our discussion of the dichotomies of right/left, upper/lower, and shell/kernel, Frank frequently sets aside Kabbalistic formulations in favor of more conventional ones.

In general, Frank is quite clear in *ZSP* that he has no interest in Kabbalistic symbolism, repudiating the Zohar even as he appears to be well versed in it.[33] Frank says in §1088, "I showed you several times in the Zohar, saying that in the whole book there was nothing I liked other than one chapter, which states: 'Who put Joseph in jail? God.—Who released him? God.—Who made him king of Egypt? God'—and many similar things." It is notable that this passage is not one of theosophical symbolism but simply that God is responsible for everything, in particular the suffering and uplifting of the faithful, with Joseph's narrative clearly a model for Frank's own. As Frank states later in the same dictum, "Who led me to Edom? God did. Who led me to Poland? God did. Who led me to prison in Częstochowa? God did. Who released me from prison? God did. And so it will be forever." But beyond that simple teaching, Frank says he has no need of Kabbalistic wisdom: "all the Zohar is not pleasing to my eyes and we don't need the books of kabbalah." Or as Frank says in §2188, "the whole Zohar and all your secret books are worth nothing," because all that matters is faith in God, and of course in Frank himself.

Not a single dictum discusses Kabbalistic terms such as *shevirat hakelim*, *nitzotzot*, or *kelipot*. In §707, Frank mockingly asks if the ten *sefirot* are "houses," then where are the outhouses? In §521 and §585, Frank mocks the Brethren's reference to *yesod*, the ninth sefirah associated with sexual potency and the righteous leader (*tzaddik*). In §521, he says the Brethren "do not know at all what it is"; Yesod, after all, is meant to be the "foundation of the world" and yet "you have nothing stable, not even in life, for there is no foundation." Only "when the time comes, there will come forth and be revealed the true *yesod*, such that one who touches it can revive something, even if it has been dead a long time." Likewise, in §585, Frank says *yesod* is meaningless when one "does not yet know what Adam is," that is, does not yet have the esoteric *Das* of how to transcend death and become a perfect human. In both dicta, Frank totally redefines *yesod* away from its traditional

---

[33] See Maciejko, *Mixed Multitude*, 81. Maciejko observes that the appellation "Zoharites" for the Frankist/Contra-Talmudist sect was actually a Hebrew translation of how the Christian authorities referred to them rather than a label taken on by the sect itself. Maciejko, *Mixed Multitude*, 83.

Kabbalistic meanings and into the Frankist myth. For Frank, theosophic symbolism is meaningless without esoteric gnosis.

In particular, there is a near total absence in *ZSP* of the Lurianic Kabbalistic themes that had become significant in Sabbateanism. Nowhere in *ZSP*, for example, is there a discussion of topics such as the "divine sparks (*nitzotzot*) of holiness and good which fell at the time of Adam's primordial sin into the impure realm of the *kelipot*."[34] As Scholem notes, these doctrines "have disappeared entirely" in Frank's teachings.[35] *Tikkun*—which, in the Sabbatean framework, is central to the messianic mission, as the messiah will repair the fractures in the godhead and the world—is pointless, Frank says in §583; what one must do is take on the attire of Esau, i.e., the outer trappings of (Christian) wealth and power. Continuing in §584, Frank speaks derisively of *tikkun*, asking, "[W]hat have you 'repaired' with your deeds until now? What good effects have come into the world?" Better, Frank says, to take on the attire of Esau (meaning, as discussed in chapter 3, the appearance, identity, and worldly power of Christianity). A few dicta later, in §586, Frank says that the fallenness of the world is evidence that it was not created by the true God, who "must repair everything to bring about complete wholeness." Real repair (here Frank does not use the Hebrew term *tikkun*) can have nothing to do with the creator of this world.

There are some limited exceptions. For example, in §305, Frank explains why he has set up fourteen sisters and twelve brothers: The fourteen sisters correlate with seven hidden kingdoms, and seven kingdoms beyond those seven. The doubling of kingdoms relates, Frank says, to everything having an "upper and lower sefirah," which Frank links to *tahira*, apparently a reference to the Sabbatean doctrine of the upper and lower *tehiru*.[36] Frank, however, reinterprets *tahira* as being related to the Yiddish word *thieren*, meaning "doors," referring to the hidden doors of the kingdoms. .[37] The fourteen sisters were meant to "unite" with the fourteen supernal rulers, who would give over the crowns of their kingdoms. It is noteworthy, in this passage, that Frank uses the term *sefirah* in an unconventional way and totally reinterprets the doctrine of the *tehiru*. That he is aware of the doctrine at all suggests a

---

[34] Scholem, *Messianic Idea*, 94.
[35] Ibid., 128.
[36] See Lenowitz's analysis in Frank, *The Collection of the Words of the Lord*, 101, n.468.
[37] Frank says the first hidden kingdom is ruled by the Queen of Sheba, the second by Sabba—perhaps Saturn. On the relationship between Saturn and Sabbatai Zevi, see Idel, "Saturn and Sabbatai Tzevi," 191–99.

somewhat high level of Sabbatean learning, but Frank changes, simplifies, de-cosmologizes, re-mythologizes, and corporealizes its meaning.

Primarily, however, Frank denigrates Kabbalah and especially Sabbateanism, making use of their doctrines when it is convenient to do so, but ignoring many principles entirely. Though scholarship has at times depicted Frank as "concerned with studying the Kabbalah and deciphering the hidden behind the revealed,"[38] in *ZSP* is dismissive of Kabbalah and skeptical of any non-physical reality. Historically, Frankism was an outgrowth of Sabbateanism, but doctrinally, it rejected most of its core principles in favor of ideas from Western esotericism. It is to that context that we now turn.

---

[38] Elior, *Jewish Mysticism*, 53.

7

"The gods of the freemasons will have to do what those two have done"

Frankism as Western Esotericism

The Frankism of the *Words of the Lord* is best understood in the context of eighteenth-century Western esotericism. Mid-eighteenth-century Europe witnessed an explosion in initiatic secret societies clustered around esoteric and occult ideas; the Frankist sect at this time was one of these, and was in touch with several others.[1] By the end of his career, when *ZSP* was dictated, Frank had transformed several times: from Sabbatean charismatic to "Contra-Talmudist" to, finally, an esoteric sect leader blending political intrigue, occultism, libertinism, and even rationalist skepticism. To be sure, Western esotericism makes extensive use of Kabbalah, usually filtered through Christian and magically oriented sources. But the orientation of *ZSP* is, as we saw in the last chapter, quite different from that of traditional or Sabbatean Kabbalah and, as we will explore in this chapter, distinctly esotericist in its teachings and social milieu. Here, I will first provide a summary of Western esotericism as understood by current scholarship and then discuss three types of connections between it and Frank: historical, doctrinal, and social.

Western Esotericism: Between Myth and Secularism

The term "esotericism" derives from the Greek *esōterikos* ("that which is inside") and first appears in Lucian's description of Aristotle as having "esoteric" and "exoteric" meanings. In the European context, the term first appears in the eighteenth century, when, as we will discuss shortly, an explosion in occult ideas and secret societies took place.[2] As the founder of the

---

[1] Faivre, *Western Esotericism*, 13; Maciejko, *Mixed Multitude*, 222–25; Maciejko, "Portrait," 555.
[2] Hanegraaf, *Western Esotericism*, 3.

contemporary academic study of Western esotericism, Antoine Faivre, has noted, the term "esotericism" obviously could refer to any secret doctrine.[3] However, following Faivre, the term "Western esotericism" has a more limited meaning among scholars: a group of specific historical-religious-philosophical currents that appear at the end of the fifteenth century in Christian Europe and continue through the contemporary period,[4] and that draw on Kabbalah, alchemy, gnosticism, Neoplatonism, and magic.[5] Faivre proposes that Western esotericism is marked by four specific beliefs: correspondences between microcosm and macrocosm, a living Nature filled with obscure forces, mediators and magical objects, and the transmutation of the initiate.[6] (At least three of these are present in *ZSP*.) Arthur Versluis, however, proposes two, broader characteristics: "1. Gnosis or gnostic insight, i.e., knowledge of hidden or invisible realms or aspects of existence (including both cosmological and metaphysical gnosis) and 2. esotericism, meaning that this hidden knowledge is either explicitly restricted to a relatively small group of people, or implicitly self-restricted by virtue of its complexity or subtlety."[7] (Those two characteristics apply to over half of *ZSP*.) Other than Faivre and Versluis, other scholars of Western esotericism whose work is relevant here include Frances Yates, Wouter Hanegraaff, Margaret Jacob, Boaz Huss, and Hilary Gatti.[8]

Thus defined, Western esotericism is essentially a Christian, European phenomenon, even though Kabbalah is one of its sources; as Faivre puts it, "Jewish Kabbalah does not belong to this 'Western esotericism,' whereas the Christian Kabbalah does."[9] Yet for centuries, there was significant interplay, in all directions, between Kabbalah and Western esoteric traditions, alchemy, and occult speculation.[10] In esoteric contexts, Kabbalah was understood not

---

[3] Faivre, *Access to Western Esotericism*, 4–10.
[4] Faivre, *Western Esotericism*, 6, 19–35.
[5] On these roots, see Faivre, *Access to Western Esotericism*, 51–55.
[6] Ibid., 10–14; idem., *Western Esotericism*, 12.
[7] Versluis, *Magic and Mysticism*, 1–2. Versluis notes that gnosis need not entail gnosticism, with its beliefs that the world was created by a hostile deity rather than by the true God. Versluis, *Magic and Mysticism*, 32. As we saw in chapter 3, Frank's theology contains both.
[8] See Versluis, *The Secret History*; Jacob, *Radical Enlightenment*; Gatti, *Giordano Bruno and Renaissance Science*; Gatti, *Giordano Bruno*; Lehrich, *Occult Mind*, 12–15, 35–64; Chajes and Huss, eds., *Theosophical Appropriations*; Hanegraaff and van der Broek, eds, *Gnosis and Hermeticism*; Hanegraaff, *Hidden Intercourse*. Yates's work on esotericism is perhaps the most popular, but also the least reliable.
[9] Faivre, *Western Esotericism* 5.
[10] See Scholem, *Alchemy and Kabbalah*; Patai, *The Jewish Alchemists*; A. P. Coudert, "Kabbalistic Messianism," 116–17. Marco Pasi has suggested that the distinction between the two is ultimately illusory. Pasi, "Oriental Kabbalah," 151–53.

as a theosophical or prophetic system but as an ancient secret science, as in the writings of Pico della Mirandola and the Christian Kabbalists, or of Georg von Welling (1652–1727), the Kabbalist-alchemist whose work Scholem discusses in *Alchemy and Kabbalah*.[11] Welling's work, according to Scholem, "was used as a main source of ideas in the formation of Freemasonry around 1780."[12] Unlike Frank, Welling makes use of the doctrines of the *sefirot*, although he does so in order to point out their effects on "spirits, angels, and earthly creatures," the kinds of magical interlocutors so important to Western esotericism.[13] Like Frank, however, Welling grafted selective Kabbalistic teachings with non-Jewish Christian and occult traditions, such as those of Lucifer and properties of minerals and metals. In all cases, Kabbalistic traditions are reinterpreted as materialistic, magical, esoteric secrets—just as in Jacob Frank.

Western esotericists themselves take a much longer view of their discipline than scholars do, believing that it goes back to ancient Egypt or Greece, and contains an ancient tradition of hidden knowledge that predates Judaism and Christianity.[14] For example, the term "Hermetic tradition," often used interchangeably with "Western esotericism" but in fact a subset of the latter, derives from the *Corpus Hermeticum*, which purports to be the writing of Hermes Trismegistus, an Egyptian priest who lived centuries before the biblical period, but which actually is a collection of texts compiled in Alexandria in the second century CE.[15] These texts combine magic, science, pseudo-science, astrology, alchemy, number mysticism, and other elements that would become familiar features of occultism, together with a natural philosophy that, despite its mythological elements, became a source for much skeptical and materialist critiques of religion. When the *Corpus* was finally published, in 1471, it ignited the phenomenon of Western esotericism as we have defined it above, and when it was translated into German in 1706, it initiated the eighteenth-century wave of European esotericism of which late Frankism is a part.[16] Leading figures of Western esotericism include, in its early period, the alchemist and occultist Paracelsus (1493–1541), the Christian Kabbalist Pico della Mirandola (1463–1494), and Marcilio Ficino (1433–1499); and in

---

[11] Scholem, *Alchemy and Kabbalah*, 94–98. See Maciejko, *The Mixed Multitude*, 219–27.
[12] Scholem, *Alchemy and Kabbalah*, 97.
[13] Ibid., 96.
[14] Faivre, *Western Esotericism*, 3.
[15] Jacob, *Radical Enlightenment*, 5–7; Katz, *The Occult Tradition*, 23–25; Faivre, *Western Esotericism* 5–7.
[16] Faivre, *Western Esotericism*, 53, 71; Jacob, *Radical Enlightenment*, 5.

the sixteenth and seventeenth centuries, Giordano Bruno (1548–1600) and Jacob Boehme (1575–1624).[17] The impact of the *Corpus* was immense; its teachings that human beings are essentially divine, creative, and immortal—more like God than unlike—not only resonated with Renaissance humanism but have continued to echo in the esotericist explosion in the eighteenth century, occult movements in the nineteenth (including Mormonism), theosophical societies in the nineteenth and twentieth, and New Thought (which has come to dominate much of American Protestantism) and the New Age in the twentieth and twenty-first centuries.

In the eighteenth century, dozens of initiatic societies appeared throughout Europe, prompting Faivre to call the eighteenth century "a century of initiations."[18] Most importantly for our purposes is the period known as Illuminism, which lasted from the 1760s through 1815 and with leading figures including "natural philosopher" Emanuel Swedenborg (1688–1772), the (in)famous "Kabbalist of London" Dr. Samuel Jacob Falk (1708–82), and "Count" Alessandro Cagliostro (*né* Joseph Balsamo, 1743–95), who cofounded the "Egyptian Rite" of Freemasonry with Falk.[19] Indeed, Falk and Cagliostro resemble more successful versions of (and perhaps models for) Frank: more assimilated into Christian society, more successful and influential, yet purveying a similar blend of Kabbalah, freemasonry, alchemy, and charlatanism.[20] The best-known of eighteenth-century initiatic societies are the various forms of "speculative" Freemasonry (as opposed to operative, practical masonry[21]), which influenced the Founding Fathers of the United States and French revolutionaries.[22] Its symbolism is on American currency, the cover of Diderot's *Encyclopedia*, and in numerous architectural features throughout Europe.[23]

Speculative Freemasonry has the same jarring combination of nonrational esoteric myth and rational, radical critique as is found in late Frankism. As early as the 1740s, Freemasonry was under attack as being subversive of state

---

[17] See Jacob, *Radical Enlightenment*, 6–9; Faivre, *Access to Western Esotericism*, 63–66; Versluis, *Magic and Mysticism*, 87–88.
[18] See Faivre, *Western Esotericism*, 63–67.
[19] Ibid., 54–55; Williams-Hogan, "The Place of Emanuel Swedenborg"; Godwin, *Theosophical Enlightenment*, 98–100; Maciejko, *Mixed Multitude*, 229.
[20] Godwin, *Theosophical Enlightenment*, 94–100; Schuchard, "Dr. Samuel Jacob Falk," 203–26.
[21] See Versluis, *Magic and Mysticism*, 93–94.
[22] See Jacob, *Radical Enlightenment*, 80–111; Faivre, *Access to Western Esotericism*, 78–81; Katz, *Occult Tradition*, 68–86. Faivre provides a bibliography of studies of freemasonry in *Access to Western Esotericism*, 311–13.
[23] Jacob, *Radical Enlightenment*, 224.

and church for its political radicalism and skepticism.[24] (As a result of these attacks, Freemasonry gradually became more conservative, eventually becoming the "fraternal society" it is today, its esoteric and occult symbolism drained of any radical political or religious meaning.) Now, when we encounter Western esotericism today, we generally see the myth and the magic. Yet that myth coexists with a radical materialism, a mechanistic alternative to traditional Christian doctrine. Consider natural philosopher Lucilio Vanini's (1585–1619) statement that "[m]an should live according to the natural law alone, because nature, which is God (because it is the principle of movement), has engraved this law in the heart of all men: as for all other laws, men should regard them as so many fictions and enticements, not invented by some malevolent genie . . . but by the princes for the education of their subjects, and by the priest with an eye to honors and riches."[25] Religion points to the truth, but the truth itself is the quasi-scientific law of nature. In Versluis's words, which again could easily be applied to Frank, "Masonic values of rationalism, deism, and nonsectarianism did help shape the modern era, with its general tendency to reject, suppress, or ignore esotericism. Yet Masonry has esoteric dimensions itself, visible most obviously in its complicated visual and ritual symbolism. Thus, there has continuously existed a tension between these opposing tendencies."[26]

By way of parallel, consider medieval Jewish astrology. As Moshe Halbertal has shown, what was objectionable about astrology was not its connection to "pagan" gods or superstitions but its notion that the universe was essentially mechanistic.[27] Astrology was not unscientific—it was overly scientific. By positing a mechanistic universe that operated according to laws which humans could understand and use to their benefit, astrology banished the monotheistic God from any relevance to the maintenance of the world. And because it was universal, it undermined claims to religious particularism.[28] Today, we may see astrology as problematic because it is superstition, but medieval religionists saw it as problematic because it was science. Likewise with both Western esotericism and Frankism: The symbolic correspondences, pseudo-Egyptian trappings, and hocus-pocus may strike

---

[24] Ibid., 209.
[25] Quoted in Jacob, *Radical Enlightenment*, 11.
[26] Versluis, *Magic and Mysticism*, 95.
[27] Halbertal, *Concealment and Revelation*, 34–48.
[28] See Idel, "Saturn and Sabbatai Tsevi," 177–78.

us today as superstition, but in their day, they were part of a radical, mechanistic alternative to theistic religion.

Historical Points of Contact

There are significant historical links between Frank and the esoteric movements of his day.[29] Frankists cofounded their own Masonic lodge, the Order of the Asiatic Brethren, or *Zur aufgehenden Sonne im Orient*. Cofounded by the Frankist Moses Dobruschka/Franz Thomas von Schönfeld/Junius Frey and Hans Heinrich von Ecker und Eckhoffen in 1780 or 1781, the Order had the explicit aim of integrating Jews into Freemasonry, and included several prominent Jewish bankers of the period.[30] The Asiatic Brethren "followed a syncretic rite that combined authentic Jewish kabbalistic teachings with elements deriving from Christian esotericism"[31] and had echoes both of Frankism and subsequent esotericist adaptations of Kabbalah. It is possible that some members were even brought to the Frankist court in Brünn for initiation.[32] However, the Asiatic Brethren, important though it is for establishing the connection between Frankism and Freemasonry, was itself a rather marginal—and persecuted—Masonic organization. It was also short-lived; it had disbanded by 1817, as conservative and antisemitic elements in Freemasonry objected to its existence.[33]

Frank also is known to have had contact with members of European eighteenth-century esoteric societies, including Masonic lodges and Rosicrucian orders, and with other esoterically-minded charlatans. With his Kabbalistic knowledge, unusual "Oriental" appearance, mysterious background, and coterie of devoted followers, Frank fit perfectly into this mysterious type, as did pseudo-Baron von Adlersthal *né* Wolf Eibeschütz. In addition to his contacts with Casanova, Frank may have also had links to the Moravian Church, which had weathered its own scandal of antinomian sexuality in the 1740s.[34] We also are aware of evidence that places the Frankist

---

[29] See Maciejko, *The Mixed Multitude*, 225–31.

[30] Katz, *Jews and Freemasons*, 555; Maciejko, "Portrait," 571; Maciejko, *The Mixed Multitude*, 162; Faivre, *Western Esotericism*, 67; Scholem, "Career of a Frankist," 144.

[31] Maciejko, "Portrait," 571; *Mixed Multitude*, 225. On this blend, discussed more in the next chapter, see Huss, "Qabalah."

[32] Maciejko, *Mixed Multitude*, 226.

[33] Churton, *Gnostic Philosophy*, 286–89; Maciejko, *Mixed Multitude*, 227.

[34] Schuchard, "From Poland to London," 260–66; Maciejko, *Mixed Multitude* 192–95, 242–43. Moravian Church antinomianism culminated in the "Sifting Time" of the 1740s, when church leader Christian Renatus Zinzendorf (known as "Christel") preached that union with Christ could

community within the underworld of European politics, using networks of Western esotericist societies to run guns, conduct trade, and build power, connections that would fuel antisemitic conspiracy theories through the present day.[35] Sabbateans were a perfect fit for this milieu: clandestine, possessed of esoteric and Kabbalistic secrets, and infused with the aroma of mystery. As Maciejko remarked, in discussing Wolf Eibeschütz and his Masonic contacts, "Thus a perfect match was achieved: the Christian esotericists' demand for directly transmitted Jewish esoteric lore was matched by the Sabbatians' desire to teach Kabbalah to non-Jews, and specifically to Christians."[36]

At the time of ZSP's dictation, Frank and the Frankists were active in a cosmopolitan, multinational milieu in which esotericism was both an ideology of materialism and an opportunity for social mobility. The Frankist sect in 1784 was part of a network of antinomian, esoterically minded, radical secret societies blending esoteric traditions with a subversive critique of religion, all with a touch of scandal and fraud.

Doctrinal Affinities

Turning from historical points of contact to doctrinal affinities, there are a handful of direct references to Western esotericism in ZSP. §678 explicitly mentions the "gods of the freemasons."[37] This utterance is important, although oracular—"The gods of the freemasons will have to do what those two have done." I interpret this dictum as referring to Frank's rejection of Sabbetai Zevi and Baruchiah Russo ("those two") in favor of the "the gods of the freemasons." Whereas in an earlier phase of Frankism (and in the assimilation of Frankism back into Sabbateanism following Frank's death),

---

be experienced in sexual intercourse (marital or extramarital) and, in 1748, conducted a ritual converting male sect members to "sisters" because all souls were female, a doctrine with parallels in Kabbalah and Sabbateanism. Like the Sabbateans, the Moravian Church often sang eroticized hymns in their rituals, and corporealized bridal mysticism played a central role. This period ended by 1760, when Christel died, and also like those of the Sabbateans, many of the records of the antinomian period were destroyed by the sect's conservative descendants. See Peucker, *A Time of Sifting*. Coincidentally, the Moravian Church's community in Herrnhaag was not far from Offenbach, where Frank would later settle in 1786.

[35] Maciejko, *Mixed Multitude*, 222–25; Scholem, "Career of a Frankist." For an example of contemporary antisemitic writing making use of Frankism and Sabbateanism, see Icke, *The Trigger*; Icke, "To Understand Sabbatian Frankism."

[36] Maciejko, "Portrait," 573. See Maciejko, *Mixed Multitude*, 220–22; Maciejko, "Portrait," 561–70.

[37] The exact word in the manuscript is "framassońscy," which appears to be an error in transcription. See Maciejko, *Mixed Multitude*, 230.

redemption was to have come through the Sabbatean-Jewish messianic project, now the "gods" of Western esotericism would be the gateway to the revised soteriological goal of immortality. In addition to this reference, Frank also makes explicit reference to alchemy in dicta such as §533, a parable in which a girl outwits an alchemist, and there is some evidence that Frank himself performed alchemical experiments.[38]

More broadly, the goal of the Frankist quest, *Das*, is likewise Western esoteric in nature. As discussed in chapter 4, *Das*, the new religion (*dat*) that transcends both Judaism and Christianity, also means gnosis (*da'at*), which Versluis put at the center of Western esotericism: a secret, esoteric gnosis that provides worldly power and transcends conventional religion. The Frankist quest has almost nothing to do with the typical Jewish messianic narrative, save perhaps the overthrow of other religions, yet it has much to do with the goals alchemists have pursued for centuries: wealth, health, spiritual perfection, and eternal life.[39] This is true in general and in detail. For example, Frank's adaptation of the myth of the *ba'alei kaben* (which had been used extensively by the Karakash sect of the *doenmeh*[40]) transforms the myth from its earlier sources into a tribe of three-bodied sages who guard a great treasure and who will be of invaluable assistance to the Brethren during their quest. It is also reminiscent of Casanova's magical ceremony to force gnomes to bring treasures to the surface of the earth.[41] Frank often speaks of signs, passwords, degrees, and keys that are necessary to progress along the path (e.g., §§266, 565, 594, 604, 1203), reminiscent of the secret signs, keys, and passwords used in some initiatic societies (and mystical ascents).[42]

Frank and Western esotericism also share a materialist orientation. Western esoteric myths often propose a radical ontology of an essentially mechanistic universe that displaces traditional Christian (and Jewish) theology, and, like Frank, blends mythology with a "religion of nature," i.e., a "religion" of scientific knowledge.[43] Illuminism is a system of mythic thinking grafted onto a materialistic metaphysics. For example, both Western esotericism and Frankism view shrines as magical places, not historically or theologically significant ones. In Western esotericism, the Temple in Jerusalem

---

[38] Maciejko, *The Mixed Multitude*, 217–18, 233; Lenowitz, "Jacob Frank Fabricates a Golem."
[39] Versluis, *Magic and Mysticism*, 85.
[40] Shai, "Antinomian Tendencies," 187.
[41] Casanova, *History of My Life*, chapter 22.
[42] It is also possible, as Lenowitz notes, that Frank's usage of the French term *billet* (ticket, signet, token) invokes Masonic terminology. Lenowitz, "The Charlatan at the *Gottes Haus*," 191–94.
[43] Jacob, *Radical Enlightenment*, xii–xiii.

is a "power place," significant not because it is dedicated to God but because it is located at a propitious geographical, energetic, and astrological location.[44] The way Frank views Częstochowa, built atop a secret cave filled with gold, is similar. In both cases, the sacred shrine is significant not because of its religious context or meaning but because it is auspiciously located at a physical place where power dwells. Not by Spirit, that is, but by Might and Power. "Every nation is sustained by some powerful thing," Frank states in §85: Israel by the Temple, Poland by Częstochowa.

Finally, consider *ZSP*'s treatment of Egypt. The Egypt of *ZSP* is not the *Mitzrayim* of Jewish tradition, but what Christopher Lehrich has usefully denoted as "Ægypt," the primordial kingdom of magic and wisdom that was the Arcadia of Western esotericism.[45] This Ægypt is the place where Hermes Trismegistus lived, whence the "Egyptian rite" of Freemasonry takes its name, and where esoteric wisdom was developed. It is a mythical place, only tangentially connected to historical Egypt, an Arcadian utopia in which the secret workings of the world were known and practiced; in Versluis's words, it was "precisely where European esotericism has always located its sources of arcane knowledge."[46] Ægypt functions in esoteric discourse much as "Ancient Greece" did in the Renaissance and for some Romantics: as the Edenic, perfect time and place in which all was harmonious and beautiful. (Indeed, after the deciphering of the Rosetta Stone in 1822, when it became clear that Ægypt had nothing to do with actual Egypt, occultists began to propose other spiritual-utopian locations such as Blavatsky's mythical Tibet.[47]) Ægypt is the reason US currency has the Masonic image of a pyramid with an eye atop it; Ægypt is why the Washington monument is an obelisk. Ægypt is the (mythical) source of the *Corpus Hermeticum*, which purports to be a record of its ancient esoteric lore, containing magical secrets to the operation of the cosmos. Egypt appears sixteen times in the Jagiellonian manuscript— as many times as Eve Frank—not counting incidental references to biblical stories. Most of the time, this Egypt is actually Ægypt. In §98, Frank states that the Egyptians know the name of one of the three gods who rule the world, which is why the Nile overflows and makes their soil fertile. In §381, Frank states that Egypt's air makes them wise regarding astrology and black

---

[44] Faivre, *Access to Western Esotericism*, 149–57, 163–76.
[45] Lehrich, *The Occult Mind*, 1–17. Lehrich borrowed the term from John Crowley's 1987 novel, *Ægypt*. See also Versluis, *Magic and Mysticism*, 88 (describing Egypt as "precisely where European esotericism has always located its sources of arcane knowledge").
[46] Versluis, *Magic and Mysticism*, 88. See also Budge, *Egyptian Magic*, 11.
[47] Lehrich, *The Occult Mind*, 132.

magic. In §§602 and 1309, he states that until the time of Pharaoh, Egypt was the best of all lands, like an Edenic garden. All of these references are deeply redolent of contemporary Western esoteric constructions of Ægypt and bear only passing resemblance to Jewish or Kabbalistic ones.

That being said, Frank has a different presentation of Egypt than his Masonic contemporaries. For Western esotericism, Ægypt is thoroughly good. In *ZSP*, the situation is more complex. In §796, Frank states that the name El Shaddai—which as we saw earlier is a magical angelic/demonic name rather than strictly a divine one—protected Abraham while he was in Egypt, suggesting that he needed such protection. In §§947, 1088, and 1225, Egypt is analogized to Edom and Poland, and Frank suggests that he will complete the proper exodus from Egypt, which in light of Frank's attitude toward Christianity, we may interpret as the overthrow of Edom/Egypt. Frank's adoption of the Western esotericist Ægypt makes use of the conventional esoteric trope but folds it into his triumphalist narrative. Western/Christian esotericism, like Christianity itself, will be overthrown by Frank. Frank here adopts the grammar and vocabulary of Western esotericism but also displaces it.

In sum, many of *ZSP*'s teachings quote or resemble those of Western esotericism: the heroic quest for eternal life, the conception of a secret gnosis that will yield that reward, a materialistic metaphysics, complex myths of hidden forces and beings, and a deep, quasi-rationalist skepticism of traditional religion, which possesses magical/technological objects but misunderstands them and imbues them with supernatural meaning. These many affinities, together with the historical links which have been established, make a strong case for understanding the Frankism of *ZSP* primarily as a form of Western esotericism.

The Frankist Court as Initiatic Society

In addition to historical and doctrinal affinities, the sociological structure of the Frankist community and the ideological foundations for that structure bear striking resemblances to contemporary secret societies.[48] The Frankist Brethren have all the hallmarks of a secret society in the Masonic mold: Like contemporary Masons, they call one another Brother and Sister.

---

[48] Lehrich, *The Occult Mind*, 230–31.

Like contemporary Masons, the Frankist company affects a hodge-podge Orientalism of exotic looks and styles.[49] And like contemporary Masons, there are varying degrees of gnosis as the inner circle grows smaller, with secret passwords required to pass from degree to degree.[50] For example, in §1203, Frank states, referring to the magical robes we discussed in chapter 4,

> Even though there is a guard who protects the entrance, if he saw those robes on you, which are the same as his, and you revealed even his secret password to him, then he himself would open the gates for you so that you could enter, because I have told you that you must go wisely and at an incline. If you had entered, no winds could have made you leave. But you did not want to, so you lost your credibility.

Considering such teachings from a functionalist perspective, recall that the deeper secrets of ZSP were intended only to be revealed to the close circle of inner disciples, while the broader apocalyptic prophecies were meant to be shared more widely. Many Masonic orders had similar relationships to Christianity, with exoteric doctrines, which conformed more or less to standard Christianity, and esoteric doctrines, which actually undermined Christianity's theistic foundations. Frankism in 1784 and 1789–1790 has a similar relationship to Sabbateanism. Outwardly, the sect appears to have perpetuated its blend of Sabbatean heresy and apocalyptic pronouncements. In the inner circle, however, Frank taught something entirely different. Similar inner/outer structures exist in numerous esoteric societies, from Freemasonry to the Theosophical Society and the circle of Aleister Crowley, which had different levels of doctrine revealed to adepts at different degrees. It appears in present-day organizations such as the contemporary Church of Scientology, which for most "members" is a somewhat quirky method of self-help but which for insiders is a front in a galactic battle with the forces of Xenu, and the Transcendental Meditation organization, which teaches an exoteric doctrine of simple meditation and an esoteric doctrine of world government and pseudo-science.[51] The initiate goes through one stage, then another, then another—not only along the esoteric quest, but, in parallel to that, within the esoteric community. Of course, this phenomenon enables sect

---

[49] Faivre, *Access to Western Esotericism*, 182–83.
[50] See Snoek, "On the Creation of Masonic Degrees," 145–90.
[51] See Faivre, *Access to Western Esotericism*, 78–81; Urban, *The Church of Scientology*, 64–86; Versluis, *Magic and Mysticism*, 138–39; Siegel, *Transcendental Deception*.

leaders to keep the faithful enticed by endlessly deferred secret teachings, but it also enables heretical societies to survive and grow, even in the face of persecution.

While we have remarked at the surprising extent of Frank's critique of particularism (which exists alongside his highly particularistic contempt for Christianity), similar trends are found in Western esotericism, which was both syncretic in its drawing from multiple religious traditions and, in the eighteenth century, often secularizing forces both intellectually and politically.[52] The 1723 "Constitution of the Freemasons," for example, preached nonsectarian tolerance. In Jacob's words, "Freemasonry was one of the most extraordinary phenomena of that 'rationalist' age, and its rise is directly linked to the triumph of a new scientific culture, to the Newtonian version of enlightenment."[53] Lodges were often meeting places for those repressed by the dominant political culture, as when Franco-Scottish Masonic lodges were established by exiled supporters of the Stuart dynasty forced to flee England.[54] Juxtapose Frank's metaphor of the three-trunked tree, which appears to be three distinct trees (i.e. religions) but is in fact one, with these lines from a 1770 Masonic address: "The whole world is but one great republic, of which every nation is a family and every particular person is a child. To revive and spread abroad those ancient maxims drawn from the nature of man, is one of the ends of our establishment."[55] Unlike the nexus between many esoteric lodges and societies and radical political movements of the seventeenth and eighteenth centuries,[56] Frank did not have a clear political program other than opportunism and self-advancement. However, before we close this chapter, it is worth noting that Freemasonry also influenced a later Sabbatean community: the *doenmeh*. In the latter part of the nineteenth century, *doenmeh* active in Freemasonic societies made up large parts of the leadership of the "Young Turks" in the Committee of Union and Progress (CUP) that would eventually bring about the modern Turkish state.[57] In Sisman's words, "with the introduction of Freemasonry into the Ottoman Empire (and, with it, masonic lodges) in the 1860s, the Dönmes found a new venue where they could express their ideas and share a bond with new

---

[52] See, e.g., Jacob, *Radical Enlightenment*, 75.
[53] Ibid., 75.
[54] Schuchard, "Dr. Samuel Jacob Falk," 204.
[55] "On the Design of Masonry. Delivered in the Union Lodge" (1770), quoted in Granziera, "Freemasonic Symbolism."
[56] Jacob, *Radical Enlightenment*, 75
[57] Sisman, *Burden of Silence*, 241–50.

people, a bond that could transcend religious and ethnic boundaries,"[58] and those lodges helped the *doenmeh* become progressive, and later revolutionary, leaders. As late as 1910, Sisman writes that *doenmeh*, Freemasons and the CUP were intimately connected both in reality and in the fevered minds of their opponents, who alleged a conspiracy.[59] This extends even to the founder of modern Turkey, Mustafa Kemal; while Sisman declines to reach a definitive conclusion about his *doenmeh* ancestry, evidence from his family members, educational background, and his own clear statements on the matter strongly suggest it.[60]

Obviously, by the nineteenth century, the *doenmeh* were in a very different temporal and geographical context from Frank. And even within the *doenmeh*, socioeconomic factors played as much a role in their revolutionary politics as their religious or ideological backgrounds. Yet it is remarkable that communities of outsiders-inside, Sabbateans, crypto-Jews, and Freemasons subscribing to transreligious or even postreligious worldviews had important secularizing cultural and political impacts on their societies. Unmoored from the religious and ethno-nationalistic foundations of those societies, Sabbateans found common cause with Freemasons seeking to reform them. Western esotericism contained not only the proto-scientific materialism that would come to define modernity but some of its incipient liberal politics as well.

In sum, the two facets of Frank's worldview—fantastical myths on the one hand, anti-religious skepticism on the other—may seem strikingly at odds with one another. But they are also joined in Western esotericism. To the outsider, secret societies may look like a vestige of superstition and magic. Inside them, however, heterodox critiques of religion, materialist science, revolutionary politics, and radical secularism are given voice, albeit in seemingly bizarre mythic language. In some ways, Frankism as Western esotericism is a halfway-house between religion and secularism, yet I will suggest in the next chapter that this house is where millions of "spiritual but not religious" people find themselves today. It has been widely observed by scholars that Frank's critiques of religious authority anticipated trends that

---

[58] Ibid., 241.
[59] Ibid., at 249.
[60] Ibid., at 266–69. According to one account, Mustafa Kemal said, "Some people seem to think that I was of a Salonican [i.e., Sabbatean] and therefore Jewish origin. Don't forget that Napoleon was of Corsican origin, Italian, as well. But he died a French man and history remembers him as being French. Everyone needs to work for the society in which they live." Id. at 268–69.

would subsequently remake the Jewish world. Yet it is less obvious that his messianic esotericism has endured as well. Though Frank's particular myths would, like the rest of his philosophy, be discarded by history, his general orientation toward a syncretic, esotericist "religion without religion" has, in surprising ways, prevailed.

8
"All religions change and go beyond the borders laid down by their ancestors"
Foreshadowing Secularism and Spirituality

The mission of Jacob Frank, as Frank himself bemoaned many times, was a failure. Not only did his sect fail to throw off Christian dominion and establish an independent Frankist kingdom; not only did it fail to gain access to the alchemical secrets of immortality; it failed even to survive, and was relegated to the dustbin of history.

Yet many of the ideas that Frank promoted—a skeptical and materialist critique of religion, a religious humanism, the liberation of women, the centrality of human action in bringing about a redeemed world, the possibility of a mythically/messianically saturated (post-)Jewish life outside of rabbinic and legal structures, and even a magically oriented esoteric practice—did, eventually, find much wider audiences. Within the Jewish world, more Jews today believe in them than in the traditional Judaism against which Frank rebelled, even if the origins of those beliefs have nothing to do with Frank. Secular Jews who are intellectual heirs to the Haskalah, and non-Orthodox Jews who are heirs to reform, share Frank's skepticism and humanistic critiques of ritual and religious stricture as ineffectual and life-denying. Early Hasidism shared the Frankist and Sabbatean innovations of Kabbalistically informed spiritual practice taking place outside of rabbinic power structures. And the diverse movements of contemporary Jewish spirituality share Frank's syncretic, "pneumatic," and protofeminist orientations. Beyond Jewish communities, the notion that one could have a spiritual life without religious stricture is now the fastest growing religious identity in the United States: the "nones" who claim no particular religious affiliation but predominantly self-define as "spiritual but not religious."[1] If a central claim of this

---

[1] See Pew Research Center, *"Nones" on the Rise*; Baggett, *Varieties*; Fuller, *Spiritual, But Not Religious*. Fuller estimates that approximately 20 percent of Americans identify as "spiritual, but not religious." Id., 5.

book has been that Jacob Frank preached a coherent, heretical philosophy, the claim of this chapter is that most of us today actually believe in it.

To be clear, this was not primarily because of Frank's, or Sabbatai Zevi's, influence. While this chapter will trace limited lines of historical influence in each of these three streams, this chapter does not allege that Frankism somehow gave birth to the Haskalah, Hasidism, or contemporary Jewish spirituality. Except in the limited examples we will explore, that is absolutely not the case. Rather, our approach in this concluding chapter (which may be deemed a kind of postscript to the previous seven) is phenomenological. Elliot Wolfson said regarding his methodology in comparing Heidegger and Kabbalah:

> Lest there be any misunderstanding, let me restate unequivocally that the question of influence—that issue that unfailingly consumes the mind of the intellectual and social historians working within the confines of the academy—is not of paramount importance to me. What is far more tantalizing is the fact that there is a constellation of thought based on conceptual correspondences.[2]

This phenomenological approach, which has yielded immensely valuable scholarship on Jewish though by Idel, Wolfson, Elior, Garb, and many others, is my approach here as well.[3]

Historically, the Frankist sect was of very limited influence. The core of the Frankist sect limped along for two decades after Frank's death in 1792, maintaining its court in Offenbach thanks to the patronage of followers in Warsaw and Prague. The leadership of Eve Frank (assisted by her two hapless sons) was largely ineffectual, and the "family business" quickly fell into debt. Meanwhile, Frank's theological innovations were lost. For example, to raise money, in 1800, three elders of the sect promulgated the so-called "Red Letters" (so named because they were written in red ink, perhaps a pun on Edom/Christianity and the Hebrew *Adom*/"red"),[4] allegedly written by Frank years earlier, and prophesying imminent catastrophe to befall the Jews unless they joined the "faith of Edom." The "Red Letters" have none of the Western esotericist doctrines or creative genius of ZSP and contain far more

---

[2] Wolfson, *Heidegger and Kabbalah*, 275.
[3] See Idel, *Kabbalah*, 22–25; Idel, *Messianic Mystics*, 3–16; Garb, *Shamanic Trance*, 3–23.
[4] See Maciejko, *Mixed Multitude*, 239–40.

conventional messianic/eschatological visions. They are also dense texts, full of biblical allusions that are, at the very least, quite different in tone from the preaching of *ZSP*. In any case, they were of little efficacy. Jews were not persuaded by an apostate whose heyday was forty years in the past. Gradually, the sect faded into irrelevance and bankruptcy, and following Eve's death in 1816, the Frankist court ceased to exist in any centralized way.

Yet remnants of the sect did survive. Following the demise of the sect, the Prague Frankists, as we will discuss below, integrated Frank into their Sabbatean worldview and their emerging sympathies with the Haskalah. In Warsaw, as Abraham Duker showed, Frank's followers who had converted to Christianity flourished, provoking antisemitic reactions that foreshadow the conspiratorial antisemitic themes of the twentieth and twenty-first centuries.[5] While at first this community was recognizably "other"—converted Jews from the backwaters of Podolia, mostly working in the beer and liquor business—gradually they assimilated and became successful as lawyers and other members of Warsaw's professional class, provoking yet more antisemitic reactions.[6] Indeed, with regard to this population, Hillel Levine's argument seems correct that Frankism offered a kind of passport to worldly success.[7] Their success was remarkable; Frankist themes even appear in the work of Poland's national poet, Adam Mickiewicz, who married into a Frankist family, and advocated for a Poland inclusive of Jews.[8] In terms of religious affiliation, the "neophytes" (the term connotes converts to Christianity generally, but in Poland came to refer to the Frankists specifically) maintained strong communal bonds[9] and continued to be active in secret societies long after the disintegration of the Frankist court itself,[10] though perhaps more for socioeconomic reasons than religious ones. The Polish Frankists were at once the preservers and the destroyers of the Frankist legacy; on the one hand, they preserved the *Words of the Lord* and other Frankist manuscripts and wrote the first Frankist histories, but on the other hand, scandalized by the rumors of their grandparents' generation, they apparently censored and suppressed the radical elements of Frankism and shaped the official histories

---

[5] Duker, "Polish Frankism's Duration"; Emeliantseva, "The Frankists in the Social Context," 105–10.
[6] Maciejko, *Mixed Multitude*, 256–61; Doktór, "Frankists and its Christian Environment," 51–53.
[7] Levine, "Frankism as Worldly Messianism," 290.
[8] See Duker, "Some Cabbalistic & Frankist Elements"; Duker, "The Mystery of the Jews"; Bosak, "Mickiewicz, Frank, and the Conquest of the Land of Israel." The extent of Mickiewicz's Frankist sympathies and background remains controversial to this day.
[9] Doktór, "Frankists and Its Christian Environment," 48–51.
[10] Duker, "Polish Frankism's Duration," 297–98, 312–13.

to suit their own apologetic purposes. Eventually, this remnant of Frankism died out as well, with most Frankist descendants unaware of their roots.[11]

Phenomenologically, however, the affinities between the teachings of Jacob Frank and significant movements in subsequent Jewish history are remarkable: a sect generally regarded as a "dead end" of Jewish history presaged the destinations where a numerical majority of Jews find themselves today. Frank's prophecies of imminent war and the triumph of Judaism over Christianity did not, of course, come to pass. But much of what he taught, surprisingly, did.

The Haskalah, Zionism, and Reform

At the same time as Jacob Frank was preaching his combination of rationalist skepticism and esoteric myth, the Jewish Enlightenment, later known as the Haskalah, was advocating its own rationalist skepticism in the urban centers of Western Europe.[12] As we will see, these very different, roughly contemporary movements did occasionally intersect. More often than not, however, they inhabited entirely different cultural and intellectual milieus, with the Haskalah beginning as a phenomenon of educated Jewish elites in urban centers, and Frankism an esoteric cult in non-Jewish Europe. And of course, the Haskalah would go on to transform the Jewish world, while Frankism died out. Yet many of the ideas championed by Frank were also advanced by the pioneers of the Haskalah, Jewish secularism, and Jewish Reform, and 250 years later, they are accepted by nearly all non-Orthodox Jews.

Gershom Scholem—as part of his meta-theory that Jewish history is self-determined and, to an extent, self-enclosed—famously argued for a more direct connection between these different phenomena. In Scholem's view, Sabbateanism and Frankism sowed the seeds for the Haskalah by destabilizing rabbinic authority; it was not the encounter with European Enlightenment figures and ideas, though they were important, but the internal dynamics of Sabbateanism and Frankism, that were the primary causes of the Haskalah. "The world of rabbinic Judaism was completely destroyed from within, quite independently of the efforts of secularist criticism," Scholem wrote.[13]

---

[11] See Kaplinski, "Discovering My Frankist Roots."
[12] See Feiner, *Origins of Jewish Secularism*; Biale, "Secularism and Sabbateans."
[13] Scholem, *Messianic Idea*, 140.

For Scholem, who was himself an anarchist for most of his life, the Frankists typified the "struggle for individual freedom against tyrannical and hypocritical institutions and in favor of free association of communities helping each other," as he said toward the end of his life.[14] Scholem calls particular attention to Prague Frankists such as Jonas Wehle and Löw Enoch Hönig von Hönigsberg, observing their peculiar blend of nonrational Sabbateanism-Frankism and rational Enlightenment thinking. According to Scholem, "in the minds of those who took part in this revolutionary destruction of old values a special susceptibility to new ideas inevitably came to exist."[15] This, Scholem says, "facilitated the transition to the new world of Judaism in the period of the emancipation."[16]

This claim has been largely refuted in the decades since Scholem made it, and has been strongly critiqued by Jacob Katz, David Biale, Hillel Levine, Ada Rapoport-Albert, Eliezer Schweid, Paweł Maciejko, and others.[17] True, the Sabbatean heresy eroded rabbinic authority; for eighty years prior to the Frankist debacle, as Elisheva Carlebach's research has shown, Sabbatean controversies had torn at rabbinic authority with disputations, investigations, polemics, and rival bids for power.[18] Indeed, the formation of Jewish Orthodoxy was as much a response to the Sabbatean controversies as to Reform, leading to the restrictions not just on Kabbalah study (perhaps Frank's greatest impact on Jewish history) but also on any form of Jewish innovation at all.[19] But while this erosion of rabbinic authority contributed to the rise of secularism, it was but one of many factors that did so, with others being far more important, including the emancipation of much of European Jewry, changes in Jewish socioeconomic status, and increasing Jewish contact with Christians, who were already rebelling against weakened clerical authorities of their own. Azriel Shohat, Shmuel Feiner, and David Biale have persuasively argued that secularization began as a cultural phenomenon in

---

[14] Scholem, "Der Nihilismus," 43. See Fagenblat, "Frankism," 48–49. As Meir and Yamamoto note, there are now a number of studies of Scholem's own ideological views in relationship to Sabbateanism. Meir and Yamamoto, *Gershom Scholem*, 24–25, citing Biale, "Shabbtai Zvi"; Maciejko, "Gershom Scholem's Dialectic," and others. They aptly describe Scholem's attitude toward Frankism as "a vacillation between repulsion and attraction." Meir and Yamamoto, *Gershom Scholem*, 25.

[15] Scholem, *Messianic Idea*, 127.

[16] Ibid., 127.

[17] See Katz, "The Suggested Relationship," 504–30; Biale, *Gershom Scholem*, 84–88; Biale, "Secularism and Sabbateans;" Levine, "Frankism as a 'Cargo Cult,' " 81–94; Rapoport-Albert and Hamann, "Something for the Female Sex"; Schweid, *Judaism and Mysticism*; Maciejko, "Gershom Scholem's Dialectic," 207–20.

[18] Carlebach, *Pursuit of Heresy*, 11–17.

[19] See Kahana, "The Allure of Forbidden Knowledge," 598–99; Carlebach, *Pursuit of Heresy*, 278.

the early eighteenth century even before it became an intellectual phenomenon in the latter half of the century.[20] Finally, most Maskilim did not come from Sabbatean or Frankist backgrounds, and late Frankism appears to have been a very small movement; Maciejko cites one source identifying only twelve Sabbatean families in Prague.[21] In sum, in Ada Rapoport-Albert's words, "most scholars have rejected Scholem's contention that the antinomian excesses of Sabbatianism undermined Judaism and encouraged secularism in favor of a sociological explanation: secularization was largely the result of increased social and intellectual contact with Christians."[22]

It is possible to discern a very narrow line of influence within the Prague Frankist community, but one far more attenuated than Scholem proposed. This community was primarily constituted not by Frankists who had converted to Christianity in 1759 but by secretly Sabbatean Jews who regarded Frank as one of their own. Indeed, Maciejko has rightly questioned whether this community is properly to be called "Frankist" at all, rather than Sabbatean with a particular affinity for Frank and the Frankist court.[23] However it is characterized, the Prague community was the site of both Sabbatean-Frankist activity and subsequent activity in the Haskalah. One example of this was discussed in chapter 5: the Prague Frankist text "Something for the Female Sex," a protofeminist (yet also misogynistic) text arguing for the liberation of women because women embody sensuality, and sensuality/sexuality should be liberated in general.[24] This unusual view more closely resembles the Frankist conception of the Maiden discussed in chapter 5 than contemporaneous feminist writing such as that of Mary Wollstonecraft. And coming as it does from the same community that subsequently became the center of the Haskalah in Prague, this would seem to be the perfect nexus at which to demonstrate the veracity of Scholem's thesis. As Rapoport-Albert has shown, however, Löw Enoch Hönig von Hönigsberg, the likely writer of "Something for the Female Sex," did not graduate, as Scholem's thesis would have it, from the heretical Kabbalah of the Frankists to the rationalist ideology of the Enlightenment. Rather, he genuinely combined two very different sources of his spiritual and intellectual inspiration, because they aligned ideologically.[25] Thus, rather than the strong case that Scholem made that Sabbateanism and

---

[20] See Biale, "Secularism and Sabbateans."
[21] Maciejko, *Mixed Multitude*, 235.
[22] Coudert, "Kabbalistic Messianism," 108. See also Katz, "Concerning the Question."
[23] Maciejko, *Mixed Multitude*, 255.
[24] Rapoport-Albert and Hamann, "Something for the Female Sex," 102–3.
[25] Ibid., 98.

Frankism lay the groundwork for the Haskalah, we can make only a weaker case: that among the sources on the bookshelf of at least one Maskilic family were Frankist critiques of religion and Enlightenment critiques of religion; that these sources diverged at points and aligned at points; and that, where they aligned, they may have reinforced one another.

Phenomenologically, however, there are close affinities between Frank's critique of religion and Haskalah, Reform, and contemporary non-Orthodox critiques of traditional religion. Frank argued that religion was ineffectual, pointless, and encrusted with superstition, and promoted a skepticism of the claims of Judaism and the binding nature of Jewish law. So did figures in the Haskalah—as well as those in the German movements for Reform, who, as Katz shows, had a very different agenda from the Maskilim but shared their critiques of superstition, law, and ritual.[26] Of course, Maskilim and Reformers alike would surely have recoiled from Frank's preposterous myths and devious manipulation of his followers. Nevertheless, Frank's skeptical antinomianism anticipated the intellectual foundation for the vast majority of non-Orthodox Jews today. Summarizing Frank's ideology, Michael Fagenblat writes that it has

> four aspects: gender roles which, in Judaism, have been arbitrarily hierarchized and thus more or less compromised since Eden; territorial autonomy, in particular as concerns the false binary of exilic subjugation and colonial appropriation; economic relations, insofar as these remain constitutive of the emancipatory bonds among human beings; and the politics of "Jewish identity" which attests to the singularity of historical collectivities while running the risk of alienation and exclusion.[27]

Once again, mutatis mutandis, these views are now widely held among non-Orthodox Jews: gender egalitarianism, Zionism, an engagement with economic life, and a complex relationship to Jewish identity and particularism. Frank's critiques of rabbinic authority, while they may not have impacted Jewish history in the way that Scholem proposed, anticipated views that are predominant today.

---

[26] Katz, "The Suggested Relationship."
[27] Fagenblat, "Frankism," 30.

Finally, both Sabbatean and Frankist messianism were seen by many important Zionist figures as an early, failed but noble attempt to attain Jewish redemption through human agency rather than divine intervention.[28] Perhaps most remarkably, Zalman Shazar, who would later become president of Israel, wrote an editorial in 1925 urging the Israeli public to celebrate. "Sabbatai Ṣevi Day" on the Ninth of Av in honor of the "generator of hope . . . whose enchanting messianic aspirations led to the establishment of the first popular movement of this sort," and even proposed a redemption of the "ruins of the House of Frank." In Shazar's words, which are an apt summary of Frankist legacy in general, "The temple, whose desolate ruins I turn towards, is foreign to me, [but] it is our destiny which was instigated in their entanglements."[29] Scholem, too, who benefited from Shazar's assistance early in his career, was likewise attracted by Frank's program of the "reconstruction of Jewish national and even economic existence,"[30] though he expressed reluctance toward the messianic implications of identifying Zionism with Sabbateanism.[31] Scholem and other scholars were quite aware that there was no historical connection between Frank's military exercises on a borrowed castle in Moravia and the activities of the Second Zionist Congress. But they saw in Sabbetai and Frank an ideological genealogy. The Zionists, like Sabbetai Zevi and Frank, did not wait for God to redeem Israel, but devoted themselves to bringing about change on earth. They, too, were animated by a radical political program that involved the self-liberation of the Jewish people, including through political and military means. And they, too, had little patience for those who refused to take matters into their own hands. In Fagenblat's words, "Frankism is precisely a case of a condemned and ridiculed idea calling for fulfillment in the present, where it assumes distorted but emancipated form."[32] Frank disappeared, but the ideas that he preached did not.

---

[28] On Sabbateanism as an inspiration for Zionism, see Verses, *Halacha v'Shabtaut*, 253–64; Meir and Yamamoto, *Gershom Scholem*, 22–25, 85–89.

[29] Meir and Yamamoto, *Gershom Scholem*, 22 (quoting Zalman Rubashov [Zalman Shazar], "Yom Shabetai Tsevi," Davar, Jul. 29, 1925, 1; *Al Tile Bet Frank (Rishme Offenbach)*, 665–74; and "Sofero shel Mashiach," ha-Shiloah 29 (1913), 47).

[30] I. Scholem, *Messianic Idea*, 127.

[31] Meir and Yamamoto, *Gershom Scholem*, 23.

[32] Fagenblat, "Frankism," 29.

Early Hasidism

Just as Frank's skeptical materialism anticipated the skeptical materialism of rationalism and reform, Frank's charismatic spirituality likewise foreshadowed the charismatic spirituality of Hasidism, which was born at the same time and in the same places where Sabbateanism had flourished. Frankism-Sabbateanism and Hasidism developed alongside one another, in the same places and times, and although one was antinomian and heretical, and the other nomian and normative, from the outside, the two could look outwardly like barely distinguishable social-religious movements. Both groups called themselves Hasidim or *ma'aminim*. Both favored their charismatic leaders over rabbinic authorities. Both were accused of sexual impropriety. Both emphasized singing, music, and joyous religious practice. Both cultivated what Idel called the "certain intensification of religious life" characteristic of messianism and mysticism, which would later become popularized as spirituality.[33] Both were perceived as a threat to the rabbinic establishment, and did indeed set up lines of authority distinct from it. And both participated in ecstatic rites, though of very different types. Indeed, as Elior has discussed at length, Frankism and Hasidism should be seen as divergent responses to late Sabbateanism, one radical and one conservative, one a failure and the other a remarkable success.[34] These proximities of geography, ideology, and social organization make it unlikely that the founders of Hasidism simply "felt that Judaism had gotten old and dry, formulaic and legalistic, and it needed to breathe the spirit back into it."[35] Rather, Hasidism domesticated, popularized, and adapted Sabbateanism and Sabbatean Kabbalah, whose messianic, mystical, and emotional "intensification of religious life" birthed what is now known as Jewish spirituality. It was not the Hasidic masters who originated this movement; it was the Sabbateans, whose approach to Jewish practice eventually triumphed over the kinds of religion that Frank critiqued.

As before, we begin with lines of historical influence before moving to wider phenomenological affinities. There are some direct references to the Frankist heresy in the Hasidic corpus. As noted in the introduction, the *Shivhei HaBesht*, published in 1814—the same year as the anti-Sabbatean *Meorot Zevi*—states,

---

[33] Idel, *Messianic Mystics*, 16.
[34] Elior, *Mystical Origins*, 173–75, 184–94.
[35] Green, "A Closing Conversation," 427.

I heard from our rabbi that the Ba'al Shem Tov said that the Shechinah wails and says, "As long as the limb is connected, there is hope for a remedy; but when it is amputated there is no remedy forever; for every Jew is a limb of the Shechinah."[36]

As we noted earlier, this was not a mere figure of speech but a reversal of the same metaphor used by Jacob Emden that the Frankist sect was like a diseased limb that had to be amputated in order to save the patient. One can only speculate as to why the Baal Shem Tov mourned the apostasy, if indeed *Shivhei HaBesht* is a reliable source here. Perhaps it was simply a belief that repentance is always available for every Jew. Or perhaps it was a deeper sense of kinship with the heretical group. Frank, like the Baal Shem Tov, offered his adherents an immediate spiritual experience, not one mediated by text, rabbinic authority, and halachic observance. Frank, like the Baal Shem Tov, urged his followers to imagine sexual relations with the immanent Divine Feminine, though Frank apparently did so literally and the Besht did so nonliterally. This, of course, is speculation; it may be only that the Baal Shem Tov was expressing concern for one's fellow Jews. But even in that case, given that the Sabbatean heresy was regarded as the deepest evil of the period—including by some other Hasidim—the statement stands out.

The most remarkable case of Sabbateanism and Frankism in the writings and actions of a Hasidic master, however, is that of Rabbi Nachman of Bratzlav.[37] R. Nachman was keenly aware of Sabbateanism/Frankism. In *Likutei Moharan* 207:1 he discusses "the matter of Sabbetai Zevi," specifically the Frankist disputations, which, R. Nachman says, says killed the Baal Shem Tov. "It made two holes in his heart," R. Nachman says. The Sabbatean movement represented both the greatest Jewish sin and its greatest spiritual potential. "When the *tzaddik* sweetens their [the heretics'] words," R. Nachman continues, "he returns them and makes words of Torah. . . . And makes a Torah of Lovingkindness [*Torat Chesed*] to teach others." This was to be part of Rabbi Nachman's mission: to succeed in sweetening the heretical words, as the Baal Shem Tov could not. Several echoes of Frankist beliefs in R. Nachman's teachings have been discussed by Yehuda Liebes, as well as by Joseph Weiss in three unpublished manuscripts presented by Jonatan Meir and Noam Zadoff. For Liebes, Sabbateanism was "the culmination of the

---

[36] See Baer ben Samuel, *In Praise of the Baal Shem Tov*.
[37] See Meir and Zadoff, "The Possibility of Frankist Traces"; Liebes, *Tikkun*.

Kabbalistic-messianic direction that had left its imprint on the previous century," and now it would fall to R. Nachman to continue it.[38] Thus R. Nachman was to "teach these modified doctrines, originally Sabbatean, to others," and "many elements in R. Nachman's doctrine were developed from Sabbatean sources."[39] Liebes catalogs several examples: the zone of the forbidden into which the righteous one must enter being associated with *Torat Chesed* (in Sabbateanism, this is Islam; in R. Nachman, it is Sabbateanism); specific images such as the "armor of repentance" which appear only in R. Nachman and Sabbatean sources; the notion of the descent for the sake of ascent and the *tzaddik* willingly placing himself in precarious situations; the "supreme religious value" of a personal tie with the *tzaddik*; even the special role of the *Akdamut* prayer.[40] R. Nachman's many instances of behaving like a small child or a fool or even a fetus—which he understood as *katnut* ("smallness")—bear a resemblance to Sabbetai Zevi's "strange acts" and Frank's "holy madness" which we discussed in chapter 1, though as Zvi Mark shows it is also typologically present in Lurianic Kabbalah.[41] The nonrational, noncognitive quality of these states also strongly resembles the Sabbatean doctrine of the *or sh'ein bo'machshavah*, the Light without Thought; the zaddik's "descent into smallness" is thus an ascent to the highest realms, which transcend the commandments and rational thought itself.[42] In addition to the examples that Liebes brings forward, Weiss's unpublished studies noted antinomian tendencies in R. Nachman's teachings that by listening to women's conversations (which is technically against halacha), one may know the status of the Shechinah, and that the merit of providing money to a Torah scholar cannot be negated by transgression.[43]

Both Liebes and Weiss devote particular attention to Rabbi Nachman's famous presentation of the *tikkun klali*, the recitation of ten psalms, as penance both for personal seminal emissions and, as the name implies, as atonement for collective sexual sin.[44] This practice was originally developed by the Sabbatean prophet Nathan of Gaza, who, incidentally, was also known

---

[38] Liebes, "*Tikkun*," 134.
[39] Ibid., 131 and 134, respectively.
[40] Ibid., 131, 134, 145, 116, and 148–49. See *ZSP* §143; *Sichot HaRan* 251.
[41] Mark, *Mysticism and Madness*, 185–97.
[42] Ibid., 205–11.
[43] Nachman of Bratzlav. *Likutei Moharan* 1:203 and 1:204. See Meir and Zadoff, "The Possibility of Frankist Traces," 409–12.
[44] See Meir and Zadoff, "The Possibility of Frankist Traces," 391–408; Liebes, "*Tikkun*," 143–47. Weiss refers to it as the "tikkun of paradox."

as MoHaRaN.[45] Moreover, as Liebes shows, R. Nachman's *tikkun klali* was instituted not because of a concern for the general spiritual lives of individual Hasidim, for which it is popular today, but as a *tikkun* for Sabbateanism.[46] R. Nachman, writes Liebes, "was concerned with the *tikkun* of the original sin that, in my view, was for him the source of all his generation's ills—Sabbateanism."[47] R. Nachman's ten "songs" were meant to heal the damage of the Sabbatean "songs"—an interesting locution if we recall that Frank characterized the sect's heretical activity at Lanckoronie as "singing songs," that the very first arrest of the *doenmeh* for heretical practices accused them of "singing songs," and that singing ecstatic songs (often Turkish melodies with new words) was a hallmark of *doenmeh* ritual observance. Perhaps "singing songs" itself connotes improper sexual activity (whether it actually entailed it or not), which is to be remedied by the *tikkun klali*. For R. Nachman, "the Sabbatean heresy was the root and the symbol of all worldly evil," and primarily sexual in nature.[48] Thus R. Nachman did battle with his own *yetzer hara* in order to do a *tikkun* for the *yetzer hara* of the entire Jewish people, which erupted in Sabbateanism. Crucially, his *tikkun* was not an outright rejection of Sabbateanism but an effort to "turn their words again to Torah."[49]

R. Nachman appears to have been uniquely interested in Frank in particular. At least two of his pilgrimages were to Kamieniec and Lwów, the sites of the two disputations with the "Contra-Talmudists"; R. Nachman said that his great-grandfather the Baal Shem Tov ordered him to go there in a dream.[50] He had his own books burned as a *tikkun* for the burning of the Talmud during the Frankist disputation period. He saw Frank as the fallen version of *mashiach ben Yosef*, who was meant to redeem Christianity/Esau, just as Sabbetai was the fallen version of *mashiach ben David*, meant to redeem Islam/Ishmael.[51] Both Frank and R. Nachman had an affinity for militaristic imagery. R. Nachman even said, "The strength to punish the wicked can only be drawn from Edom," a dictum that could easily have come from *ZSP*'s valorizations of the might of Edom and exhortations to the Frankist company to seize it. "The blessed king is even found in heresy," taught R. Nachman

---

[45] Liebes, "*Tikkun*," 143–44. As discussed earlier, Nathan of Gaza's ascetic impulse eventually yielded within the Sabbatean movement to the more libertine ethos of Sarah Ashkenazi. See also Van Der Haven, *From Lowly Metaphor*, 40–45.
[46] Mark, "Contemporary Renaissance," 108.
[47] Liebes, "*Tikkun*," 116.
[48] Ibid., 128.
[49] Ibid., 131.
[50] Ibid., 146–47.
[51] Ibid., 200.

in *Sichot HaRan* 102.[52] The most striking affinities between Frankism and Bratzlav Hasidism, however, lie in the unconventional, often unpredictable tales told by the two charismatic leaders, each seeming to have no equivalent in the literature—unless one knows of both.[53] The two sets of tales are unlike any others, but they resemble each other tonally and occasionally substantively. They share motifs: that of the lost virgin; that of exchanging sons; Satan appearing as an old man.[54] Both had a sense of impending doom and violence.

And at least once, it seems that R. Nachman has retold a tale of Frank's directly: the well-known "tale of the rooster-prince," which appears in no other source except R. Nachman and *ZSP*. Says Liebes, unless another source becomes known, "I shall believe that Rabbi Nachman took it from Jacob Frank."[55] When one is living in an insane world, one must don the garb of insanity in order to slowly wean the student from her or his delusion into sanity. Here is the tale in Rabbi Nachman's version:

> A prince once became mad and thought that he was a rooster. He felt compelled to sit naked under the table, pecking at bones and pieces of bread, like a rooster. All the royal physicians gave up hope of curing him of this madness. The king grieved tremendously. A sage arrived and said, "I will undertake to cure him." The sage undressed and sat naked under the table, next to the prince, picking crumbs and bones. "Who are you?" asked the prince. "What are you doing here?" "And you?" replied the sage. "What are you doing here?" "I am a rooster," said the prince. "I'm also a rooster," answered the sage. They sat together like this for some time, until they became good friends. One day, the sage signaled the king's servants to throw him shirts. He said to the prince, "What makes you think that a rooster can't wear a shirt? You can wear a shirt and still be a rooster." With that, the two of them put on shirts. After a while, the sage again signaled and they threw him pants. As before, he asked, "What makes you think that you can't be a rooster if you wear pants?" The sage continued in this manner until they were both completely dressed. Then he signaled for regular food, from the table. The sage then asked the prince, "What makes you think that you will

---

[52] *Likutei Moharan* 1:20; *Sichot HaRan* 102. See Weiss, *Studies in Bratslav Hasidism*, 244–48.
[53] See Green, *Tormented Master*, 172–74; Mark, *Mysticism and Madness*, 247–82 (discussing the story of the "humble king"); Mark, "Ma'aseh me-ha-Shiryon."
[54] See *ZSP* §1021.
[55] Liebes, "*Tikkun*," 149.

stop being a rooster if you eat good food? You can eat whatever you want and still be a rooster!" They both ate the food. Finally, the sage said, "What makes you think a rooster must sit under the table? Even a rooster can sit at the table." The sage continued in this manner until the prince was completely cured.[56]

And here is almost the same tale (with interesting differences) in §986 of *ZSP*:

> There once was a merchant who had seven ships at sea which normally would not return to shore for seven years. The merchant waited seven years, and then an eighth year, but heard nothing of the ships. Even though he had great riches at home, he went mad after experiencing such a great loss. Having stripped himself of his robes, he began to act like a rooster: he ate and drank like a rooster, and when the time came to crow, he would slap his buttocks with his hands the way a rooster does with his wings, and then he would begin to crow like a rooster. There was not a single doctor who could remedy it, until a wise man came, who employed the following ruse: he also took off his robes and walked into the same room where he was and did the same as he did. Same as he did, he ate and drank seeds like a rooster. The merchant-rooster asked him: "Who are you?" The wise man answered: "You are a plain rooster, but I am a wild rooster and the elder of all roosters." At midnight, the new rooster woke up the old one: "It is time to crow!" He stood crowing alongside him to the point that the two grew very accustomed to each other. Then he said: "Now we can break bread into pieces, like seeds, instead of only eating seeds, and we will still be roosters." He then ordered that broth be served and said: "We can sprinkle bread in it and eat it like this, and still be roosters." He [the merchant] heeded this, too. Then he [the wise man] said: "We can even eat a piece of meat, and we will still be roosters." He [the merchant] also acquiesced to this. Then he [the wise man] persuaded him: "We can sleep in beds, because a rooster will still be a rooster." But halfway through the night he made him get out of bed: "It's time to crow!" he said. Then he persuaded him: "We can even drink good wine and sleep in bed, and still be roosters." The former one fell into a good sleep after having drunk. When the new rooster began to wake

---

[56] Rabbi Avraham Chazan, *Kochvei Ohr*, 26–27. For a contemporary retelling of this tale, see Schwartz, *Palace of Pearls*, 186–87. For a slightly different rendering of it, see Green, *Tormented Master*, 172–73.

him up, the former one had already come to his senses and said: "Leave me alone and be yourself a rooster, I don't want to be one anymore."

Clearly, despite their minor differences, these two tales are the same tale. And that raises the tantalizing question of how Rabbi Nachman of Bratzlav came into contact with the tale, whether in a manuscript of *ZSP*, which was seemingly intended only for a small group of Frank's closest disciples, or in some other form. Rabbi Nachman was born in 1772, the same year Frank was imprisoned; Liebes surmises that he "may have come across Frankists who had remained Jews, of whom there were many in Podolia."[57] Since it is unlikely that these communities would have had copies of *ZSP*, this would suggest that Frank had told the story in other contexts that had been committed to writing or memory. The differences between the tales are interesting: Frank's character is a greedy merchant who goes mad waiting for his (literal) ship to come in; Nachman's is a prince whose madness is unexplained. Frank's hero has to resort to more tricks than Rabbi Nachman's, and Frank's merchant eventually quits out of annoyance whereas Nachman's prince is cured. But the basic story is the same, as are the themes of "holy madness" (which we touched on in chapter 1) and the sage appearing to be in a degraded state but actually in service of truth. (In Sabbateanism, this would be understood as a "descent for the sake of ascent; Frank's iteration of this symbol is different, as we explored in chapter 6.) One might even read it as a meta-comment on Rabbi Nachman's entering the realm of the *kelipot* of Sabbatean heresy to liberate the holiness hiding in its depths.

To be sure, the case of Rabbi Nachman is at the extreme end; practically alone among Hasidic figures, he shows the direct influence not only of Sabbateanism but also of Jacob Frank. Yet as in the case of the Haskalah, these narrow historical connections point to much broader phenomenological ones. First and foremost, Frankism, Sabbateanism, and Hasidism each offer a magical, mystical, messianic spirituality that either replaces normative, legalistic Judaism (in Frank and Sabbateanism) or sits within it (in Hasidism). Both redefine messianism from the historical to the personal; for example, in the Baal Shem Tov's famous letter describing his visionary ascent to heaven (itself the kind of prophetic trance experience that was widespread in the Sabbatean movement), the Messiah tells him that he will come when

---

[57] Liebes, "*Tikkun*," 148.

everyone can do spiritual practices the way the Baal Shem Tov just did.[58] (The Baal Shem Tov also combined his visionary experiences with claims to magical powers that could cure diseases, as Frank did.[59]) Both were also centrally magical movements: As Moshe Idel and others have observed, Hasidism, like Frankism, was heavily invested in magical performance and worldly benefit.[60] Indeed, Rapoport-Albert suggests that Hasidic texts, especially *Shivhei HaBesht*, played down the importance of magic in order to distance the Hasidim from Sabbateanism.[61] Both movements use eroticized ritual as a way of experiencing that messianic reality, the Frankist and Sabbatean versions being, at least to some extent, physical eroticism and the Hasidic one being spiritualized or sublimated into ecstatic-erotic prayer (indeed, numerous Hasidic texts speak approvingly of transcending the physical entirely, which would be anathema to Frank).[62] And Sabbateanism-Frankism and Hasidism both invested charismatic leaders with unique relationships to the divine and to redemption and demanded that followers cleave closely to them; Scholem suggests that the type of the *tzaddik* is essentially the Sabbatean type of the "prophet-messiah," which Frank obviously embodied,[63] while Rapoport-Albert argues that Hasidism "shared the Kabbalistic legacy of Sabbatianism, and adopted, or at least independently reproduced, its most distinctive mode of prophetic-charismatic leadership."[64]

In these ways, early Hasidism was a kind of domestication of the spiritual experience of Sabbateanism and Frankism. Frankism, Scholem said, was "the attempt of a minority to maintain, in the face of persecution and vituperation, certain new spiritual values which correspond to a new religious experience."[65] That new religious experience was "neutralized" or personalized

---

[58] Idel, *Messianic Mystics*, 214–20.
[59] Ibid., 214–20.
[60] Idel, *Hasidism*, 147–88.
[61] Rapoport-Albert, *Women*, 286. This was not always successful; consider the words of R. Chaim Hacohen Rapaport of Lwów, a bitter opponent of both Frankism and Beshtian Hasidism, who said of the latter, "I have heard of your intentions to turn to a witch doctor who calls himself 'Ba'al Shem.' God forbid, heaven forfend because this is a great evil, it is a scam. It would be exactly like throwing your money in the garbage." Translated by and quoted in Meir, "Marketing Demons," 28.
[62] See Green and Holtz, *Your Word Is Fire*, 80; Idel, *Messianic Mystics*, 235 (citing texts which describe *hitpashtut hagashmiut*, the divestment of corporeality, as the redemption of humanity).
[63] Idel, "The Tsadik"; Scholem, *Major Trends*, 233–34; Liebes, "Tikkun," 117–18.
[64] Scholem, *Major Trends*, 333–34; Rapoport-Albert, *Women and the Messianic Heresy*, 264. See also Goldish, *Sabbatean Prophets*, 41–55 (discussing links between messianism and prophecy).
[65] Scholem, *Messianic Idea*, 127.

mystical messianism, and as we will see in a moment, it becomes even more central to later trends in Jewish spirituality and New Age Judaism. Indeed, Weiss notes that when Hasidic masters were accused of being "prophets," that was essentially an accusation of being Sabbatean.[66] Haviva Pedaya, reflecting on the Baal Shem Tov's model of spiritual expression and revelation, writes,

> In Sabbateanism, extroverted ecstatic revelation was intimately linked with the message of messianism, and continued the structures of experience that had developed since the Expulsion from Spain. For the Besht, ecstatic extroverted revelation during prayer supported his public mission and his capacity to redeem souls.... [I]n certain ways, the Besht maintained structural continuity with the former experiences of revelation and messianism through his language and practice.[67]

In a sense, the entire spiritual grammar of Hasidism is, like Frankism, a displacement of the Sabbatean messianic impulse into here-and-now spiritual experience, led by a charismatic/prophetic leader from outside the rabbinic hierarchy, and a critique of overly legalistic observance as deadening.

Of course, there were many differences as well. Frankism did not possess Hasidism's panentheistic theology that would later become central in neo-Hasidism and New Age Judaism.[68] Frankism rejected practices that were central to Hasidism, such as repentance, prayer, and conformity with Jewish law. And while both Frankism and Hasidism took triumphalist positions vis-à-vis non-Jews, Frankism did not possess the ontological hierarchy that many Hasidic masters, such as R. Levi Yitzhak of Berdichev and R. Schneur Zalman of Liady, postulated, in which Jews possess fundamentally different (and higher) souls than non-Jews.[69] On the contrary, as we saw in chapter 2, Late Frankism put forth a quasi-universalism. Nevertheless, in terms of their prioritization of what would later come to be called spiritual experience, as well as in many of the ways in which that experience would be articulated, Frankism and Hasidism are sister branches of Sabbateanism, though one withered and the other flourished.

---

[66] Weiss, *Studies*, 29–30.
[67] Pedaya, "*Iggeret HaKodesh*," 348–49.
[68] See Michaelson, *Everything Is God*, 63–74.
[69] See Rose, "Hasidism and the Religious Other," 114–17.

New Age Judaism

Shaul Magid has described Jewish Renewal, a movement of Jewish spirituality associated with the phenomenon known as the "New Age,"[70] as "Sabbateanism on the other side of modernity."[71] The phenomenological similarities are indeed striking. As Frank did, New Age Jewish movements critique normative Jewish observance; embrace a syncretic and universalized iteration (and simplification) of Jewish mysticism;[72] see sexuality as an enactment of liberation; and emphasize the personal and spiritual over the communal and historical. Like Frankism, New Age Judaism, in its various forms, generally emphasizes this-worldly spirituality and subjective experience over nomic observance or study of traditional legal topics; the "shamanic" leader who ventures to other worlds, has transformative spiritual experiences, and then returns to tend to the material and spiritual needs of his/her community;[73] boundary-crossing ecumenism and syncretism; antitextualism;[74] the emphasis on personal transformation rather than communal-historical affiliation;[75] and a rejection of Jewish strictures that are seen to be ascetic or otherwise anti-humanistic.

More broadly, in Hanegraaff's words, the New Age emphasizes the "primacy of personal religious experience and a this-worldly holism, but expresses criticisms of Western culture in terms of the secular premises of that culture."[76] What Boaz Huss has described as postmodern spirituality, including the New Age, emphasizes self-transformation over collective destiny,[77] as does late Frankism. Even the notion of a Jewish "spirituality," as Boaz Huss describes, itself reflects this dynamic, insofar as it denotes a Jewish praxis centered on internal, subjective religious/mystical experience rather

---

[70] On these trends in Judaism, see Magid, *American Post-Judaism*, 115–32; Salkin, "New Age Judaism"; Ariel, "From Neo-Hasidism to Outreach Yeshivot"; Weissler, "Performing Kabbalah"; Garb, *Chosen*, 80; Rothenberg & Vallely, eds., *New Age Judaism*. On the New Age and "spiritual revolution" in Western religion and postreligion, see Hanegraaff, *New Age Religion*, 324–27; Heelas and Woodhead, *The Spiritual Revolution*; Fuller, *Spiritual, But Not Religious*; Forman, *Grassroots Spirituality*. The term "New Age" is often used in a derogatory fashion, but that is not my intention here. As we will see, it refers to a set of cultural, spiritual, and economic processes that can be analyzed without a normative or theological position on their value. See Huss, "Spirituality," 47–49.
[71] Magid, *American Post-Judaism*, 131.
[72] Salkin, "New Age Judaism," 366–67; Posen, "Beyond New Age," 73.
[73] Garb, *Shamanic Trance*, 3.
[74] See Ariel, "From Neo-Hasidism to Outreach Yeshivot," 28; Myers, "Kabbalah for the Gentiles"; Weissler, "Performing Kabbalah"; Magid, *American Post-Judaism*, 115–16.
[75] Hanegraaff, *New Age Religion*, 331–61.
[76] Ibid., 524.
[77] Huss, "The New Age of Kabbalah," 107–25.

than on nomic observance or tribal affiliation, and the "notion that spirituality can exist outside of the realm of religion."[78] Indeed, while there are no direct historical connections between Frank and New Age Judaism, these and other phenomenological similarities are so great that it can often seem as though New Age Judaism is, rather as Magid describes, Frankism for the twenty-first century.

The phenomenological affinities are not coincidental. As Hanegraaff has shown, the New Age in general is a direct descendent of Western esotericism, the movement of which late Frankism was a part, and shares many of its central preoccupations.[79] These include (pseudo-)science, a quasi-Romantic critique of normative religious structures, emphases on energies and correspondences, a syncretic approach to multiple wisdom traditions; and a psychologized understanding of personal spiritual experience. The streams of Western esotericism that flowed into the New Age also include Kabbalah (or, as it is often spelled in this context, "Qabalah"), reread in terms of magic, myth, and a kind of universal science.[80] The most influential expressions of Kabbalah that influenced the New Age come not from classical Jewish sources but from late nineteenth- and early twentieth-century occultists, figures such as S. L. MacGregor Mathers, Eliphas Levi/Alphone Louise Constant (whose work Scholem described as being, like that of Frank, "supreme charlatanism"[81]), and Aleister Crowley.[82] Thus with New Age Judaism, a curious evolution of Kabbalah has come full circle: Kabbalah influenced Christian/esoteric Kabbalah; Christian/esoteric Kabbalah (and sometimes, including Sabbatean Kabbalah via figures like Frank and Eibeschütz) influenced Western esotericism; Western esotericism influenced the syncretic Kabbalah of the nineteenth century; that syncretic Kabbalah influenced the New Age; and the New Age influenced New Age Judaism, including its presentations of Kabbalah.

Once again, however, there are more ideological and sociological affinities than historical points of contact. Primarily, as noted above, there is the conception of "spirituality" itself: a practice centered on internal experience rather than communal norms, on personal transformation rather than historic change, and on personal fulfillment as a goal in and of itself.[83] If

---

[78] Huss, "Spirituality," 47–49.
[79] Hanegraaff, *New Age Religion*, 324–27; Sutcliffe, *Children of the New Age*. Other influences include Romanticism, transcendentalism, theosophy, and the psychology of religious experience.
[80] See Asprem, "Kabbalah Recreata," 149–50; Huss, "Qabbalah, the Theos-Sophia of the Jews."
[81] Scholem, *Kabbalah*, 203.
[82] See Feuerstein, *Holy Madness*, 59–63; Urban, "The Beast with Two Backs."
[83] See Huss, "Spirituality," 47–49.

Hasidism domesticated the "intensification of religious life" from Sabbatean messianism, rendering it "kosher" within Jewish normative frames (a project continued by contemporary neo-Hasidism), more radical forms of New Age Judaism rewilded it. Indeed, it did so to a greater extent than Frankism, which ultimately reserved such experiences for the Brethren; in New Age Judaism, mystical experience—at least as defined by practitioners—is said to be available to everyone. New Age Judaism is also more universalist than Frankism; if we again recall Frank's metaphor of the tree that appears to be three branches (Christianity, Judaism, and Islam) but is in reality only one, New Age Judaism embraces the entire pluralistic tree, including non-Western and non-Northern religions as well—a deep ecumenicism in part inherited from Western esotericism. Hasidism adapted Sabbatean spiritual grammar into a normative Jewish frame; New Age Judaism does away with that frame and expands the ecumenical and spiritual project well beyond its original contours. And although New Age Judaism does retain some Jewish ritual practices, it does so not on the basis of a covenantal theology of obligation (as do Hasidism and neo-Hasidism) but because those practices are in the service of spiritual ends, which is to say, personalized messianic ends, in which prophecy (and, in both Frank and New Age Judaism, unusual vitality and power) is available to those who seek it.

This extends even to many New Age Jewish presentations of Kabbalah. First, as Chava Weissler has said, "As much as the use of actual Kabbalistic texts, concepts and practices, a state of communion with the Divine, achieved through contemplative or ecstatic means, *is* Kabbalah to Renewal Jews."[84] In Weissler's depiction, the Kabbalah of Jewish Renewal is a seemingly oxymoronic Kabbalah without text; it is whatever leads to the spiritual experience, just as Frank said in *ZSP* §1088, "we don't need the books of Kabbalah." Second, New Age Judaism often interprets Kabbalah through the prism of Western esotericist "Qabalah," which is magical rather than theoretical, universalistic rather than particularistic, and syncretically aligned with other spiritual maps and disciplines.[85] Though the lineage may be unknown to practitioners of New Age Judaism, the "Kabbalah" they experience is, in fact, filtered through Western esotericism, then through the New Age, then "back" into New Age Judaism.

---

[84] Weissler, "Performing Kabbalah," 41.
[85] Huss, "Qabbalah"; Huss, "New Age of Kabbalah." In some cases, especially in the eighteenth century, it was explicitly Sabbatean. See Maciejko, "A Portrait of the Kabbalist," 573.

New Age Judaism (and, here, Neo-Hasidism) also shares with Frankism the rejection of a Judaism obsessed with mourning and loss. In Yaakov Ariel's words, Jewish Renewal leaders

> thought that the unhappy elements of Jewish history as a persecuted minority, including the trauma of the Holocaust, made some people associate Judaism with a morbid, joyless tradition. They believed that a renewed version of Hasidic Judaism, modified to the needs of the time, could instill joy, comfort, enthusiasm and a sense of elevation into an otherwise dull Jewish scene. Bringing back the "fun" into Judaism became one of their aims.[86]

Compare that with Frank's statement in *ZSP* §988, quoted in chapter 2:

> Your way is not my way, because you fasted for your gods and lay prostrate in mourning because mourning is their due. . . . But this is not my way. When my aid arrives, I will furnish my court and keep it in festive garments. I will provide all comfort in food and drink, I will have my own music, my own theater, my own actors, and everyone will rejoice and dance together . . . because my God does not rest just anywhere, but only where joy and merriment reside.

Frank's "aid" never came to him, of course, but his theological claim that God is present where there is joy and merriment is now widespread in mainstream American Judaism, influenced as it has been by New Age Judaism, Jewish Renewal, and neo-Hasidism.

In addition to these spiritual commitments, New Age Judaism shares the Sabbatean movement's egalitarianism, and its emphasis on sexual liberation and women's liberation. In the twentieth and twenty-first centuries, of course, these concerns play out quite differently than in the eighteenth, with unambiguous egalitarianism with respect to gender and sexuality. Recall from chapter 5 Rapoport-Albert's characterization of Sabbateanism as "an untimely eruption of female spirituality—a powerful force prematurely unleashed which was now to be stowed away, kept out of sight, and securely contained until the appointed time for its discharge, which was not to be until some unknown point in the distant messianic future.[87] That force has been

---

[86] Ariel, "From Neo-Hasidism to Outreach Yeshivot," 23. See also Magid, *American Post-Judaism*, 219–30 (discussing Jewish Renewal as a post-Holocaust Judaism).

[87] Rapoport-Albert, *Women and the Messianic Heresy*, 296, see also 265–75.

more fully unleashed in New Age Judaism, which features not only women leaders and egalitarian changes in ritual practice and textual interpretation but also goddess-language (including numerous prayers to and invocations of the Shechinah), imagery, myth, and veneration of the Divine Feminine that exceeds Frank's own.[88]

As we have already said, there is little awareness of these phenomenological affinities within New Age Jewish communities. The foremost exception to this is Rabbi Zalman Schachter-Shalomi, who himself emerged from a hybrid secular and Hasidic education to become first an emissary of the messianic Chabad movement and later the founder of Jewish Renewal and an immensely creative and innovative figure in twentieth-century Judaism.[89] Schachter-Shalomi was familiar with Sabbatean and Frankist texts (he and I discussed them together), and wrestled with the specter of Sabbateanism within both Hasidism and his own Jewish Renewal enterprise. In 1991, Schachter-Shalomi presented a discourse at a gathering of the Jewish Renewal community titled "Renewal Is Not Heresy: How We Differ from the Sabbatians," which, ironically, is one of the best summations of the two movements' similarities.[90] The text provides an apt conclusion for this chapter.

In "Renewal is Not Heresy," Schachter-Shalomi discusses several aspects of Sabbateanism. First, regarding sexual liberation, he says,

> The power of this [sexually] repressive message was very great and, from the perspective of someone in the 1600s, universally pervasive. On the other hand, what is it that makes *davvenen* [prayer] so exciting? It is the same kind of urge, a longing and yearning for the Divine Beloved. Since the object of longing could no longer be a physical beloved, the object of the longing gets sublimated. . . . Needing to put that longing someplace, it gets invested in the messianic. Loving the *mashiach* is acceptable and if, within the circles of those who believe in and are therefore freed by the *mashiach*, it is possible to enjoy sex in a way not possible before, and not

---

[88] See, e.g., Hammer and Shere, *The Jewish Priestess*; Firestone, *The Receiving*. Of course, these developments were influenced by Jewish feminism, the secular feminist movement in general, ecofeminism, and contemporary paganism, not Frankism or Sabbateanism, and many of their doctrinal and ritual changes are also found in mainstream liberal Judaism. However, the extent to which goddess language, imagery, worship, and myth its present in Jewish Renewal and other forms of New Age Judaism is distinct to those movements.

[89] See Posen, "Beyond New Age," 73–91; Michaelson, "Reb Zalman"; Magid, *American Post-Judaism*, 48–56, 64–73.

[90] An edited version of the talk was published as Schachter-Shalomi, *Renewal Is Judaism NOW*.

only within marriage, then you can have a sense of the power of this person and possibility.

We experienced some of that power in the 1960s. It was in the air; it was strong and thick. It was something like the vernalizing of seed—when you take seed and it has to get kicked into starting to grow. It's almost as if the "Greening of America," the beginning of a certain consciousness, was vernalized by the fantastic "itch" that was around for those of us who lived through the sixties. This may be another way for some of us to get a glimpse of what it felt like at the time of Shab'tai Zvi, how powerful that must have been.[91]

For Schachter-Shalomi, as perhaps for Frank, that which Scholem referred to as the "pneumatic" element in mysticism generally and Sabbateanism and Hasidism in particular, is essentially a kind of sublimated eros. The ecstatic, eroticized aspect of Hasidic prayer is well known; Schachter-Shalomi here rightly applies it to Sabbatean messianism as well. Reflecting on Jewish Renewal's similar embrace of eros in both spiritual and relational contexts, Schachter-Shalomi speculates that the experience of the sexual liberation movement may provide a prism for understanding the power of sublimated sexuality displaced onto the messianic in the case of Sabbateanism. Yet that same sublimation of sexuality into longing for the *mashiach* is re-eroticized and embodied in Frankism, with its eroticized female messiah and occasional, if limited, sexual ritual.

Yet, Schachter-Shalomi says, that Sabbateanism failed because it was "only a dream, something whose existence was mostly in the mind."[92] This echoes Frank's criticism in §2124 that Sabbetai did not convince the nations of the world, and that the Sabbatean messianic age existed only on some spiritual plane. Instead, says Schachter-Shalomi, the version of Jewish messianism that succeeded was Zionism, which (like Frankism) focused on the physical world, physical liberation, and a physical homeland. Zionism was pragmatic where Sabbateanism was "inept"—once again, a criticism Frank himself made several times. The Sabbatean response to crisis failed; the Zionist one succeeded (albeit, Schachter-Shalomi says, incompletely, because of its lack of spiritual foundation).

---

[91] Ibid., 52.
[92] Ibid., 116.

Finally, Schachter-Shalomi says that Jewish Renewal is in fact more radical than Sabbateanism because it represents a move away from the traditional Jewish worldview:

> There is another level of difference between the Jewish Renewal of today and the Sabbatian messianism, if we take Shab'tai Zvi as a representative of the way in which the expectation for the fulfilment of history has been expressed in spiritual language. The Sabbatians were playing out the messianic dream on the classical chessboard, while we say that this chessboard itself is no longer where the game is being played. Thus, our messianism is not an effort to restore, but part of our larger effort at renewal.
>
> On one level, then, it can be said that we are greater heretics than the Sabbatians. The Sabbatians at least bought into the reality map of Luria and played the game according to those rules. They said, "Do you want to release sparks? We can show you how to release sparks the way it can be done in the messianic period. . . . All you need to do is plunge into the depth of that evil, maintaining your consciousness and all its fervor. Then, pull out that spark, experience the experience, take it back, offer it to God!" They had a fantastic sense of the drama involved in entering into and experiencing that which had always been called so evil that it had to be avoided by everyone without exception. But this was still the old, static stage on which they were playing.[93]

Sabbateanism, for Schachter-Shalomi, represents "the expectation for the fulfillment of history . . . in spiritual language." But the Sabbatean movement still used the traditional Jewish map of reality; Renewal does not. Once again, Schachter-Shalomi here sets forth an almost Frankist critique of Sabbateanism. Frankism, too, saw itself as moving beyond the Jewish framework into a universalist one, and one more directly engaged with history. Frankism, too, rejected the "classical chessboard" of Jewish messianism and replaced it with a new millennialism of personal transformation and worldly power, albeit of a very different flavor from twentieth-century humanism. And yet despite that universalism, Frankism also shares the "real concern about what will happen to the Jewish people in this new age,"[94] although of course its prophecies are quite different. In sum, the Jewish Renewal

---

[93] Ibid., 119–20. See also Naor, *Post-Sabbatean Sabbateanism*, 6.
[94] Schachter-Shalomi, *Renewal is Judaism NOW*, 120.

movement, as described by its leading exponent, maintains the messianic/erotic charge of Sabbateanism (rendered even more clearly in Frankism) that comes as a response to profound crisis, but goes further than Sabbateanism in leaving behind the Jewish "reality map" in which the former messianic movement was contained—just as Frank had done. Schachter-Shalomi's talk was titled "Renewal Is Not Heresy," but the substance of the talk echoed the most notorious Jewish heresy of the modern period.

As Frankism and Hasidism did, New Age Judaism in general, and Jewish Renewal in particular, present a mystical-messianic intensity that has been "neutralized," that is to say, displaced from the historical onto the personal and experiential, and to some degree onto the erotic.[95] Like Frankism (and unlike Hasidism), it does so apart from the normative universe of Jewish law and tradition, and in a syncretic and partially universalized context that owes a great deal to the New Age's adaptation of Western esotericism. And like Frankism, it exists in a semi-heretical posture with respect to that normative Judaism, at once a part of the Jewish communal experience and apart from it.

This manifestation of Judaism, then, even more so than the skeptical-rationalist Haskalah or charismatic-mythic Hasidism, is a remarkable instance in which Frank's teachings in *ZSP* anticipate a later trend in Jewish modernity or postmodernity. In hindsight, Frank was correct that great masses of people would come to reject Judaism and Christianity, in part on skeptical grounds. He was also correct that an ideology of personal transformation would come to supplant traditional religious observance, that gender roles would be significantly loosened, and that spiritual practice could endure without the *nomos*. But he could not foresee how these changes could be brought about, absent magical beings and quasi-divine intervention. He lacked community, power, and historical timing. And ultimately, he died a failure, a seeker of immortality stricken by old age and disease, a pretender to worldly power bluffing his way through a carnival of ludicrous pretense. Yet in charting a new course for Judaism and post-Judaism, the problem was not that Jacob Frank was insufficiently radical. On the contrary, as a prophet, he was not radical enough.

---

[95] See Idel, *Messianic Mystics*, 212–14.

Acknowledgments

In 1955, Gershom Scholem wrote to Hannah Arendt regarding his research into Sabbateanism that "After fifteen years of unbelievable mining and nosing around, I've amassed so much fantastical material that I can scarcely use any of my earlier manuscripts and drafts, and nearly everything has to be completely rethought."[1]

Certainly, that has been my experience as well. Like many of its type, this book has had a long gestation, beginning with my own seduction by Jacob Frank in the Hebrew University libraries in 2005. I had intended to write my doctoral dissertation on a nondualistic Hasidic master. But after stumbling on Frankist texts shelved alongside those of Hasidism, I found myself "cheating" on my research with this bizarre figure who was so unpredictable, so complex, and so weird. Primary thanks are due to my dissertation advisor, Professor Rachel Elior, who patiently worked through two proposals on Hasidism with me before encouraging me to yield to my curiosity, and helping me to craft the dissertation that was the predecessor to this book. Fortunately, in those days, Dr. Paweł Maciejko's office was right down the hall, and I found myself chatting over coffee, vodka, and wine with some of the world's leading scholars on this subject. I am profoundly grateful for Paweł's guidance and patience, and for his exemplary model of scholarship and erudition. Sadly, another major influence on this work, Professor Ada Rapoport-Albert, passed away before its completion; I was deeply honored to have her on my dissertation committee and learn from her creativity, doggedness, and insightfulness as well. And warm thanks to Professors Matt Goldish, Boaz Huss, Moshe Idel, Steven T. Katz, Adam Shear, Samuel Hayim Brody, Shaul Magid, Ronit Meroz, Jill Hammer, Nathaniel Berman, Pinchas Giller, Cengiz Sisman, Brian Ogren, Jonatan Meir, Alexander van der Haven, Jeremy Dauber, Michael Zogry, Chava Weissler, David Halperin, Hadar Feldman Samet, and Arthur Green, for their invaluable input and for

---

[1] Arendt, *Correspondence*, 182. The Scholem letter quoted in the epigraph to this book may be found in the Scholem Archive, Correspondence, Folder 2506. The full letter is quoted and discussed in Meir and Yamamoto, *Gershom Scholem*, 70–71.

opportunities to share this work at various stages along the way. Thanks also to Hebrew University's Shmuel Feiner, Lee Israel Levine, Miriam Levine, Tova Gottesman, and Elka Tirnover.

I am grateful to my colleagues at Chicago Theological Seminary, in particular Ken Stone, Alice Hunt, Scott Haldeman, and Rachel Mikva, for the remarkable work they do and the opportunity to be part of such a dynamic and supportive community. Some of the last work on this volume was completed while I was a visiting research fellow at the Center for LGBTQ and Gender Studies in Religion, a program of the Pacific School of Religion; warm thanks to Jane Rachel Litman and Bernard Schlager for their support. Thanks to the community at the Jagiellonian University in Krakow, where I learned Polish and worked with the manuscripts of *ZSP* in a collegial and supportive atmosphere. Thanks also to the helpful commenters at the Association for Jewish Studies conferences in 2012, 2013, 2014, and 2021; the Summer Workshop on Kabbalah Research at the Van Leer Institute in 2012; and the Comparative Religion Section of the American Academy of Religion conference in 2018, where portions of this research were presented.

Thanks to Theo Calderara and Brent Matheny at Oxford University Press, especially for their forbearance during the pandemic and the missed deadlines it caused. Deep thanks to colleagues, collaborators, and assistants who have helped bring this project to completion: Luiza Newlin-Lukowicz, Joshua Fesi, Geoffrey McFarland, Rachel Dobkin, Sarah Chandler, and Andrew Novak. And thanks to teachers and fellow travelers outside the academy who encouraged and assisted me in this work, including Rabbi Zalman Schachter-Shalomi z"l, Ohad Ezrachi, Baris Telimen, and Avraham Leader. Finally, of course, none of these 95,000 + words could have been written and edited without the support, love, and childcare provided by my husband Paul Dakin, to whom my deepest thanks are due.

APPENDIX

Review of Scholarship and Textual Notes

Review of Scholarship

Frankism has been the subject of study for just over 125 years, beginning with Alexandr Kraushar in 1895. In recent years, however, the history of the Frankist movement has been understood in new and provocative ways by Paweł Maciejko and Jan Doktór, and its religious themes have been discussed by Rachel Elior, Ada Rapoport-Albert, and others. Here, I begin with a list of the Frankist primary sources at our disposal today, then review the contributions of Scholem, Elior, Maciejko, Rapoport-Albert, Lenowitz, Doktór, and Levine. Prominent contemporary scholars of Frankism also include Jonatan Meir,[1] Matt Goldish,[2] and Yehuda Liebes,[3] as well as Shinichi Yamamoto, Michael Fagenblat, Aviva Sela, Shmuel Feiner, Michael Galas, Shmuel Verses, and others.[4] Earlier scholars include Kraushar,[5] Meir Bałaban,[6] Heinrich Graetz,[7] Abraham Brawer,[8] Ben Zion Wacholder,[9] Chone Shmeruk,[10] Jacob Allerhand,[11] and Avraham Duker.[12]

As noted in chapter 1, there are few primary Frankist sources at our disposal today. While there are many sources that refer to Frank,[13] texts written by the Frankists themselves are few, with some perhaps destroyed by later generations seeking to conceal their radical or scandalous nature,[14] and others lost during the two world wars. What we now possess, in manuscript form, are:

---

[1] Meir, "Jacob Frank."
[2] Goldish, "Jacob Frank's Innovations"; Goldish, "Messianism and Ethics"; Goldish, *The Sabbatean Prophets*.
[3] Liebes, "*Tikkun*," 115–50; Liebes, "'Al Kat Yehudit Notsrit"; Liebes, "Sabbateanism and the Bounds of Religion."
[4] Yamamoto, "The Last Step"; Fagenblat, "Frankism"; Sela, "A Study of One Three-fold Tale of Jacob Frank"; Feiner, *Origins of Jewish Secularization*, 66–83; Galas, "The Influence of Frankism"; Galas, "Sabbateanism in the Seventeenth-Century Polish-Lithuanian Commonwealth"; Verses, *Haskalah and Sabbateanism*.
[5] Kraushar, *Jacob Frank: The End to the Sabbatian Heresy*.
[6] Bałaban, *Toward a History of the Frankist Movement*.
[7] Graetz, *Frank and the Frankists*.
[8] Brawer, *Studies in Galician Jewry*, 197–275. Brawer's study devotes only its final eight pages to the Frankist movement after the Lwów disputation.
[9] Wacholder, "Jacob Frank and the Frankists."
[10] Shmeruk, "Jacob Frank's Book"; Shmeruk, "The Frankist Novels."
[11] Allerhand, "The Frankist Movement and Its Polish Context."
[12] Duker, "Frankism as a Movement;" Duker, "Polish Frankism's Duration"; Duker, "Some Cabalistic and Frankist Elements."
[13] See Emden, *Sefer Shimush*; Rabinowicz, "Jacob Frank in Brno"; Scholem, "The Career of a Frankist," 128–29; Maciejko, *Mixed Multitude*, 325–35.
[14] See Brawer, *Studies in Galician Jewry*, 197–98; Duker, "Polish Frankism's Duration," 330–31.

- Two editions of *Zbiór Słów Pańskich w Brünnie Mówionych* ("The Collection of the Words of the Lord Spoken in Brünn") in the Krakow Jagiellonian Library, Mss. 6868 and 6969. Ms. 6968 contains 927 pages, and dicta 1–756. Ms. 6969, in multiple parts, contains the same dicta 1–756, dicta 757–1069, and dicta numbered 1065–1318, with an apparent numbering error, since 1065–69 are different. Following Lenowitz and Doktór, I refer to these second dicta 1065–69 as 1065A–69A.
- *Dodatek do Zbióru Słów Pańskich w Offenbach Mówionych* ("Addition to the Collection of the Words of the Lord Spoken in Offenbach"), with dicta 2120–88, together with a one-dictum "Addition to the Words of the Lord Spoken in Brünn" contained in Lublin Hieronim Łopaciński Library, Ms. 2118 (the "Lublin manuscript").
- *Widzenia Pańskie* ("Visions of the Lord"), a compilation of Frank's visions and dreams from 1775 to 1786, included in the Lublin manuscript, dicta 2189–2286.
- *Rozmaite adnotacyie, przypadki, czynności, i anektody Pańskie* ("Various notes, occurrences, activities, and anecdotes of the lord"), an incomplete narrative of Frank's career apparently compiled in the early nineteenth century, included in the Lublin manuscript.
- Additional excerpts of ZSP published by Hipolit Skimborowicz in 1866 as *Żywot, skon i nauka Jakóba Józefa Franka ze spółczesnych i dawnych źródeł oraz z 2 rękopisów*, and by Aleksander Kraushar in 1895 in his book *Frank i Frankisci polscy, 1726–1816*. Kraushar possessed two manuscripts, both now lost, one with 2191 dicta and the other with 2292.
- Two texts circulated after Frank's death, the "Red Letters" and the "Prophecies of Isaiah." Although said by Frank's followers to have been written by Frank, they are written in a very different style from ZSP, dense in biblical allusions and full of prophecies of impending apocalypse.[15]
- Assorted documents from Frankist followers, including the quasi-feminist treatise *Etwas fuer dem weibliche geschlecht die hoffen oyf das was Gott machen wird und seine heilige Hilfe naher angeht* ("Something for the Female Sex, Which Hopes for That Which God Will Do, and Concerning His Imminent Holy Help," discussed in chapter 5), probably written c. 1800 by the Prague Frankist Löw Enoch Hönig von Hönigsberg; the memoirs of Moses Porges which describe a short stay in Eve Frank's court; and various Frankist documents first published by Scholem.[16]

Jan Doktór published a printed recension of the two manuscripts of ZSP in 1997, which modernized the language and combined the two different versions of the text. Two translations of ZSP have been prepared but never published officially: Rachel Elior has prepared an "interim version" of Fania Scholem's Hebrew translation, and Harris Lenowitz has prepared an English translation that has been circulated as well. The numbering of the different recensions of the text of ZSP differ slightly, and at least three editions of the manuscript were lost in World War II, leaving only the two extant today. Hillel Levine published a Polish/Hebrew version of *Various Notes* under the title *The Kronika*, which Lenowitz has translated as well.

---

[15] See Maciejko, *Mixed Multitude*, 244. Maciejko believes that the letters were written by Frank during the Częstochowa imprisonment. Maciejko, *Mixed Multitude*, 239. Other scholars disagree. See Brawer, *Studies in Galician Jewry*, 269–75; Wacholder, "Jacob Frank and the Frankists."

[16] Scholem, "A Frankist Interpretation"; Scholem, "A Frankist Letter"; Scholem, "A Sabbathaian Will."

Gershom Scholem was the first scholar to treat Sabbateanism and Frankism as serious religious-historical phenomena, and presented Frankism as a late, extreme manifestation of Sabbateanism focused on the false messianic pretentions of Jacob Frank. On the one hand, Scholem saw Frank as "a truly corrupt and degenerate individual."[17] On the other, in the landmark essay "Redemption through Sin," Scholem pointedly criticizes those historians who regarded "the entire movement [as] a colossal hoax perpetuated by degenerates and frauds"[18] and, as we observed in chapter 2, clearly regarded Frankist "nihilism" as, in part, a liberating force. In Scholem's words:

> It is undoubtedly true that Jacob Frank was every bit the depraved and unscrupulous person he is supposed to have been, and yet the moment we seriously ponder his "teachings," or attempt to understand why masses of men should have regarded him as their leader and prophet, this same individual becomes highly problematic.... Whatever we may think of Sabbatai Zevi and Jacob Frank, the fact is: their followers ... were sincere in their faith, and it is the nature of this faith, which penetrated to the hidden depths and abysses of the human spirit, that we wish to understand.[19]

Many of these claims have been critiqued in the body of the present volume, in particular the description of Frank's character and the assertion of ideological continuity between Sabbateanism and Frankism. In general, I agree with Maciejko that "Redemption through Sin," initially written in 1936, is "unquestionably the most influential, arguably the most original, and . . . also the most misleading interpretation of Frankism."[20] Maciejko's critique centers on (1) Scholem's dialectical approach to Jewish history, which overdetermined the historical causes of Frankism and unduly minimized those causes which did not fit Scholem's metatheory; (2) Scholem's belief, stated in *Major Trends in Jewish Mysticism*, that "Lurianic Kabbalism, Sabbateanism, and Chasidism are after all three stages of the same process"; and (3) Scholem's projection onto Sabbateanism aspects of Jewish anarchism.[21] Indeed, even the title of Scholem's influential essay is problematic. The original Hebrew title is *Mitzvah haba'ah ba'averah*, the rabbinic concept of "a commandment which is fulfilled by means of a transgression." Under rabbinic law, such a commandment is null and void, but the Sabbateans inverted the meaning of this principle into antinomianism, holding that commandments are fulfilled through sin.[22] That is not Frank's view; he rejects the religion of commandments in general. Nor is sin "redemption" in any traditional sense, except insofar as it contributes to the Brethren's redemption from religion and, eventually, mortality. But the thrust of the title is Sabbatean, not Frankist; it implies the effect of hastening a historical-messianic redemption by a deliberately sinful act, perhaps because it uplifts "sparks" or "fills the kelipah with holiness," as the Sabbatean Nehemiah Hayon describes, in a passage quoted by Scholem, with traditional Kabbalistic language that one never finds in ZSP.[23]

---

[17] Scholem, *Messianic Idea*, 126–27.
[18] Ibid., 82.
[19] Ibid., 86.
[20] Maciejko, "Development," 198.
[21] Ibid.; Maciejko, "Gershom Scholem's Dialectic of Jewish History," 207–20.
[22] Scholem, *Messianic Idea*, 99.
[23] Ibid., 119–20.

After Scholem, the most sustained readings of Frankism as a religious phenomenon have been provided by Rachel Elior, particularly in a lengthy article on *ZSP* and its theology[24] in a two-volume anthology on Sabbateanism which she edited,[25] a chapter comparing Frank's life and thought with that of the Baal Shem Tov,[26] and a version of Fania Scholem's Hebrew translation of *ZSP*. Elior's article discusses Frank's theology, the language and manuscripts of the text, and the chronology of Frank's career.[27] In the article, Elior begins by depicting Frank as a man without shame and therefore, in a sense, without civilization, a liminal and marginal figure who lived in many countries but was of none; who spoke many languages but had, in a sense, no native tongue; and who half-voluntarily lived a life of marginalization, transgression, and wandering.[28] Following this introduction, Elior discusses several themes within Frankist thought: questions of genre[29] and language,[30] the "shamelessness" of Frankist antinomianism,[31] Jacob and Esau,[32] myth,[33] gender and sexuality,[34] nihilism, Frank's alienation from the Jewish world,[35] and themes of violence, suffering, impurity, and others.[36] Drawing on these themes, Elior often reflects on the "destructive and nihilistic power" of Frank's Sabbatean messianic vision, stating that Frankism is a "carnival of the grotesque in total contravention of the existing order" or a nihilistic carnival.[37] Elior also discusses how Frankism and Hasidism can be seen as divergent responses to late Sabbateanism.[38]

Paweł Maciejko's *Mixed Multitude*, based on his earlier dissertation on Frankism,[39] is the largest sustained study of Frankism as a movement, and his significant research has altered our understanding of Frankism as a historical phenomenon in many critical ways. First, as discussed above, it has greatly aided our understanding of how Frankism shifted over time, a theme we have already discussed, and how it diverged from Sabbateanism. Second, Maciejko's historical research has greatly enriched our understanding of Frankism as a movement, throughout its various stages. For example, it has borne out the evidence adduced by Israel Halperin[40] that, contrary to popular perceptions, the apostasy was essentially forced on the Frankists by the mainstream rabbinic community.[41] And Maciejko's remarks on the relationship between Frankism and eighteenth-century charlatanism forms the basis for my analysis in chapter 7. Maciejko's treatment of Frankism is

---

[24] Elior, "Jacob Frank."
[25] Elior, ed., *Ha-Halom v'Shivro*.
[26] Elior, *Mystical Origins*, 173–94.
[27] Elior, "Jacob Frank," 544–48.
[28] Ibid., 471–74.
[29] Ibid., 541–42.
[30] Ibid., 542–44.
[31] Ibid., 487–88.
[32] Ibid., 495–97.
[33] Ibid., 506–14.
[34] Ibid., 497–502.
[35] Ibid., 484–85.
[36] Ibid., 486.
[37] Ibid., 502–5.
[38] Ibid., 482.
[39] Maciejko, "Development."
[40] Halperin, ed., *Pinkas*. See also Ben Samuel, *Shivḥei ha-Besht*, 107–8.
[41] Maciejko, *Mixed Multitude*, 127–60; Maciejko, "Baruch me-Eretz Yavan," 333–54. Maciejko argues in this article that the disputation essentially created Frankism as we know it, transforming the sect from one of many Sabbatean groups to a distinct community headed by the charismatic Frank—notwithstanding the fact that Frank himself did not participate in the disputation itself.

primarily from a historical point of view: "The Development of the Frankist Movement" devotes one chapter to Frank's religious ideas and another to a literary/linguistic analysis of *ZSP*, though the bulk of this material was not included in *Mixed Multitude*. With regard to theology, Maciejko discusses the deliberate break *ZSP* makes from traditional Kabbalistic textual forms,[42] the notion of boundary-crossing,[43] the strikingly gnostic character of Frankist thought,[44] the goal of "Life,"[45] nihilism and antinomianism,[46] and the Frankist attitude toward Christianity and Poland.[47] Maciejko also provides a persuasive historical account of the Jewish community's decision to expel the Frankists rather than attempt to reform them,[48] a discussion of Christian elements in early Frankism,[49] and a comparison of Frank with contemporary European charlatans who also used occult and esoteric knowledge to advance themselves in the world.[50]

Ada Rapoport-Albert has greatly enriched our understanding of the roles of women, sexuality, prophecy, and ecstasy in Frankism and Sabbateanism, as well as the relationship between theology and social practice in Frankist communities, primarily in two works: her monograph *Women and the Messianic Heresy of Sabbetai Zevi* and her article, cowritten with Cesar Merchan Hamann, included as an appendix to that volume, "Something for the Female Sex: A Call for the Liberation of Women, and the Release of the Female Libido from the 'Shackles of Shame,' in an Anonymous Frankist Manuscript from Prague c. 1800." Rapoport-Albert shows that not only did women have markers of authority in the Frankist camp[51] but also they took meaningful leadership and prophetic roles in Frankist and Sabbatean circles, such figures including Chaya Shorr as well as Eve Frank herself.[52] Rapoport-Albert discusses in detail the Kabbalistic framework that legitimated this change, as applied both to earlier Sabbateanism and Frankism, particularly in Prague.[53] In particular, Rapoport-Albert and Hamann's study of the fascinating text "Something for the Female Sex," likely authored by the Prague Frankist Löw Enoch Hönig von Hönigsberg, sheds enormous light on how Frankist approaches to gender were adapted by the Haskalah-influenced community in Prague, and is discussed in chapters 5 and 8.[54]

Harris Lenowitz has authored a number of short studies of Frankism and prepared an English-language edition of *ZSP* in 2004 that he has since published online.[55] Most of Lenowitz's studies focus on the literary character of *ZSP* as well as Lenowitz's psychological-literary studies of Frank.[56] His 1982 "Introduction to the *Sayings* of Jacob

---

[42] Maciejko, "Development," 194.
[43] Ibid., 196–97.
[44] Ibid., 205–7.
[45] Ibid., 201–2. Maciejko relates Frankist chiliasm to the typologies of Karl Mannheim. See Mannheim, *Collected Works*. Vol. 1, *Ideology and Utopia*, 190–92.
[46] Maciejko, "Development," 203–4.
[47] Ibid., 212–14.
[48] Maciejko, "Baruch me-Eretz Yavan."
[49] Maciejko, "Christian Elements."
[50] Maciejko, "Sabbatean Charlatans." Much of this material was included in idem., *Mixed Multitude*, 199–261.
[51] Rapoport-Albert, *Women and the Messianic Heresy*, 261.
[52] Ibid., 163–64, 171–72.
[53] Ibid., 262–308.
[54] Rapoport-Albert and Hamann, "Something for the Female Sex," 87–88.
[55] See http://archive.org/stream/TheCollectionOfTheWordsOfTheLordJacobFrank/.
[56] See Lenowitz, "The Three-Fold Tales"; idem., "The Three-Fold Tales of Jacob Frank"; idem., "Jacob Frank Fabricates a Golem"; idem., The Tale of Zahak in Frank Jacob's 'Collection of the Words

Frank" remains a concise summary of issues of composition, language, and dating, together with speculative phenomenological comparisons to myths from other cultures.[57] Lenowitz's characterization of Frank as an "ethnographer, mythopoet, and charlatan" is a provocative one.[58] Lenowitz has also provided a schema for understanding how Frank's tales have exoteric, esoteric, and hagiographical layers to them, each of which mutually reinforces the others.[59]

The Polish scholar Jan Doktór has prepared a redaction of the Polish texts of *ZSP* and *Various Notes*, thus greatly increasing access to the Frankist corpus.[60] Doktór's own views of Frankism are summarized in numerous articles.[61] Like Maciejko, Doktór observes that Frankism evolved so greatly between the 1750s (the post-Częstochowa period) and the period following Frank's death that "we are faced with different Messianic doctrines."[62] Doktór describes the initial doctrine as a synthesis of Sabbatean and Christian elements, based largely on the teachings of Baruchiah Russo, but sometimes identifying Frank as Christ incarnate, and the second period as taking shape in the Częstochowa monastery, disavowing claims to Frank's divinity and orienting toward the Cult of the Virgin at Jasna Gora, where, according to Doktór, Frank believed the Shechinah was "imprisoned."[63] Parting with Maciejko, Doktór describes a sect pulled in different directions by Frank and other messianic pretenders, and by different iterations of the sect's mission.[64]

The sociologist of religion Hillel Levine made valuable and controversial contributions to our understanding of the Frankist movement, primarily as translator and compiler of *Various Notes*, but also by providing a socioeconomically oriented analysis of Frankism as a movement. In "Frankism as Worldly Messianism," Levine attributes Frankism's success to social changes in the status of Jews in Poland: Jews, formerly dependent on the king, found themselves adrift as the monarchy's power waned in the eighteenth century, amid rising tides of economically motivated antisemitism.[65] At precisely this time, Frank adopted a religious ideology of outward assimilation and embracing the dominant religion.[66] Similarly, in "Frankism as a 'Cargo Cult,'" Levine argues that the reasons Polish Frankists converted while Moravian Frankists did not are chiefly attributable to differences in the motives Jews had to convert (higher in Poland than in Moravia).[67] Noting how myths transform into ideologies under particular social circumstances, Levine suggests an analogy to Melanesian "cargo cults," in which indigenous populations came to believe themselves to be the rightful owners of colonizers' cargo, eventually

---

of the Lord.'" Other literary treatments of the Frankist corpus include Sela, "A Study in One Three-Fold Tale of Jacob Frank"; Heitner-Siev, "Avraham Esav Yaakov."

[57] Lenowitz, "An Introduction."
[58] Lenowitz, "Charlatan at the *Gottes Haus*."
[59] Lenowitz, "The Three-Fold Tales of Jacob Frank."
[60] Unfortunately, Doktór modernized the language of *ZSP* in his edition in ways which occasionally lose some of the original meaning.
[61] Doktór, "Jakub Frank"; Doktór, "The Non-Christian Frankists"; Doktór, "Frankism: The History of Jacob Frank"; Doktór, "Lanckoroń in 1756."
[62] Doktór, "Jakub Frank," 53.
[63] Ibid., 64.
[64] Doktór, "Frankism: The History of Jacob Frank."
[65] See Doktór, "Jakub Frank," 287–90.
[66] Ibid., 293–94.
[67] Levine, "The Lublin Manuscript," 83–92. Levine also produced a short study of the Lublin manuscript of *ZSP* and *RA*. Levine, "The Lublin Manuscript."

adopting worldly means to bring its restoration about.[68] Levine's account addresses the curiosity of how a group of rational, wealthy Prague Haskalah Jews retained a sense of loyalty to the nonrational, nearly-bankrupt Jacob Frank—an anomaly observed by members and descendants of the Prague community itself, from Moses Porges to Louis Brandeis.

Zbiór Słów Pańskich: Date of Composition and Statistical Analysis

What is *Zbiór Słów Pańskich*? And what it is about? As discussed in chapter 1, these seemingly simple questions have proven remarkably difficult to answer in scholarship, first because the text was not accessible and second because, on the surface at least, there is no other text like it: part autohagiography, part theology, part record of an abusive sect leader, and many other parts as well, all in a form that, at first, admits of little editing or organization. In brief, ZSP is a chronologically organized collection of Jacob Frank's oral teachings from the late period of the Frankist career, and its themes are primarily Frank himself, his critique of religion, his esotericist myth, and the mission of the Frankist company, together with a wide variety of teachings on the end times, magic, folklore, and other topics.

Since Maciejko, Doktór, and Lenowitz have engaged in great depth with the textual issues regarding ZSP and the manuscripts in which it is contained, I limit my analysis here to two questions: the editing and ordering of the text on the one hand, and a statistical analysis of the topics it covers on the other.

ZSP is not organized thematically and indeed has often been regarded as a random assemblage of recorded oral teachings. However, a close reading of the Jagiellonian manuscript of ZSP reveals that it was more or less chronologically recorded over the course of the year 1784. Only a few of the dicta contain specific dates, but many of the recorded dreams do. With the exception of §§450 and 451 (Oct. 20, 1784), and §1223 (Nov. 17), all of the "dream dicta" appear in chronological order: 495 (Jan. 7), 750 (May 5), 839 (July 1), 886 (July 26), 915 (Aug. 12), 970 (Sept. 4), 971 (Sept. 5), 998 (Sept. 11), 999 (Sept. 12), 1033 (Oct. 18), 1045 (Oct. 24), 1069 (Oct. 28), 1081 (Nov. 1), 1092 (Nov. 2), 1168 (Nov. 24), 1187 (Dec. 6), and 1187A (Dec. 8). Interpolating the dream dicta with the few other dicta with dates, the chronological order of the manuscript becomes clear. The dated dicta of all types are:

450: October 20
451: October 20
495: January 7
750: May 5
827: June 19–21
839: July 1
886: July 2
915: August 12
970: September 4
971: September 5
998: September 11

[68] Ibid., 89–90.

999: September 12
1007: October 6
1027: October 15
1033: October 18
1045: October 24
1069: October 28
1081: November 1
1092: November 2
1142: November 17
1168: November 24
1169: November 24
1170: November 26
1187: December 6
1223: December 17
1253: December 3

As can readily be seen, this nearly complete chronological ordering strongly suggests that the material in the Jagiellonian manuscript is a roughly chronological record of words spoken by the fifty-eight-year-old Frank in Brünn, Moravia, during the year 1784. Indeed, the "Words Spoken in Brünn" practically begins in January and ends in December, as if the arc of that particular recension was to be a "year in the life" of Frank. Why 1784? It is possible that §75, which states oracularly that "in the year 1783 began the last days," reflects the real or purported impetus for the commitment of ZSP to writing. Perhaps Frank suggested to the Brethren that with the end nigh—an event that, as described in chapter 4, would require Frank to be sundered from the Brethren for some period of time—now was the time to commit his teachings and tales to writing. But there is no direct evidence for this, and the "end of the world is nigh" theme is, of course, hardly unique to Frank or 1784.

The "Words Spoken in Offenbach" contained in the Lublin manuscript have a similar, though less full, chronological order:

2137: October 22, 1789
2164: Sukkot, 1789
2166: June 30, 1790
2168: July, 1790
2174: August 16, 1790
2175: August 19, 1790
2176: August 22, 1790
2177: September 15, 1790
2184: November 25, 1790

ZSP is not organized thematically. There are some sequences of topical concern, but these are not sustained, not set off by any introductory or transitional phrases, and not in any way thematically developed. In my view, the occurrences of these sequences are best explained by the suggestion that the text is a chronological record of Frank's homiletical and other statements, with various topics ebbing and flowing over time. Consider the first three hundred dicta of the text. Dicta 1–60 contain a high number of autobiographical statements, stories of "contrary deeds" and Frank's youth. This genre then nearly vanishes for the next hundred dicta, which are primary theological, many dealing with Jacob and Esau (§§131–35, 150–68). From §210 to §276, Frank is chiefly concerned with the Maiden, coming to Esau, and the coming end-times. Then from §278 to §301, the text contains a series of bawdy tales of Frank harassing Jews, exposing hypocrisy, and so forth. This pattern recurs throughout the text. The "Words Spoken in Offenbach" contains far less esoteric-mythological material, and more imminent prophecies (§§2120, 2123, 2125, 2150, 2153, 2158, 2162, 2163, 2172, 2180, 2182, 2185), as Frank's health and finances ebbed and he perhaps felt it necessary to reassure (or berate) any followers who might have been losing faith. In general, except for the long tale in §2186, there is less creative material in this section, which ends on a tragic, if not pathetic, note.

There is some controversy regarding the original language of the Frankist corpus. The text of ZSP as we have it today exists in Polish. However, as described in detail by Maciejko, scholars disagree as to the original language of the text's composition.[69] Scholem, Bałaban, Brawer, Duker, Levine, Shmeruk, and Elior all suggest that the text was originally written down in Hebrew or Yiddish, in turn based on oral teachings perhaps given in a polyglot of Hebrew, Yiddish, Ladino, and other languages, and then subsequently translated into Polish.[70] Doktór, Schreiner, and Maciejko believe that the original language of the manuscripts was Polish,[71] though they maintain (Maciejko with reservations) that it is unlikely the teachings were originally spoken in that language, as Frank's Polish was poor, and it appears that Frank and his disciples spoke Yiddish in daily conversation. Linguistically, as other scholars have noted, there are some turns of phrase that only make sense in Yiddish (§1106) and some puns that only work in Polish (§1193). Many times, Frank uses Hebrew, Yiddish, Ladino, and Polish terms, both in quotations and in his colloquial speech. As Maciejko notes, there is no reference anywhere, in any Frankist text, to a Hebrew or Yiddish master edition of ZSP, and no evidence whatsoever of a translation of the text in toto. Thus, the working assumption at this time is that the teachings of ZSP were likely spoken in Yiddish peppered with other languages, and were written down by Frank's disciples, primarily Mateusz Matuszewski, in Polish.[72]

In general, ZSP is not a carefully edited volume. The recension and editing of ZSP is visible both textually and on the manuscripts themselves. The Jagiellonian manuscript 6969, as I examined it in the Jagiellonian library in Krakow, is clearly written in different hands. (Indeed, there are actually several Jagiellonian manuscripts. Ms. 6968 contains §§1–653 of ZSP. Ms. 6969/1 contains §§1–193, with a slight variation in numbering. Ms. 6969/2 contains §§442–894 and then concludes "*koniec pierwszego Tomu*" (the end of the first volume). What Lenowitz refers to as Ms. 6969/3 then picks up with §§895–1070, and 6969/3b has §§1065A–1318 (actually 1324). As Lenowitz observes, there are often

---

[69] Maciejko, "Development," 179–92.

[70] See Shmeruk, "Jacob Frank's Book," (citing Yiddish puns, locutions, and grammar, and discussing Frank's own linguistic abilities); Elior, "Jacob Frank," 542–44 (discussing the views of Doktór and Kraushar, among others).

[71] Doktór and Maciejko tie the language of the text to Frankist theories of adopting local customs and crossing boundaries. Maciejko, "Development," 191–97; Frank, *Księga Słów Pańskich*, 25. Lenowitz observes that the text as we have it contains puns that make sense only in Polish or German, but concludes that it is impossible to know which language is the original. Lenowitz, "An Introduction," 96–97.

[72] Maciejko, "Development," 179–92.

numbering errors (resulting in the duplication of some dicta numbers, such as §1065) and mistakes. This was compounded in Doktór's version, which contains a numbering error at §1182. (I follow Lenowitz in referring to duplicate dicta as 1065A and 1182A. I follow Doktór's numbering, however, in the body of this book.) There are also some clear transcription errors; for example, §1241 refers to "those 12 years in Brünn," but it clearly means to refer to Częstochowa.

The editorial voice is often silent, then suddenly intrusive. For example, in §1098, in the middle of a direct record of a statement, an editorial voice breaks in, saying, "then the lord continued in this way...," and continues the record. In several dicta, it appears that simplistic morals on the value of faithfulness have been tacked on to more complex and subtle tales. For example, §96, discussed in chapter 5, tells a long and paradoxical tale of a prince being seduced by a lesser-rank princess because his princely nature causes him to trample on customs and ignore inversions. This clearly is one of many examples of Frank teaching that the truly noble one distinguishes himself by transgression, but its "moral" at the end is that the Brethren should have listened to Frank. Another example: in §576, Frank relates that on the Shavuot holiday, his father showed him a collection of twigs and told a tale of Adam creating a tree with twigs that can be used to punish children, with more twigs on the tree than sins. The young Frank responds impudently that his father should wait until tomorrow, when there will be more sins to punish! This tale is one of many examples of Frank ridiculing religion and its threats of punishment. Yet the moral simply states, "So is it with you . . . you did not want to be punished." Other examples of an apparent editorial hand missing the point of the tale itself include §§485, 491, 576, 695, 800, 840, 1189, and 1265. In all these cases, the moral that is drawn has to do with faithfulness and unfaithfulness. I suggest that these morals were added to the text at a later time, perhaps after Frank's death, as part of Eve Frank's efforts to enforce discipline and demand faithfulness. If this is true, Frank's complex mythic stories were flattened into simple exhortations for later polemical purposes—and if that is true, then the question of editorial hand in other areas (particularly in regard to censorship regarding sexuality and other controversial topics) must remain open. If the text is edited here, perhaps it has been edited elsewhere as well.

The following quantitative analyses divide *ZSP* first by topic, then by genre. (I include here both the Jagiellonian manuscripts and the Lublin manuscript, thus including both the dicta from Brünn and those from Offenbach. I do not include the "Visions of the Lord" or "Various Notes." Because some dicta are about multiple topics, the total number listed here is greater than the number of dicta in the manuscripts.) The following are the topics indexed here, together with the number of dicta in which they appear and the chapter in this book that discusses them:

1. Frank's Character (Chapter 1): 250

Braggadocio/Frank's strength	48
Bucharest, period in	45
Explanation of Frank's conduct	35
Frank's chosenness and relationship to God	37
Frank as "fool"/*prostak*	24
Dreams and visions	43 (plus 97 in *Visions of the Lord*)
Hermeneutics/How to understand teachings	18

APPENDIX 219

2. Critique of Religion, Philosophy of Transgression (Chapter 2): 237

Carnival, hypocrisy, nihilism, tricksterism	73
Religion: disrespecting; hypocrisy	67
Religion: transcending particularism	56
Transgression, inversion, boundary-crossing	41

3. Myth, Philosophy, and Theology (Chapter 3): 415

God	33
Big Brother/world behind the curtain	40
Fallenness/"gnostic" theology, three who rule the world	48
Ethical teachings (conventional)	31
Exegesis: Jacob and Esau	86
Exegesis: Other patriarchs	57
Exegesis: Other	42
Lowest to Highest/Shell/kernel	78

4. Frankist Mission and Community (Chapter 4): 655

Baptism, Edom, *Das*	58
Brothers and Sisters	45
Burden of Silence (*Ma'asah dumah*)	16
Concealment, silence	31
Deeds rather than words	20
Eve Frank	16
Followers, berating	169
Followers: demanding faith	94
Followers, relying on	30
Followers: will get worse but then better	42
Openness, visibility	21
Parables for Frankist mission	87
Specific members of the Brethren	26

5. Prophecy: 188

Prophecies: apocalyptic	156
Prophecies: transformation into new people, life	32

6. The Maiden and Sexuality (Chapter 5): 164

Dark Mother	7
Maiden	110
Sexuality	47

220   APPENDIX

7. Magic and Folklore: 233

General	62
Asmodeus	13
Balaam	10
Ba'alei kaben	23
Benayahu	7
Demonology	21
Egypt/Nile	16
Golden Thread	11
Illness and Healing	22
Queen of Sheba	22
Solomon	26

8. Judaism: 170

Jews	43
Kabbalah	38
Prayer	26
Sabbetai/Nathan of Gaza/Baruchiah/Sabbateans	56
Torah	7

9. Other Topics: 212

Humor	12
Jesus/Christianity	29
Money	66
Poland/Częstochowa	41
Teachers and Other Figures	11
Unclear/Uncertain Meaning	9
Violence	44

As this quantitative analysis shows, the dominant subject matters of *ZSP* are the Frankist mission and myth, including berating the followers for their failure; Frankist theology, including a radical critique of religion and an esoteric replacement for it; and Frank's own character. Apocalyptic prophecy, which is central to the "Red Letters," plays only a secondary role, though it appears much more in the 1789–1790 "Words Spoken in Offenbach" rather than the 1784 "Words Spoken in Brünn." Sexuality appears as a secondary theme. And references to magic and folklore greatly outnumber those to normative Judaism, Torah, and Kabbalah. These data are represented graphically on the following chart:

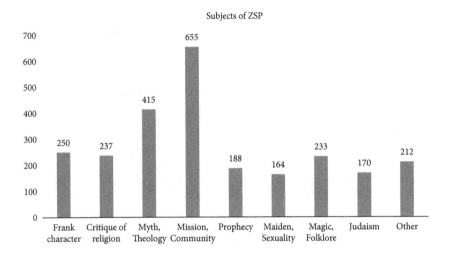

Genre

ZSP is a collection of oral teachings that span many genres, including autobiographical statements (many of which, clearly, are fanciful), interpretations of dreams and visions, biblical exegesis, exhortations to the Brethren, long and short theological utterances, tales and parables, and other material. This quantitative analysis categorizes the text of *ZSP* (again, I do not include either the "Various Notes" or the "Visions of the Lord") into eight genres with three subgenres. Where a dictum includes multiple genres, e.g., an autobiographical statement followed by a theological one, I have selected the genre that is predominant.

1. Autobiography/Hagiography: 188
1, 2, 7, 8, 10, 11, 12, 13, 14, 15, 16, 17, 18, 19, 20, 21, 22, 23, 24, 25, 26, 27, 28, 29, 30, 32, 33, 34, 35, 36, 37, 38, 39, 40, 41, 42, 43, 44, 45, 46, 47, 48, 49, 50, 51, 52, 53, 54, 55, 116, 119, 147, 150, 151, 152, 220, 223, 272, 279, 280, 282, 283, 284, 285, 286, 287, 288, 289, 290, 291, 292, 293, 294, 295, 296, 297, 298, 299, 300, 301, 325, 329, 333, 356, 365, 366, 388, 390, 395, 401, 402, 420, 427, 436, 437, 453, 458, 479, 512, 515, 522, 525, 527, 528, 532, 556, 557, 574, 575, 576, 579, 587, 621, 653, 659, 676, 686, 692, 694, 695, 707, 709, 726, 727, 751, 762, 789, 797, 819, 873, 879, 889, 904, 908, 913, 935, 936, 942, 943, 945, 951, 952, 953, 966, 994, 1006, 1007, 1017, 1019, 1025, 1026, 1031, 1036, 1039, 1053, 1074, 1075, 1076, 1077, 1078, 1079, 1083, 1128, 1136, 1137, 1157, 1173, 1199, 1200, 1202, 1219, 1232, 1234, 1236, 1237, 1240, 1252, 1256, 1263, 1265, 1276, 1284, 1297, 1298, 1308, 1311, 1313, 1314.

2. Dreams (of Frank Unless Noted): 42 (Not Including the 97 Dicta of *Visions of the Lord*)
450, 451, 452, 480, 495, 504, 748, 750 (Eve), 591, 592, 759, 791, 792, 793, 804, 822, 823, 839 (Eve), 842 (Matuszewski), 843, 852 (Eve), 856, 857, 886, 915, 970, 971, 998, 999, 1015 (Eve), 1033 (Eve), 1045 (Eve), 1069, 1081, 1092, 1093 (Matuszewski), 1094, 1168 (Eve), 1187, 1187A, 2159 (Matuszewski), 2160 (Matuszewski).

222 APPENDIX

3. Epigrammatic Statements: 40
58, 61, 89, 101, 137, 165, 221, 222, 224, 228, 231, 253, 335, 336, 363, 534, 601, 610, 642, 678, 683, 702, 715, 728, 785, 841, 863, 956, 1048, 1071, 1110, 1123, 1156, 1165, 1215, 1225, 1291, 2143, 2151, 2177.

4. Biblical Exegesis (as Primary Form Rather Than Mere Citation): 120
31, 63, 65, 68, 69, 70, 73, 74, 76, 77, 83, 84, 92, 93, 107, 117, 122, 123, 124, 131, 132, 134, 135, 136, 147, 148, 149, 156, 160, 164, 175, 178, 185, 191, 192, 196, 198, 208, 240, 242, 264, 267, 268, 275, 310, 324, 339, 340, 344, 348, 349, 350, 392, 403, 407, 462, 463, 464, 465, 466, 562, 563, 577, 581, 583, 596, 613, 614, 657, 693, 697, 732, 798, 835, 846, 851, 871, 874, 876, 877, 897, 914, 918, 921, 924, 925, 938, 944, 948, 957, 974, 975, 989, 1016, 1027, 1032, 1040, 1058, 1065, 1072, 1080, 1113, 1114, 1205, 1224, 1233, 1235, 1243, 1254, 1261, 1269, 1277, 1288, 1312, 2120, 2131, 2147, 2165, 2173, 2179, 2183.

5. Exhortations to the Followers about Mission, the Brethren's Failure, and Faith: 125
6, 66, 79, 104, 105, 111, 120, 129, 133, 144, 146, 172, 176, 183, 206, 230, 239, 241, 248, 261, 270, 281, 306, 308, 330, 362, 396, 400, 405, 409, 411, 417, 423, 424, 428, 440, 442, 449, 454, 469, 471, 478, 498, 506, 536, 538, 539, 541, 546, 550, 553, 568, 582, 595, 599, 608, 610, 612, 617, 630, 644, 648, 649, 650, 652, 701, 703, 719, 730, 733, 734, 743, 766, 774, 787, 800, 802, 824, 825, 848, 882, 883, 919, 928, 931, 932, 950, 958, 961, 963, 991, 1044, 1047, 1068A, 1102, 1111, 1121, 1124, 1127, 1129, 1130, 1131, 1132, 1133, 1146, 1147, 1155, 1182A, 1208, 1226, 1283, 1286, 2122, 2133, 2139, 2144, 2148, 2155, 2156, 2166, 2170, 2174, 2175, 2181, 2185.

6. Exhortations with Mythic/Theological Content: 127
112, 114, 168, 174, 197, 203, 214, 217, 218, 243, 249, 257, 271, 274, 343, 374, 406, 412, 414, 415, 421, 441, 443, 444, 446, 447, 448, 450, 459, 460, 462, 474, 476, 488, 493, 494, 496, 514, 530, 542, 543, 555, 558, 561, 565, 566, 567, 571, 584, 585, 597, 614, 634, 636, 658, 660, 666, 667, 681, 682, 684, 685, 689, 690, 691, 698, 710, 711, 755, 765, 770, 771, 779, 788, 801, 821, 875, 878, 887, 888, 895, 896, 902, 939, 964, 993, 1013, 1052, 1061, 1062, 1070, 1101, 1115, 1116, 1126, 1134, 1144, 1162, 1163, 1183, 1197, 1201, 1212, 1217, 1230, 1248, 1251, 1258, h1262, 1271, 1287, 1293, 1296, 1304, 1305, 1316, 2129, 2130, 2132, 2135, 2140, 2146, 2150, 2168, 2171, 2176, 2187.

7. Myth/Theology Statements—Long: 145
85, 86, 115, 126, 127, 142, 143, 145, 153, 154, 166, 170, 179, 188, 190, 195, 201, 202, 211, 232, 233, 236, 252, 258, 263, 265, 266, 305, 307, 314, 315, 319, 320, 322, 326, 327, 331, 337, 338, 341, 346, 347, 358, 361, 370, 375, 376, 377, 378, 379, 380, 381, 396, 397, 399, 410, 416, 418, 431, 513, 516, 531, 564, 573, 578, 600, 627, 628, 647, 656, 665, 679, 700, 708, 716, 725, 744, 746, 753, 775, 776, 781, 796, 813, 832, 869, 891, 901, 922, 955, 965, 977, 978, 982, 988, 990, 992, 1005, 1009, 1018, 1022, 1023, 1029, 1067A, 1082, 1088, 1089, 1096, 1097, 1100, 1106, 1140, 1153, 1171, 1174, 1175, 1178, 1180, 1181, 1190, 1194, 1195, 1196, 1198, 1203, 1206, 1210, 1220, 1221, 1227, 1244, 1259, 1266, 1267, 1270, 1273, 1274, 1275, 1280, 1282, 1285, 1290, 1299, 1302, 2184.

8. Myth/Theology Statements—Short (i.e., 1–3 lines): 195
5, 9, 62, 64, 78, 91, 95, 98, 99, 100, 102, 103, 106, 108, 109, 110, 128, 130, 157, 158, 159, 177, 186, 187, 200, 205, 209, 219, 234, 237, 238, 254, 256, 269, 302, 303, 321, 334, 345, 351,

352, 353, 354, 357, 359, 368, 369, 385, 386, 387, 393, 394, 400, 413, 422, 433, 438, 455, 461, 468, 470, 475, 486, 487, 497, 502, 503, 507, 508, 509, 510, 517, 518, 521, 524, 526, 535, 548, 549, 552, 559, 586, 588, 590, 594, 598, 602, 619, 620, 622, 623, 625, 629, 632, 635, 638, 641, 646, 662, 664, 668, 671, 673, 714, 721, 723, 729, 731, 745, 749, 757, 760, 761, 764, 767, 769, 772, 773, 778, 807, 810, 855, 864, 865, 866, 867, 868, 881, 923, 926, 930, 941, 946, 962, 967, 968, 969, 981, 995, 997, 1001, 1002, 1008, 1043, 1046, 1049, 1050, 1051, 1064, 1067, 1068, 1069A, 1087, 1103, 1104, 1107, 1108, 1110, 1112, 1117, 1135, 1141, 1145, 1150, 1159, 1182, 1184, 1191, 1204, 1228, 1238, 1239, 1278, 1279, 1292, 1294, 1303, 1306, 1309, 1315, 2121, 2126, 2127, 2128, 2136, 2138, 2142, 2145, 2152, 2154, 2157, 2162, 2169, 2178, 2188.

9. Prophecy (Including Conditional Statements of What "Would Have Happened"): 180
56, 59, 60, 67, 72, 75, 81, 82, 87, 88, 90, 94, 113, 155, 163, 167, 173, 184, 194, 199, 207, 210, 212, 215, 216, 225, 226, 227, 229, 235, 245, 250, 251, 259, 260, 262, 276, 304, 311, 312, 313, 316, 317, 318, 342, 355, 367, 371, 372, 373, 384, 398, 404, 429, 432, 439, 445, 477, 482, 483, 499, 500, 501, 519, 520, 523, 529, 537, 558, 560, 580, 589, 604, 605, 606, 607, 609, 615, 624, 631, 633, 639, 645, 651, 654, 655, 661, 672, 677, 687, 699, 717, 718, 720, 756, 782, 784, 799, 801, 803, 805, 806, 808, 809, 811, 817, 818, 826, 827, 828, 829, 831, 849, 859, 860, 885, 890, 892, 909, 910, 916, 921, 929, 940, 947, 959, 987, 1003, 1010, 1012, 1024, 1030, 1041, 1059, 1060, 1063, 1065A, 1066A, 1098, 1099, 1105, 1118, 1119, 1151, 1154, 1158, 1161, 1167, 1169, 1170, 1172, 1176, 1177, 1179, 1192, 1211, 1216, 1229, 1241, 1242, 1245, 1253, 1301, 1310, 2123, 2124, 2125, 2134, 2137, 2141, 2149, 2153, 2158, 2161, 2163, 2164, 2167, 2172, 2180, 2182.

10. Tales and Parables—Frankist Mission: 100
3, 4, 57, 59, 71, 80, 120, 121, 125, 213, 247, 273, 323, 328, 408, 425, 426, 457, 467, 473, 484, 485, 489, 490, 491, 511, 533, 540, 544, 547, 551, 569, 570, 626, 674, 706, 713, 722, 747, 752, 754, 783, 786, 812, 815, 816, 844, 845, 862, 906, 907, 920, 934, 937, 954, 960, 972, 979, 996, 1000, 1020, 1021, 1028, 1035, 1042, 1054, 1055, 1056, 1057, 1086, 1125, 1138, 1139, 1142, 1143, 1148, 1149, 1152, 1160, 1164, 1185, 1189, 1193, 1207, 1209, 1213, 1214, 1222, 1223, 1231, 1247, 1249, 1257, 1260, 1268, 1272, 1289, 1307, 1317, 2186.

11. Tales and Parables—Other/Theology: 76
96, 97, 118, 124, 138, 139, 140, 141, 171, 180, 181, 189, 193, 204, 244, 246, 255, 277, 278, 332, 360, 364, 382, 383, 389, 391, 419, 556, 593, 603, 616, 618, 648, 663, 675, 696, 705, 763, 777, 794, 820, 830, 836, 838, 870, 872, 880, 898, 899, 900, 911, 927, 933, 949, 973, 976, 983, 985, 986, 1004, 1011, 1034, 1037, 1038, 1073, 1084, 1085, 1090, 1091, 1166, 1246, 1250, 1255, 1264, 1281, 1318.

Grouping together the subcategories yields the following overall totals:

Autobiography	188
Dreams	42
Epigrams	40
Exegesis	120
Exhortations	252
Myth/Theology	340
Prophecy	180
Tales	176

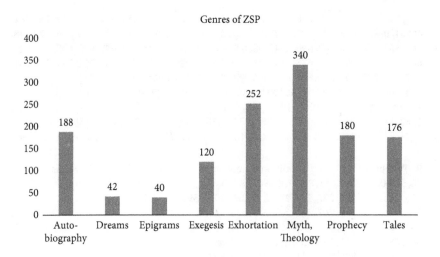

This statistical analysis suggests that ZSP is primarily a work of exhortation, myth, and theology, and secondarily one of prophecy, tales, and autobiography. Primarily, Frank is teaching his theology and exhorting his followers to stay on the right path. In terms of genre, it is not unlike contemporaneous Hasidic texts, which were often records of oral teachings, recorded chronologically as they were spoken, and concerned primarily with matters of theology and exhortations to the *tzaddik*'s followers. In this regard, Frank was not unlike a heretical *rebbe*.

Bibliography

B.1. Primary Sources

Frank, Jacob. *Zbiór Słów Pańskich (ZSP)*. See the following editions:
  a. *Księga Słów Pańskich: Ezoteryczne wykłady Jakuba Franka*. Edited by Jan Doktór. Warsaw: Semper, 1997.
  b. *Zbiór słów pańskich w Brünnie mówionych*. Biblioteka Jagiellonskia, Krakow, mss. 6968, 6969.
  c. *The Collection of the Words of the Lord*. Translated by Harris Lenowitz. Available online at https://docshare.tips/jacobfrankmsslenowitz_58785cd1b6d87fbfa28b4b5d.html.
  d. *Divrei Ha'Adon*. Translated by Fania Scholem. Edited by Rachel Elior. On file with author.

Frank, Jacob. *Rozmaite adnotacyie, przypadki, czynności, i anektody pańskie (RA)*. See the following editions:
  a. *Rozmaite adnotacyje, przypadki, czynności, i anektody Pańskie*. Edited by Jan Doktór. Warsaw: Tikkun, 1996.
  b. Levine, Hillel. *The Kronika: On Jacob Frank and the Frankist Movement*. Jerusalem: Israel Academy of Sciences and Humanities, 1984 [Hebrew].
  c. *Various Notes, Occurrences, Activities, and Anecdotes of the Lord*. Translated by Harris Lenowitz. On file with author.

Frank, Jacob. *Widzenia Pańskie*. In *Księga Słów Pańskich: Ezoteryczne wykłady Jakuba Franka*. Edited by Jan Doktór. Warsaw: Semper, 1997.

Frank, Jacob (ascribed). "Red Letters." See the following editions:
  a. Wacholder, Ben Zion. "Jacob Frank and the Frankists. Hebrew Zoharic Letters." *Hebrew Union College Annual* 53 (1982): 265–93.
  b. Brawer, Abraham. *Galitsiya ve-Yehudeha*. Jerusalem: Mosad Bialik, 1964.

Kraushar, Alexandr. *Frank i Frankisci polscy, 1726–1816: Monografia historyczna osnuta na źródłach archiwalnych i rękopiśmiennych* [Frank and the Polish Frankists]. Krakow: Gebethnera, 1895. See the following editions:
  a. *Jacob Frank: The End to the Sabbatian Heresy*. Edited and translated by Herbert Levy. Lanham, MD: University Press of America, 2001.
  b. *Frank ve-Adato*. Warsaw: M. Lewinsky, 1895.

Porges, Moses. *Memoirs*. Translated by Arnold Von der Porten. http://www.porges.net/MosesPorgesMemoirs_English.html.

Von Hönigsberg, Löw Enoch Hönig (probable). Letter ["A Frankist Letter on the History of the Faith"], transcribed by S. Zucker. Jewish National & University Library, Scholem Archive 4o 1499/155.1 and 155.2. Edited by Gershom Scholem in idem., "A Frankist

Letter on the History of the Faith." *Studies in Sabbateanism*, 634–51. Tel Aviv: 'Am 'Oved, 1991.

Von Hönigsberg, Löw Enoch Hönig (probable). *Etwas fuer dem weibliche geschlecht die hoffen oyf das was Gott machen wird und seine heilige Hilfe naher angeht* ["Something for the female sex, which hopes for that which God will do, and concerning his imminent holy Help"], Jewish National & University Library 80 2921, 99a–103a. Translated by Ada Rapoport-Albert and Cesar Merchan Hamann in Rapoport-Albert, *Women and the Messianic Heresy of Sabbatai Zevi, 1666–1816*, 297–98. Liverpool: Liverpool University Press, 2011.

B.2. Additional Primary Sources

Rabbi Avraham Chazan. *Kochvei Ohr*. Safed: Keren, 2016.

Attias, Moshe, and Gershom Scholem, eds. *Shirot ve-Tishbachot shel ha-Shabbetaim*. Tel Aviv: Yad Ben Zvi, 1947.Ben Samuel, Dov Baer. *In Praise of the Baal Shem Tov: The Earliest Collection of Legends about the Founder of Hasidism*. Translated by D. Ben Amos and J. R. Mintz. New York: Schocken, 1984.

Ben Samuel, Dov Baer. *Shivḥei ha-Beshṭ: Mahadurah muʿeret u-mevo'eret*. Edited by Avraham Rubinstein. Jerusalem: Re'uven Mas, 2005.

Blake, William. "The Marriage of Heaven and Hell." In *The Complete Poetry and Prose of William Blake*, edited by David V. Erdman, 33–45. Berkeley: University of California Press, 1982. First published 1793.

Boehme, Jacob. *Mysterium Magnum*. Vol. 1. San Rafael, CA: Hermetica Press, 2007.

Cardoso, Abraham Miguel. "Drush Zeh Eli ve-Anvehu." In *Meḥḳarim u-meḳorot le-toldot ha-Shabtaʾut ve-gilguleha*, edited by Gershom Scholem, 365–67. Jerusalem: Mosad Bialiḳ, 1974.

Cardoso, Abraham Miguel. *Selected Writings*. Translated by D. J. Halperin. Mahwah, NJ: Paulist Press, 2001.

Caro, Joseph. *Maggid Mesharim* (Hebrew), available at https://www.sefaria.org/Maggid_Meisharim.1. First published 1646.

Casanova, Giacomo. *History of My Life*. Translated by Willard R. Trask. Baltimore: Johns Hopkins University Press, 1997.de Laclos, Choderlos. "On the Education of Women." In *The Libertine Reader: Eroticism and Enlightenment in Eighteenth-Century France*, edited by Michel Feher, 113–68. Cambridge, MA: Zone, 1997.

de La Mothe Le Vayer, François, "Of Divinity." Translated by Richard Watson. In *Skepticism: An Anthology*, edited by Richard H. Popkin and José R. Maia Neto, 205–11. Amherst, NY: Prometheus Books, 2007.

Eibeshütz, R. Jonathan. *V'avo hayom el ha'ayin*. Edited by Paweł Maciejko. Los Angeles: Cherub Press, 2014.

Emden, R. Jacob. *Sefer Shimush*. Altona, 1760.

Glanvill, Joseph. *Essays on Several Important Subjects in Philosophy and Religion*. Ann Arbor, MI: Text Creation Partnership, 2003.

Halperin, Israel, ed. *Pinkas Vaʿad Arba' Aratzot* [The Records of the Council of the Four Lands]. Jerusalem: Mossad Bialik, 1945. New ed., revised and edited by Israel Bartal, 1990.

Hobbes, Thomas. *Leviathan*. Edited by Crawford Brough Macpherson. London: Penguin, 1985.

Maciejko, Paweł, ed. *Sabbatian Heresy: Writings on Mysticism, Messianism, and the Origins of Jewish Modernity*. Waltham, MA: Brandeis University Press, 2017.
Nachman of Bratzlav. *Likutei Moharan*. Safed: Keren, 1994.
Nachman of Bratzlav. *A Palace of Pearls: The Stories of Rabbi Nachman of Bratslav*. Retold by Howard Schwartz. New York: Oxford University Press, 2018.
Nachman of Bratzlav. *Rabbi Nachman's Stories*. Translated by Aryeh Kaplan. Jerusalem: Breslov Research Institute, 1983.
Nachman of Bratzlav. *Sichot HaRaN*. Safed: Keren, 1985.
Rousset de Missy, Jean (probable). *Traité des trois imposteurs*. Sydney, Australia: Wentworth Press, 2018.
Schachter-Shalomi, Zalman, *Renewal Is Judaism NOW: To See the Power of Heart in Our Time*. Edited by Daniel Siegel. Philadelphia: ALEPH: Alliance for Jewish Renewal, 2004. https://searchworks.stanford.edu/view/6911177.
Scholem, Gershom, ed. "A Frankist Interpretation of 'Hallel.'" In *Yitzhak F. Baer Jubilee Volume*, edited by Salo W. Baron and B. Dinur, 409–30. Jerusalem: Historical Society of Israel, 1960.
"Testament of Solomon: A New Translation and Introduction." Translated by Dennis C. Duling. In *The Old Testament Pseudepigrapha*. Vol. 1, *Apocalyptic Literature and Testaments*, edited by James H. Charlesworth, 935–87. New York: Doubleday, 1983.
Wollstonecraft, Mary. *A Vindication of the Rights of Woman: With Strictures on Moral and Political Subjects*. Boston: Peter Edes, 1792.

B.3. Secondary Sources

Allerhand, Jacob. "The Frankist Movement and Its Polish Context." In *Proceedings of the Conference on "Poles and Jews: Myth and Reality in the Historical Context" Held at Columbia University, March 6–10, 1983*, edited by John S. Micgiel, Robert Scott, and Harold B. Segel, 93–110. New York: Columbia University Institute on East and Central Europe, 1986.
Allison, Dale C. "Ezekiel, UFOs, and the Nation of Islam." In *After Ezekiel: Essays on the Reception of a Difficult Prophet*, edited by Paul M. Joyce and Andrew Mein, 247–57. The Library of Hebrew Bible/Old Testament Studies 535. New York: T&T Clark, 2010.
Alpert, Reuven. *Caught in the Crack: Encounters with the Jewish-Muslims of Turkey—A Spiritual Travelogue*. Spring Valley, NY: Orot, 2002.
Alvarez, Gonzalo, Francisco C. Ceballos, and Celsa Quinteiro. "The Role of Inbreeding in the Extinction of a European Royal Dynasty." *PLoS ONE* 4, no. 4 (2009): e5174. https://doi.org/10.1371/journal.pone.0005174.
Arendt, Hannah, and Gershom Scholem. *The Correspondence of Hannah Arendt and Gershom Scholem*. Edited by Marie Luise Knott. Translated by Anthony David. Chicago: University of Chicago Press, 2017.
Ariel, Yaakov. "From Neo-Hasidism to Outreach Yeshivot: The Origins of the Movements of Renewal and Return to Tradition." In *Kabbalah and Contemporary Spiritual Revival*, edited by Boaz Huss, 17–38. The Goldstein-Goren Library of Jewish Thought 14. Beer Sheva: Ben-Gurion University of the Negev Press, 2011.
Ascarelli, Roberta. "The Unfortunate Encounters of Moses Dobrushka." In *Along the Road to Esau: Studies on Jakob Frank and Frankism*, edited by Roberta Ascarelli and Klaus Davidowicz, 131–51. Rome: Bibliotheca Aretina, 2011.

Ascarelli, Roberta, and Klaus Davidowicz, eds. *Along the Road to Esau: Studies on Jakob Frank and Frankism*. Rome: Bibliotheca Aretina, 2011.

Attias, Moshe. *The Psalms and Hymns of the Sabbateans* [Hebrew]. Tel Aviv: Dvir, 1947.

Baader, Benjamin Maria, Sharon Gillerman, and Paul Lerner, eds. *Jewish Masculinities: German Jews, Gender, and History*. Bloomington: Indiana University Press, 2012.

Bader, Chris. "When Prophecy Passes Unnoticed: New Perspectives on Failed Prophecy." *Journal for the Scientific Study of Religion* 38 (1999): 119–31. https://doi.org/10.2307/1387588.

Baeck, Leo. "Romantic Religion." In *Judaism and Christianity: Essays*, edited by Walter Kaufmann, 189–291. Philadelphia: Jewish Publication Society, 1958.

Baer, Mark David. *The Dönme: Jewish Converts, Muslim Revolutionaries, and Secular Turks*. Stanford, CA: Stanford University Press, 2009.

Baer, Mark David. "Revealing a Hidden Community: Ilgaz Zorlu and the Debate in Turkey over the Dönme/Sabbateans." *Turkish Studies Association Bulletin* 23, no. 1 (Spring 1999): 68–75.

Baggett, Jerome P. *The Varieties of Nonreligious Experience: Atheism in American Culture*. New York: New York University Press, 2019.

Baker, J. Wayne. "*Sola Fide, Sola Gratia*: The Battle for Luther in Seventeenth-Century England." *Sixteenth Century Journal* 16 (1985): 115–33.

Bakhtin, Mikhail. *Rabelais and His World*. Translated by Hélène Iswolsky. Cambridge, MA: MIT Press, 1973.

Bałaban, Meir. *Toward a History of the Frankist Movement* [Hebrew]. Tel Aviv: Dvir, 1935.

Barasch, Frances K. *The Grotesque: A Study in Meanings*. Boston: de Gruyter, 1971.

Bar-Ilan, Meir. "Between Magic and Religion: Sympathetic Magic in the World of the Sages of the Mishnah and Talmud." *Review of Rabbinic Judaism* 5 (2002): 383–99. https://doi.org/10.1163/15700700260431013.

Barnai, Jacob. "Christian Messianism and the Portuguese Marranos: The Emergence of Sabbateanism in Smyrna." *Jewish History* 7, no. 2 (1993): 119–26. https://doi.org/10.1007/BF01844625.

Barnai, Jacob. "From Sabbateanism to Modernization: Ottoman Jewry on the Eve of the Ottoman Reforms and the Haskala." In *Sephardi and Middle Eastern Jewries: History and Culture in the Modern Era*, edited by Harvey E. Goldberg, 73–80. Bloomington: Indiana University Press, 1996.

Barnai, Jacob. "Outbreak of Sabbateanism: The Eastern European Factor." *Journal of Jewish Thought and Philosophy* 4 (1994): 171–83.

Barnai, Jacob. "The Sabbatean Movement in Smyrna: The Social Background." In *Jewish Sects, Religious Movements, and Political Parties: Proceedings of the Third Annual Symposium of the Philip M. and Ethel Klutznick Chair in Jewish Civilization Held on Sunday–Monday, October 14–15, 1990*, edited by Menahem Mor, 113–22. Omaha, NE: Creighton University Press, 1992.

Barnai, Jacob. "The Spread of the Sabbatean Movement in the Seventeenth and Eighteenth Centuries." In *Communication in the Jewish Diaspora: The Pre-Modern World*, edited by Sophia Menache, 313–38. Brill's Series in Jewish Studies 16. Leiden: Brill, 1996.

Bartal, Israel. "Dov of Bolechów: A Diarist of the Council of Four Lands in the Eighteenth Century." *Polin: Studies in Polish Jewry* 9 (1996): 187–91.

Bataille, Georges. *Erotism: Death and Sensuality*. Translated by Mary Dalwood. San Francisco: City Lights, 1986.

Battis, Emery. *Saints and Sectaries: Anne Hutchinson and the Antinomian Controversy in the Massachusetts Bay Colony.* Chapel Hill: University of North Carolina Press, 1962.

Begg, Ean. *The Cult of the Black Virgin.* New York: Routledge & Kegan Paul, 1985.

Belser, Julia Watts. "Rabbinic Trickster Tales: The Sex and Gender Politics of the Bavli's Sinful Sages." In *Talmudic Transgressions: Engaging the Work of Daniel Boyarin,* edited by Charlotte Fonrobert, Ishay Rosen-Zvi, Aharon Shemesh, and Moulie Vidas, 274–92. Boston: Brill, 2017.

Ben-Amos, Dan. "On Demons." In *Creation and Re-Creation in Jewish Thought: Festschrift in Honor of Joseph Dan on the Occasion of His Seventieth Birthday,* edited by Rachel Elior and Peter Schäfer, 27–38. Tübingen: Mohr Siebeck, 2005.

Ben-Zvi, Y. "Doenmeh" [Hebrew]. In *Encyclopedia Hebraica,* edited by Alexander Peli, 12:194–96. Tel Aviv: Massadah, 1968.

Benarroch, Jonatan. *Sava and Yanuqa: God, the Son and the Messiah in Zoharic Narratives* [Hebrew]. Jerusalem: Magnes Press, 2018.

Berman, Nathaniel. *Divine and Demonic in the Poetic Mythology of the Zohar: The "Other Side" of Kabbalah.* IJS Studies in Judaica 12. Leiden: Brill, 2018.

Biale, David. "The Afterlives of Shabbatai Zvi: A Lecture on the Memory of Heresy." Lecture at YIVO Institute for Jewish Research (2018). Video, 1:09:23, June 27, 2019. https://www.youtube.com/watch?v=PykXebNmnyo.

Biale, David. *Gershom Scholem: Kabbalah and Counter-History.* Cambridge, MA: Harvard University Press, 1982.

Biale, David. "Gershom Scholem on Nihilism and Anarchism." *Rethinking History: The Journal of Theory and Practice,* July 23, 2014, 1–11.

Biale, David. "Shabbtai Zvi and the Seductions of Jewish Orientalism." In *The Dream and Its Interpretation,* edited by Rachel Elior, 85–110. Jerusalem: Institute of Jewish Studies, Hebrew University of Jerusalem, 2001.

Biale, David. "Secularism and Sabbateans." *Jewish Review of Books* (Winter 2012). https://jewishreviewofbooks.com/articles/215/secularism-and-sabbateans/

Biale, David, David Assaf, Benjamin Brown, Uriel Gellman, Samuel Heilman, Moshe Rosman, Gadi Sagiv, and Marcin Wodziński. *Hasidism: A New History.* Princeton, NJ: Princeton University Press, 2018.

Bohak, Gideon. *Ancient Jewish Magic: A History.* Cambridge: Cambridge University Press, 2008.

Bosak, Meir. "Mickiewicz, Frank, and the Conquest of the Land of Israel" [Hebrew]. *Molad* 13, no. 87 (1955): 440–43.

Boswell, John. *Christianity, Social Tolerance, and Homosexuality: Gay People in Western Europe from the Beginning of the Christian Era to the Fourteenth Century.* Chicago: University of Chicago Press, 1980.

Boyarin, Daniel. *Carnal Israel: Reading Sex in Talmudic Culture.* Berkeley: University of California Press, 1993.

Boyarin, Daniel. *A Radical Jew: Paul and the Politics of Identity.* Berkeley: University of California Press, 1997.

Boyarin, Daniel. *Unheroic Conduct: The Rise of Heterosexuality and the Invention of the Jewish Man.* Berkeley: University of California Press, 1997.

Boyarin, Daniel, Daniel Itzkovitz, and Ann Pellegrini, eds. *Queer Theory and the Jewish Question.* New York: Columbia University Press, 2003.

Braiterman, Zachary. "Critical Reflections re: American Post-Judaism (Shaul Magid)." *Jewish Philosophy Place* (2013). http://jewishphilosophyplace.wordpress.com/2013/05/28/small-worlds-more-post-american-judaism-shaul-magid/.

Brawer, Abraham Ya'akov. *Studies in Galician Jewry* [Hebrew]. Jerusalem: Mosad Bialik, 1964.

Breslauer, S. Daniel, ed. *The Seductiveness of Jewish Myth: Challenge or Response?* SUNY Series in Judaica: Hermeneutics, Mysticism, and Religion. Albany: State University of New York Press, 1997.

Breuner, Nancy Frey. "The Cult of the Virgin Mary in Southern Italy and Spain." *Ethos* 20 (1992): 66–95.

Buck, Christopher. *Religious Myths and Visions of America*. Santa Barbara, CA: Praeger, 2009.

Budge, E. A. Wallis. *Egyptian Magic*. New York: Dover, 1971.

Bull, Graham E. "Desire in Psychoanalysis and Religion: A Lacanian Approach." *Pacifica* 13 (2000): 310–25. https://doi.org/10.1177/1030570X0001300305.

Burns, Douglas F. "Charisma and Religious Leadership: An Historical Analysis." *Journal for the Scientific Study of Religion* 17 (1978): 1–15. https://doi.org/10.2307/1385423.

Butler, Judith. *Bodies That Matter: On the Discursive Limits of "Sex."* New York: Routledge, 1993.

Butler, Judith. *Gender Trouble*. New York: Routledge, 1990.

Burton, Tara Isabella. "The Biblical Story the Christian Right Uses to Defend Trump." *Vox*, March 5, 2018. https://www.vox.com/identities/2018/3/5/16796892/trump-cyrus-christian-right-bible-cbn-evangelical-propaganda.

Campbell, Jan. *Arguing with the Phallus: Feminist, Queer and Postcolonial Theory: A Psychoanalytic Contribution*. London: Zed Books, 1999.

Campbell, Joseph. *The Hero with a Thousand Faces*. Cleveland, OH: Meridian, 1956.

Carlebach, Elisheva. *The Pursuit of Heresy: R. Moses Hagiz and the Sabbatean Controversies*. New York: Columbia University Press, 1990.

Carlebach, Elisheva. "Sabbatianism and the Jewish-Christian Polemic." *Proceedings of the World Congress of Jewish Studies C*, no. 2 (1989): 1–7.

Carroll, Michael P. *The Cult of the Virgin Mary*. Princeton, NJ: Princeton University Press, 1992.

Chajes, J. H. "*Entzauberung* and Jewish Modernity—On 'Magic,' Enlightenment, and Faith." *Jahrbuch des Simon-Dubnow-Instituts* 6 (2007): 191–200.

Chajes, J. H., and Yuval Harari. "Practical Kabbalah." *Aries—Journal for the Study of Western Esotericism* 19 (2019): 1–5.

Chajes, Julie, and Boaz Huss. *Theosophical Appropriations: Esotericism, Kabbalah and the Transformation of Traditions*. The Goldstein-Goren Library of Jewish Thought 21. Beer Sheva: Ben-Gurion University of the Negev Press, 2016.

Churton, Tobias. *Gnostic Philosophy from Ancient Persia to Modern Times*. Rochester, VT: Inner Traditions, 2005.

Clark, Christopher M. *The Politics of Conversion: Missionary Protestantism and the Jews in Prussia 1728–1941*. Oxford: Clarendon Press, 1995.

Crosby, Donald. "Nihilism." In *Routledge Encyclopedia of Philosophy*. doi 10.4324/9780415249126-N037-1. https://www.rep.routledge.com/articles/thematic/nihilism/v-1.

Cohn, Norman. *The Pursuit of the Millennium*. London: Secker and Warburg, 1957.

Cohn, Yehudah. "Were Tefillin Phylacteries?" *Journal of Jewish Studies* 59 (2008): 39–61. https://doi.org/10.18647/2773/JJS-2008.

Comstock, Gary David, and Susan E. Henking. *Que(e)rying Religion: A Critical Anthology*. New York: Continuum, 1997.

Corber, Robert J., and Stephen M. Valocchi, eds. *Queer Studies: An Interdisciplinary Reader*. Malden, MA: Blackwell, 2006.

Coudert, A. P. "Kabbalistic Messianism versus Kabbalistic Enlightenment." In *Millenarianism and Messianism in Early Modern European Culture*. Vol. 1, *Jewish Messianism in the Early Modern World*, edited by Matt D. Goldish and Richard H. Popkin, 107–24. Boston: Kluwer, 2001.

Crowley, Aleister. *Portable Darkness: An Aleister Crowley Reader*. Edited by Scott Michaelsen. New York: Harmony Books, 1989.

Cryle, Peter, and Lisa O'Connell, eds. *Libertine Enlightenment: Sex, Liberty and License in the Eighteenth Century*. New York: Palgrave Macmillan, 2004.

Cryle, Peter, and Lisa O'Connell. "Sex, Liberty, and Licence in the Eighteenth Century." In *Libertine Enlightenment*, edited by Peter Cryle and Lisa O'Connell, 1–14. New York: Palgrave Macmillan, 2004.

Dahan-Kalev, Henriette. "Gender, Sexuality and Queer in Modern Jewish Studies." *Journal of Modern Jewish Studies* 18, no. 2 (2019): 139–41. https://doi.org/10.1080/14725886.2019.1595497.

Dan, Joseph. "Christian Kabbalah: From Mysticism to Esotericism." In *Western Esotericism and the Science of Religion*, edited by Antoine Faivre and Wouter J. Hanegraaff, 117–29. Gnostica 2. Leuven: Peeters, 1998.

Dan, Joseph, ed. *Gershom Scholem (1897–1982): In Memoriam*. Jerusalem Studies in Jewish Thought 21. Jerusalem: Hebrew University, 2007.

Davidowicz, Klaus. "The Frankist Court at Offenbach in the Mirror of Contemporary Sources." In *Along the Road to Esau*, edited by Roberta Ascarelli and Klaus Davidowicz, 29–44. Rome: Bibliotheca Aretina, 2011.

Davidson, Hilda Roderick Ellis, ed. *Boundaries and Thresholds: Papers from a Colloquium of the Katharine Briggs Club*. Stroud, UK: Thimble Press, 1993.

Davies, Norman. *God's Playground: A History of Poland*. New York: Columbia University Press, 1982.

Dawson, Lorne L. "When Prophecy Fails and Faith Persists: A Theoretical Overview." *Nova Religio: The Journal of Alternative and Emergent Religions* 3 (1999): 60–82. https://doi.org/10.1525/nr.1999.3.1.60.

Dein, Simon. "What Really Happens When Prophecy Fails: The Case of Lubavitch." *Sociology of Religion* 62 (2001): 383–401. https://doi.org/10.2307/3712356.

Deveney, John Patrick. "The Two Theosophical Societies: Prolonged Life, Conditional Immortality, and the Individualized Immortal Monad." In *Theosophical Appropriations: Esotericism, Kabbalah and the Transformation of Traditions*, edited by Julie Chajes and Boaz Huss, 93–114. The Goldstein-Goren Library of Jewish Thought 21. Beer Sheva: Ben-Gurion University of the Negev Press, 2016.

DiCenso, James J. "Symbolism and Subjectivity: A Lacanian Approach to Religion." *Journal of Religion* 74 (1994): 45–64. https://doi.org/10.1086/489286.

Doktór, Jan. "Frankism and Its Impact on the Mutual Perceptions of Christians and Jews in Poland." *Kwartalnik Historii Żydów* 212 (2004): 486–91.

Doktór, Jan. "Frankism: The History of Jacob Frank or of the Frankists." In *New Directions in the History of the Jews in the Polish Lands*, edited by Antony Polonsky, Hanna Węgrzynek, and Andrzej Żbikowski, 261–79. Boston: Academic Studies Press, 2018.

Doktór, Jan. "Frankists and its Christian Environment in Old Poland." In *Along the Road to Esau*, edited by Roberta Ascarelli and Klaus Davidowicz, 45–64. Rome: Bibliotheca Aretina, 2011.

Doktór, Jan. "Jakub Frank, a Jewish Heresiarch and His Messianic Doctrine." *Acta Poloniae Historica* 76 (1997): 53–74.

Doktór, Jan. "Lanckoroń in 1756 and the Beginnings of Polish Frankism: An Attempt at a New Outlook." *Jewish History Quarterly* 3, no. 255 (September 2015): 396–411.

Doktór, Jan. "The Non-Christian Frankists." *Polin: Studies in Polish Jewry* 15 (2002): 131–44.

Dolansky, Shawna. *Now You See It, Now You Don't: Biblical Perspectives on the Relationship between Magic and Religion*. Winona Lake, IN: Eisenbrauns, 2008.

Douglas, Mary. *Purity and Danger: An Analysis of Concepts of Pollution and Taboo*. London: Routledge, 1966.

Dowman, Keith. *The Divine Madman: The Sublime Life and Songs of Drukpa Kunley*. Kathmandu: Pilgrim's Book House, 2000.

Duerr, Hans Peter. *Dreamtime: Concerning the Boundary between Wilderness and Civilization*. New York: Blackwell, 1985.

Duker, Abraham. "Frankism as a Movement of Polish-Jewish Synthesis." *East European Monographs* 13 (1975): 133–64.

Duker, Abraham. "The Mystery of the Jews in Mickiewicz's Towianist Lectures on Slav Literature." *The Polish Review* 7, no. 3 (1962): 40–66.

Duker, Abraham. "Polish Frankism's Duration: From Cabbalistic Judaism to Roman Catholicism and from Jewishness to Polishness." *Jewish Social Studies* 25, no. 4 (1963): 287–333.

Duker, Abraham. "Some Cabbalistic & Frankist Elements in Adam Mickiewicz's 'Dziady.'" In *Studies in Polish Civilization: Selected Papers Presented at the First Congress of the Polish Institute of Arts & Sciences in America*, edited by Damian S. Wandycz, 213–35. New York: Columbia University Institute on East and Central Europe, 1971.

Dynner, Glenn, ed. *Holy Dissent: Jewish and Christian Mystics in Eastern Europe*. Detroit: Wayne State University Press, 2011.

Ehrlich, M. Avrum. "Sabbatean Messianism as Proto-Secularism." In *Turkish-Jewish Encounters: Studies on Turkish-Jewish Relations through the Ages*, edited by Mehmet Tutuncu, 273–306. Haarlem: SOTA, 2001.

Eilberg-Schwartz, Howard. *God's Phallus: And Other Problems for Men and Monotheism*. Boston: Beacon Press, 1994.

Elior, Rachel. "Breaking the Boundaries of Time and Space in Kabbalistic Apocalypticism." In *Apocalyptic Time*, edited by Albert I. Baumgarten, 187–97. Leiden: Brill, 2000.

Elior, Rachel. *Freedom on the Tablets: The Mystical Origins and Kabbalistic Foundations of Hasidic Thought* [Hebrew]. Tel Aviv: Misrad HaBitachon, 2000.

Elior, Rachel, ed. *The Dream and Its Interpretation: The Sabbatian Movement and Its Aftermath: Messianism, Sabbatianism and Frankism*. 2 vols. Jerusalem Studies in Jewish Thought 17. Jerusalem: Institute of Jewish Studies, Hebrew University of Jerusalem, 2001.

Elior, Rachel. "Hasidism: Historical Continuity and Spiritual Change." In *Gershom Scholem's Major Trends in Jewish Mysticism: 50 Years After*, edited by Peter Schäfer and Joseph Dan, 303–24. Tübingen: Mohr Siebeck, 1993.

Elior, Rachel. "Jacob Frank and His Book *The Sayings of the Lord*: Anarchism as a Restoration of Myth and Metaphor" [Hebrew]. In *The Dream and Its Interpretation*, 2 vols., edited by Rachel Elior, 2:471–548. Jerusalem: Institute of Jewish Studies, Hebrew University of Jerusalem, 2001.

Elior, Rachel. *Jewish Mysticism: The Infinite Expression of Freedom*. Portland, OR: Littman Library of Jewish Civilization, 2010.

Elior, Rachel. *The Mystical Origins of Hasidism*. Portland, OR: Littman Library of Jewish Civilization, 2006.

Elior, Rachel. "The Paradigms of *Yesh* and *Ayin* in Hasidic Thought." In *Hasidism Reappraised*, edited by Ada Rapoport-Albert, 168–79. London: Littman Library, 1996.

Elior, Rachel. *The Three Temples: On the Emergence of Jewish Mysticism*. Portland, OR: Littman Library of Jewish Civilization, 2005.

Ellens, J. Harold, ed. *The Destructive Power of Religion: Violence in Judaism, Christianity, and Islam*. Vol. 2, *Religion, Psychology, and Violence*. London: Praeger, 2004.

Ellens, J. Harold, ed. *The Destructive Power of Religion: Violence in Judaism, Christianity, and Islam*. Vol. 3, *Models and Cases of Violence in Religion*. London: Praeger, 2004.

Elqayam, Avraham. "Bury My Faith: A Letter from Sabbatai Zevi in Exile" [Hebrew]. *Peamim* 55 (1993): 4–37.

Elqayam, Avraham. "Sabbetai Zevi's Holy Zohar" [Hebrew]. *Kabbalah* 3 (1998): 345–87.

Elqayam, Avraham. "*Shirot ve-Tishbaḥot* of the Sabbatians: A Critical Study of Gershom Scholem's Handwritten Annotations" [Hebrew]. *Kabbalah* 31 (2013): 119–68.

Elqayam, Avraham. "To Know the Messiah: The Dialectics of the Sexual Discourse in the Messianic Thought of Nathan of Gaza" [Hebrew]. *Tarbiz* 65 (1996): 637–70.

Elqayam, Avraham. "The Horizon of Reason: The Divine Madness of Sabbatai Sevi." *Kabbalah* 9 (2003): 7–61.

Endelman, Todd. *Jewish Apostasy in the Modern World*. New York: Holmes and Meier, 1987.

Endelman, Todd. "Jewish Converts in Nineteenth-Century Warsaw: A Quantitative Analysis." *Jewish Social Studies* 4, no. 1 (1997): 28–59.

Evans, Dave. *The History of British Magic after Crowley: Kenneth Grant, Amado Crowley, Chaos Magic, Satanism, Lovecraft, the Left Hand Path, Blasphemy and Magical Morality*. Harpenden, UK: Hidden Publishing, 2007.

Fagenblat, Michael. "Frankism and Frankfurtism: Historical Heresies for a Metaphysics of Our Most Human Experiences." *Bamidbar; Journal for Jewish Thought and Philosophy* 7, no. 1 (2014): 21–55.

Faivre, Antoine. *Access to Western Esotericism*. Albany: State University of New York Press, 1994.

Faivre, Antoine. *The Eternal Hermes: From Greek God to Alchemical Magus*. Grand Rapids, MI: Phanes Press, 1995.

Faivre, Antoine. *Western Esotericism: A Concise History*. Albany: State University of New York Press, 2010.

Faivre, Antoine, and Wouter J. Hanegraaff, eds. *Western Esotericism and the Science of Religion*. Gnostica 2. Leuven: Peeters, 1998.

Feher, Michel. "Libertinisms." In *The Libertine Reader: Eroticism and Enlightenment in Eighteenth-Century France*, edited by Michel Feher, 10–47. Cambridge, MA: Zone Books, 1997.

Feiner, Shmuel. *The Origins of Jewish Secularization in Eighteenth-Century Europe*. Translated by Chaya Naor. Philadelphia: University of Pennsylvania Press, 2010.

Felsenstein, Frank. *Anti-Semitic Stereotypes: A Paradigm of Otherness in English Popular Culture*. Baltimore: Johns Hopkins University Press, 1999.

Festinger, Leon. *When Prophecy Fails: A Social and Psychological Study of a Modern Group That Predicted the Destruction of the World*. New York: Harper & Row, 1964.

Feuerstein, Georg. *Holy Madness: The Shock Tactics and Radical Teachings of Crazy-Wise Adepts, Holy Fools, and Rascal Gurus*. New York: Paragon House, 1991.

Feuerstein, Georg. *Sacred Sexuality: The Erotic Spirit in the World's Great Religions*. Rochester, VT: Inner Traditions, 2003.

Firestone, Tirzah. *The Receiving: Reclaiming Jewish Women's Wisdom*. San Francisco: HarperCollins, 2003.

Fishman, Talya. "A Kabbalistic Perspective on Gender-Specific Commandments: On the Interplay of Symbols and Society." *AJS Review* 17 (1992): 199–245. https://doi.org/10.1017/S0364009400003676.

Fitzgerald, Timothy. *The Ideology of Religious Studies*. Oxford: Oxford University Press, 2004.

Fogel, M. "The Feminine in Jacob Frank: Cultural and Jungian Perspectives" [Hebrew]. Seminar paper, Hebrew University, 1997.

Forman, Robert K. C. *Grassroots Spirituality: What It Is, Why It Is Here, Where It Is Going*. Charlottesville, VA: Imprint Academic, 2004.

Freud, Sigmund. *Totem and Taboo: Some Points of Agreement between the Mental Lives of Savages and Neurotics*. Translated by James Strachey. New York: Routledge, 2001.

Fromm, Erich. *The Anatomy of Human Destructiveness*. New York, Chicago, and San Francisco: Holt, Rinehart and Winston, 1973.

Fuller, Robert C. *Spiritual, But Not Religious: Understanding Unchurched America*. Oxford: Oxford University Press, 2001.

Funkenstein, Amos. "Gershom Scholem: Charisma, *Kairos* and the Messianic Dialectic." *History and Memory* 4, no. 1 (1992): 123–42.

Galanter, Marc. *Lowering the Bar: Lawyer Jokes and Legal Culture*. Madison: University of Wisconsin Press, 2005.

Galanter, Marc. "The Three-Legged Pig: Risk Redistribution and Antinomianism in American Legal Culture." *Mississippi College Law Review* 22 (2002): 47–55.

Galas, Michael. "The Influence of Frankism on Polish Culture." *Polin: Studies in Polish Jewry* 15 (2002): 153–59.

Galas, Michael. "Sabbateanism in Polish Historiography." In *Jewish Studies in a New Europe: Proceedings of the Fifth Congress of Jewish Studies in Copenhagen 1994 under the Auspices of the European Association for Jewish Studies*, edited by Ulf Haxen, Karen Lisa Salamon, and Hanne Trauterb-Kromann, 240–46. Copenhagen: C. A. Reitzel, 1998.

Galas, Michael. "Sabbateanism in the Seventeenth-Century Polish-Lithuanian Commonwealth: A Review of the Sources." In *The Dream and Its Interpretation*, edited by Rachel Elior, 1:51*–63*. Jerusalem: Institute of Jewish Studies, Hebrew University of Jerusalem, 2001. https://www.jstor.org/stable/23365059.

Galland, China. *Longing for Darkness: Tara and the Black Madonna*. New York: Penguin, 2007.

Galley, Susanne. "Holy Men in Their Infancy: The Childhood of *Tsadikim* in Hasidic Legends." *Polin: Studies in Polish Jewry* 15 (2002): 169–86.

Garb, Jonathan. *The Chosen Will Become Herds: Studies in Twentieth-Century Kabbalah*. Translated by Yaffah Berkovits-Murciano. New Haven: Yale University Press, 2009.

Garb, Jonathan. "Gender and Power in Kabbalah: A Theoretical Investigation." *Kabbalah* 13 (2005): 79–107.
Garb, Jonathan. *Shamanic Trance in Modern Kabbalah*. Chicago: University of Chicago Press, 2011.
Gatti, Hilary. *Giordano Bruno and Renaissance Science*. Ithaca, NY: Cornell University Press, 1999.
Gatti, Hilary. *Giordano Bruno: Philosopher of the Renaissance*. Aldershot, UK: Ashgate, 2002.
Gelber, Nahum. "Three Documents about the History of Frankism in Poland" [Hebrew]. *Zion* 2 (1937): 326–32.
Gellman, Jerome. "Hasidic Mysticism as an Activism." *Religious Studies* 42 (2006): 343–49. https://doi.org/10.1017/S0034412506008468.
Girard, René. *Violence and the Sacred*. Translated by Patrick Gregory. Baltimore: Johns Hopkins University Press, 1979.
Godwin, Joscelyn. *The Theosophical Enlightenment*. Albany, NY: State University of New York Press, 1994.
Goldish, Matt. "Jacob Frank's Innovations in Messianic Leadership." In *Along the Road to Esau*, edited by Roberta Ascarelli and Klaus Davidowicz, 11–28. Rome: Bibliotheca Aretina, 2011.
Goldish, Matt. "Kabbalah, Academia, and Authenticity." *Tikkun* (September/October 2005): 63–67.
Goldish, Matt. "Messianism and Ethics." In *Rethinking the Messianic Idea in Judaism*, edited by Michael L. Morgan and Steven Weitzman, 157–73. Bloomington: Indiana University Press, 2014.
Goldish, Matt. "Sabbatai Zevi and the Sabbatian Movement." In *The Cambridge History of Judaism, Vol. VII: The Early Modern World, 1500–1815*, edited by Jonathan Karp and Adam Sutcliffe, 491–521. Cambridge: Cambridge University Press, 2018.
Goldish, Matt. *The Sabbatean Prophets*. Cambridge, MA: Harvard University Press, 2004.
Goldish, Matt. "Toward a Reevaluation of the Relationship between Kabbalah, Sabbateanism, and Heresy." In *Rabbinic Culture and Its Critics: Jewish Authority, Dissent, and Heresy in Medieval and Early Modern Times*, edited by Daniel Frank and Matt Goldish, 393–407. Detroit: Wayne State University Press, 2008.
Goldish, Matt, and Daniel Frank, eds. *Rabbinic Culture and Its Critics: Jewish Authority, Dissent, and Heresy in Medieval and Early Modern Times*. Detroit: Wayne State University Press, 2008.
Goldish, Matt, and Richard Popkin, eds. *Millenarianism and Messianism in Early Modern European Culture*. Vol. 1, *Jewish Messianism in the Early Modern World*. Boston: Kluwer, 2001.
Govinda, Anagarika. "Principles of Tantric Buddhism." In *2500 Years of Buddhism*, edited by P. V. Bapat, 357–58. New Delhi: Government of India, 1959.
Graetz, Heinrich. *Frank and the Frankists* [German, 1868]. Frankfurt: Salzwasser-Verlag, 2020.
Granziera, Patrizia. "Freemasonic Symbolism and Georgian Gardens." *Esoterica* 5 (2003): 41–72.
Green, Arthur. "Three Warsaw Mystics." *Jerusalem Studies in Jewish Thought* 13 (1996): 1–58.

Green, Arthur. *Tormented Master: The Life and Spiritual Quest of Rabbi Nahman of Bratzlav*. Woodstock, VT: Jewish Lights, 1992. First published 1979 by University of Alabama Press.

Green, Arthur, and Barry Holtz. *Your Word Is Fire: Hasidic Masters on Contemplative Prayer*. Woodstock, VT: Jewish Lights, 1993.

Green, Arthur, and Ariel Evan Mayse, eds. *A New Hasidism: Branches*. Philadelphia: Jewish Publication Society, 2019.

Green, Arthur, and Ariel Evan Mayse, eds. *A New Hasidism: Roots*. Philadelphia: Jewish Publication Society, 2019.

Green, Arthur, and Ariel Evan Mayse, "A Closing Conversation." In *A New Hasidism: Branches*, edited by Arthur Green and Ariel Evan Mayse, 425–49. Philadelphia: Jewish Publication Society, 2019.

Green, Arthur, and Zalman Schachter-Shalomi. "A Dialogue on the Beginnings of Neo-Hasidism in America." *Spectrum: A Journal of Renewal Spirituality* 3 (2007): 10–18.

Grözinger, Karl Erich. "Tzadik and Baal Shem in East European Hasidism." *Polin: Studies in Polish Jewry* 15 (2002): 159–68.

Halbertal, Moshe. *Concealment and Revelation: Esotericism in Jewish Thought and Its Philosophical Implications*. Translated by Jackie Feldman. Princeton, NJ: Princeton University Press, 2007.

Hall, David D., ed. *The Antinomian Controversy, 1636–1638: A Documentary History*. Durham, NC: Duke University Press, 1990.

Hallett, Cynthia, ed. *Scholarly Studies in Harry Potter: Applying Academic Methods to a Popular Text*. Lewiston, NY: Edwin Mellen Press, 2005.

Halperin, David J. "Abraham Cardozo and the Woman on the Moon." *Kabbalah* 8 (2003): 51–64.

Halperin, David M. *One Hundred Years of Homosexuality*. New York: Routledge, 1990.

Halperin, David J. *Sabbatai Zevi: Testimonies to a Fallen Messiah*. London: Littman Library, 2012.

Hammer, Jill and Taya Shere. *The Jewish Priestess: Ancient and New Visions of Jewish Women's Spiritual Leadership*. Teaneck, NJ: Ben Yehuda Press, 2015.

Hanegraaff, Wouter J. "The Beginnings of Occultist Kabbalah: Adolphe Francke and Eliphas Levi." In *Kabbalah and Modernity: Interpretations, Transformations, Adaptations*, edited by Boaz Huss, Marco Pasi, and Kocku von Stuckrad, 107–28. Aries Book Series 10. Leiden: Boston, 2010.

Hanegraaff, Wouter J. "Forbidden Knowledge: Anti-Esoteric Polemics and Academic Research." *Aries* 5 (2005): 225–54. https://doi.org/10.1163/1570059054761703.

Hanegraaff, Wouter J. *Hidden Intercourse: Eros and Sexuality in the History of Western Esotericism*. New York: Fordham University Press, 2010.

Hanegraaff, Wouter J. *New Age Religion and Western Culture: Esotericism in the Mirror of Secular Thought*. Albany: State University of New York Press, 1998.

Hanegraaff, Wouter J. *Western Esotericism: A Guide for the Perplexed*. London: Bloomsbury, 2013.

Hanegraaff, Wouter J., and Roelof van der Broek, eds. *Gnosis and Hermeticism from Antiquity to Modern Times*. Albany: State University of New York Press, 1997.

Harari, Yuval. "'Practical Kabbalah' and the Jewish Tradition of Magic." *Aries—Journal for the Study of Western Esotericism* 19 (2019): 38–82.

Hardyck, Jane Allyn, and Marcia Braden. "Prophecy Fails Again: A Report of a Failure to Replicate." *Journal of Abnormal and Social Psychology* 65 (1962): 136–41.

Hartigan, Emily Albrink. "Unlaw." *Buffalo Law Review* 55 (2007): 841–61.
Hawthorne, Nathaniel. *Tales and Sketches*. New York: Library of America, 1982.
Heelas, Paul, and Linda Woodhead. *The Spiritual Revolution: Why Religion Is Giving Way to Spirituality*. Oxford: Oxford University Press, 2008.
Heitner-Siev, Irit. "Avraham Esav Yaakov: The Biblical Hermeneutics of Jacob Frank" [Hebrew]. Master's thesis, Hebrew University, 2000.
Hellner-Eshed, Melila. *A River Flows from Eden: The Language of Mystical Experience in the Zohar*. Translated by Nathan Wolski. Stanford, CA: Stanford University Press, 2011.
Holquist, Michael. *Dialogism: Bakhtin and His World*. New York: Routledge, 1990.
Hundert, Gershon David. "Bandits in Bolechów: Eighteenth-Century Jewish Memoirs in Context." *Jewish History* 22 (2008): 373–85. https://doi.org/10.1007/s10 835-008-9067-6.
Hundert, Gershon David. "The Introduction to *Divre Binah* by Dov Ber of Bolechów: An Unexamined Source for the History of Jews in the Lwów Region in the Second Half of the Eighteenth Century." *AJS Review* 33 (2009): 225–69. https://doi.org/10.1017/S0364009409990018.
Hundert, Gershon David. "Jewish Popular Spirituality in the Eighteenth Century." *Polin: Studies in Polish Jewry* 15 (2002): 93–103.
Huss, Boaz, ed. *Kabbalah and Contemporary Spiritual Revival*. The Goldstein-Goren Library of Jewish Thought 14. Beer Sheva: Ben-Gurion University of the Negev Press, 2011.
Huss, Boaz. "The New Age of Kabbalah." *Journal of Modern Jewish Studies* 6, no. 2 (2007): 107–25.
Huss, Boaz. "'Qabbalah, the Theos-Sophia of the Jews': Jewish Theosophists and Their Perceptions of Kabbalah." In *Theosophical Appropriations: Esotericism, Kabbalah and the Transformation of Traditions*, edited by Julie Chajes and Boaz Huss, 137–66. The Goldstein-Goren Library of Jewish Thought 21. Beer Sheva: Ben-Gurion University of the Negev Press, 2016.
Huss, Boaz. "Sabbatianism and the Reception of the Zohar." [Hebrew]. In *The Dream and Its Interpretation*, edited by Rachel Elior, 1:53–71. Jerusalem: Institute of Jewish Studies, Hebrew University of Jerusalem, 2001.
Huss, Boaz. "Spirituality: The Emergence of a New Cultural Category and Its Challenge to the Religious and the Secular." *Journal of Contemporary Religion* 29, no. 1 (2014): 47–60. http://dx.doi.org/10.1080/13537903.2014.864803.
Icke, David. *The Trigger: The Lie That Changed the World*. Cambridge: David Icke Books, 2019.
Icke, David. "To Understand Sabbatian Frankism Is to Understand the World." Video, 52:41, December 28, 2019. https://www.youtube.com/watch?v=ZcsGNdfBgkg.
Idel, Moshe. *Absorbing Perfections: Kabbalah and Interpretation*. New Haven, CT: Yale University Press, 2002.
Idel, Moshe. "East European Hasidism: The Emergence of a Spiritual Movement." *Kabbalah* 32 (2014): 37–63.
Idel, Moshe. *Hasidism: Between Ecstasy and Magic*. Albany: State University of New York Press, 1995.
Idel, Moshe. "The Interpretations of the Secret of Incest in Early Kabbalah" [Hebrew]. *Kabbalah* 12 (2004): 89–199.
Idel, Moshe. *Kabbalah and Eros*. New Haven, CT: Yale University Press, 2005.
Idel, Moshe. *Messianic Mystics*. New Haven, CT: Yale University Press, 1998.

Idel, Moshe. "'One from a Town and Two from a Clan'—The Diffusion of Lurianic Kabbala and Sabbateanism: A Re-Examination." *Jewish History* 7 (1993): 79–104. https://doi.org/10.1007/BF01844623.

Idel, Moshe. "On Judaism, Jewish Mysticism and Magic." In *Envisioning Magic: A Princeton Seminar and Symposium*, edited by Peter Schäfer and Hans G. Kippenberg, 195–214. Studies in the History of Religions 75. Leiden: Brill, 1997.

Idel, Moshe. "On Prophecy and Early Hasidism." In *Studies in Modern Religions, Religious Movements, and the Bābī-Bahā'ī Faiths*, edited by Moshe Sharon, 41–76. Leiden: Brill, 2004.

Idel, Moshe. "On Prophecy and Magic in Sabbateanism." *Kabbalah* 8 (2003): 7–50.

Idel, Moshe. "Perceptions of Kabbalah in the Second Half of the 18th Century." *Journal of Jewish Thought and Philosophy* 1 (1991): 55–78. https://doi.org/10.1163/105369992790231059.

Idel, Moshe. "Saturn and Sabbatai Tsevi: A New Approach to Sabbateanism." In *Toward the Millennium: Messianic Expectations from the Bible to Waco*, edited by Peter Schäfer and Mark R. Cohen, 173–202. Studies in the History of Religions 77. Leiden: Brill, 1998.

Idel, Moshe. "Sexual Metaphors and Praxis in the Kabbalah." In *The Jewish Family: Metaphor and Memory*, edited by David C. Kraemer, 179–224. Oxford: Oxford University Press, 1989.

Idel, Moshe. "The Tsadik and His Soul's Sparks: From Kabbalah to Hasidism." *Jewish Quarterly Review* 103 (2013): 196–240. https://doi.org/10.1353/jqr.2013.0013.

Idel, Moshe. "Universalization and Integration: Two Concepts of Mystical Union in Jewish Mysticism." In *Mystical Union in Judaism, Christianity, and Islam: An Ecumenical Dialogue*, edited by Moshe Idel and Bernard McGinn, 27–58. New York: Continuum, 1989.

Ivanov, Sergey A. *Holy Fools in Byzantium and Beyond*. Translated by Simon Franklin. New York: Oxford University Press, 2006.

Jacob, Margaret C. *The Radical Enlightenment: Pantheists, Freemasons and Republicans*. New Orleans: Cornerstone, 2006.

Janowitz, Naomi. *Icons of Power: Ritual Practices in Late Antiquity*. University Park: Pennsylvania State University Press, 2002.

Jarzębski, Jerzy, and Joanna Trzeciak Huss. "Olga Tokarczuk's Portrait of Jacob Frank against the Backdrop of His Times." *The Polish Review* 66, no. 2 (2021): 118–27.

Jenks, Chris. *Transgression*. London: Routledge, 2003.

Jonas, Hans. *The Gnostic Religion: The Message of the Alien God and the Beginnings of Christianity*. Boston: Beacon Press, 1958.

Jordan, Mark D. *The Silence of Sodom: Homosexuality in Modern Catholicism*. Chicago: University of Chicago Press, 2000.

Jung, Carl G. *Answer to Job*. London: Routledge & Paul, 1954.

Jung, Carl G. "On the Psychology of the Trickster-Figure." In *The Archetypes and the Collective Unconscious*, 3–41. Translated by R. F. C. Hull. London: Routledge, 1959.

Kahana, Maoz. "The Allure of Forbidden Knowledge: The Temptation of Sabbatean Literature for Mainstream Rabbis in the Frankist Moment, 1756–1761." *Jewish Quarterly Review* 102, no. 4 (Fall 2012): 589–616.

Kahana, Maoz. "An Esoteric Path to Modernity: Rabbi Jacob Emden's Alchemical Quest." *Journal of Modern Jewish Studies* 12, no. 2 (2013): 253–75. https://doi.org/10.1080/14725886.2013.796154.

Kann, Nitza. "Yichud Rachel and Leah: Same-Sex Kabbalistic/Poetic Hermeneutics." *Women in Judaism: A Multidisciplinary E-Journal* 8, no. 2 (2011). Retrieved from https://wjudaism.library.utoronto.ca/index.php/wjudaism/article/view/16025.

Kantner, Katarzyna, and Marta Aleksandrowicz. "Olga Tokarczuk's *The Books of Jacob*: The Revolution in Language." *The Polish Review* 66, no. 2 (2021): 80–104.

Kaplinski, Jaan. "Being Frank? Discovering My Frankist Roots." Dockument (blog). *Journal of Levantine Studies* (2016). https://levantine-journal.org/being-frank-discovering-my-frankist-roots/.

Katz, David. *The Occult Tradition: From the Renaissance to the Present Day*. London: Jonathan Cape, 2005.

Katz, Jacob. "The First Controversy over Accepting Jews as Freemasons" [Hebrew]. *Zion* 25 (1965): 171–205.

Katz, Jacob. *Jews and Freemasons in Europe, 1723–1939*. Translated by Leonard Oschry. Cambridge, MA: Harvard University Press, 1970.

Katz, Jacob. "The Suggested Relationship between Sabbatianism, Haskalah, and Reform." In *Divine Law in Human Hands: Case Studies in Halakhic Flexibility*, edited by Jacob Katz, 504–30. Jerusalem: Magnes Press, 1998.

Kayser, Wolfgang. *The Grotesque in Art and Literature*. Translated by Ulrich Weisstein. Bloomington: Indiana University Press, 1963.

Kennedy, Duncan. "A Semiotics of Critique." *Cardozo Law Review* 22 (2001): 1147–89.

Kestenberg-Gladstein, Ruth. "The National Character of the Prague Haskalah" [Hebrew]. *Molad* 23 (1965): 221–33.

Kieval, Hillel J. *Languages of Community: The Jewish Experience in the Czech Lands*. Berkeley: University of California Press, 2000.

Kinney, Jay. *The Masonic Myth: Unlocking the Truth about the Symbols, the Secret Rites, and the History of Freemasonry*. San Francisco: HarperOne, 2009.

Koepping, Klaus-Peter. "Absurdity and Hidden Truth: Cunning Intelligence and Grotesque Body Images as Manifestations of the Trickster." *History of Religions* 24 (1985): 191–214. https://doi.org/10.1086/462997.

Kripal, Jeffrey. *Roads of Excess, Palaces of Wisdom: Eroticism and Reflexivity in the Study of Mysticism*. Chicago: University of Chicago Press, 2001.

Kugel, James. *Traditions of the Bible: A Guide to the Bible as It Was at the Start of the Common Era*. Cambridge, MA: Harvard University Press, 1999.

Kunin, Seth Daniel. *The Logic of Incest: A Structuralist Analysis of Hebrew Mythology*. Journal for the Study of the Old Testament Supplement Series 185. Sheffield: Sheffield Academic Press, 1995.

Landes, David. *The Wealth and Poverty of Nations: Why Some Are So Rich and Some So Poor*. New York: W. W. Norton, 1998.

Landes, Richard. *Heaven on Earth: The Varieties of the Millennial Experience*. Oxford: Oxford University Press, 2011.

Lang, Amy Shrager. *Prophetic Woman: Anne Hutchinson and the Problem of Dissent in the Literature of New England*. Berkeley University of California Press, 1987.

Laurence, Dan H., ed. *Bernard Shaw: Collected Letters, Vol. 3: 1911–1925*. New York: Viking, 1985.

Lehrich, Christopher. *The Occult Mind: Magic in Theory and Practice*. New Delhi: Munshiram, 2009. First published 2007 by Cornell University Press.

Leiman, Sid. "Rabbi Jonathan Eibeschuetz's Attitude towards the Frankists." *Polin: Studies in Polish Jewry* 15 (2002): 145–51.

Leiman, Sid. "When a Rabbi Is Accused of Heresy: R. Ezekiel Landau's Attitude toward R. Jonathan Eibeschütz in the Emden-Eibeschütz Controversy." In *From Ancient Israel to Modern Judaism: Intellect in Quest of Understanding: Essays in Honor of Marvin Fox*. Vol. 3, *Judaism in the Middle Ages: Philosophers, Hasidism, Messianism in Modern Times, the Modern Age: Philosophy*, edited by Jacob Neusner, 179–94. Brown Judaic Studies 174. Atlanta: Scholars Press, 1989.

Lenowitz, Harris. "The Charlatan at the *Gottes Haus* in Offenbach." In *Millenarianism and Messianism in Early Modern European Culture*. Vol. 1, *Jewish Messianism in the Early Modern World*, edited by Matt Goldish and Richard Popkin, 189–202. Boston: Kluwer, 2001.

Lenowitz, Harris. "An Introduction to the *Sayings* of Jacob Frank." *Proceedings of the World Congress of Jewish Studies* C (1981): 93–98.

Lenowitz, Harris. "Jacob Frank Fabricates a Golem." In *Rabbinic Culture and Its Critics: Jewish Authority, Dissent, and Heresy in Medieval and Early Modern Times*, edited by Daniel Frank and Matt Goldish, 409–34. Detroit: Wayne State University Press, 2008.

Lenowitz, Harris. *The Jewish Messiahs: From the Galilee to Crown Heights*. Oxford: Oxford University Press, 2001.

Lenowitz, Harris. "Leaving Turkey: The Dönme Comes to Poland." *Kabbalah* 8 (2003): 65–113.

Lenowitz, Harris. "*Me'ayin yavo 'ezri*? The *Help* of Jacob Frank and His Daughter, Ewa." In *Holy Dissent: Jewish and Christian Mystics in Eastern Europe*, edited by Glenn Dynner, 281–308. Detroit: Wayne State University Press, 2011.

Lenowitz, Harris. *Sayings of Jacob Frank*. Berkeley: Tree/Tzaddikim, 1978.

Lenowitz, Harris. "The Struggle over Images in the Propaganda of the Frankist Movement." *Polin: Studies in Polish Jewry* 15 (2002): 105–30.

Lenowitz, Harris. "The Tale of Zahak in Frank Jacob's 'Collection of the Words of the Lord.'" In *Persian Studies in North America: Studies in Honor of Mohammad Ali Jazayery*, edited by Mehdi Marashi, 339–52. Bethesda, MD: Iranbooks, 1994.

Lenowitz, Harris. "The Three-Fold Tales of Jacob Frank." *Proceedings of the World Congress of Jewish Studies, Division C: Jewish Thought and Literature* 9 (1985): 117–24.

Lenowitz, Harris. "The Visions of the Lord by Jacob Frank." *Proceedings of the World Congress of Jewish Studies, Division C: Jewish Thought and Literature* 2 (1990): 9–16.

Lenowitz, Harris, and Dan Chopyk. "Fifty Sayings of the Lord Jacob Frank." *Alcheringa: Ethnopoetics* 3, no. 2 (1977): 32–51.

Lerner, Robert. *The Heresy of the Free Spirit in the Later Middle Ages*. Notre Dame, IN: University of Notre Dame Press, 1972.

Levine, Hillel. "Jacob Frank as Christian Kabbalist." In *The Christian Kabbalah: Jewish Mystical Books and Their Christian Interpreters*, edited by Joseph Dan, 181–87. Cambridge: Harvard College Libra, 1997.

Levine, Hillel. *Economic Origins of Antisemitism: Poland and Its Jews in the Early Modern Period*. New Haven, CT: Yale University Press, 1991.

Levine, Hillel. "Frankism as a 'Cargo Cult' and the Haskalah Connection: Myth, Ideology, and the Modernization of Jewish Consciousness." In *Essays in Modern Jewish History: A Tribute to Ben Halpern*, edited by Frances Malino and Phyllis Cohen Albert, 81–94. Madison, NJ: Fairleigh Dickinson University Press, 1982.

Levine, Hillel. "Frankism as Worldly Messianism." In *Gershom Scholem's Major Trends in Jewish Mysticism: 50 Years After*, edited by Peter Schäfer and Joseph Dan, 283–300. Tübingen: Mohr Siebeck, 1993.

Levine, Hillel. "The Lublin Manuscript of the Frankist *Księga Słów Pańskich*: Some Themes." *Proceedings of the World Congress of Jewish Studies, Division C: Jewish Thought and Literature* 9 (1985): 109–16.

Lewis, James L., and Jesper Aagaard Petersen, eds. *Controversial New Religions*. Oxford: Oxford University Press, 2004.

Lieb, Michael. *Children of Ezekiel: Aliens, UFOs, the Crisis of Race, and the Advent of End Time*. Durham, NC: Duke University Press, 1998.

Liebes, Yehuda. "On a Jewish Christian Sect Based in Sabbateanism" [Hebrew]. In *The Secret of the Sabbatean Faith: Collected Papers*, 212–37. Jerusalem: Mosad Bialik, 1995.

Liebes, Yehuda. "Sabbatianism and the Bounds of Religion." [Hebrew]. In *The Dream and Its Interpretation*, edited by Rachel Elior, 1:1–22. Jerusalem: Institute of Jewish Studies, Hebrew University of Jerusalem, 2001.

Liebes, Yehuda. *The Secret of the Sabbatean Faith: Collected Papers* [Hebrew]. Jerusalem: Mosad Bialik, 1995.

Liebes, Yehuda. "*Ha-Tikkun Ha-Kelali* of R. Nahman of Bratslav and Its Sabbatean Links." In *Studies in Jewish Myth and Messianism*, translated by Batya Stein, 115–50. SUNY Series in Judaica. Albany, NY: State University of New York Press, 1993.

Lorde, Audre. "The Use of the Erotic: Erotic as Power." In *Sexuality and the Sacred: Sources for Theological Reflection*, 2nd ed., edited by Marvin Ellison and Kelly Brown Douglas, 73–77. Louisville: Westminster John Knox, 2010.

Maciejko, Paweł. "Baruch me-Eretz Yavan and the Frankist Movement: Intercession in an Age of Upheaval." *Jahrbuch des Simon-Dubnow-Instituts* 4 (2005): 333–54.

Maciejko, Paweł. "Christian Elements in Early Frankist Doctrine." *Gal-Ed* 20 (2006): 13–41.

Maciejko, Paweł. "Coitus Interruptus in *And I Came This Day unto the Fountain*." In *V'avo hayom el ha'ayin*, edited by Paweł Maciejko, ix–lii. Los Angeles: Cherub Press, 2014.

Maciejko, Paweł. "The Development of the Frankist Movement in Poland, the Czech Lands, and Germany (1755–1816)." D.Phil. thesis, Hertford College, 2003.

Maciejko, Paweł. "Gershom Scholem's Dialectic of Jewish History." *Journal of Modern Jewish Studies* 3 (2004): 207–20.

Maciejko, Paweł. "Jacob Frank and Jesus Christ (with an Excursus on Nathan of Gaza)." In *Jesus among the Jews: Representation and Thought*, edited by Neta Stahl, 119–31. London: Routledge, 2012.

Maciejko, Paweł. "A Jewish-Christian Sect with a Sabbatian Background Revisited." *Kabbalah* 14 (2006): 95–113.

Maciejko, Paweł. "The Jews' Entry into the Public Sphere: The Emden-Eibeschütz Controversy Reconsidered." *Jahrbuch des Simon-Dubnow-Instituts* 6 (2007): 135–54.

Maciejko, Paweł. "The Literary Character and Doctrine of Jacob Frank's 'The Words of the Lord.'" *Kabbalah* 9 (2003): 175–210.

Maciejko, Paweł. *The Mixed Multitude: Jacob Frank and the Frankist Movement, 1755–1816*. Philadelphia: University of Pennsylvania Press, 2011.

Maciejko, Paweł. "The Perils of Heresy, the Birth of a New Faith: The Quest for a Common Jewish-Christian Front against Frankism." In *Holy Dissent: Jewish and Christian Mystics in Eastern Europe*, edited by Glenn Dynner, 223–49. Detroit: Wayne State University Press, 2011.

Maciejko, Paweł. "A Portrait of the Kabbalist as a Young Man: Count Joseph Carl Emmanuel Waldstein and His Retinue." *Jewish Quarterly Review* 106 (2016): 521–76. https://doi.org/10.1353/jqr.2016.0037.

Maciejko, Paweł. "Sabbatian Charlatans: The First Jewish Cosmopolitans." *European Review of History/Revue européenne d'histoire* 3, no. 17 (2010): 361–78.

Magid, Shaul. *American Post-Judaism: Identity and Renewal in a Postethnic Society*. Religion in North America. Bloomington: Indiana University Press, 2013.

Magid, Shaul. *Hasidism on the Margins*. Madison: University of Wisconsin Press, 2001.

Magid, Shaul. "Rainbow Hasidism in America: The Maturation of Jewish Renewal," *The Reconstructionist* 68, no. 2 (Spring 2004): 34–60.

Mandel, Arthur. *The Militant Messiah, or the Flight from the Ghetto*. Atlantic Highlands, NJ: Humanities Press, 1979.

Mandel, Arthur. "Some Marginalia to the Later History of the Frankist Movement" [Hebrew]. *Zion* 43 (1978): 68–74.

Mannheim, Karl. *Collected Works*. Vol. 1, *Ideology and Utopia*. Wilmington, CA: Harvest Press, 1997.

Marcuse, Herbert. *Eros and Civilization: A Philosophical Inquiry into Freud*. Boston: Beacon Press, 1974.

Margalit, Natan. "Why Neo-Hasidism?" *Spectrum: A Journal of Renewal Spirituality* 3 (2007): 5–9.

Mark, Zvi. "*Ma'aseh me-ha-Shiryon* (the Tale of the Armor): The Hidden Secret of Bratslav Censorship" [Hebrew]. *Zion* 72 (2005): 191–216.

Mark, Zvi. "The Contemporary Renaissance of Braslav Hasidism: Ritual, *Tiqqun* and Messianism." In *Kabbalah and Contemporary Spiritual Revival*, edited by Boaz Huss, 101–16. The Goldstein-Goren Library of Jewish Thought 14. Beer Sheva: Ben-Gurion University of the Negev Press, 2011.

Mark, Zvi. *Mysticism and Madness: The Religious Thought of Rabbi Nachman of Bratslav*. Kogod Library of Judaic Studies 7. London: Continuum, 2009.

Marshall, Gordon. *In Search of the Spirit of Capitalism*. New York: Columbia University Press, 1983.

Martin, Stoddard. *Art, Messianism and Crime: A Study of Antinomianism in Modern Literature and Lives*. New York: St. Martin's Press, 1986.

McCutcheon, Russell T. *Manufacturing Religion: The Discourse of Sui Generis Religion and the Politics of Nostalgia*. Oxford: Oxford University Press, 2002.

McIntosh, Christopher. *The Rose Cross and the Age of Reason: Eighteenth-Century Rosicrucianism in Central Europe and Its Relationship to the Enlightenment*. Leiden: Brill, 1992.

Meir, Jonatan. "Haskalah and Esotericism: The Strange Case of Elyakim Getzel Hamilzahgi (1780–1854)." *Aries—Journal for the Study of Western Esotericism* 18 (2018): 153–87.

Meir, Jonatan. "Jacob Frank: The Wondrous Charlatan" [Hebrew]. *Tarbiz* 80, no. 3 (2012), 463–74.

Meir, Jonatan. "Marketing Demons: Joseph Perl, Israel Baal Shem Tov and the History of One Amulet." In *Kabbalah and Contemporary Spiritual Revival*, edited by Boaz Huss, 35–77. The Goldstein-Goren Library of Jewish Thought 14. Beer Sheva: Ben-Gurion University of the Negev Press, 2011.

Meir, Jonatan. "Me'ora'ot Tsvi and the Construction of Sabbatianism in the Nineteenth Century." *Making History Jewish: The Dialectics of Jewish History in Eastern Europe and the Middle East, Studies in Honor of Professor Israel Bartal*, edited by Paweł Maciejko and Scott Ury, 30–51. Series: Studia Judaeoslavica, Vol. 12. Leiden: Brill, 2020.

Meir, Jonatan, and Shinichi Yamamoto, *Gershom Scholem and the Research of Sabbatianism*. Translated by Samuel Glauber-Zimra. Jerusalem: JTS—Schocken Institute for Jewish Research and Blima Books, 2021.

Meir, Jonatan, and Noam Zadoff. "The Possibility of Frankist Traces in the Teachings of Rabbi Nachman of Bratslav: Three Passages from the Archives of Joseph Weiss" [Hebrew]. In *Gershom Scholem (1897–1982): In Memoriam*, edited by Joseph Dan, 385-413. Jerusalem: Hebrew University, 2007.

Melton, J. Gordon, Jr. "Spiritualization and Reaffirmation: What Really Happens When Prophecy Fails." *American Studies* 26 (1985): 17–29.

Michaelson, Jay. "Chaos, Law and God: The Religious Meanings of Homosexuality." *Michigan Journal of Gender and Law* 15 (2008): 41–119.

Michaelson, Jay. "Conceptualizing Jewish Antinomianism in the Teachings of Jacob Frank." *Modern Judaism: A Journal of Jewish Ideas and Experience* 37 (2017): 338–62. https://doi.org/10.1093/mj/kjx031.

Michaelson, Jay. *Everything Is God: The Radical Path of Nondual Judaism*. Boston: Trumpeter, 2009.

Michaelson, Jay. *God vs. Gay? The Religious Case for Equality*. Boston: Beacon Press, 2011.

Michaelson, Jay. "Hating the Law for Christian Reasons: The Religious Roots of American Antinomianism." In *Jews and the Law*, edited by Ari Mermelstein and Victoria Saker Woeste, 270–78. New York: Quid Pro Books, 2014.

Michaelson, Jay. "'I Do Not Look to Heaven, but at What God Does on Earth': Materialism, Sexuality and Law in the Jagellonian Manuscript of Jacob Frank's *Zbior Slow Panskich*." PhD diss., Hebrew University of Jerusalem, 2012.

Michaelson, Jay. "In Praise of the Pound of Flesh: Legalism, Multiculturalism, and the Problem of the Soul." *Journal of Law in Society* 6 (2005): 98–153.

Michaelson, Jay. "Kabbalah and Queer Theology: Resources and Reservations." *Theology and Sexuality* 18 (2012): 42–59. https://doi.org/10.1179/1355835813Z.0000000003.

Michaelson, Jay. "Rabbi-Professor: Neo-Hasidism as Spiritual Bricolage." Presentation, Van Leer Institute, 2012.

Michaelson, Jay. "Reb Zalman: The Prophet of Both-And." *Forward*, July 3, 2014. https://forward.com/news/201398/reb-zalman-the-prophet-of-both-and/

Miller, Michael L. *Rabbis and Revolution: The Jews of Moravia in the Age of Emancipation*. Palo Alto: Stanford University Press, 2010.

Miller, Michael L. "Reluctant Kingmakers: Moravian Jewish politics in Late Imperial Austria." *Jewish Studies at the Central European University* 3 (2002–2003): 111–23.

Miller, Michael L. "Voice and Vulnerability: The Vagaries of Jewish National Identity in Habsburg Moravia." *Jahrbuch des Simon-Dubnow-Instituts* 5 (2006): 159–71.

Mollenkott, Virginia Ramey. "Reading the Bible from Low and Outside: Lesbitransgay People as God's Tricksters." In *Take Back the Word: A Queer Reading of the Bible*, edited by Robert Goss and Mona West, 13–22. Cleveland, OH: Pilgrim Press, 2000.

Mopsik, Charles. "Union and Unity in Kabbalah." In *Between Jerusalem and Benares: Comparative Studies in Judaism and Hinduism*, edited by Hananya Goodman, 223–42. Albany: State University of New York Press, 1994.

Moss, Leonard, and Stephen C. Cappannari. "In Quest of the Black Virgin: She Is Black Because She Is Black." In *Mother Worship: Theme and Variations*, edited by James J. Preston, 53–74. Chapel Hill: University of North Carolina Press, 1982.

Myers, Jody. *Kabbalah and the Spiritual Quest: The Kabbalah Centre in America*. Westport, CT: Praeger, 2007.

Myers, Jody. "Kabbalah for the Gentiles: Diverse Souls and Universalism in Contemporary Kabbalah." In *Kabbalah and Contemporary Spiritual Revival*, edited by Boaz Huss, 181–212. The Goldstein-Goren Library of Jewish Thought 14. Beer Sheva: Ben-Gurion University of the Negev Press, 2011.

Naor, Bezalel. *Post-Sabbatian Sabbatianism*. Spring Valley, NY: Orot, 1999.

Needleman, Jacob. "Tibet in America." In *The New Religions*, 170–93. New York: Crossroad, 1970.

Neitz, Mary Jo, and Marion S. Goldman, eds. *Sex, Lies, and Sanctity: Religion and Deviance in Contemporary North America*. London: JAI Press, 1995.

Niditch, Susan. *Underdogs and Tricksters: A Prelude to Biblical Folklore*. San Francisco: Harper & Row, 1987.

Oakes, Leonard. *Prophetic Charisma: The Psychology of Revolutionary Religious Personalities*. Syracuse, NY: Syracuse University Press, 1997.

Ott, Ludwig. *Fundamentals of Catholic Theology*. Charlotte, NC: TAN Books, 2009. First published 1955 by Herder.

Packer, J. I. *Concise Theology: A Guide to Historic Christian Beliefs*. Carol Stream, IL: Tyndale House, 2001.

Panek, Adrian, dir. *Daas*. Poland, 2011, DVD.

Pasi, Marco. "Oriental Kabbalah and the Parting of East and West in the Early Theosophical Society." In *Kabbalah and Modernity: Interpretations, Transformations, Adaptations*, edited by Boaz Huss, Marco Pasi, and Kocku von Stuckrad, 151–64. Aries Book Series 10. Leiden: Boston, 2010.

Pasierb, Janusz. *The Shrine of the Black Madonna at Częstochowa*. Warsaw: Interpress, 1989.

Patai, Raphael. *The Hebrew Goddess*. New York: Discus, 1978.

Patai, Raphael. *The Jewish Alchemists*. Princeton, NJ: Princeton University Press, 1995.

Patai, Raphael. *The Messiah Texts*. Detroit: Wayne State University Press, 1979.

Pedaya, Haviva. "The *Iggeret HaKodesh* of the Baal Shem Tov: The Style of the Text and Its Worldview—Messianism, Revelation, Ecstasy, and Sabbateanism" [Hebrew]. *Zion* 70, no. 3 (2005): 311–54.

Persico, Tomer. "Neo-Hasidic Revival: Expressivist Uses of Traditional Lore." *Modern Judaism: A Journal of Jewish Ideas and Experience* 34 (2014): 287–308. https://doi.org/10.1093/mj/kju016.

Pettman, Dominic. *After the Orgy: Toward a Politics of Exhaustion*. Albany: State University of New York Press, 2002.

Peucker, Paul. *A Time of Sifting: Mystical Marriage and the Crisis of Moravian Piety in the Eighteenth Century*. University Park, PA: Penn State University Press, 2016.

Pew Research Center. *"Nones" on the Rise: One-in-Five Adults Have No Religious Affiliation*. Washington, DC: The Pew Forum on Religion and Public Life, 2012.

Plaut, Gunther. *The Man Who Would Be Messiah*. New York: Mosaic Press, 1988.

Popkin, Richard H. "Introduction." In *Millenarianism and Messianism in Early Modern European Culture*, edited by Matthew Goldish and Richard Popkin, xv–xx. New York: Kluwer Academic, 2001.

Popkin, Richard H. "Jewish-Christian Relations in the Sixteenth and Seventeenth Centuries: The Conception of the Messiah." *Jewish History* 6 (1992): 161–77. https://doi.org/10.1007/BF01695217.

Popkin, Richard H. "Three English Tellings of the Sabbatai Zevi Story." *Jewish History* 8 (1994): 43–54. https://doi.org/10.1007/BF01915907.

Popkin, Richard H., and Jose R. Maia Neto, eds. *Skepticism: An Anthology*. Amherst, NY: Prometheus Books, 2007.

Popkin, Richard H., and Arjo Vanderjagt, eds. *Scepticism and Irreligion in the Seventeenth and Eighteenth Centuries*. Leiden: Brill, 1993.

Posen, Marie-Joseé. "Beyond New Age: Jewish Renewal's Reconstruction of Theological Meaning in the Teachings of Rabbi Z. Schachter-Shalomi." In *New Age Judaism*, edited by Rothenberg, Celia E., and Anne Vallely, 73–91. Portland, OR: Vallentine Mitchell, 2008.

Preston, James J. *Mother Worship: Themes and Variations*. Chapel Hill: University of North Carolina Press, 1992.

Rabinowicz, Oskar K. "Jacob Frank in Brno." *Jewish Quarterly Review* 57 (1967): 429–45. https://doi.org/10.2307/1453507.

Radin, Paul. *The Trickster: A Study in American Indian Mythology*. New York: Schocken, 1987. First published 1956 by Bell Publishing Co.

Rapoport-Albert, Ada. *Women and the Messianic Heresy of Sabbatai Zevi, 1666–1816*. London: Littman Library of Jewish Civilization, 2011.

Rapoport-Albert, Ada, and Cesar Merchan Hamann. "Something for the Female Sex: A Call for the Liberation of Women, and the Release of the Female Libido from the 'Shackles of Shame,' in an Anonymous Frankist Manuscript from Prague c. 1800." In *Gershom Scholem (1897–1982): In Memoriam*, edited by Joseph Dan, 2:77–135. Jerusalem: Hebrew University, 2007.

Raschke, Carl A. "God and Lacanian Psychoanalysis: Toward a Reconsideration of the Discipline of Religious Studies." In *Religion, Society, and Psychoanalysis*, edited by Donald Capps, 230–39. Boulder, CO: Westview Press, 1997.

Rawson, Philip. *The Art of Tantra*. Oxford: Oxford University Press, 1978.

Reinkowski, Maurus. "Hidden Believers, Hidden Apostates: The Phenomenon of Crypto-Jews and Crypto-Christians in the Middle-East." In *Converting Cultures: Religion, Ideology of Transformations of Modernity*, edited by Dennis Washburn, 409–33. Leiden: Brill, 2000.

Rich, Adrienne. *The Fact of a Doorframe: Selected Poems 1950–2001*. New York: W. W. Norton & Company, 2002.

Rose, Or. "Hasidism and the Religious Other." In *A New Hasidism: Branches*, edited by Arthur Green and Ariel Evan Mayse, 105–28. Philadelphia: Jewish Publication Society, 2019.

Rose, Or. "Reb Zalman, Neo-Hasidism, and Inter-Religious Engagement: Lessons from My Teacher." *Tikkun* 32, no. 4 (2017): 40–47. https://doi.org/10.1215/08879982-4252983.

Rosen, Tova, ed. *Unveiling Eve: Reading Gender in Medieval Hebrew Literature*. Philadelphia: University of Pennsylvania Press, 2013.

Rothenberg, Celia E., and Anne Vallely, eds. *New Age Judaism*. Portland, OR: Vallentine Mitchell, 2008.

Salkin, Jeffrey K. "New Age Judaism." In *The Blackwell Companion to Judaism*, edited by Jacob Neusner and Alan J. Avery-Peck, 354–70. Malden, MA: Blackwell Publishing, 2003.

Samet, Hadar Feldman. "Ottoman Songs in Sabbatian Manuscripts: A Cross-Cultural Perspective on the Inner Sources of the Ma'aminim." *Jewish Quarterly Review* 109, no. 4 (Fall 2019): 567–97.

Saperstein, Marc, ed. *Essential Papers on Messianic Movements and Personalities in Jewish History*. Essential Papers on Jewish Studies 2. New York: New York University Press, 1992.

Schacter, Jacob J. "Rabbi Jacob Emden, Sabbatianism, and Frankism: Attitudes toward Christianity in the Eighteenth Century." In *New Perspectives on Jewish-Christian Relations*, edited by Elisheva Carlebach and Jacob J. Schacter, 359–96. Leiden: Brill, 2011.

Schäfer, Peter, and Mark R. Cohen, eds. *Toward the Millennium: Messianic Expectations from the Bible to Waco*. Studies in the History of Religions 77. Leiden: Brill, 1998.

Schatz Uffenheimer, Rivka. *Hasidism as Mysticism: Quietistic Elements in Eighteenth-Century Hasidic Thought*. Translated by Jonathan Chipman. Princeton, NJ: Princeton University Press, 1993.

Schleiermacher, Friedrich. *On Religion: Speeches to Its Cultured Despisers*. Translated and edited by Richard Krouter. Cambridge: Cambridge University Press, 1996.

Scholem, Gershom. *Alchemy and Kabbalah*. Translated by Klaus Ottmann. Putnam, CT: Spring Publications, 2006.

Scholem, Gershom. "Baruchiah, the Sabbatian Heresiarch in Salonica" [Hebrew]. *Zion* 6 (1941): 119–47, 181–202.

Scholem, Gershom. "The Career of a Frankist: Moshe Dobrushka and His Transformations" [Hebrew]. *Zion* 35 (1970): 127–81.

Scholem, Gershom. "A Frankist Document from Prague." In *Salo Wittmayer Baron Jubilee Volume on the Occasion of His Eightieth Birthday*, edited by Saul Lieberman and Arthur Hyman, 2:787–814. Jerusalem: American Academy for Jewish Research, 1974.

Scholem, Gershom. "A Frankist Interpretation of 'Hallel'" [Hebrew]. In *Yitzhak F. Baer Jubilee Volume*, edited by Salo W. Baron and B. Dinur, 409–30. Jerusalem: Historical Society of Israel, 1960.

Scholem, Gershom. "A Frankist Letter on the History of the Faith" [Hebrew]. In idem., *Studies in Sabbateanism*, 634–51. Tel Aviv: 'Am 'Oved, 1991.

Scholem, Gershom. "Jacob Frank and the Frankists." In idem., *Kabbalah*, 274–305. New York: Meridian, 1987. https://www.amazon.com/Kabbalah-Meridian-Gershon-Scholem/dp/0452010071/

Scholem, Gershom. "A Letter from Rabbi Hayim Malach" [Hebrew]. *Zion* 11 (1946): 168–74.

Scholem, Gershom. *Major Trends in Jewish Mysticism*. New York: Schocken Books, 1995.

Scholem, Gershom. *The Messianic Idea in Judaism and Other Essays on Jewish Spirituality*. New York: Schocken, 1988. First published 1971 by Schocken.

Scholem, Gershom. "Der Nihilismus als Religiöses Phänomen" [Nihilism as a Religious Phenomenon]. In *Judaica*, Vol. 4, edited by Gershom Scholem, 129–88. Frankfurt: Suhrkamp, 1988.

Scholem, Gershom. *Sabbatai Ṣevi: The Mystical Messiah 1626–1676*. Translated by R. J. Z. Werblowsky. Bollingen Series 93. Princeton, NJ: Princeton University Press, 1973.

Scholem, Gershom. "The Sabbatean Movement in Poland" [Hebrew]. In *Studies and Texts on the History of Sabbateanism and Its Incarnations*, 68–140. Jerusalem, 1964.

Scholem, Gershom. "A Sabbathaian Will from New York." *Miscellanies (Jewish Historical Society of England)* 5 (1948): 193–211.

Scholem, Gershom. *Studies and Texts on the History of Sabbateanism and Its Metamorphoses* [Hebrew]. Jerusalem: Bialik Institute, 1974.
Scholem, Gershom. *Studies in Sabbateanism* [Hebrew]. Tel Aviv: 'Am 'Oved, 1991.
Schuchard, Marsha K. "Dr. Samuel Jacob Falk: A Sabbatian Adventurer in the Masonic Underground." In *Millenarianism and Messianism in Early Modern European Culture*. Vol. 1, *Jewish Messianism in the Early Modern World*, edited by Matt Goldish and Richard Popkin, 203–26. Boston: Kluwer, 2001.
Schuchard, Marsha K. *Emanuel Swedenborg, Secret Agent on Earth and in Heaven: Jacobites, Jews, and Freemasons in Early Modern Sweden*. Leiden: Brill, 2011.
Schuchard, Marsha K. "From Poland to London: Sabbatean Influences on the Mystical Underworld of Zinzendorf, Swedenborg, and Blake." In *Holy Dissent: Jewish and Christian Mystics in Eastern Europe*, edited by Glenn Dynner, 250–80. Detroit: Wayne State University Press, 2011.
Schuchard, Marsha K. *Why Mrs. Blake Cried: William Blake, and the Sexual Basis of Spiritual Vision*. London: Century, 2006.
Schwartz, Howard. *Lilith's Cave: Jewish Tales of the Supernatural*. Oxford: Oxford University Press, 1988.
Schwartz, Howard. *A Palace of Pearls: The Stories of Rabbi Nachman of Bratslav*. Oxford: Oxford University Press, 2018.
Schweid, Eliezer. *Judaism and Mysticism according to Gershom Scholem: A Critical Analysis and Programmatic Discussion*. Translated by David Weiner. Atlanta: Scholars Press, 1985.
Scott, Eugene. "Comparing Trump to Jesus, and Why Some Evangelicals Believe Trump Is God's Chosen One." *Washington Post*, December 18, 2019. https://www.washingtonpost.com/politics/2019/11/25/why-evangelicals-like-rick-perry-believe-that-trump-is-gods-chosen-one/
Sedgwick, Eve Kosofsky. *Epistemology of the Closet*. Berkeley: University of California Press, 1990.
Segol, Marla. *Kabbalah and Sex Magic: A Mythical-Ritual Genealogy*. University Park: Pennsylvania State University Press, 2021.
Sela, Aviva. "A Study of One Three-Fold Tale of Jacob Frank." Master's thesis, Department of Languages and Literature, University of Utah, 1988.
Sela, Aviva. "A Study in One Three-Fold Tale of Jacob Frank" [Hebrew]. *Proceedings of the World Congress of Jewish Studies* C, no. 2 (1989): 8–14.
Shachar, Isaiah. *The Judensau: A Mediaeval Anti-Jewish Motif and Its History*. Warburg Institute Surveys 5. London: Warburg Institute, 1974.
Shai, Eli. "Antinomian Tendencies in the Ethics of Marriage Amongst the Sects of the Doenmeh" [Hebrew]. D. Phil thesis, Hebrew University, 2003.
Shai, Eli. *The Messiah of Incest* [Hebrew]. Tel Aviv: Yediot Ahronot, 2002.
Sharot, Stephen. *Messianism, Mysticism and Magic: A Sociological Analysis of Jewish Religious Movements*. Chapel Hill: University of North Carolina Press, 1982.
Shatzky, Jacob. "Alexander Kraushar and His Road to Total Assimilation." *YIVO: Annual of Jewish Social Science* 7 (1952): 146–74.
Shmeruk, Chone. "The Frankist Novels of Isaac Bashevis Singer." In *Literary Strategies: Jewish Texts and Contexts*, edited by Ezra Mendelsohn, 118–27. Oxford: Oxford University Press, 1996.
Shmeruk, Chone. "Jacob's Frank's 'Book of the Words of the Lord': Its Metamorphosis from Yiddish to Poland" [Hebrew]. *Gal-Ed* 14 (1995): 23–36.

Shmeruk, Chone. "Notes on Jacob Frank's Childhood Memoirs" [Hebrew]. *Gal-Ed* 15–16 (1997): 35–42.
Shrine of Częstochowa Association. *History of the Painting of the Blessed Mother of Częstochowa*. Częstochowa: Shrine of Częstochowa Association, 1982.
Siegel, Aryeh. *Transcendental Deception: Behind the TM Curtain*. Los Angeles: Janreg Press, 2018.
Singelenberg, Richard. "'It Separated the Wheat from the Chaff': The '1975' Prophecy and Its Impact among Dutch Jehovah's Witnesses." *Sociology of Religion* 50 (1989): 23–40. https://doi.org/10.2307/3710916.
Singer, Isaac Bashevis. *Satan in Goray*. Austin, TX: Bard Press, 1974.
Sisman, Cengiz. *The Burden of Silence: Sabbatai Sevi and the Evolution of the Ottoman-Turkish Dönmes*. Oxford: Oxford University Press, 2015.
Sisman, Cengiz. *A Jewish Messiah in the Ottoman Court: Sabbatai Sevi and the Emergence of a Judeo-Islamic Community* (1666–1720). Doctoral thesis, Department of Middle Eastern Studies, Harvard University, 2004.
Sisman, Cengiz. "The Redemptive Power of Sexual Anarchy." *AJS Perspectives*, Spring 2017. http://perspectives.ajsnet.org/transgression-issue/the-redemptive-power-of-sexual-anarchy/
Sloat, Donald. "Imposed Shame: The Origin of Violence and Worthlessness." In *The Destructive Power of Religion: Violence in Judaism, Christianity, and Islam*, Vol. 3, edited by J. Harold Ellens, 175–92. New York: Praeger, 2003.
Smith, Jonathan Z. *Relating Religion: Essays in the Study of Religion*. Chicago: University of Chicago Press, 2004.
Snoek, J. A. M. "On the Creation of Masonic Degrees: A Method and Its Fruits." In *Western Esotericism and the Science of Religion*, edited by Antoine Faivre and Wouter J. Hanegraaff, 145–90. Gnostica 2. Leuven: Peeters, 1998.
Sperber, Daniel. *Magic and Folklore in Rabbinic Literature*. Ramat Gan: Bar Ilan University Press, 1994.
Sproul, R. C. *Essential Truths of the Christian Faith*. Carol Stream, IL: Tyndale House, 1992.
Stallybrass, Peter, and Allon White, *The Politics and Poetics of Transgression*. Ithaca, NY: Cornell University Press, 1986.
Stanislawski, M. "The State of the Debate over Sabbatianism in Poland: A Review of the Sources." In *Proceedings of the Conference on "Poles and Jews: Myth and Reality in the Historical Context" Held at Columbia University, March 6–10, 1983*, edited by John S. Micgiel, Robert Scott, and Harold B. Segel, 58–69. New York: Columbia University Institute on East and Central Europe, 1986.
Stone, Jon, ed. *Expecting Armageddon: Essential Readings in Failed Prophecy*. London: Routledge, 2000.
Stone, Jon, ed. "Introduction." In *Expecting Armageddon: Essential Readings in Failed Prophecy*, edited by Jon Stone, 1–30. London: Routledge, 2000.
Stone, Jon, ed. "Prophecy and Dissonance: A Reassessment of Research Testing the Festinger Theory." *Nova Religio: The Journal of Alternative and Emergent Religions* 12, no. 4 (2009): 72–90. https://doi.org/10.1525/nr.2009.12.4.72.
Stone, Ken. *Practicing Safer Texts: Food, Sex and Bible in Queer Perspective*. Queering Theology Series New York: T&T Clark, 2005.
Stone, Ken, ed. *Queer Commentary and the Hebrew Bible*. Cleveland, OH: Pilgrim Press, 2001.

Sullivan, Nikki. *A Critical Introduction to Queer Theory*. New York: New York University Press, 2003.

Sutcliffe, Steven. *Children of the New Age: A History of Spiritual Practices*. London and New York: Routledge, 2003.

Świderska, Hanna. "Three Polish Pamphlets on Pseudo-Messiah Sabbatai Sevi." *British Library Journal* 15 (1989): 212–16.

Teter, Magda. *Jews and Heretics in Catholic Poland*. Cambridge: Cambridge University Press, 2006.

Tishby, Isaiah. "Between Sabbateanism and Hasidism: The Sabbateanism of the Kabbalist R. Ya'akov Koppel Lifshitz of Mezritch" [Hebrew]. In *Pathways of Faith and Heresy*, 204–26. Jerusalem: Magnes Press, 1982.

Tokarczuk, Olga. *The Books of Jacob*. Translated by Jennifer Croft. New York: Riverhead Books, 2022.

Tokarczuk, Olga. *Księgi Jakubowe*. [The Books of Jacob] [Polish]. Kraków: Wydawnictwo Literackie, 2014.

Trachtenberg, Joshua. *Jewish Magic and Superstition: A Study in Folk Religion*. Philadelphia: University of Pennsylvania Press, 2004. (First published 1939).

Tumminia, Diana. "How Prophecy Never Fails: Interpretive Reason in a Flying-Saucer Group." *Sociology of Religion* 59 (1998): 157–70. https://doi.org/10.2307/3712078.

Turner, Jonathan, and Alexandra Maryanski. *Incest: Origins of the Taboo*. Boulder, CO: Paradigm, 2005.

Turner, Victor. *Dramas, Fields, and Metaphors: Symbolic Action in Human Society*. Ithaca, NY: Cornell University Press, 1974.

Turner, Victor. *The Forest of Symbols: Aspects of Ndembu Ritual*. Ithaca, NY: Cornell University Press, 1967.

Turner, Victor. "Liminality, Kabbalah, and the Media." *Religion* 15 (1985): 205–17.

Turner, Victor. *The Ritual Process: Structure and Anti-Structure*. Piscataway, NJ: Transaction Publishers, 1995. First published 1969 by Aldine Publishing Company.

Urban, Hugh. "The Beast with Two Backs: Aleister Crowley, Sex Magic, and the Exhaustion of Modernity." *Nova Religio* 7, no. 3 (2004): 7–25.

Urban, Hugh. *Church of Scientology: A History of a New Religion*. Princeton, NJ: Princeton University Press, 2011.

Urban, Hugh. "The Cult of Ecstasy: Tantrism, the New Age, and the Spiritual Logic of Late Capitalism." *History of Religions* 39 (2000): 268–304. https://doi.org/10.1086/463593.

Urban, Hugh. *Magia Sexualis: Sex, Magic, and Liberation in Modern Western Esotericism*. Berkeley: University of California Press, 2006.

Urban, Hugh. "The Omnipotent OOM: Tantra and Its Impact on Modern Western Esotericism." *Esoterica* 3 (2001): 218–59.

Urban, Hugh. "Religion and Secrecy in the Bush Administration: The Gentleman, the Prince, and the Simulacrum." *Esoterica* 7 (2005): 1–38.

Urban, Hugh. *Tantra: Sex, Secrecy, Politics and Power in the Study of Religion*. Berkeley: University of California Press, 2003.

Van der Haven, Alexander. "The Earliest Footprint of a Messianic Queen: Sarah the Ashkenazi in Amsterdam." *Zutot: Perspectives on Jewish Culture* 17 no. 1 (2019): 15–21.

Van der Haven, Alexander. *From Lowly Metaphor to Divine Flesh: Sarah the Ashkenazi, Sabbatai Tsevi's Messianic Queen and the Sabbatian Movement*. Menasseh ben Israel Instituut Studies 7. Amsterdam: Menasseh ben Israel Instituut, 2012.

Van Fossen, Anthony. "How Do Movements Survive Failures of Prophecy?" In *Expecting Armageddon: Essential Readings in Failed Prophecy*, edited by Jon Stone, 175–90. London: Routledge, 2000.

Vasquez, Manuel. *More Than Belief: A Materialist Theory of Religion*. Oxford: Oxford University Press, 2011.

Verses, Samuel. *Haskalah and Sabbateanism* [Hebrew]. Jerusalem: Merkaz Zalman Shazar le-Toldot Yisrael, 1988.

Versluis, Arthur. *Magic and Mysticism: An Introduction to Western Esoteric Traditions*. London: Rowman & Littlefield, 2007.

Versluis, Arthur. "Mysticism and the Study of Esotericism, Part II." *Esoterica* 5 (2003): 27–40.

Versluis, Arthur. *The Secret History of Western Sexual Mysticism*. Rochester, VT: Destiny Books, 2008.

Versluis, Arthur. (2002). "What Is Esoteric? Methods in the Study of Western Esotericism." *Esoterica* 4 (2002): 1–15.

Versnel, H. S. "Some Reflections on the Relationship Magic-Religion." *Numen* 38 (1991): 177–97.

Vytrhlik, Jana. "A History of the Jewish People in Bohemia and Moravia." In *Precious Legacy: Treasures from the Jewish Museum in Prague*, edited by Jana Vytrhlik, 14–23. Sydney: Powerhouse, 1998.

Wacholder, Ben Zion. "Jacob Frank and the Frankists: Hebrew Zoharic Letters." *Hebrew Union College Annual* 53 (1982): 265–93.

Waldron, Jeremy. "'Dead to the Law': Paul's Antinomianism." *Cardozo Law Review* 28 (2006): 301–32.

Walker, Benjamin. *Tantrism: Its Secret Principles and Practices*. Wellingborough, Northamptonshire: Aquarian Press, 1982.

Wallis, Roy. "Sex, Violence, and Religion." *Update* 7, no. 4 (1983): 3–11.

Walzer, Michael. *The Revolution of the Saints: A Study in the Origins of Radical Politics*. Cambridge, MA: Harvard University Press, 1965.

Ware, Kallistos. "The Holy Fool as Prophet and Apostle." *Sobornost* 6 (1984): 6–28.

Webb, Eugene. "Recent French Psychoanalytical Thought and the Psychology of Religion." *Religious Studies and Theology* 8 (1988): 31–44.

Weber, Max. *On Charisma and Institution Building: Selected Papers*. Edited by S. N. Eisenstadt. Chicago: University of Chicago Press, 1968.

Weber, Max. *The Protestant Ethic and the Spirit of Capitalism*. Edited and translated by Peter Baehr and Gordon C. Wells. New York: Penguin, 2002. First published 1905 by Mohr Siebeck.

Weininger, Otto. *Sex and Character: An Investigation of Fundamental Principles*. Translated by Ladislaus Löb. Bloomington: Indiana University Press, 2005. First published 1903 by Braumüller.

Weinryb, Bernard D. *The Jews of Poland: A Social and Economic History of the Jewish Community in Poland from 1100 to 1800*. Philadelphia: Jewish Publication Society of America, 1973.

Weissinger, Catherine. *The Oxford Handbook of Millennialism*. Oxford: Oxford University Press, 2011.

Weiss, Joseph. *Studies in Bratslav Hasidism* [Hebrew]. Jerusalem: Mosad Bialik, 1974.

Weiss, Joseph. *Studies in East European Jewish Mysticism and Hasidism*. Edited by David Goldstein. Oxford: Oxford University Press, 1985.

Weissler, Chava. "Performing Kabbalah in the Jewish Renewal Movement." In *Kabbalah and Contemporary Spiritual Revival*, edited by Boaz Huss, 39–74. The Goldstein-Goren Library of Jewish Thought 14. Beer Sheva: Ben-Gurion University of the Negev Press, 2011.

Werblowsky, R. J. Zwi. "Comments on Sabbetai Sevi by Gershom Scholem" [Hebrew]. *Molad* 15 (1957): 539–46.

Whited, Lana A., ed. *The Ivory Tower and Harry Potter: Perspectives on a Literary Phenomenon*. Columbia: University of Missouri Press, 2002.

Wilde, Oscar. "The Picture of Dorian Gray." In *Collected Works*, 1–154. Hertfordshire: Wordsworth Editions, 1997. First published 1890.

Williams-Hogan, Jane. "The Place of Emanuel Swedenborg in Modern Western Esotericism." In *Western Esotericism and the Science of Religion*, edited by Antoine Faivre and Wouter J. Hanegraaff, 201–52. Gnostica 2. Leuven: Peeters, 1998.

Winquist, C. "Lacan and Theology." In *Post-Secular Philosophy: Between Philosophy and Theology*, edited by Phillip Blond, 305–17. London: Routledge, 1998.

Winthrop, John. *Antinomianism in the Colony of Massachusetts, 1636–1638*. Boston: The Prince Society, 1894.

Witkowska, Aleksandra. "The Cult of the Virgin Mary in Polish Religiousness from the 15th to the 17th Century." In *The Common Christian Roots of the European Nations: International Colloquium in the Vatican*, 2:467–78. Florence, Italy: Le Monnier, 1982.

Wolfson, Elliot R. *Circle in the Square: Studies in the Use of Gender in Kabbalistic Symbolism*. Albany, NY: State University of New York Press, 1995.

Wolfson, Elliot R. "Circumcision, Secrecy, and the Veiling of the Veil." In *The Covenant of Circumcision: New Perspectives on an Ancient Jewish Rite*, edited by Elizabeth Wyner Mark, 58–70. Boston: Brandeis University Press, 2003.

Wolfson, Elliot R. "Constructions of the Shekhinah in the Messianic Theosophy of Abraham Cardoso with an Annotated Edition of Derush ha-Shekhinah." *Kabbalah: Journal for the Study of Jewish Mystical Texts* 3 (1998): 11–143.

Wolfson, Elliot R. "The Engenderment of Messianic Politics: Symbolic Significance of Sabbatai Ṣevi's Coronation." In *Toward the Millennium: Messianic Expectations from the Bible to Waco*, edited by Peter Schäfer and Mark R. Cohen, 203–58. Studies in the History of Religions 77. Leiden: Brill, 1998.

Wolfson, Elliot R. *Heidegger and Kabbalah: Hidden Gnosis and the Path of Poiēsis*. Bloomington: Indiana University Press, 2019.

Wolfson, Elliot R. "Immanuel Frommann's Commentary on *Luke* and the Christianizing of Kabbalah." In *Holy Dissent: Jewish and Christian Mystics in Eastern Europe*, edited by Glenn Dynner, 171–222. Detroit: Wayne State University Press, 2011.

Wolfson, Elliot R. *Language Eros Being: Kabbalistic Hermeneutics and Poetic Imagination*. New York: Fordham University Press, 2005.

Wolfson, Elliot R. "Left Contained in the Right: A Study in Zoharic Hermeneutics." *AJS Review* 11, no. 1 (Spring 1986: 27–52.

Wolfson, Elliot R. "Phantasmagoria: The Image of the Image in Jewish Magic from Late Antiquity to the Early Middle Ages." *Review of Rabbinic Judaism* 4 (2001): 78–120. https://doi.org/10.1163/157007001X00045.

Wolfson, Elliot R. *Through a Speculum That Shines: Vision and Imagination in Medieval Jewish Mysticism*. Princeton, NJ: Princeton University Press, 1997.

Wolfson, Elliot R. "'Tiqqun ha-Shekhinah': Redemption and the Overcoming of Gender Dimorphism in the Messianic Kabbalah of Moses Hayyim Luzzatto." *History of Religions* 36, no. 4 (May, 1997): 289–332.

Ya'ari, Avraham. "The Burning of the Talmud in Kaminiez, Podolia" [Hebrew]. *Sinai* 21 (1940): 294–306.

Ya'ari, Avraham. "A History of the Campaign of the Sages of Poland against the Frankist Movement" [Hebrew]. *Sinai* 35 (1954): 170–82.

Yamamoto, Shinichi. "The Last Step of Jacob Frank's Odyssey for the True Religion." Lecture at Center for the Study of Conversion and Inter-Religious Encounters, Ben Gurion University of the Negev, March 6, 2018. Video, 1:37:32, March 8, 2018. https://www.youtube.com/watch?v=0ghTCSDJeVc.

Yamamoto, Shinichi. "The Origin and Development of Sabbatean Antinomism." PhD dissertation, University of Tokyo, 2011.

Yates, Frances. *Giordano Bruno and the Hermetic Tradition*. Chicago: University of Chicago, 1991.

Index

For the benefit of digital users, indexed terms that span two pages (e.g., 52–53) may, on occasion, appear on only one of those pages.

Tables and figures are indicated by *t* and *f* following the page number

Abraham, 6–7, 61–62, 65, 74, 94, 124–25, 162–63, 177
Adam, 85–86, 96–97, 98–99, 145, 157, 158, 165–66, 218
alchemy, 1–4, 23–25, 33, 60, 87, 91n.1, 105–6, 112–13, 152, 168–71, 174–75, 182
Alpert, Reuven/ Bezalel Naor, 4n.7, 15n.11, 205n.93
"And I Came This Day unto the Fountain." See *V'Avo Hayom El Ha'Ayin*
animals, power over, 92–93, 105
antinomianism, 6, 10–11, 16–17, 26–27, 83, 154–55, 174, 186–87, 190, 191–92, 211, 212–13
   definition of, 48–51
   distinguished from mere disobedience, 49–50
   history of, 48–49
   in Jacob Frank, 46–48, 52–55, 56–63, 64–68, 69–70, 85
   and Martin Luther, 48–49
   pronouncing the Tetragrammaton/ Ineffable Name, 58, 63–64
   sexual, 8–9, 55, 68, 108–9, 114, 115–16, 120–23, 139–41, 148–49, 151
   turning fast days into feast days, 14–15, 63–64
   types and meanings of, 50–22
antisemitism, 20, 21, 22, 42, 152–53, 173, 184–85, 214–15
   Frankism's legacy within, 1–2, 1n.1, 173–74, 184–85
   See also blood libel
apostasy, 1–2, 5, 21–23, 55, 58, 155, 183–84, 191, 212–13

Ariel, Yaakov, 199n.70, 202
Asch, Sholem, 4–5
Ashkenazi, Sarah. *See* Sarah Ashkenazi
Austria. *See* Hapsburg Empire

Ba'alei kaben, 30, 72–73, 81–82, 83–84, 84n.36, 105–6, 175, 220
Baal Shem Tov, 10–11, 19–20, 113, 191–92, 193–94, 196–98, 212
Babel, Tower of, 88–89, 96–97
Baer, Mark, 15n.11
Bakhtin, Mikhail, 39–40, 39n.89
Balaam, 9–10, 71–72, 220
baptism, 93, 95, 111–12, 121, 122, 128, 137, 138–39, 219
Baruchiah Russo, 5, 9–10, 16–17, 32–33, 57, 83, 85–86, 108, 124, 143–44, 157, 164–65, 174–75, 214, 220
   as Osman Baba, 16–17, 143–44
Biale, David, 17–19, 53, 85n.38, 186–87
Bible, 35, 44, 55–56, 71–72, 74, 85, 86–87, 176–77, 183–84, 210, 219, 221, 222
   "As a dog returns to its vomit" (Proverbs 26:11), 6–7, 58–59
   "I will tread the wine press" (Isaiah 63:3), 53–54, 59–60, 91–92
   Nimrod and the Tower of Babel (Genesis 10:10), 96–97
biblical interpretation, Frankist, 3–4, 6, 79–80, 124–25, 137, 154–55, 219
Big Brother, 3–4, 7–8, 32–33, 64–65, 71–73, 74–75, 80–81, 84–85, 92–94, 96–97, 99–102, 103, 128, 155–56, 161, 219
   as intermediary, 88–89, 97–98
   and Jesus, 98–99

Black Virgin of Częstochowa, 3–4, 7, 23, 71–72, 75, 76, 78–79, 95, 98–99, 105, 110, 112–13, 115, 126, 128–29, 131, 132–34, 136, 163–64, 214
Blake, William, 37–38, 161–62
blood libel, 21, 26–27
Books of Jacob, The, 1–2, 4–5
    See also Tokarczuk, Olga
Boyarin, Daniel, 142–43, 142–43n.65
Brandeis, Louis, 1–2, 26, 214–15
Brethren (Frankist Sect), 8–10, 29, 31–35, 46–47, 48–49, 56, 62, 64–65, 68–69, 71–76, 77–78, 84–85, 87–88, 91–113, 116–34, 138–39, 141, 144–45, 157, 159–60, 162–64, 165–66, 173, 175, 177–78, 200–1, 211, 216, 218, 219, 221, 222
    as brothers and sisters, 8, 73, 80–81, 84–85, 93, 94–95, 97–100, 101, 114–15, 120–21, 124, 219
Brethren of the Free Spirit, 49n.8, 116–18
Brünn, 17–19, 23–25, 33n.77, 84, 173, 216, 217–18
Bucharest, 13–14, 29–30, 42–43, 218
burden of silence, 31, 96, 219

Cagliostro, "Count" Alessandro, 5n.11, 60, 171
Cardoso, Abraham Miguel, 71–72, 76n.17, 85, 86–87, 130–31, 155n.11, 156n.14
"Cargo Cult," Frankism as, 34, 214–15
    See also Levine, Hillel
Carlebach, Elisheva, 15–16, 18n.26, 114, 186–87
Casanova, Giacomo, 3–4, 10, 34n.78, 44, 55–56, 60, 173–74, 175
charlatanism, 5, 10, 27, 33–34, 60, 171, 173–74, 178–79, 200, 212–14
Chaucer, Geoffrey, 39–40
Christianity, 1–2, 65–66, 200–1, 220
    Evangelical, 35–36, 48–49, 161–62
    Frank's conversion to, 1–2, 21–23, 60, 83, 84–85, 96–97, 103, 111–12, 120n.25, 121, 139–40, 211, 214–15
    in Frankist doctrine, 25–26, 61–62, 79–80, 93, 95, 96–97, 177, 183–84, 193–94
    in Frankist sexual ritual, 19–20, 69, 120–21
    Holy Spirit in, 6n.14, 49n.10, 50, 136–37
    mockery of, 40–42, 58, 125
    triumph over, 41–42, 79–80, 91–93, 125, 177, 185, 212–13
    See also baptism
cognitive dissonance. *See* Festinger, Leon
Collection of the Words of the Lord. See Zbiór Słów Pańskich
"Contra-Talmudists," 20–22, 26–27, 109, 165n.33, 168, 193–94
corporealization, 8–9, 17–19, 30, 70, 91–92, 151, 166–67
Corpus Hermeticum, 170–71, 177
Crowley, Aleister, 140–41, 178–79, 200
curtain, the world behind the. *See* hidden world
Częstochowa, 7, 22–23, 30, 33–34, 37–38, 44, 75, 76, 78–79, 101–2, 110, 115, 121n.27, 122, 128, 133–34, 163–64, 165, 175–76, 210n.15, 214, 217–18, 220
    See also Black Virgin of Częstochowa

Daniel, Book of, 66, 72–73, 89
Das, 3–4, 31, 34, 92–93, 103, 165–66, 219
    and *da'at*, 77–78, 95
    meaning of, 95–97
    and Western esotericism, 8, 96–97, 175
de La Mothe Le Vayer, François, 54–55, 66
death, 58–59, 66
    angel of, 43–44
    as condition of fallen world, 86, 89–90
    and the Foreign Woman, 136, 147
    religion is from the side of, 46, 52–53, 64
    See also immortality, pursuit of
Dębowski, Jędrzej, 102, 122
deeds (not words), 47–48, 91–103, 122–23, 132, 159–60, 219
Dembowski, Bishop Mikołaj, 20–21
demons, 7–9, 17–19, 45, 71–72, 74, 75, 81, 82–85, 105–6, 110, 132, 135, 137, 164–65, 177, 220
    See also *Shedim*
Dervish Effendi, 16–17, 63–64

Dobruschka, Moses, 12, 23–25, 127, 152–53, 173
  as Junius Frey, 23–25, 127, 173
  as Thomas von Schönfeld, 23–25, 173
Dobruschka, Schöndl, 17–19, 23–25
doenmeh, 1n.1, 8–9, 16–17, 18n.26, 31, 58, 63–64, 65–66, 68, 83, 116–18, 139–40, 143–44, 175, 179–80, 192–93
  Karakash sect, 17, 65–66, 118–19, 143–44, 175
Doktór, Jan, 2n.4, 4–5, 17–19, 23n.51, 157n.17, 209, 210, 214, 215, 217–18

ecstasy. *See* pneumatic (ecstatic/prophetic/charismatic) practices
Eden, Garden of, 59–60, 75, 102, 145, 176–77, 188
Edom, 7–8, 55, 75, 77–78, 80–81, 110, 129, 162–63, 165, 219
  as Christianity, 25–26, 61–62, 79–80, 93, 95, 96–97, 177, 183–84, 193–94
Egypt, 75, 81, 88–89, 94, 105–6, 124–25, 129, 132, 165, 170–73, 176–77, 220
  as Ægypt, 176–77
Eibeschütz, Jonathan, 5n.11, 15–16, 19–20, 50n.17, 200
Eibeschütz, Wolf, 5n.11, 18n.29, 60, 173–74
El Shaddai. See *Shaddai*
Elijah, 42–43, 46–47, 53–54, 76, 105–6, 130–31, 154–55,
Elior, Rachel, 4–5, 30, 39, 51–52, 59–60, 73, 76, 77–78, 83, 84, 99n.17, 153n.5, 154, 155n.9, 183, 190, 207–8, 209, 210, 212, 217
Emden, Jacob, 17–20, 21–22, 68, 83, 91n.1, 116–18, 118n.13, 119–20, 191
Enlightenment, 1–2, 10, 12, 179–80, 185–86, 187–88
  and rationalism, 3–4, 6, 10–11, 25, 51–52, 67–68, 134–35, 155, 168, 171–72, 175–76, 177, 179–80, 185–88, 190, 206, 214–15
eros. *See* sexuality
Esau, 61–62, 67, 75n.8, 95, 193–94
  garments of / robes of, 31, 79–80, 93, 96–97, 166

  Jacob and, 6–7, 77–81, 93, 95, 96–97, 98–99, 128, 130–31, 142–43, 164–65, 212, 216–17, 219
  masculinity of, 6–7, 142–43
esotericism. *See* Western esotericism
Esther, 136–37, 143–44
eunuchs, 144–45

Fagenblat, Michael, 4–5, 52–53, 145–46, 188, 192, 209
failure, 1–2, 5–6, 8, 9–10, 17–19, 33, 35, 77–79, 80–81, 92, 94–95, 96–97, 102, 109–13, 139–40, 142–43, 149, 153, 156, 160, 162, 182, 189, 190, 206, 220, 222
faith
  in Frank, 31, 77–78, 84–85, 93–94, 98–99, 102–3, 104–5, 108, 110–13, 124–25, 162–64, 165, 211, 216–17, 218, 219, 222
  in God, 53–54, 68, 75, 84–85, 87–88
  in Sabbateanism, 9–10, 154–55, 157
  Sod HaEmunah, 9–10
Faivre, Antoine, 104n.20, 168–69, 171
Falk, Dr. Samuel Jacob, 15n.11, 171
"false messiah," 2, 9–10, 161–64
  See also failure; Festinger, Leon; messianism
femininity, 160
  and Messianism, 8–9, 128, 139
  and misogyny, 80, 116, 147, 150, 187–88
  and Shechinah (*see* Kabbalah; Shechinah)
  and the Divine Feminine, 26, 144–45, 191
  and The Foreign Woman (*see* Foreign Woman, The)
  and The Maiden (*see* Maiden, The)
  and women's liberation/feminism, 8–9, 80, 116, 129, 145–51, 182–83, 187–88, 203n.88, 210
Festinger, Leon, 9–10, 111–13, 161–62
Feuerstein, Georg, 44–45
folklore, 45, 71–72, 81–83, 84n.36, 105, 164–65, 215, 220, 221
  healing and disease, 39, 42, 43–44, 81, 105, 196–97, 220

folklore (*cont.*)
　magic and, 10, 28, 75–76, 81–82, 105–6, 164–65, 215, 220, 221
　witchcraft, 72, 76, 81–82, 85, 105–6, 108, 110
fool/idiot (*prostak*), 27–28, 34–45, 104–6, 218
　holy madness, 5, 34–35, 38–39, 44, 191–92
　as literary device, 29
"Foreign Woman," The, 8–9, 111–12, 116, 123, 134–38, 143–45, 147–48, 219
Foucault, Michel, 114
Frank, Eve, 3–4, 5, 23–25, 114, 127, 128, 146–47, 176–77, 219, 221
　as Frank's successor, 25–26, 35–36, 183–84, 213, 218
　as the Maiden/messiah, 8–9, 23, 46n.1, 115, 121–22, 126, 129, 132–33, 161, 163–64
Frank, Jacob
　biography of, 1–2, 5, 13–26, 173–74, 221, 223, 224
　as charlatan, 5, 10, 27, 33–34, 60, 171, 173–74, 178–79, 200, 212–14
　death of, 1–3, 10–11, 12, 23–26, 112, 153–54, 174–75, 183–84, 206, 210, 214, 218
　as holy fool, 27–28, 29–30, 34–39, 45, 104–5, 218
　influence of, 3–4, 10–11, 184–88, 190–98, 199–200
　as literary character, 4–5, 34–45, 221
　theology of, 2–5, 7–8, 10, 27–34, 42–43, 53–55, 59–60, 64–68, 71–76, 81–90, 128–51, 154–56, 174–77, 202, 212–13, 219, 220, 221, 222, 223–24
　as trickster, 5, 34–35, 38–45, 58, 59–60, 77–78, 219
Frank, Hannah, 16–17, 120n.26, 121–22, 125, 132–33, 148
Frankism/Frankists
　after death of Frank, 25–27, 183–84
　and Sabbateanism, 9–10, 14–21
　apostasy of Sect, 21–22, 26–27, 34, 79–80, 83, 212–13, 214–15
　in Prague, 10–11, 115n.5, 184–86
　in Warsaw, 25–26

　phases of, 16–27
　quest (*see* Quest, Frankist)
　scholarship on, 8–9, 209–15
　sect and communities of, 52–53, 174, 184–85, 187–88, 196
　texts and manuscripts, 2–3, 4–5, 11–12, 27–28, 115n.5, 147–48, 209–10, 215–24
　See also Brethren
Freemasonry, 3–4, 12, 23–25, 55–56, 71–72, 75, 96–97, 104n.20, 152–53, 168–72, 173–81
　Order of the Asiatic Brethren, 1–2, 173
French Revolution, 1–2, 12, 23–25, 85, 152–53, 173–74
fruit jam, 43, 122–23

Garb, Jonathan, 17n.21, 32n.74, 100n.18, 183
Glanvill, Joseph, 72
gnosticism
　in Frank, 3–4, 8, 25, 31, 34, 71–72, 77, 85–90, 93, 95, 98–99, 165–66, 212–13, 219
　in Sabbateanism, 74, 85, 86–87
　in Western esotericism, 8, 10, 168–73
　See also Das
God
　Frankist conception of, 6, 31, 36, 51–52, 53–54, 56–57, 61–62, 67, 71–72, 74–75, 81–82, 85–86, 97–99, 131, 218, 219
　gnostic conception of, 85–90, 169n.7, 174–75
　See also gnosticism; *Shaddai*
Goldish, Matt, 4–5, 14n.4, 15n.9, 17n.21, 27, 33, 119n.22, 207–8, 209
Graetz, Heinrich, 26–27, 209
Green, Arthur, 190, 193–94, 196–97
grotesque, 8–9, 33–34, 35, 39–40, 44, 51–52, 212, 219

Hagiz, Moshe, 15n.12, 86–87
halacha, 37–38, 149, 191–92
Halbertal, Moshe, 172–73
Hammer, Jill, 203n.88, 207–8
Hanegraaff, Wouter, 168–69, 199–200

Hapsburg Empire, 12, 23–25, 56n.37, 152–53, 163–64
court of, 26, 127
Harry Potter, 75, 82
Hasidism
  Bratzlav (*see* Nachman of Bratzlav)
  Chabad, 203
  Frankism's affinities with, 8–9, 37–38, 50, 92, 112–13, 139–40, 154, 196–98, 202, 204, 205–6, 212, 224
  Frankism's differences from, 198
  Frankism's influence on, 3–4, 10–11, 190–96
  See also Judaism; Neo-Hasidic
Haskalah, 1–2, 3–4, 10–11, 26, 152–53, 182–83, 184–89, 196–97, 206, 213, 214–15
  Scholem's theory of Frankist influence on, 10–11, 52–53, 67–68, 185–88, 211
Hayon, Nehemiah, 77n.19, 86–87, 211
Hebrew, 2n.4, 4–5, 44, 62, 87, 146, 165n.33, 166, 183–84, 210, 211, 212, 217
heresy, 5, 15–16, 19–20, 47–49, 85n.38, 87, 116–18, 119, 128, 139–40, 178–79, 186–87, 190–94, 196, 203–6
  heresiology and, 17–19, 114–15, 118n.13
hidden world/world behind the curtain, 3–4, 7–8, 32–33, 71–72, 74–75, 82, 89–90, 93, 97–103, 130–31, 141, 175, 178–79, 219
high vs. low. *See* low vs. high
Hobbes, Thomas, 46–47
Holy Spirit. *See* Christianity; Holy Spirit
humanism, 3, 6, 50, 55–63, 69–70, 170–71, 182–83, 199, 205–6
Huss, Boaz, 168–69, 199–200, 207–8
hybridity, 23, 71–72, 84–85, 92, 113

Icke, David, 1n.1
Idel, Moshe, 15n.9, 115, 138–40, 166n.37, 183, 190, 196–97, 207–8
Illuminism, 3–4, 91, 102, 171, 175–76
immortality, pursuit of, 2–3, 7–8, 12, 23–25, 31, 46–47, 69–70, 71–72, 79, 84–85, 87, 88–89, 91–103, 105, 112–13, 141, 152, 155, 161, 163–64, 174–75, 178–79, 182, 206, 219
incest
  accusations of, 8–9, 19–20, 94, 114, 118n.13, 124
  symbolism of, 94, 114–15, 118n.16, 123–24
Ishmael. *See* Islam
Islam, 56n.37, 57–58, 65–66, 157, 161–62, 163–64, 200–1
  Frank's conversion to, 20, 21, 22
  Ishmael, 67, 193–94
  mockery of, 40–42
  Sabbatean conversion to, 15–16, 83, 191–92, 193–94
  and sexuality, 41–42
  See also Sufism
Israel, Land of, 14–15, 75, 161, 189, 192
Iwanie, 36–37, 112–13

Jacob, 23n.52, 62, 88–89, 159, 175
  effeminacy of, 6–7, 41–42, 77, 80–81, 142–43, 147
  Esau and, 6–7, 77–81, 93, 95, 96–97, 98–99, 128, 130–31, 142–43, 164–65, 212, 216–17, 219
Jakubowski, Piotr, 35, 73–74, 122
Jehovah's Witnesses, 34, 111–12
Jesus, 56n.37, 161, 220
  and Big Brother, 93–94, 97–99
  disciples of, 93–94, 98–99
  See also Christianity
joy
  humor in tales, 39, 42–43, 220
  as religious value, 3, 6–7, 56–57, 190, 202
Judaism/Jews, 65–66, 200–1, 220, 221
  body of / tree of, 19–20, 21–22, 26–27, 191
  critique of, 2–3, 61–62, 137, 142–43, 182–83, 185–86, 188
  Neo-Hasidic, 198, 200–1, 202
  New Age, 10–11, 26, 152–53, 197–98, 199–206
  Orthodox, 15–16, 49–50, 182–83, 185, 186–87, 188
  Reform, 1–2, 53–54, 185, 192
  Renewal, 10–11, 199, 201, 202, 203–6

258 INDEX

Judaism/Jews, (cont.)
  role in apocalypse, 9–10, 41–42, 75, 79–80, 89, 91, 161, 162–63, 185, 219
  and secularism, 1–2, 60, 103, 130, 180–81, 182–83, 185–87
Jung, Carl, 44

Kabbalah, 15–16, 19–20, 65–66, 76, 94, 99–100, 118n.16, 123–24, 135, 139–41, 143, 144–46, 186–87, 196–97, 200–1, 211, 219
  Christian, 60, 168, 173, 200
  Frank's attitudes toward, 2–3, 30, 35, 53–54, 55–56, 77–78, 93–94, 153–60, 164–67, 212–13
  Lurianic, 14–15, 99–100, 139, 145–46, 154, 164–65, 166, 191–92, 211
  and New Age "Qabalah," 200, 201
  references in *ZSP*, 9–10, 81–82, 211, 220
  sefirot, 46n.1, 49–50, 53–54, 77–78, 93–94, 95, 97, 130–31, 155n.11, 165–67, 169–70
  Shechinah, 3–4, 6, 71–72, 75n.9, 93, 97, 115, 128–31, 132, 133–34, 143, 149, 191–92, 202–3, 214
  Tikkun, 55–56, 83, 152, 161, 166, 192–94
  Tikkunei Zohar, 83–84, 118n.16, 123–24, 129
  and Western Esotericism, 51n.20, 71–73, 88–89, 168–73, 174–77, 200, 201
  Zohar, 17, 20, 27–28, 35, 37–38, 51–52, 62, 63–64, 77n.20, 89, 93–94, 130–31, 133–34, 135, 145, 146, 155n.11, 158, 158n.20, 164–66, 201
Kraushar, Alexandr, 22n.48, 26–27, 209, 210
Kripal, Jeffrey, 140–41, 143
Krysa, Yehuda Leib, 20–21, 47–48

Ladino, 217
Lanckoronie, incident at, 17–20, 31, 116–18, 120, 192–93
Landes, Richard, 9–10, 161–62
Lenowitz, Harris, 2n.4, 4–5, 57n.40, 77n.18, 83n.34, 120n.25, 123n.29, 129n.35, 166n.36, 175, 209, 210, 213–14, 215, 217–18, 217n.71

Levine, Hillel, 4n.6, 23–25, 26–27, 34, 67–68, 95n.6, 184–85, 186–87, 207–8, 209, 210, 214–15, 217
  See also "Cargo Cult," Frankism as
libertinism, 3–4, 10, 34–35, 44, 49n.12, 50–51, 52, 55–56, 60–61, 69–70, 116–18, 119–20, 124, 125, 127, 168, 173–74n.34, 193n.45
Liebes, Yehudah, 10–11, 155n.11, 161, 191–93, 194, 196, 209
Lilith, 75n.9, 135
liminality, 13–14, 58, 63–64, 66, 84, 113, 180–81, 212
literalism, of *ZSP*, 30, 33, 42–44, 72–73, 103
Lorde, Audre, 116, 150–51
low vs. high, 28–30, 35–38, 39–42
Luther, Martin, 48–49
Lwów, 21–22, 26–27, 83, 121, 193–94, 197n.61, 209n.8, 211

ma'aminim. *See doenmeh*
ma'asah dumah. *See* burden of silence
Maciejko, Paweł, 2n.4, 4–5, 13, 19–20, 21, 22n.48, 25n.62, 52, 53–54, 67–68, 75n.8, 77n.20, 79–80, 98–99, 103, 110, 116–18, 128, 132, 153, 153n.5, 155–56, 165n.33, 173–74, 186–88, 207–8, 209, 210n.15, 211, 212–13, 213n.45, 214, 215, 217
madness, 25, 28, 34–35, 38–39, 44, 194–96
  as diagnosis for the marginalized, 14n.6, 26–27
  See also fool/idiot [*prostak*]
magic, 12, 28, 33, 67–68, 71–76, 140–41, 152–53, 164–65, 182–83, 196–97, 201
  and magical beings, 1–2, 3–4, 7, 30, 32–33, 47, 71–72, 75, 82–85, 88–90, 105–6, 169–70, 175, 206, 220, 221
  replacing religion, 6, 10, 61–62, 67–68, 71–76, 105–6, 175, 219, 220, 221
  in the tales, 43–44, 58–59, 81–85, 103–9, 147–48
  terafim as magical objects, 23, 72, 75, 78–81, 82, 92–94, 96–97, 99–100, 104–6, 108–9, 147–48,

168–69, 175, 177–78 (*see also* Esau: garments of / robes of)
and transformation, 8, 75, 76, 87, 89–90, 91–103, 109, 112–13, 115, 141, 144–45, 152, 163–64, 219
"uniting with" superhuman beings, 8, 74, 84–85, 99–100, 101, 142–43, 166–67
See also Folklore: magic and
Magid, Shaul, 50, 63, 199–200, 207–8
Maiden (*Panna*), The, 3–4, 8–10, 23, 40, 46n.1, 64–65, 69–70, 71–72, 78–80, 93–94, 95, 97–99, 101, 102, 110, 112–13, 114–16, 122–23, 128–38, 141–51, 175, 187–88, 216–17, 219, 221
and the Black Virgin, 23, 76, 110, 115, 131, 163–64, 214
as messiah, 9–10, 115, 128–34, 141, 155, 161, 163–64
in Frank's tales, 99–100, 103–5, 106–7, 108, 125–27
Maimonides, 31, 147
masculinity, 8–9, 41–42, 80–81, 116, 139, 141–46, 156, 160
See also queer theory
Mashiach. See messianism
Mashiach Ben Yosef, 9–10, 161, 193–94
materialism, 6, 7–8, 12, 27, 28, 46, 52, 55–56, 57, 63–64, 66, 69–70, 71–76, 81–85, 88–89, 99–100, 101–2, 105–6, 113, 115, 125, 149, 151, 157, 169–72, 174, 175–76, 177, 180–81, 182–83, 190
Matuszewski, Mateusz, 102, 122, 217, 221
Meir, Jonatan, 52–53, 191–92, 196–97
Meroz, Ronit, 89, 207–8
messianism, 1–3, 8–11, 14–19, 22–23, 26, 27–28, 36, 51–52, 53–54, 63–64, 68, 69–70, 73, 79–80, 83, 89–90, 91, 92, 93–94, 95n.6, 98–99, 102, 103, 110, 112–13, 115, 116, 121–22, 128–34, 138–41, 143–44, 145–47, 148–49, 152, 154–56, 157, 158–59, 161–64, 174–75, 182–83, 187–88, 189–90, 196–98, 200–1, 202–6, 211, 212, 214
and the Maiden, 9–10, 115, 128–34, 141, 155, 161, 163–64

Frank's disclaiming of, 161–64
Mickiewicz, Adam, 1–2, 26, 184–85
Midrash, 89, 96, 123, 129
millennialism, 9–10, 62, 69, 103, 111, 158–59, 161–63
Moravia, 1–2, 23–25, 173–74, 192, 212–13, 214–15, 216
Moravian Church, 38, 173–74
Mormonism, 3–4, 34, 75
Moses, 13, 56n.37, 62, 87–88, 136, 155
music, 6, 56–57, 190, 202
and "singing songs," 17–19, 31, 116–18, 120, 190, 192–93
mysticism, 15–16, 32–33, 62, 99–100, 139–40, 143, 175, 190, 196–98, 199–201
myth
Frankist, 7–9, 25, 30, 34, 35–45, 46–47, 51–52, 75, 84–85, 92, 121–22, 128, 132–33, 152–53, 164–66, 175–76, 180–81, 182–83, 185, 188, 202–3, 213–14, 219, 220, 221, 222–23, 224
mythic elements in *ZSP*, 28–34, 84, 105–6

Nachman of Bratzlav, 10–11, 38–39, 108–9, 191–97
Nathan of Gaza, 14–15, 33, 46–47, 63–64, 71–72, 119–20, 154, 164–65, 192–93, 220
neo-Hasidism. *See* Judaism; Neo-Hasidic
Nephilim, 7–8, 71–72
New Age Judaism. *See* Judaism; New Age
New Testament, 37–38, 48, 64, 98–99, 147
See also Christianity
Nihilism, 50, 51–55, 57, 60–63, 64–65, 69–70, 85, 212, 219
See also antinomianism

Offenbach, 23–25, 33n.77, 153n.5, 154, 173–74n.34, 183–84, 218
Order of the Asiatic Brethren. *See* Freemasonry: Order of the Asiatic Brethren
Osman Baba. *See* Baruchiah
Ottoman Empire, 5, 13–16, 20–21, 23–25, 66, 142–43n.65, 146, 163–64, 179–80

Packer, J. I., 48–49
Panek, Adrian, 4–5
panentheism, 50n.18, 198
Paul, Apostle, 37–38, 48, 63
Pettman, Dominic, 69
pneumatic (ecstatic/prophetic/ charismatic) practices, 182–83, 190, 200–1
  and messianism, 190, 196–97
  and Sabbateanism, 68–70, 197–98
Podolia, 5, 13–14, 16–17, 45, 184–85, 196
Poland, 1–2, 5, 13–14, 20–23, 25–26, 30, 33, 35–36, 52–53, 76, 152, 175–76, 184–85, 213, 214–15, 220
  Dziurdziów, 40–41, 77–78
  as promised land, 75, 78, 95, 96–98, 101, 102, 110, 162–63, 165, 177, 220
  Warsaw, 22–26, 55, 94, 98–99, 102, 110, 124, 153, 183–85
  See also Częstochowa; Lanckoronie; Lwów
Polish, 208
  as language of *Words of the Lord*, 2–3, 4–5, 57n.40, 62, 123n.29, 128, 210, 214, 217
Prague, 1–2, 10–11, 23–25, 26, 153, 183–88, 210, 213, 214–15
  See also Frankism: in Prague
prayer, 8–9, 17, 37–38, 40–41, 115, 116, 131, 163–64, 191–92, 196–97, 198, 203–4, 220
  uselessness of, 42, 53–54, 56, 58, 61–62, 75, 198
"Prophecies of Isaiah," 11–12, 210
prophecy, 8, 9–10, 11–12, 15–16, 17n.21, 27–28, 32–35, 38–39, 51–52, 68, 72–73, 75–76, 92, 96–97, 102–3, 111–13, 125, 127, 142, 146–48, 149, 158–59, 161, 162–64, 178–79, 183–84, 185, 196–98, 200–1, 206, 210, 211, 213, 216–17, 219, 220, 221, 223, 224
  See also trance

Queen of Sheba, 9–10, 71–72, 77–78, 81–82, 99–101, 103, 166–67, 220
queer theory, 8–9, 44n.99, 116, 142–45, 150

Quest, Frankist, 6, 8, 31, 46–47, 52, 69–70, 74, 76, 77–79, 80–81, 84–85, 89–90, 91–113, 116, 141, 142–43, 152, 161, 175, 177, 221
  failure of (*see* failure)
  tales of, 103–9, 219, 223

rabbinic authority, 1–2, 21–22, 121, 182–83, 198
  disputations, 20, 21–22, 26–27, 35, 128, 186–87, 191–92, 193–94, 209n.8, 211, 212n.41
  threats toward, 2, 10–11, 20–21, 185–87, 188, 190, 211
Rachel, 6, 23n.52, 56–57, 77, 78–79, 80, 129n.35, 130–31, 137, 175
Rapoport-Albert, Ada, 4–5, 10–11, 17–19, 46n.1, 54–55, 69–70, 80, 116–18, 119–20, 129, 130–31, 132–33, 138–40, 146, 147, 149, 186–88, 196–97, 202–3, 207–8, 209, 213
"Red Letters," 11–12, 25–26, 92, 112, 161, 183–84, 210, 220
redemption, Frankist conception of, 7, 30, 41–42, 51–52, 57, 61–62, 70, 72–73, 74–75, 79, 89–90, 91, 98–99, 102, 113, 115, 147, 148–49, 151, 152, 157, 158, 161–63, 174–75, 182–83, 189, 192
religion
  and hypocrisy, 6, 42, 44, 52–53, 55–56, 60–61, 216–17, 219
  and particularism, 6, 65–66, 67–68, 77, 172–73, 201, 219
Rich, Adrienne, 150
right and left, 61–62, 64, 108, 111–12, 157, 159–60, 164–65
Rozmaite adnotacyie, przypadki, czynności, i anektody Pańskie ("Various Notes"), 11–12, 69, 114–15, 122–23, 210, 214, 218, 221
Russia, 22–26, 22n.48, 102
Russo, Baruchiah. *See* Baruchiah

Sabbateanism
  Frankism's displacement of, 2–3, 9–11, 30, 71–72, 113, 115, 153–60
  Frankism's origins in, 5, 14–21, 153

influence of, 183, 185–88, 189 190, 191–93, 196–97, 202–6
religious antinomianism of, 47, 51, 63–64
theology of, 154–56, 219
See also *doenmeh*
Sabbetai Zevi, 2, 14–16, 17–19, 23, 26, 34, 36, 37–38, 47, 57, 58, 68–69, 83, 85–86, 110, 118–19, 130–31, 136, 146, 154, 155, 157n.17, 163–64, 191–92, 193–94, 220
criticism of, 10–11, 108, 116, 126, 143–44, 161, 174–75, 204
Sade, Marquis de, 44, 60–61
Saint-Germain, Comte de, 5n.11, 60
Salonica, 5, 13–14, 15n.11, 16–17, 20, 22, 47, 57, 73, 83, 180n.60
Samael, 61–62, 77–78
Samet, Hadar Feldman, 120, 207–8
Sarah, 65, 124–25
Sarah Ashkenazi, 14–15, 17–19, 119–20, 119n.22, 143–44, 193n.45
satire. *See* tales: satirical
Schachter-Shalomi, Zalman, 203–6, 208
Scholem, Gershom, 14–15, 17, 53, 68–69, 83–84, 86–87, 115, 130–31, 152–53, 155–56, 166, 169–70, 196–97, 204, 207, 209, 210
attitudes toward Frankism, v, 2, 12, 35, 51–53, 85, 154, 197–98, 200, 211–12, 217
"Redemption Through Sin," 4n.6, 153n.4, 158n.19, 211
Sabbatai Ṣevi, 14n.4, 155n.9
theory of Jewish history, 10–11, 52–53, 67–68, 185–88, 211
Scientology, 34, 73n.4, 178–79
sefirot. *See* Kabbalah: *sefirot*
sexuality, 219, 220, 221
and antinomianism, 8–9, 55, 68, 108–9, 114, 115–16, 120–23, 139–41, 148–49, 151
and Frank's character, 5, 35–36, 45, 122–23, 125–26
and group identity, 69, 94, 187–88
and incest (*see* incest)

liberation of, 8–9, 46–47, 80, 116, 129, 145–51, 173–74, 182–83, 187–88, 199, 203–4, 203n.88, 210
as messianic experience, 118–19, 139–41
repression of, 40, 80, 116, 125, 134–38, 150, 218
in ritual, 2–3, 17–20, 26, 49n.11, 69, 120, 121–24, 126–27, 166–67
and Sabbateanism, 16–21, 114, 116–20, 139
sensationalist rumors of, 2–3, 17–20, 26–27, 116–18
sexual inclination as the messiah, 129, 133–34
and symbolic homoeroticism, 143–45, 165–66
taboos regarding, 39–40, 48–49, 54–55, 63–64, 138–39, 140–41
as "uniting with," 98, 99–100, 106–7, 142–44, 166–67
shamelessness, 58–60, 145, 147, 212, 213
Shaddai, 7–8, 74–75, 97–98, 177
Shaw, George Bernard, 38n.86
Shazar, Zalman, 189
Shechinah, 191–92, 202–3
and the Maiden, 3–4, 23, 71–72, 73, 75, 75n.9, 115, 128–29, 130–31, 132–34, 143, 149, 214
as metaphor for Frankist apostasy, 19–20, 191
See also Kabbalah
shedim, 7–8, 72–73, 74, 84
Shorr, Chaya, 17–19, 68, 138–39, 146–47, 213
silence, 31–32, 95–96, 219
See also burden of silence
Singer, Isaac Bashevis, 4–5
Sisman, Cengiz, 4–5, 13, 14–15, 18n.26, 25–26, 63–64, 139, 143n.69, 179–80, 207–8
skepticism, 6, 10–11, 12, 27, 53–63, 69–70, 180–81, 182–83
Solomon, King, 3–4, 67, 72, 75, 81–82, 99–100, 103, 104–5, 137, 220
Sołtyk, Kajetan, 21
"Something for the Female Sex," 147, 153n.5, 187–88, 210, 213

spirituality, 68–69, 190, 199–200
    definition of, 200–1
    See also pneumatic (ecstatic/prophetic/charismatic) practices
Sufism, 146
    See also Islam
Swedenborg, Emanuel, 171
syncretism, 3–4, 8–9, 10, 12, 23, 65–66, 67–68, 76n.17, 79–80, 93–94, 95n.6, 97–98, 128, 155–56, 173, 182–83, 199, 200, 201, 205–6, 211

tales, 223–24
    of Bucharest, 13–14, 29–30, 42–43, 218
    as disclosure, 29–32
    exposing hypocrisy, 42–45, 216–17, 219
    of Frank's disrespect for religion, 40–42, 44–45
    of Frank as holy fool, 34–38
    of Frankist quest, 103–9
    interpretation of, 5, 13, 27–34, 218
    of maidens, 103–5, 125–26
    satirical, 34–45
    scatological, 39–40, 42, 122–23
    tale of
        the Congregation of the Prophet Elijah, 42–43, 53–54, 76, 105–6
        conning sick people with *Adon Olam*, 42
        debunking the bogeyman, 105–6
        defecating on the Torah, 42, 122–23
        drilling the pearl, 36–37
        forcing Muslims and Christians to transgress, 40–41
        God as a powerful sorcerer, 81
        mistaking the challah for Shabbat, 37–38
        Mohammed assaulting St. Peter, 41–42
        outwitting the scheming peasants, 82
        priests leaving the priesthood, 58–59
        smoking a pipe during Ramadan, 40–42
        stealing fruit jam, 43
        the "lion" of Judah, 42–43
        the man who questions the sun, 108–9
        the merchant/prince who thought he was a rooster, 38–39, 194–96
        the prince who becomes a field marshal, 104–5
        the prince who cannot be judged, 126–27
        the prince who cures the royal family, 105
        the prince who doesn't care about propriety, 106–7
        the prince who is faithful to the goddess, 108
        the servant girl with magical silk, 104–5
        the thief who wins the princess, 107–8
        the three-branched tree, 65–66
        tricking the Angel of Death, 43–44
    trickster, 38–39, 42–45
Talmud, 17, 20–21, 26–27, 44n.99, 53–54, 81n.28, 96n.11, 108, 133–34, 147, 193–94, 211
    See also Contra-Talmudists
Tantra, 48–49, 140–41
Temple, 62, 72, 75–76, 137, 175–76, 192
three demigods who rule the world, 7–8, 71–72, 88–90, 98, 101, 136, 176–77, 219
Tokarczuk, Olga, 1–2, 4–5
Torah, 17–19, 28, 52–53, 74, 79–80, 86–87, 135, 146, 191–92, 220
    as "law," 61–62
    scroll of, 13, 34–35, 42, 122–23, 155
    Two Torahs, Sabbatean doctrine of, 14–15, 63–64, 139
Tova, Yehudah Levi. *See* Dervish Effendi
trance, 99–100, 142
    and prophecy, 32–33, 69n.61, 196–97
    in Sabbatean communities, 5, 16–17, 196–97
tree, 105, 106–7, 108–9, 218
    of death, sexual repression as, 66, 136
    of Knowledge of Good and Evil, 14–15, 62, 63–64, 155n.9
    of Life, 14–15, 62, 63–64, 77–78, 155n.9
    three-trunked, 65–66, 200–1, 205–6
tricksterism, 5, 34–35, 38–45, 58, 59–60, 77–78, 219
Trismegistus, Hermes, 170–71, 176–77

INDEX 263

Trump, Donald, 35–36
Turkey, founding of, 16, 179–80
tzaddik, figure of, 83, 165–66, 191–92, 196–97, 224

UFOs, 73n.4, 111
universalism, 6, 58, 65–68, 198

Van der Haven, Alexander, 119–20, 193n.45
Various notes, occurrences, activities, and anecdotes of the lord. See *Rozmaite adnotacyie*
V'Avo Hayom El Ha'Ayin ("And I Came This Day unto the Fountain"), 118–19
Versluis, Arthur, 10, 91n.1, 168–69, 171–72, 175, 176–77
violence, 27, 30, 41–42, 47, 54–55, 56, 57–58, 107–8, 122–23, 142–44, 193–94, 212, 220
Virgin Mary, 23, 46n.1, 97, 98–99, 128, 131, 132, 136, 155–56, 214
  See also Black Virgin of Częstochowa
visions and dreams, 28, 32–33, 56–57, 87, 88, 96n.14, 108–9, 125–26, 133–34, 141–42, 146–47, 183–84, 193–94, 196–97, 204, 210, 215, 218, 221, 223, 224
Visions of the Lord. See *Widzenia Pańskie*
von Hönigsberg, Löw Enoch Hönig, 153n.5, 185–86, 187–88, 210, 213
Vonnegut, Kurt, 38–39
vulgarity. *See* low and high

Wehle, Jonas, 153n.5, 185–86
Weiss, Joseph, 10–11, 191–93, 197–98

Western Esotericism, 10, 28, 60, 67–68, 75, 88–89, 91, 92, 96–97, 105–6, 112–13, 152–53, 167, 173–81, 200–1, 205–6
  and alchemy (*see* alchemy)
  definition of, 168–70
  esotericism vs. exotericism, 34, 168–69, 178–79, 213–14
  history of, 169–73
  materialism of, 67–68, 175–76, 180
  Rosicrucianism, 23–25, 173–74
  See also Freemasonry
Widzenia Pańskie, 11–12, 32–33, 103–4, 125–26, 210, 218, 221
Wilde, Oscar, 134–35
witchcraft. *See* Folklore: witchcraft
Wolfson, Elliot, 143, 145–46, 183
Wollstonecraft, Mary, 146
world, hidden. *See* hidden world
Words of the Lord. See *Zbiór Słów Pańskich*

Yamamoto, Shinichi, 118–19, 153, 185–86
Yiddish, 5, 166–67, 217

Zbiór Słów Pańskich (ZSP) (*Collection of the Words of the Lord*):
  chronology of, 28, 92, 215–16
  editing of, 11–12, 118, 126–27, 217–18
  genres of, 11–12, 28, 221–24
  literary character of, 27–45
  manuscripts of, 2n.4, 4–5, 28, 62, 118, 174n.37, 176–77, 184–85, 196, 208, 209–10
Zionism, 1–2, 10–11, 142–43, 152–53, 188, 192
  affinity for Sabbateanism, 189, 192, 204
Zohar. See Kabbalah: *Zohar*

Printed in the USA
CPSIA information can be obtained
at www.ICGtesting.com
CBHW051350111124
17247CB00004B/125